REVOLUTION AND DISENCHANT- MENT

Theory in Forms

A SERIES EDITED BY NANCY ROSE HUNT
AND ACHILLE MBEMBE

REVOLUTION AND DISENCHANTMENT

ARAB MARXISM AND

THE BINDS OF EMANCIPATION

× × × × × × *Fadi A. Bardawil*

Duke University Press   Durham and London   2020

Printed in the United States of America on acid-free paper ∞
Cover designed by Drew Sisk
Typeset in Garamond Premier Pro by Westchester Publishing Services

Library of Congress Cataloging-in-Publication Data

Names: Bardawil, Fadi A., [date] author.
Title: Revolution and disenchantment : Arab Marxism and the binds of
    emancipation / Fadi A. Bardawil.
Description: Durham : Duke University Press, 2020 | Series: Theory in forms |
    Includes bibliographical references and index.
Identifiers: LCCN 2019028452 (print)
LCCN 2019028453 (ebook)
ISBN 9781478006169 (hardcover)
ISBN 9781478006756 (paperback)
ISBN 9781478007586 (ebook)
Subjects: LCSH: New Left—Lebanon—History. | Socialism—Lebanon—History. |
    Lebanon—Politics and government—1946–
Classification: LCC HX378.A6 B37 2020 (print) | LCC HX378.A6 (ebook) |
    DDC 320.53/15095692—dc23
LC record available at https://lccn.loc.gov/2019028452
LC ebook record available at https://lccn.loc.gov/2019028453

Cover art: *Socialist Lebanon*, Issue 5, April 1967

Publication of this open monograph was the result of Duke University's
participation in TOME (Toward an Open Monograph Ecosystem), a collaboration
of the Association of American Universities, the Association of University Presses,
and the Association of Research Libraries. TOME aims to expand the reach of
long-form humanities and social science scholarship including digital scholarship.
Additionally, the program looks to ensure the sustainability of university press
monograph publishing by supporting the highest quality scholarship and
promoting a new ecology of scholarly publishing in which authors' institutions
bear the publication costs. Funding from Duke University Libraries made it
possible to open this publication to the world.

To Abdo and Gisèle Bardawil
and
Zouheir Aniss Rahhal

في هذا العدد

× × × × × × × × × × × × × × × × × × × ×

* الافتتاحية :

من التهم البالية : التروتسكية

* ماذا يجري في نقابة المعلمين

* زاوية التثقيف النظارى:

نصوص مختارة من " ما العمل ؟ "

لينين ١٦٠٢٥

* مشكلة السكن

× × × × × × × × × × × × × × × × × × × ×

افتتاحية

من التهم البال

١ ٠ ماذا يعني الاتهام بالترو

يطلق حزب الثورة الاشترا

الاشتراكي " ٠ لماذا هذه ال

" سوفياتيين " ولا " لينيين "

ماركسيين لينينيين وحسب ! و

العدد ٥ فلم يعد حزب الثورة

التروتسكية لماذا ٠ هل بمعنى

الاشتراكية حاولوا تحديد معنى

سبب اللجوء الى التروتسكية كـ

التحديد ٠ في الخلاف الصيني

تهمة التروتسكية دونما اى احـ

وهو بالنسبة لحزب الثورة الاشتراكية ، المارق ، الذى لا نقاش معه ولا عمل

الاختفاء بحملات متخفية عن طريق تبادل النشرات ! اذن ، لا مبرر لمحاول

الاختلاف والاتفاق وتحديد ما ٠ وبذلك تتقرر الحرية الماركسية العمالـ

التجاه التي ولدت الانعزال التنظيمي والهزال النظارى والتي ادت الـ

يد الاحزاب الشيوعية ٠

ولكن اذا كان فريق من الرفاق الماركسيين يرفض التهم ، فهل يق

برفض مماثل ؟ حتما لا ٠ اذ ان السكوت او الاحتجاع (بحجة المساس

تبقي الموضوعني الاطار الذي يطرح فيه ٠ و هذا الاطار هو الذ ولد ب

الماركسي يشكو منه حتى الان ٠ لذلك سيكون جوابنا محاولة تحديد موقف

٢ ٠ ما هي التروتسكية ؟

المقصود من طرح السؤال بهذا الشكل هو البرهان على ان التر

الى القيام بعمل قادر على استيعاب الواقع اللبناني والعربي ٠ بذلك يت

لتجربة هي من تجارب العمل الماركسي ــ بعيوبها ونقائصها ش لاعن ال

وهذا هو الموقف الوحيد الجدير بماركسيين يثقون بالتحليل العلمي ٠ وال

Contents

A Note on Transliteration and Translation

I use the common transliteration of Arabic names when used by authors in their non-Arabic works, most of which rely on a simplified French transliteration system. For example, I use Waddah Charara and Fawwaz Traboulsi instead of Waḍḍāḥ Sharāra and Fawwāz Ṭrābulsī. I adopt the same convention for cities—for example, Beirut instead of Bayrūt. I otherwise follow a simplified transliteration system based on the *International Journal of Middle East Studies* (*IJMES*). All diacritical marks, except for the ʿayn (ʿ) and hamza (ʾ), are omitted. All translations are mine unless noted otherwise.

Prologue

Je voudrais sans la nommer vous parler d'elle.
—GEORGES MOUSTAKI

At a fundamental level, I am preoccupied in *Revolution and Disenchantment* with the question of theory and practice. More precisely, I explore the seductions, authority, and pragmatics of theory in revolutionary political organizations and academic settings. My modes of investigation are therefore historical and ethnographic, in contrast to a philosophical one that offers, say, an a priori account of how theory ought to relate, or not, to practice. I pursue these questions by tacking back and forth between the long overlooked archive of the 1960s Lebanese New Left and the critical theories produced in the Euro-American academy.[1] In particular I examine the beginnings, high tides, and vicissitudes of Lubnan Ishtiraki (Socialist Lebanon, 1964–70), a small Marxist organization, composed for the most part of militant intellectuals. In this work, I do not reconstruct a comprehensive history of the Lebanese Left, its political fortunes, and the multiple theoretical streams that nourished it, and the ones it produced. Rather, I revisit a minority Marxist tradition, which produced conceptually sophisticated diagnostic works, and a revolutionary movement that splintered. In taking the Marxist tradition as my major site of investigation, the question of theory and practice is thought concomitantly with the dialectic of revolutionary hope and political disenchantment.

I do not revisit the theoretical works and political trajectories of an older generation of militants because I think they provide answers to a present characterized by both a heightened state of communal and nationalist fragmentation and an increased interconnectedness fostered by the accelerated circulation of capital, people, and technologies. Having said that, more than a handful of the questions this generation of militant intellectuals confronted have regained intellectual and political relevance in the wake of the Arab revolutions and the global anticapitalist mobilizations: Who is the revolutionary subject? What are the different forms a political organization can take, and when does an agency of emancipation turn into one of power that stifles the people's initiatives in their own name? What are the privileged sites of political practice, and its multiple scales? Do militant intellectuals translate *texts* to educate the masses? Or translate themselves to working-class neighborhoods and jobs to learn from the masses (*établissement*)? How does one mobilize across difference?[2] If power is primarily conceptualized as exploitation, how are other forms of power conceptually apprehended and politically articulated with a class-based politics? More specifically, what is the political status of forms of communal solidarity in a revolutionary project? What forms of class-based national politics are possible when the political is not autonomous from the social—sectarian, regional, and kinship divisions—and when these multiple communal constituencies share the state's sovereignty? These questions about theory and practice that seek to elucidate the subject and agent of revolution, as well as the modalities, scales, forms, and telos of political practice, are confronted by militants in their daily practice. In the Marxist tradition, which holds theoretical analysis in the highest regard, these questions are tethered to the generative labors of translation and interpretation that produce its universality in practice, through the global circulation of texts—think Karl Marx, Vladimir Lenin, Rosa Luxemburg, Antonio Gramsci, Mao Tse-Tung, Che Guevara. In *Revolution and Disenchantment*, I weave the story of revolutionary hope and disenchantment with the answers the Lebanese New Left articulated in practice to three fundamental issues that generations of Marxists worldwide confronted and were divided by: the question of intellectuals, as the vectors (or not) of revolutionary theory; the debate around the organization, as the mediator (or not) between theory and practice; and last but not least the anxiety generated by nonemancipatory—non-class-based solidarities—attachments, such as national and communal ones, as impediments (or not) to revolutionary practice.

The problem-space of beginnings is radically different from the one of completion. Much has happened in the world since I began feeling my way around some of the material that ended up in this book. This project initially took shape in the US in the wake of the September 11, 2001, attacks, characterized by the imperial wars in Afghanistan and Iraq and the polarization it effected among Arab intellectuals. This period witnessed the increasing public visibility of intellectuals critical of Arab culture and society grouped under the catch-all banner of "Arab liberals," a substantial number of whom previously belonged to leftist political parties. At the time, it did not seem that there was any possibility to break free from the political deadlock that presented itself as the impossible choice between "national sovereignty" under tyrants hiding behind a thin veneer of anti-imperialist rhetoric and a potential "democracy" to come brought about by foreign sanctions and occupations epitomized by the invasion of Iraq. In this conjuncture *theoretical* anti-imperialism, as practiced in the US academy, resonated loudly, and affectively, as an ersatz political anti-imperialism. As the tanks rolled in, the least one could do is put on a postcolonial armor to debunk the claims of intellectuals deriding Arab culture for its atavisms or calling for the "liberation" of Muslims, particularly Muslim women, from the yoke of religious fundamentalists as rigged faulty knowledges in cahoots with imperial ideologies.

The project was first articulated as an attempt to understand the shifts in political ideologies from Marxism to liberalism in the Arab world. At the time, the opposition to the Iraq War and the US plans in and for the region in its aftermath came hand in hand with a critical attitude toward universals, such as liberal democracy and human rights, as vectors of imperial violence cloaked in ideologies of liberation. In brief, the polarized present justified the interest in, and the will to critique of, liberalism. The first part of the question—Marxism—however, was a different story altogether. It was nourished by older subterranean political-affective veins, which were carved out in the early 1990s, as I was coming of age, in the aftermath of the Lebanese civil and regional civil wars (1975–90), the cradle of my generation's political consciousness. The 1960s and 1970s Left, with its militants, thinkers, novelists, playwrights, poets, and musicians, became then a site of deep political-affective investment. For one, that tradition was generative of theoretical-aesthetic-political explorations far more seductive and engrossing than the intellectually tenuous, politically provincial, and aesthetically kitschy productions of the nationalist and sectarian (Christian/Muslim) forces. For those of us escaping the provinces of families, regions, and sectarian communities and meeting in Beirut, for the most part in university halls, a few years after the fighting stopped, the Left was also a name for a project that held the promise of a political community much wider, and more inclusive, than the stifling compounds of, predominantly but not exclusively, sectarian communities. The Left, it is needless to assert, also held the promise of a more socially just world. The conceptual resources of the tradition also enabled the beginnings of a critical apprehension of the postwar economic policies and privatized reconstruction projects in the mid-1990s that were opposed by a number of former leftist militants. Last but not least, the 1960s Left was on the right side of history. It supported, and allied itself, with the Palestinian revolution, against the predominantly Christian Lebanese nationalist forces, who during the wars (1975–90) were backed by Israel. For all these reasons and more, it seemed like the 1960s generation was the last great revolutionary, and intellectual, generation. The fact that this generation failed to achieve its revolutionary goals did not dampen the melancholic tones of this attachment. Melancholy, though, should not to be confused with assent. The attachment did not preclude an intergenerational, critical at times, dialogue. This was a melancholy for a time that precedes my birth in the first years of the civil wars and my generation's formative experiences. At least then there was a possibility of emancipatory political practice that escapes the times of repetition of inter- and intracommunal fighting. History, at that point in time, could have been made. It was a youth that was traversed, in part, in the future anterior tense, sustained by endless streams of revolutionary song, some texts, and a dearth of political experience.

So when I began the project theoretical anti-imperialism and political anti-imperialism came hand in hand. The first, particularly in the form of the theoretical epistemology critique of the universalist or essentializing discursive assumptions of Arab intellectuals and militants, or both, was in tension with the political-affective attachment to the Left tradition as a project of total emancipation. I did not release the tension in one direction or another. Bit by bit, and after meeting some of these disenchanted Marxists and talking with them at length about their political lives and conceptual works, I grew increasingly skeptical about the suitability of epistemology critique to capture the stakes that animated their projects, and the multiple articulations of theory and practice I was unearthing as I lingered over and reconstructed aspects of this generation's spaces of experience and horizons of expectation.[3] In part this was a well-known story of ethnographic humility, which consisted of testing the limits in practice of certified theoretical contraptions to immediately capture an entire world upon landing there. That said, the narrative of ethnographic humility was entangled in a more personal (dare I say postcolonial?) two-step move. The first step consists of confusing the latest metropolitan theoretical moves with the most sophisticated ones that are assumed to have a universal validity. In practice, this reproduction of the colonial divide takes the form of assuming that "abstract theory" is produced in the metropoles and "concrete facts" are found in the Global South. It also takes the form of pinpointing the lack of conceptual sophistication, or the old-fashioned nature, of theorists in the peripheries. To say this is to underscore both that the West was taken to be the land of theoretical opportunities and that a certain idea of what constitutes "theory" was assumed to be the most prized form of thinking. The seductions of academic metropolitan theory are also compounded by a spotty knowledge of the works of previous generations and a dearth of critical engagement with it in the present (step two). This is too large an issue to be broached here, but suffice it to say that generational transmission, which is in part related to postcolonial state and educational institutions, is a very difficult and fraught question that leaves its marks on works and lives: Where do you begin from and how?

While I grew increasingly skeptical of theoretical anti-imperialism as the primary conceptual lens to approach the archive of modernist and contemporary Arab thought, I was still attached to political anti-imperialism as the prime contradiction that ought to dictate political alignments. Then the Arab revolutions happened (2011–). The event broke the political paralysis resulting from the deadlock of having to choose between authoritarian nationalists and imperial democrats. The long eclipsed subject and agent of emancipation—the people—occupied center stage again. The revolutions were a seismic pan-Arab event. They displaced the West from the heart of modern Arab mass politics in rearticulating popular sovereignty outside the orbit of imperial decolonization. Unlike the twentieth-century mass movements, the revolutions that mobilized millions of citizens against their own regimes were not propelled by anti-imperialist engines. This does not mean that anti-imperialist concerns were completely absent but that they were not the main drive of the revolutions. Earlier mass political movements in the region carried successively the banner of decolonization from political domination (independence movements), political and economic dependence (radical national liberation movements and the Left), and Western cultural alienation (Islamists). The Arab Left thought the questions of external economic independence and internal class contradictions together, but for the most part these twentieth-century movements articulated multiple visions of political, economic, and cultural sovereignty from imperial orbits. The first wave of revolutions (2011–) ushered in a new structure of feeling, which, in my case at least, put to rest the melancholic attachment to the 1960s generation as the marker of the last great leap into emancipation.

Looked at from the perspective of the aftermath of the Arab revolutions, we seem to be entering into "post-postcolonial" times that are beginning the process of decentering the West in practice after it has been subjected to multiple iterations of theoretical decenterings in the past.[4] This is not only because of the practice of the revolutionaries but also because of the recent geopolitical conjuncture, which dislodged the post–Cold War arrangement during which the West, and particularly the US, was the supreme intervening military power. Arab, regional, and non-Western international powers are increasingly and unabashedly involved in the region. Two caveats. First, unlike its decentering in theory, which is staged as a liberatory act of decolonization, its decentering in practice certainly did not usher in an era of progressive politics. A quick glance at the Russian, Iranian, Turkish, and Israeli involvements in Syria, in addition to Western ones, and the destruction they brought on are enough to put an end to the automatic association of the decentering of the West with a horizon of justice. Having said that, this is certainly not a cause for imperial nostalgia and to begin lamenting "the decline of Western civilization." The legacies of the wars in Afghanistan and Iraq and the never-ending "War on Terror" are still unfolding in our political present, not to mention the continuing US support of the Israeli colonization of Palestinian lands. Moreover, the multipolar interventions today are in part the consequences of the recent US interventions in the region. This decentering is a crucial fact to be reckoned with, without celebration or lamentation, and it's not an easy thing to do since clear-cut binary antagonisms and the logic of the "main contradiction" are hard to dislodge from political alignments.

The limits on anti-imperialism, as the main contradiction, animating both theory and politics is clearly revealed in the growing chasm separating oppositional, diasporic or not, intellectuals in the metropoles and critical thinkers, artists, and revolutionaries at home and those of them who recently found sanctuary in the metropoles. The political alliance between metropolitan oppositional culture and revolutionary forces at home that Edward Said wrote so eloquently about, and that he embodied in his own practice, today seems like a relic from a bygone age.[5] Critical strategies that rely exclusively on speaking back to the West through marshaling a set of binaries—West/non-West; homogenization/difference; universal/particular; secular/nonsecular; westernized elite/nonwesternized masses; liberal Muslim/nonliberal Muslim—that retain the West at the heart of their deepest attachments have become increasingly problematic in the wake of the Arab revolutions. They cannot account for political practice outside of its relation, and opposition, to imperial orbits, obliterating the revolutionaries' attempts to make their own history, and reinscribing in the process the West as the main subject and agent of history.[6] These critical theories also fail to critically account for the multiple societal divisions that result from the entanglement of the political in the webs of the social fabric and for the interventions of non-Western powers. In other words, forms of revolutionary practice, the logics of communal solidarities (sectarian, ethnic, regional, kin), and interventions by non-Western powers whose coordinates cannot be plotted on the axis of the West remain invisible in theory. At most, these critical strategies point out, and rightly so, that communal solidarities are the offspring of modernity—imperialism, capitalism, the nation-state. Non-Western interventions in the region can be condemned politically and morally, but these critical theories do not have the resources to apprehend them conceptually.

Lest you think that there is an "Arab exceptionalism" lurking in the situation I am describing, I will bring this preface to a close by undertaking a historical and regional translation. More than a decade ago, Rey Chow interrogated the self-referentiality of the knowledge produced by area studies that, by focusing on "targeting or getting the other," ends up consolidating "the omnipotence and omnipresence of the sovereign 'self'/'eye'—the 'I'—that is the United States."[7] Chow, who herself grew up among survivors of Japan's invasion of China between 1937 and 1945, remembers how, as a child, she was used to hearing more about the wartime atrocities committed by the Japanese against the Chinese than she did about the US violence against Japan. The arrival of the Americans, she recalls, was considered "a moment of 'liberation'" (Chow, *Age of the World Target*, hereafter AWT, 25–26). These childhood oral narratives will persist in her mind as a "kind of emotional dissonance, a sense of something out-of-joint" (AWT, 26). "It is as if the sheer magnitude of destruction unleashed by the bombs," Chow writes, "demolished not only entire populations but also the memories and histories of tragedies that had led up to the apocalyptic moment, the memories and histories of those who had been brutalized, kidnapped, raped, and slaughtered in the same war by other forces" (AWT, 26). The erasure and silencing of these multiple, non-US-centric experiences results, she notes by drawing on Harry Harootunian's work, in the haunting of area studies by the "problem of the vanishing object." In brief, the events, "whose historicity does not fall into the epistemically closed orbit of the atomic bomber—such as the Chinese reactions to the war from a primarily anti-Japanese point of view," Chow asserts, "will never receive the attention that is due to them" (AWT, 41). Chow's reminiscences, particularly the out-of-jointness between one's violent experiences, and emotions, and what metropolitan disciplines and critical theories take as their object of study and critique, resonates deeply with the generation of disenchanted revolutionaries whose story this book recounts. Self-referentiality may render these metropolitan works provincial, but that does not subtract from their authority, which is not necessarily an epistemological effect—say, of their theoretical superiority—but a consequence of their institutional location. Metropolitan scholars, diasporic or not, have the luxury to, and selectively do, ignore works by Arab thinkers and militants at home in a way that the latter cannot afford to do.

You may, at this point, detect a tension in my argument between the case I am making for the necessity of taking stock of the decentering West in practice—by revolutionaries and non-Western interventions—and my reinscription of the hegemony of its knowledges and educational institutions. I don't think there is a tension here. Again, we are living in times when English is still the strongest global language, in a time when the educational institutions of the West, particularly those of the US, are still hegemonic and opening offshore outlets in different parts of the world; *and yet* the multiple political, economic, and military developments, particularly in the Arab world today, steer us toward not collapsing critique exclusively with opposition to the West. In this conjuncture, what are the analytical, political, and ethical costs of insisting that critical theory equals a critique of the West and its discourses? If "Europe is no longer the center of gravity of the world," then how does this "fundamental experience of our era" impact the modalities of operation of critical practices and the political compass that guides metropolitan oppositional alignments?[8]

INTRODUCTION

Yet the shadows that cling to Marxism
cannot be dispelled solely by desk lamps.
—RUSSELL JACOBY

We know, of course, that anthropologists, like other academics,
learn not merely to use a scholarly language, but to fear it,
to admire it, to be captivated by it.
—TALAL ASAD

Revolution and Disenchantment is preoccupied with an earlier episode of Arab political hope and despair. It takes a step back to the 1960s to excavate for our present the lost archive of the Lebanese New Left. It is at once a history of the rise of the New Left and its subsequent ebbing away, as well as an anthropological inquiry into the production, circulation, and uses of revolutionary and critical theory. In doing so, I am less motivated by an encyclopedic drive of inquiry that seeks to fill a gap in the literature by examining an archive that has not yet been explored—although that is also important in itself. Rather, I ask, how does the reconstruction of revolutionary lives and the excavation of an overlooked theoretical tradition shed light on the *metropolitan unconscious* of our critical—anthropology, critical theory, and Middle East studies—traditions?

Unlike the much older Arab communist parties—the Lebanese CP was founded in 1924—that revolved in the Soviet orbit, the New Left emerged out of the ideological and militant constellations of Arab nationalisms. The New Left militants were the generation of the Palestinian revolution that came to embody revolutionary hopes in a future of sovereignty and social justice after the swift military defeat of the Arab regimes against Israel in June 1967. I focus primarily on the trajectory and theoretical writings of Waddah Charara (1942–), a prominent Lebanese transdisciplinary thinker whose major works bridge the social sciences and history, in addition to multiple forays into the Arab-Islamic *turath* (traditions) and translations of theory and poetry. Charara cofounded Socialist Lebanon (1964–70) with a handful of comrades.[1] I also close in on segments of the political and critical paths of Fawwaz Traboulsi (1941–) and Ahmad Beydoun (1942–). Traboulsi was cofounder of the organization and alongside Charara was one of its main dynamos before becoming a prolific historian, sociologist, and translator, and a major public face of the political and intellectual Left in Lebanon. Beydoun, who joined the group about a year and half later, would go on to become a distinguished historiographer and cultural critic, who also wrote poetry and the script of *Beirut, the Encounter* (1981), one of the cult movies of the Lebanese civil and regional wars (1975–90). In brief, the underground Marxist organization was a hub of militant intellectuals who much later, in the wake of successive waves of political disenchantment, became prominent intellectuals.

In 1970 Socialist Lebanon merged with the Organization of Lebanese Socialists, the radicalized Lebanese branch of the Arab Nationalist Movement, which severed its ties with President Gamal Abdel Nasser after the 1967 defeat, to found the Organization of Communist Action in Lebanon (OCAL). Charara, who was instrumental in the fusion between both organizations, subsequently led a substantial internal opposition movement along Maoist lines that was expelled from OCAL in 1973. At the beginning of the Lebanese civil and regional wars Charara's shock in the face of the sectarian—Christian/ Muslim—forms that wartime practices of fighting, killing, pillaging, and destroying took led him very early on to put an end to nearly two decades of political militancy and exit from the Marxist tradition of thought. The sectarian divisions of the masses during the war revealed the difficulty of practicing a class-based politics of emancipation. Political practice could not be extricated from the webs of the social fabric. Communal solidarity eclipsed class interest. In the wake of disenchantment, Charara turned to a minute sociological investigation of the modalities of operation of communal—sectarian, regional, kin—power. Charara was probably the first of his cohort of militant intellectuals to take his distance from, and become critical of, leftist politics and ideologies, which, even if they did not themselves arise on sectarian grounds, did not manage to break free from the dominant communal polarizations dividing Lebanese society.

In excavating first Socialist Lebanon's forgotten archive from the 1960s and then focusing on Charara's theoretical texts in the wake of disenchantment, I unearth a minoritarian tradition of immanent critical Arab thought that diagnosed the logics and practices of power and examine the vicissitudes of a revolutionary project that sought to articulate an autonomous leftist practice. This diagnostic tradition, as I will develop throughout the book, steers away from the dominant topoi of contemporary Arab thought. Its diagnostic imma-nent edge, which focused first on the practices of anticolonial regimes and Left political parties before examining communal logics of subjugation, did not get caught up on the ideological battleground of authenticity. It moved away from the comparison of "Arab" and "Islamic" values with "Western" ones, ushering a critique of the latter from the standpoint of the former, or translating one set into the other. When the promise of revolutionary emancipation was eclipsed, the critique of communal solidarities did not revert either to a Marxist histori-cism or a liberal critique of the social fabric and culture from the standpoint of a detached, context-less abstract reason. These political communal solidarities were not "traditional," "pre-capitalist remainders," Charara argued very early on in the mid-1970s, but modern products. They are partially the result of the logics of formal subsumption at work in Lebanese capitalism and the divisions of the Lebanese nation-state. Charara and Beydoun retained from their Marx-ist past a reflexive stance, which thinks the conditions of possibility of a critical work's own conceptual building blocks, and the critic's positionality, as it is thinking its object. It is this attachment to reflexive critique, in the wake of their realization that class is no longer the universal engine propelling political practice, that led them to formulate an immanent sociological and historical critique of community that is not grounded in universal reason. This critique worked by detecting the cracks in the communities' own mythologizing dis-courses about themselves, highlighting in the process contingencies, hetero-geneities, and divisions and the gaps separating discourses from practices. This patient diagnostic tracking of the layers of sedimented narratives and the vaga-ries of actual political practices can't be more different than blanket culturalist statements that critique Arab societies from "the mythical space" of Western normative liberal theory.[2] But why reopen today the archive of a generation that was formed during the high tides of Arab nationalism, founded the New Left, and adhered to the Palestinian revolution before ending up as detached, disenchanted critics of communal logics dwelling in the ruins of futures past? What is the purchase in and for the present of revisiting this story of a genera-tion that moved from nation to class to community?

History, First. This generation, born for the most part on the eve of in-dependence in Lebanon (1943) and Syria (1945), lived through, acted in, and thought about major political turning points. It was marked very early on by the Palestinian Nakba, or Catastrophe (1948), before being swept by the high tides of the Ba'th and Nasser's anticolonial nationalism in the 1950s. By the 1960s, they became Marxist critics of both anticolonial Arab nationalisms and pro-Western Arab governments. This generation of New Left militants revolving outside the Soviet communist orbit and within a wider Third World-ist network of internationalist solidarity—the Chinese, Algerian, Cuban, and Vietnamese Revolutions—produced very early prescient Marxist critiques of imperialism, the national liberation regimes, and the Arab bourgeoisie. The Marxist ground that dialectically held these external (imperialism) and internal (regimes in power and the bourgeoisie) critiques together was premised on the presence of "the people," the revolutionary subject capable of embodying this program in its revolutionary practice. The ground began to crumble with the beginning of the Lebanese civil and regional wars (1975–90). A few years later, the Iranian Revolution (1979) constituted a seismic event, whose aftermath began to radically alter the Lebanese political landscape by adding a militant Islamist component to the sectarian divisions already at work. Meanwhile, the 1980s witnessed the ebbing away of the Lebanese Left and the Palestinian resistance a few years after the Israeli invasion (1982); increased violence of the neighboring authoritarian regimes, such as the Syrian Ba'th's Massacre in Hama (1982); devastating regional conflicts, such as the Iran-Iraq War (1980–88); and increased Islamist militancy (Hizbullah, 1985 to the present, and Hamas, 1987 to the present). After 1982, Israel, the postcolonial regimes, Islamist militancy, and sectarian confrontations all contributed to dashing the revolutionary hopes of those militants and thinkers who would come to be known as the 1960s Left generation.

This string of events resulted in the fragmentation of the members of this generation who were bound by their anti-imperialism, support of the Palestinian revolution, and a commitment to a horizon of social justice, in different political and ideological directions. Charara and Beydoun retreated from militancy into a life of writing, and some of the comrades converted into, or became fellow travelers of, Islamist anti-imperialism.[3] Others retreated to the fold of their own sectarian communities—Christian, Sunni, Shi'i, Druze—that they had initially broken away from when they joined Marxist political parties in the 1960s. Looked at from the perspective of their "Palestinian years"—from their early childhood memories of the Nakba (1948) to the invasion of Beirut (1982)—this generation lived through successive seismic transformations. Their story, one of a generation captivated by the dialectic of revolutionary exhilaration and political despair in an ideologically saturated world and in compressed political times, deserves to be told.

Theory, Second. These militant intellectuals inaugurated a sophisticated minoritarian tradition of revolutionary and critical Arab theory, characterized by "a transversality of knowledges," which defied the logics of professionalization, expertise, and disciplinarity.[4] They weaved their works by engaging authors such as Karl Marx, Vladimir Ilyich Lenin, Rosa Luxemburg, Mao Tse-Tung, Leon Trotsky, Antonio Gramsci, Louis Althusser, Vo Nguyen Giap, Ibn Khaldun, Che Guevara, Maurice Merleau-Ponty, Pierre Bourdieu, Cornelius Castoriadis, Michel Foucault, and Abdal-Rahman al-Jabarti, among others. Excavating this archive provides multiple "ex-centric" vantage points, located outside of hegemonic centers, their institutions, disciplines, and languages, which bypass the colonial divide assigning the Global South as locus of "concrete facts" and the North the manufacturer of "abstract theory."[5] In doing so, there is a gain in reflexivity generated by highlighting how the questions, stakes, modes of criticism, and practices of engagement of disenchanted Marxist intellectuals speak back to the ones practiced in critical anthropology, area studies, and postcolonial studies—what I earlier called the critical disciplines' metropolitan unconscious.

In fact, it is this metropolitan unconscious that is in part responsible for the neglect of the archive of Arab Marxism and the examination of the production and circulation of critical theory from what is now referred to in shorthand as the Global South. Except for the brief Third Worldist interlude of the 1960s, when militant intellectuals like Mao, Giap, and Guevara were read and commented on, Western Marxists did not, for the most part, seek out, translate, and converse with the tradition's non-Western theorists.[6] Moreover, Arab Marxists were either criticized or neglected by critics whose reading practices condemned them for what they dubbed their Orientalist, historicist, and modernist discursive assumptions. Their "epistemological complicity" with Empire turned them from revolutionaries to discursive compradors.[7] You know you're really out of luck when both Eurocentric Marxists and their postcolonial critics agree to ignore you. Moreover, the imbrication of scholarship on the Middle East in Western political agendas sidelined militants who were neither bound by the frontiers of the nation-state nor the boundaries of religious tradition and were therefore on the margins of nationalism and Islamism.[8] Last but not least, these militant intellectuals, who shared many of the same texts that later came to constitute the body of academic theory that social scientists drew on, appeared, at first sight, to be much closer to these disciplines' theoretical skin than, say, Salafi Muslims. Their low coefficient of "Otherness" pushes to the limit the question of who occupies the slot of anthropological understanding and is a subject of charitable interpretation and who is the object of critical condemnation.

This is why, in recovering this history, my aim is to bypass the treatment of modern and contemporary Arab intellectuals as falling into one of two camps: either imitators of the West, call them self-Orientalizing and westernized natives if you want, or autochthonous—religious thinkers engaging in an immanent critique of their societies.[9] I hope I have managed to convey that what I am engaged in is far from a study of the unilinear reception by Arab thinkers of Western revolutionary and critical theorists, which at times announces itself with sensationalist titles à la *Reading Althusser in Ras Beirut,* anticipating the metropolitan dazzlement at the wonderful conjunction of reading a "universal" text in a "particular" location. Reception presumes a priori an origin and a destination, an authentic and a copy, while I am making a case for the primacy of multidirectional streams of translation.[10]

Having said that, Arab thought and literature have, in the past hundred years, also been produced from the Global North, a fact exacerbated by the massive displacements of people in the wake of the Arab revolutions. Successive waves of migration resulting from economic hardship, colonialism, relentless imperial interventions, authoritarian regimes, and civil wars resulted in the dispersion of Arab thinkers; just think of the Palestinians, who became a stateless diaspora after the first wave of eviction from their homeland that took place with the establishment of the state of Israel in 1948. Arab thinkers and militants could be at home, in the diaspora, in exile, refugees, or shuttling back forth between their homes and a more secure location depending on political circumstances.

This dispersion is also linguistic: in addition to Arabic, they mostly also write in English or French or in more than one of these languages. While *Revolution and Disenchantment* focuses primarily on the travels, trajectories, and works of militant intellectuals who founded Socialist Lebanon, it does so by engaging their labors in the same analytic frameworks as Arab thinkers in the metropoles. It aims to incorporate into the spaces of contemporary Arab thought those distinguished exilic contributors, such as Edward Said, who rubbed shoulders with these thinkers in the same pro-Palestinian political and intellectual spaces, but are not included in the pantheon of contemporary Arab thinkers.[11] Without folding these intellectuals into the same tradition, scholarship will fail to address the shifting conditions of production of Arab thought, and it will reproduce the colonial divide. Arab thinkers at home will continue to be objects of study, while those in the diaspora will be addressed as colleagues to be engaged or as theorists whose work is used to frame the works and lives of others. This act of folding acquires an added significance in the wake of the Arab revolutions (2011–), which led to an increase in the global dispersion of Arabs from São Paolo to Istanbul. Former revolutionaries and militant intellectuals are today visiting researchers, professors, scholars at risk, and graduate students around the world.

To put it briefly, the book makes an argument for considering Edward Said not only as a cosmopolitan and postcolonial theorist but also as an Arab intellectual among others intimately impacted by, and engaged with, the unfolding of political events in the region—and for understanding the disenchanted Marxists at home, not as "local, autochthonous" intellectuals but as theorists at the crossroads of transnational streams of discourses. Of course, the mere fact that Edward Said is absent from compendia of contemporary Arab thought, or that his work is marshaled as the theoretical paradigm that frames the work of others, is symptomatic of the metropolitan unconscious of area studies disciplines. Otherwise, I wouldn't have to make a case to include Edward Said in the same analytical frame as Fawwaz Traboulsi, Waddah Charara, Sadik al-Azm, Ahmad Beydoun, and Mahdi 'Amil. In other words, I seek in this work to hold the tension between the interconnectedness of our world and the structural imbalance of power that makes some intellectual theorists to be engaged and others autochthonous intellectuals to be studied, or native informants to be used. I seek to avoid both highlighting an interconnectedness, which does not take power into account, and an erasure of interconnectedness, which is itself a symptom of power.

Political Present, Third. Last but not least, unearthing this archive in, and for, our political present is a timely affair. I certainly do not intend to collapse the distance separating the past of the New Left militants from our present. The political conjuncture they inhabited and acted in, and the answers they articulated exclusively in a Marxian idiom before abandoning it, is not exactly ours today. I am also not attracted to retrospectively judging whether they were right or wrong in their analysis and political wagers. To recover the theoretical labors and visions of emancipation of a previous generation of militants and thinkers is not only an antidote to public amnesia but an exercise that clarifies the distinct contours of our present and an invitation to an intergenerational conversation around the possibilities and binds of emancipation.

In addition to revisiting the theoretical-political questions they were preoccupied with, and which have become salient today in the wake of the Arab popular uprisings (2011) and the recent global anticapitalist mobilizations that I mentioned in the prologue, I am also driven to revisit their dual legacy: revolutionary exhilaration and political despair. Hope and disenchantment; revolutions and murderous regimes, foreign interventions and civil wars; and citizens and communal subjects are all constitutive of our very recent past and our present. It is in this sense that we are inheritors of the dual legacy of hope and despair of the 1960s Left. To do so, I carve a path between a corrosive Left melancholy that disparages an uncertain and increasingly precarious present while drinking to stories of the 1960s, the golden age of internationalist solidarity, on the one hand, and a liberal and Islamist triumphalism that banishes this past's relevance to our present by dismissing this Marxist generation's critical labors and practice because of the collapse and disintegration of socialist regimes or their cultural alienation from their society, on the other.[12]

Fieldwork in Theory

In examining the transnational travels and translations of critical theory in different spaces such as political party cells and academic settings, as well as its uses and appropriations in political projects, the book engages in what I call "fieldwork in theory." It looks into the different social lives of theory. I ask not only how theory helps us understand the world but also what kind of work it does in it: how it seduces intellectuals, contributes to the cultivation of their ethos and sensibilities, and authorizes political practices for militants. Anthropology has produced a rich reflexive tradition that, by turning the discipline's critical gaze inward, has interrogated the epistemological assumptions undergirding its concepts and its practices of representation.[13] The book shifts the focus away from the critique of the discursive assumptions of theoretical discourses to the ethnography of their production, circulation, and political effects in nonacademic settings.[14] As the frames of inquiry become the objects of ethnographic investigation, the anthropological frontiers between the worlds of slick, context-less, abstract, and frequent flying theories and the concrete stickiness of ethnographic empirical worlds become increasingly muddied.[15]

Fluency in theory was, and remains, a prized good in anthropology despite recent observations that the discipline has taken an empiricist turn.[16] For one, dabbling in abstractness makes for a more fluid circulation and a wider readership, as any editor would tell you. In anthropology, it also provides a common lingua franca that rises above the particularities of the discipline's geographic subdivisions, joining its practitioners together in a more encompassing disciplinary space of arguments. For instance, in the mid-1970s, Middle East anthropology was considered a marginal subfield that had by and large failed to both attract an audience beyond area specialists and contribute to disciplinary theoretical debates.[17] By the late 1980s Middle East anthropology managed to escape its parochialism. It was home to two influential theorists—Clifford Geertz and Pierre Bourdieu—as well as some key figures of "reflexive anthropology" (Vincent Crapanzano, Paul Rabinow, and Kevin Dwyer).[18]

At least since Geertz recast doing fieldwork as an act of interpretation, strict separation between observation and "data collection," on the one hand, and interpretation and theoretical reflection, on the other, became harder to maintain.[19] This separation was roughly mapped on a temporal and spatial structure. First, the anthropologist travels somewhere to do fieldwork. This is the moment of participant observation, the ethnographer's gaze, and experiences, supposedly to be recorded in field notes and diaries—a moment of discovery and self-discovery. And then there is the second moment, a consequence of the anthropologist's privilege of departure, for metropolitan anthropologists, who for the most part do not permanently reside in the societies they study.[20] This is the time when the anthropologist comes back from the field and sifts through her notes, audio recordings, pictures, and archives to compose a text presenting the collected material.[21] This is when the "raw material" gets processed and made to *speak back* to theoretical concerns, when it gets fashioned into a recognizable text complying with the styles and academic conventions of the field. After years of mentorship, writing manuals and boot camps, procrastination and drafts of drafts, the initial ethnographic gaze is, at last, translated into a disciplinary trace.

Having said that, anthropological practice is still by and large structured around a distinction between the anthropologist's theory and the people's lives and intellectual traditions, which she studies during her fieldwork. This leads anthropologists to struggle with a few things, mainly the epistemological status of their accounts of people's lives, practices, and discourses, which are mediated by their own theoretical tools. Anthropologists are no longer authoritatively affirming, like Ernest Gellner did in his study of Muslim Moroccan Berbers, that "what appears to be *vox dei* is in reality *vox populi*."[22] The epistemic authority of the anthropologists' theoretical discourses remains, nonetheless, a vexed question. As Michael Jackson recently asked, "But why not place Sophocles' drama of Oedipus, Freud's model of the psyche, and Kalabari [Nigeria] and Tallensi [Ghana] myths on a par?," undoing therefore the distinction between art, theory, and myth.[23] Because thought, Jackson says, requires some distance from the empirical field while underscoring that distancing is not a "sign of superior intellectual skill," nor are the accounts produced as a result endowed "with a superior epistemological truth-value."[24] Philosophy, he adds, is a strategy to take our distance from the sensory and social worlds of experience, in contrast to ethnography, which is one for close and "intersubjective encounters."[25] In brief, we encounter again the distinction between the sticky materiality and intersubjectivity of the lived empirical world, and the slick, abstract, conceptual universe that hovers above it.

This distinction is also upheld by authors who do not argue for what is gained by the use of philosophy and theory but what is potentially lost. "People," João

Biehl and Peter Locke write, "are plural and ambiguous, irreducible to history and populations, norms and social forces."[26] In this case, theory, which is put to use to provide an account of a particular ethnographic encounter, risks, through its powers of subsumption, ironing out the complexities of the world. It also stifles "conceptual innovation" from the ethnographic ground up. Calls were also issued to return to ethnographic theory, as a response to a diagnosis of the discipline as descending into a parochialism as a result of its conceptual subservience to Continental philosophy coupled with a neglect of its own history, debates, and concepts, such as mana, taboo, and totemism.[27] In contrast to the discipline's past, when philosophers, social theorists, and psychoanalysts could not avoid wrestling with its ethnographic concepts, today anthropologists churn out studies that apply "the concept-of-the-month" in a game that no one outside the discipline cares about.[28]

These current debates about theory in anthropology are symptomatic of the discipline's anxiety regarding the political and epistemic authority of its discourses vis-à-vis the forms of life it inquires about (are its concepts superior to other traditions of intellectual inquiry?) and their intellectual authority vis-à-vis the big ideas produced by philosophy (are they subservient to Continental philosophy?). Anthropologists, and sociologists, have held philosophy in such awe that it has led them to oscillate between getting as close as possible to it and trying to dethrone it.[29] The French genealogy of the social sciences, which provides US academia with much of what it considers to be its theory, reveals—from Émile Durkheim to Pierre Bourdieu—different attempts to displace the authority of philosophy by arguing that the social sciences provide better, and more reflexive, answers to philosophical questions than the mother discipline herself.[30] These debates also bring out the question of anthropology's status today as a discipline that tries to be accountable to multiple constituencies, both internal and external to it, that are driven by different questions and attachments. It has to be wary of accusations of colonial violence, which can take the form of reifying difference, or of culturally appropriating a concept from its everyday uses in its form of life and "elevating it" to the status of theory, while simultaneously striving to be theoretically innovative and autonomous from the hegemony of ideas produced by philosophers. Can it manage to carve out a space for itself that does not fall back on the epistemological violence it was accused of in the past, when it generated its ethnographic concepts from below, without being epistemologically subservient to Continental theory?

The distinctions between the concreteness and messiness of the field and the abstractness and slickness of theory, as well as the one between the bottom-up ethnographic theorizing and the top-down application of Continental theory, do not hold when one's "raw material" and "fieldwork experiences" include translations of, glosses on, and engagements with works and authors that form the canons of political and social theory. When one observes strands of one's own "theory" in the field—but not exclusively so, let me add—the presumed "innocence" of the supposed first moment of immersion, observation, and experience evaporates, since the frames through which one sees, classifies, and records are themselves, in this particular case, the objects of inquiry. The back and forth between the stickiness, concreteness, and senses-drenched materiality of the field and the slick world of abstract theory comes to a halt. In this case, the conceptual distance separating the tradition doing the inquiring and the one inquired about diminishes. For this is an internal traffic in theory. Yet the initial conservative pleasure of recognition, which overcomes the anthropologist as a result of her acquaintance with these theorists in the classroom (say, Marx, Gramsci, Bourdieu, Althusser), quickly recedes from view. It vanishes as the researcher encounters the multiple social and political lives of concepts, which are translated, transfigured, and embedded in emancipatory projects by members belonging to a different *generation* whose spaces of experiences and horizons of expectation were fashioned by different times and places. This is why doing fieldwork in theory, and tackling the question of theory from the South, cannot restrict itself to picking a few concepts, or authors away from their spaces of argument, to call into question some aspect of, or highlight an absence in, metropolitan critical theory.[31]

Fieldwork in theory moves away from the reification of discursive assumptions toward the labors of excavation of traditions of intellectual inquiry and the reconstitution of the theoretical, ideological, and political stakes at play in order to understand the numerous translations and modulations of critical theory.[32] Moreover, far too often revisiting the works of earlier critical thinkers focuses on assessing the purchase of their theories, either by making a case for the usefulness of their concepts for understanding the contemporary moment or by going in the opposite direction by seeking to denaturalize our present by underlining the difference separating their labors of conceptualization from ours. In both cases, their theories are what are mainly at stake in the excavation operation. In this work, I am also driven by a desire to recover something more than their concepts. I will pay attention to their critical ethos, their intellectual sensibilities, their sense of positionality, their ways of navigating the terrains of social accountability and intellectual autonomy and of theoretical production and political practice. In paying attention to these extra-epistemological issues, I avoid collapsing the inquiry into the social lives of theory, into a reified conceptual analysis of Marxist, Islamic, or secular discourses. In doing so, we get a better sense of the political struggles and the stakes animating the spaces in which these theoretical works were produced, circulated, and appropriated. I am driven to do so by a desire not only to provide a more complex picture of the intellectual life and political struggles in the Arab world but also to curtail an instrumental appropriation of "Arab theory" and to forestall the reproduction in critical scholarly discourses—and disciplinary institutions—of ideological distinctions, such as between the secular and the religious.[33] In *Revolution and Disenchantment*, I intentionally *hold the tension* between narrative (historical and ethnographic) and theory without seeking to release it in one of the two directions.[34]

Time of History: Traveling Militants and Theories

This generation of intellectuals came into a world that had already been radically altered by capitalist modernity and forces of European hegemony.[35] They were the products of a modern schooling system in Lebanon, which at the time taught French, and English to a lesser extent, alongside Arabic.[36] Both Waddah Charara and Ahmad Beydoun moved between private and public Francophone schools in their youth. Fawwaz Traboulsi, on the other hand, attended a private Anglophone boarding high school. The choice of where to go for higher education was, as would be expected, determined by the second language one possessed. Beydoun and Charara received grants to study in France, while Traboulsi traveled to England and studied at the American University of Beirut.[37] Sadik Jalal al-Azm (1934–2016), the Syrian philosopher and fiery public intellectual, did his graduate work at Yale University after studying at the American University of Beirut. The Lebanese University, the only institution of public higher learning in Lebanon, was founded in 1951, a bit less than a decade after Lebanon's independence. After exiting from revolutionary political practice, Charara, Beydoun, and a handful of other comrades from Socialist Lebanon would teach at the public university, while Traboulsi would join the private Anglophone universities.[38]

This generation's travels to the metropoles to study their own societies, coming back to lead revolutionary lives before finding sanctuary in the university in the wake of political disenchantment, is a familiar postcolonial story. Yet Socialist Lebanon's militant intellectuals traveled in the opposite direction of some of the best known public intellectuals of their generation.[39] Sadik Jalal al-Azm and Edward Said were detached ivory tower academics who did their graduate work on Immanuel Kant and Joseph Conrad, respectively. Struck by the 1967 blitzkrieg, they converted. They moved out of the university and into the world, inaugurating a life of public engagement that came to define their legacy. Socialist Lebanon's militants, on the other hand, had always found themselves swimming in political streams before an event—the Lebanese civil war, in the case of Charara and Beydoun—left them high and dry. They moved from the world and into the academy. The crisscrossing lives of these revolutionaries turned academics and academics turned public intellectuals intersected at the Palestinian juncture. The high tides of the Palestinian revolution during the late 1960s and early 1970s brought them together. They either joined the revolution or became its allies before going their separate political and theoretical ways at different points in the next decade.

It is difficult to conceive of the lives of this generation of leftist militant intellectuals without dwelling on their intimate relation to the practice of translation. During the days of militancy, one translated for purposes of political education, as a strategy to give Marxist political arguments a different gloss on a doctrinal point and to anchor a political line in a theoretical ground. Later on, one translated a text to make it available for students in a seminar, and, of course, translation is always one way to earn some income.[40] These translations, especially those associated with the Marxist tradition, were not translated from their original languages (Marx: German; Lenin and Trotsky: Russian; Gramsci: Italian; Guevara: Spanish), but mostly from their French or English translations. At times an Arabic text was produced by simultaneously translating from English and French translations. In the particular case of a translation from a translation, which I will explore further in chapter 2, the metropole's languages, publishing houses, and publications, such as Éditions Maspero, *Le Monde Diplomatique*, *Les Temps Modernes*, *Historical Materialism*, and *New Left Review*, were pivotal institutional bridges that made, via metropolitan languages, the ideas and experiences of different militants and theorists from the South and the North accessible to each other.[41] I say one, because this globally interconnected world, which was fashioned by the practice and travels of militants as well as the intense circulation and translation of texts, did not always transit through metropolitan universities, periodicals, and publishers. It was also fostered by the art festivals, publications, and intellectual, political, and military institutions of the nonaligned and socialist worlds.

Besides their labors of linguistic translation, these militant intellectuals effected an additional act of translation. The knowledges these militants produced, relying on the transnational discourses of Marxism, Leninism, and Third Worldist radical thought, were not merely representations of their societies but rather interventions in them that were part and parcel of their revolutionary political practice. They underscored the centrality of adapting Marxist concepts for the formulation of a communist politics attentive to the particularities of their political present, which went under the heading of the "Arabization of Marxism." These were acts of transfiguration that "refunction a text . . . for different demanding-sites," moving away from translation's problematic of meaning and its attendant questions.[42] These acts of linguistic translations from translations and conceptual transfigurations were fueled more by the impediment of revolutionary practice than by a fidelity to an original text. They were not mediations between a self and an other, an attempt to bridge supposed incommensurabilities between cultures, or an initiation of a dialogue between different intellectual traditions. Theirs was not an attempt that sought, as many critical and anthropological works do, to render what seems unfamiliar at first glance familiar or, going in the opposite direction, to denaturalize what we take for granted. They did not aim toward a rediscovery of one's own commitments in a different theoretical language or to reveal the contingency of one's own norms when refracted through a different prism. Rather, the practice of theorizing, which includes translation and transfiguration, was part and parcel of the arsenal of revolutionary politics, which was rendered possible by a deeply held belief in a shared horizon of an emancipation to come.

These practices, discourses, and institutions assumed and produced a global interconnectedness, a political universality of sorts premised on internationalist solidarity, the urgency of political practice, and multidirectional translation—North-South; South-South—that dodged the usual trap of *recognition* and consecration of authors from the colonies by the strong institutions of the metropole. "The structures of power the colonized writer confronts," Talal Asad wrote a while ago, "are institutional, not textual." "When someone pleads with the colonizer to make a judgment in a particular writer's favor, to have him or her translated and read 'seriously,' what is sought," Asad added, is "the modern world culture's transcendent power to redefine that writer's value as 'universal.'"[43] In the case Asad is describing, the metropole's institutions are the gatekeepers that grant an author access to "the universal," enabling the global circulation and multiple translations of the work—even though it is often a universal that always falls short of attaining true universality. Literary criticism in the Anglo-American academy, Rosalind Morris notes, "tends to attribute to the third world literary text an irreducible particularity." "The resistance here," she writes, "is not of or by the third world writer and/or her writings, let alone by the subaltern; it is the resistance of dominance to its possible displacement from the exclusive claim to universality."[44]

These militant intellectuals were fashioned by and contributed to fashioning a globally interconnected world that cannot be captured adequately by an ahistorical deployment of East/West or North/South binaries. Nor was its commonality synonymous with a homogeneity and an epistemological naïveté. Their theories cannot be reduced to a wholesale operation of the importation of Left varieties of modernization theory, even if some of them dabbled in them, and to self-Orientalizing discourses. To do so is to mistake multipolar acts of translation and transfiguration for a one-way colonial imports business. The figure of the internationalist militant intellectual/translator, not that of the westernized discursive comprador, is at the heart of the first part of this book—chapters 1 to 3.

In highlighting these points, I aim to underscore three different pathways to attain universality. The first is the a posteriori outcome of *political articulation*. It is sustained by an ethos of internationalist solidarity that, through traveling theories and militants, and multiple acts of translation/transfiguration, fashions a common world. True, this pathway was premised on positing class as the universal grammar of inequality, but its universality is socially mediated and needed to be activated through the practices of transfiguration and militancy.[45] The second pathway privileges context-less, supposedly a priori universal concepts, say, rights, reason, and freedom, which subsume, and are in no need of, the double movement of transfiguration and militancy.[46] The third—metropolitan institutional consecration—is an outcome of power.

Times of the Sociocultural: Civil Wars, Communal Solidarities, and Metropolitan Epistemology Critique

Difference at the time of Marxist militancy was not yet articulated on the ground of communal—sectarian, regional, familial—solidarities. It was a function of the particularity of the political present that through a diagnosis of the political forces, and attention to possibilities for practice, also steered the militants of Socialist Lebanon away from grounding difference in historicist evolutionary terms, which in communist politics took the form of stagism.[47] Militant Arab Marxism and anthropology articulated mirror images of difference. The first articulated difference in historical terms (historicist stagism, or the anticipation of a revolutionary future), while the second articulated difference in sociocultural terms.

The compressed years of the 1970s revealed clearly the differences between the slow temporalities of academic disciplines and the fast pace of political events. Around the time when metropolitan disciplines were taking stock of events such as decolonization, the Vietnam War, and the increased racialization of Arabs in the wake of 1967, by interrogating the entanglements of their knowledges with colonial power, particularly by diasporic scholars (e.g., Talal Asad and Edward Said), there was a swift unraveling of a political world, through the sectarian violence of a civil war, that dislodged Marxist concepts—"revolutionary masses," "organic intellectuals," "revolutionary theory"—from the world they were supposed to capture and transform. To put it briefly, by the time these disciplines were slowly beginning the process of their own decolonization from ahistorical assumptions in the mid-1970s, Marxist militant intellectuals were beginning to cast away their revolutionary conceptual arsenal to examine the wartime communal logics. As diasporic intellectuals began their critical forays into the politics of theory, the shocked revolutionaries called into question their own previously cherished theory of politics. At a time when metropolitan disciplines dealing with the non-Western world were emerging from their prehistory, breaking away from the authoritative repetitions of Orientalist structures, the disenchanted Marxists, betrayed by history's promise of emancipation, were entering into a posthistorical world that was characterized by the repetitions of communal wars.

Those years not only witnessed disenchanted Marxists at home and metropolitan critical scholarship going in opposite critical directions (History →←Society/Culture).[48] What these divergent critical directions shared was, as I will develop in chapters 4, 5, and 6, a sidelining of ideological distinctions—Left and Right, progressives and reactionaries—as fundamental criteria of theoretical and political discernment. The autonomy of the ideological was called into question from two radically different corners: the discursive and the sociological. Thinkers in the metropoles, such as Edward Said, who were influenced by Michel Foucault's work, sidelined *theoretically* the ideological distinctions between right-wing authors and Marxists by showing how both groups, despite their ideological differences, partake in the same Orientalist discursive assumptions (chapter 6). While Charara, who was closely observing the unfolding of the fighting during the Lebanese civil and regional wars, noted that despite the ideological divisions separating the fighters on opposite sides of the trenches (Left and Right), the more fundamental divide, which dictated common modalities of practice for both sides, was communal—primarily sectarian, but regional and kin solidarities also played a role (chapter 5).

The Euro-American epistemological critique of Western knowledges of the non-West, which took off in the late 1970s and 1980s, inaugurated what would come to be known as postcolonial studies; it was also contemporaneous with a crisis of Marxism in Europe. Those same years witnessed the ebbing of the vigorous debates that sought in different ways to think the question of the political—Mao, Gramsci, Althusser—away from economic reductionism. Critical works, sometimes undertaken by former Marxist militants such as Jean-François Lyotard, subjected master narratives, universals, and notions of totality to a corrosive theoretical skepticism.[49] While poststructuralist and postcolonial thinkers were theoretically calling into question the discursive assumptions shared by liberals and leftists for their violence and their exclusions, the disenchanted Lebanese Marxists were experiencing the political breakdown of the Lebanese state and of a common world of ideological distinctions. Theirs was a world fragmented into blocs governed by subfactions of fighting militias in Beirut or by the regimes that increasingly colonized every sphere of social life—political, educational, judicial—and subjugated them to the will of the sovereign. They did not necessarily have a theoretical longing for universals or the application of Western liberal models. Rather, they longed for a dignified life in *common* that escapes oscillating between a world fragmented by sectarian warlords and identitarian communal discourses, on the one hand, and one that is colonized by tyrants who subjugate their citizens for decades on end in the name of the coming battle against imperialism, on the other. The final chapter of the book traces the fork in critical and political agendas in the wake of the communal fragmentation of the militants' common world and the Iranian Revolution between those intellectuals who not so long ago worked side by side in support of the Palestinian revolution.

On Method

Edward Said critically addressed the intelligentsia in the postcolonies, noting that one of the indications of cultural domination resided in its auxiliary status to Western trends.[50] "Impressive evidence for this," he wrote, "is found in the social sciences and, surprisingly enough, among radical intellectuals whose Marxism is taken wholesale from Marx's own homogenizing view of the Third World."[51] Whether gravitating in the Soviet or US orbits, the rigged concepts, which were at the heart of Arab intellectuals' thought and guiding their political practice, risked turning them from emancipators into unknowing dupes partaking in their own domination. Over time this mode of epistemological criticism has gained more and more traction in the scholarship on the Middle East and keeps on adding new objects to its critical mill. The critique of discursive assumptions, whose focal point was the interrogation of modernist, liberal, feminist, and Marxist assumptions about nation, gender, religion, and culture, has more recently extended its terrain to focus on new objects of investigation: secular and LGBTQ discursive assumptions. The insurrectional acts these modes of reading enabled at first withered away as they became increasingly doxic procedures of a researcher's domain.[52]

Despite the fact that it has become normalized, and hegemonic in anthropology and Middle East studies, this reading practice never ran out of steam. In geopolitical conjunctures, characterized by US imperial interventions and invasions that were buttressed by ideologies of liberation, this defensive and oppositional practice of criticism constituted a much-needed corrective to the enlisting of discourses—such as feminism and liberalism—in military imperial ventures.[53] This critique of the entanglement of discourses, say, Orientalist or universalist, with imperial power did not lose its impetus, precisely because of the sense of political urgency generated by the geopolitical conjuncture that propelled it and bestowed upon this theoretical critique its anti-imperialist *lettres de noblesse*.[54] Moreover, for those of us who teach in the US, and who witness in our everyday lives institutional and personal racist acts of violence against Arabs and Muslims, these critical reading practices, which seek to disrupt the reproduction of racist tropes, at the very least in the classroom, acquire an added importance. "The web of racism, cultural stereotypes, political imperialism, dehumanizing ideology, holding in the Arab or the Muslim is very strong indeed," Said wrote regarding life in the West, and particularly in the US, "and it is this web which every Palestinian has come to feel as his uniquely punishing destiny."[55]

These critical reading practices are still much needed as pedagogical tools and *strategic* modalities of public intervention in the Euro-American domestic battles of representation. Having said that, they have become increasingly problematic as a hegemonic theoretical apparatus in the academic fields of knowledge production and in public interventions *about* the Arab world. In the wake of the initial insurrectionary works by Talal Asad and Edward Said, this mode of criticism morphed from a practice that teases out the different layers of mediation between knowledge and power into one of ideological adjudication. The nonintended effect of the Saidian rewiring of the Foucauldian genealogies that marked the power/knowledge couplet (colonial power/imperial knowledge) and imbricated it within a political anticolonial antagonism with a dominant subject (the West) and a dominated one (the Orient) is that it produced a form of discursive-ideology critique that unmasks the rigged discursive assumptions undergirding thinkers' thought to reveal a class of "westernized natives" who are discursively, and at times economically, allied with Empire. The "Oriental" subjects who are fashioned by "Orientalist" knowledges (ontology) put them to use (epistemology), like the colonialists and imperialists, to undermine from the inside their own societies (politics). Perhaps the most memorable sentence that encapsulates the workings of this modality of criticism that collapsed ontology and politics into epistemology is contained in Leila Ahmed's powerful revisionist critique of the nineteenth-century Egyptian thinker Qasim Amin, who was often hailed as a feminist pioneer in the Arab world. After noting that Amin's work is the rearticulation "of the colonial thesis of the inferiority of the native and Muslim and the superiority of the European" in a "native upper-middle class voice, the voice of a class economically allied with colonizers," Ahmed quips that "far from being the father of Arab feminism, then, Amin might more aptly be described as the son of Cromer [the British proconsul general in Egypt from 1877 to 1907] and colonialism."[56]

Three decades after the insurrectionary critical contraption came into being to criticize the authority, and claims to neutrality and objectivity, of Western knowledges of the non-West, it was repurposed as an ersatz anti-imperialist implement wielded to condemn Arab thinkers and militants from the nineteenth century to our present for internalizing "colonial taxonomies" and being discursive compradors of sorts.[57] What disappeared with this repurposing is the crucial initial concern with the question of the authority of discourses, which Talal Asad was particularly preoccupied with. The question of authority cannot be separated from the loci of enunciation of these discourses' authors, their institutional sites of production, and their spheres of circulation, in addition to their discursive backbone.[58] Evacuating the question of authority risks collapsing the two meanings of representation—re-presentation as portrait (art, philosophy) and representation as proxy (speaking for, politics)—into each other.[59] The irony of the matter lies in the fact that the epistemology critique of Arab thinkers took off at the point of their political and military defeat, and at times imprisonment and assassination, by Israel, the authoritarian regimes, and the rising sectarian and religious political forces. Their words came to be criticized as their worlds began falling apart.

This modality of criticism remains "parasitic" on a particular idea of the West.[60] In an older Maoist jargon the West constitutes the main contradiction for these critics, which is why these critiques cannot account for the complexities and internal divisions of Arab and Muslim societies. Its main move, vis-à-vis those Arab thinkers whose discursive assumptions are dubbed to be in alliance with Empire, is a strategy of inversion that never surrenders its attachment to the West. By only taking up an oppositional stance toward the attempts of the West and "westernized natives" to refashion these forms of life, without dialectically relating these attempts to the internal historical dynamics and contradictions of these societies, this modality of criticism falls very close to reinscribing the argument that the engine of historical transformation is external to these societies, but instead of welcoming it like twentieth-century modernization theory did, it now has to be resisted.

In fact, the archive of contemporary Arab thought is primarily examined, like the older generation of scholars did, through the anxiety of influence of the West. In the introduction to his magisterial *Arabic Thought in the Liberal Age*, Albert Hourani wrote about the pitfalls of focusing on individual thinkers in contrast to schools of thought.[61] In doing so, there is a risk, Hourani wrote, "of giving the impression that they were more important and original than they really were; most of them (although not quite all) were derivative thinkers of the second or third rank of importance."[62] Highlighting this tradition's reproduction of Orientalist and colonial taxonomies, and doubting the originality of secular Muslim thought, underscores, like Hourani, the derivative nature of this tradition. Again, the difference lies in inverting the normative charges associated with this common diagnosis. While Hourani focuses on these thinkers because they are vectors of modernization, the oppositional metropolitan critics underscore the epistemological and ontological violence at the heart of these intellectuals' visions that seeks to bring about Western hegemony. What gets foreclosed in the process is an engagement with modern and contemporary Arab and Muslim thought that does not reinscribe the West as its sovereign subject. Moreover, critiques of Arab and Muslim intellectuals as self-Orientalizing, unoriginal, and plagued by colonial taxonomies reproduce the historicism and theories of lack that are criticized in these thinkers' works by unwittingly reinscribing once more the Arab world as lagging behind, this time around in the production of original thought.

Therefore, if one is interested, like I am in this project, in understanding the travails of this generation of thinkers, the questions they posed, the answers they proposed, and the different positions they were arguing against or aligning themselves with, a practice of criticism premised on unmasking "faulty," or not, epistemological assumptions will not be of any help. What it will do is erase the historicity of these fields of argument and obscure the *character* of these specific interventions. It also forecloses the investigation of how theories, which are embedded in language games and political projects, help fashion the ethos of militant intellectuals and later of disenchanted solitary critics. For instance, in just focusing on universal—say, secular or liberal—discursive assumptions, and aligning them a priori with the US empire and human rights imperialism and epistemological violence, these critical strategies risk reifying these universals by erasing the logics of political practice, the powers of institutions, and the transfiguring acts of translation that repurpose these discourses and embed them in different projects. It does so through eliding central histori-cal and ethnographic questions. How are they put to use? By whom? In what conjuncture and to what end? How do their international travels change them and their adherents? What projects do they enable and foreclose as they are put to practice? While the unmasking of Eurocentric knowledges parading as uni-versals proved to be salutary against the effortlessly thrown historicist charges of the "backwardness" of non-Western cultures, it also risks naturalizing the conceptual universal/particular distinction on a geographical West/East one.[63] This will again participate in either hailing difference as a form of resistance to the homogenizing power of the West or claiming it to be a traditional, or "pre-capitalist," remainder that needs to be overcome to safely reach the much awaited and always deferred shores of modernity.[64]

In investigating these questions, I will mainly draw sustenance from the methodology developed by the Ludwig Wittgenstein and John L. Austin–inspired work of Quentin Skinner and David Scott's notion of a problem-space. The central tenet of Skinner's method is captured in "Wittgenstein's remark 'that words are also deeds.'"[65] Skinner posited that in order to under-stand the *historical meaning* of the text, one has to view it as an intervention in argument and ask about the *character* of the intervention[66] through asking questions such as "What is this text doing? What is the author doing in this text?"[67] "How is it positioned in relation to existing arguments? What kind of an intervention does it constitute? What does it accept, reject, repudiate, satirize, ignore in existing discussions?"[68] The import of R. G. Collingwood's "logic of question and answer," put to use in Skinner's work, was its insight that it is helpful to approach any intentional object of the human mind (a building, a piece of music, a philosophical work) as a solution to certain prob-lems, and hence the historian's task is "to find out the questions to which the text was the answer."[69]

David Scott elaborates the concept of a problem-space, mainly out of his reading of Collingwood and Skinner, "though in the background of it," he tells the late Stuart Hall, one can "discern the trace of Wittgenstein, J. L. Austin and Foucault."[70] In *Conscripts of Modernity: The Tragedy of Colonial Enlightenment* (2004), Scott notes that

> a "problem-space," in my usage, is meant first of all to demarcate a dis-cursive context, a context of language, but it is more than a cognitively intelligible arrangement of concepts, ideas, images, meanings, and so on—though it is certainly this. It is a context of argument, and therefore one of intervention. A problem-space, in other words, is an ensemble

of questions and answers around which a horizon of identifiable stakes (conceptual as well as ideological-political stakes) hangs.[71]

Moreover, what this concept allows Scott to do is to gauge the temporality of different spaces of arguments, how in a new conjuncture "old questions may lose their salience, their bite, and so lead the range of old answers that once attached to them to appear lifeless, quaint, not so much wrong as irrelevant."[72] In emphasizing the temporality of problem-spaces, Scott is after a rethinking of the relation of past to present, to avoid understanding the past in the terms of the present, to sidestep the "presentism that reads the past as a naive or mistaken version of the present"[73] by reconstructing the character of an intervention in its own space of arguments. Scott, however, is also interested in an additional question following the historical act of reconstruction, that of interrogating the saliency of the reconstructed move for the critic's present. Is the question still worth answering?, he asks. In that sense, Scott adds a normative edge, an engaged posture, to the labors of historical reconstruction, noting the insufficiency of the detached reconstructing of the past practiced by Skinner, "who bows and exits just at the point at which the question arises of determining and judging the stakes in the present of the rehistoricizing intervention."[74] The labors and responsibility of the historian are not to stop at the present's doorstep, by denaturalizing and revealing the constructedness of what we now take for granted.[75] It is not enough to show how things were different in the past, and therefore infer that our present could possibly have different contours; rather, Scott urges the critic to knock on this door and seek "to make the present yield more attractive possibilities for alternative futures."[76]

In this project I will build on Scott's insights, drawing attention to the problem-spaces, not only of different generations of critics but of differently located contemporary critics. While Scott's interest lies mostly in the temporality of problem-spaces, I will put this notion to work to also help us understand the dynamics of synchronous fields of argument in the Levant and in the North American academy.[77] Moreover, in times when oppositional culture in the metropoles is growing farther and farther away from the thinkers and movements of emancipation on the ground in the Arab world—unlike the earlier generation's solidarity and alliance with the Palestinian national liberation movements—these critics are answerable to a variant of Scott's critique of Skinner's detachment. So you've shown from afar how the discursive assumptions that Marxist and feminist militants and thinkers are using are all deeply entangled with power. This reveals that you have mastered the application of critical tool, but is that enough? Can't theory go beyond oppositional critique toward "positing a new imaginary figure/model of intelligibility," as Cornelius Castoriadis suggested—one that can be tethered to a reimagining of political futures.[78]

Coda

This book is best approached like a musical fugue. Its major voice is the Lebanese New Left. Diasporic critical theorists, like Edward Said and Talal Asad, and the impact that their critical work had on metropolitan disciplines, are its minor voice. It has two more minor voices, which appear every now and then. The first is the work of scholars associated with the South Asian Subaltern Studies collective, who shared in their beginnings a common Maoist and Gramscian lineage with the theorists of Socialist Lebanon but put it to use differently. The second is the 1960s French Left. Socialist Lebanon's militant intellectuals were in touch with some of its factions and kept track of its theoretical productions and militant strategies. As the fugue unfolds, its main subject—emancipation, particularly from colonialism and imperialism—goes through a succession of inversions and counterpoints that are still unfolding in time.

The form of the book reflexively reenacts this generation's dialectic of revolutionary hope and political disenchantment. In part I—Time of History—I reconstruct the coming into being and high tides of the New Left by examining Socialist Lebanon's archive. In doing so, I underscore how the members of this generation were bound together by a collective project of emancipation, which inscribed itself within an internationalist constellation of revolutionary movements. In examining the multiple binds confronting the revolutionary project in part II—Times of the Sociocultural—I move from the reconstruction of a collective project of emancipation to an in-depth examination of Waddah Charara's own militant trajectory and critical work. The scale and focus of the chapters mirrors the transubstantiation of a collective of underground militant intellectuals writing anonymous clandestine texts in the service of the revolution into disenchanted, isolated critics in a wartorn polis.

PART I.
TIME OF
HISTORY

One was dealing with oneself as if under a constant demand, as an employee of History, or an employee of some other power, with many tasks to achieve.

—ABBAS BEYDOUN

1. O YOUTH, O ARABS, O NATIONALISTS

Recalling the High Tides of Anticolonial Pan-Arabism

Pick a pen and take note: the Muslims make the pilgrimage to Mecca, the Christians to the Vatican and the national liberation movements to Algiers!
— AMILCAR CABRAL

We will never repeat the past. . . . We will get rid of the past by regaining our rights in the Suez Canal. . . . O citizens—when we build the high dam we also build the dam of honor, freedom, and dignity, and we get rid of the dams of degradation and humiliation and declare all of Egypt one front. . . . All of Egypt will fight until its last drop of blood.
— GAMAL ABDEL NASSER, SPEECH ON THE FOURTH ANNIVERSARY
OF THE REVOLUTION IN ALEXANDRIA

Prelude

Revisiting *Arabic Thought in the Liberal Age*, a little bit more than two decades after its publication, Albert Hourani made a series of observations on the problem-space the book inhabited, as well as on the alternative directions the project could take, or maybe should have taken. These retrospective historiographical comments, included in the preface to the 1983 edition, fall into two overlapping sets of concerns. First, Hourani draws his readers' attentions to the insufficiency of a "pure" history of ideas and to the need to supplement it "by asking how and why the ideas of my writers had an influence on the minds of others."[1] The histories of ideas and arguments, Hourani suggested, would benefit from an anchoring in social history, an attentiveness to a finer scale of analysis that pays attention to intra-Arab distinctions, and an examination of the processes of mediation of thought via such vectors as poetry, which disseminate it to wider publics.[2]

In the second series of comments, Hourani recalled a guiding assumption of the project: focusing on breaks and discontinuities with the past. "To some extent," he wrote twenty years later, "I may have distorted the thought of the writers I studied, at least those of the first and second generations: the 'modern' element in their thought may have been smaller than I implied, and it would have been possible to write about them in a way which emphasized continuity rather than a break with the past."[3] Hourani's late interest in the question of historical continuity went beyond his retrospective worry regarding the emphasis placed on reading more "echoes of European thought" (discontinuity) than "echoes of Islamic political thought" (continuity) in the works of Arab thinkers he dealt with, as he put it a few years later in a rich autobiographical interview.[4] It took the form of a call to write about other kinds of writers. Those were the ones not given their due in the book. In the process Hourani alerted his readers to how the historian's present is refracted through the formation of historical objects, and how they are interpreted by making explicit the decisions he made in the early 1960s regarding who to include in his pantheon of Arab thought. "Those," as he put it, "who still lived in their inherited world of thought, whose main aim was to preserve the continuity of its tradition, and who did so in accustomed ways, writing and teaching within the framework of the great schools, the Azhar in Cairo or the Zaytuna in Tunis, or of the Sufi brotherhoods," were the authors who had remained dominant throughout the nineteenth century.[5] "In the present century they have lost much of their domination," noted the veteran historian, "or so it seemed at the point in time when I was writing my book." Hourani's "or so it seemed" gives his readers a clue to how his emerging interest in the question of continuity registers the transformations altering the political landscape in the Arab world in the two decades since he first published his book. "It is clearer now than it was then, at least to me," Hourani wrote, "that the extension of the area of political consciousness and activity, the coming of 'mass politics,' would bring into the political processes men and women who were still liable to be swayed by what the Azhar said or wrote, and what the shaykhs of a brotherhood might teach."[6]

Revisiting futures past in 1983, with an emphasis on continuity rather than its opposite, Hourani subtly revised some of the conclusions of his book's epilogue, "Between Past and Future," which addressed the post–World War II era from the vantage point of the early 1960s. There, the picture drawn was of the passing of a world divided into East and West, and the birth of a new modern world. The West had managed to carry out "its historic mission of creating a new and unified world."[7] "The world was one," Hourani concluded, during the age of independence and national liberation. Not only was it unified on the levels of material techniques and science but, more importantly for our purposes, "politically too the world had become one: there was a single universe of political discourse. There were of course different political systems, but the differences could not be explained simply in terms of regional or national character or tradition."[8] Differences, during the age of ideologies, were no longer predicated on the *particularities* of region, nation, or tradition. Rather, the differences were themselves contained within a single *universal* terrain of political discourse. "The most important of all changes which came to the surface in these twenty years," Hourani added in his depiction of the postwar era, "was this: the past was abolished whether it were the past of 'westernization' or the more distant past of the traditional societies."[9] The pasts of tradition, and westernization, seemed then to have passed for good to usher in a universal modernity at the pinnacle of anticolonial passions a decade after the coming to power of the Free Officers in Egypt (1952) and in the last hours of the Algerian struggle for national liberation. This was the time that preceded the Islamic revival and the Iranian Revolution. The promise of anticolonial nationalism had not yet been "followed by the crisis of the third-world-state, and the culture wars became identified with chauvinism, ethnic hatred, and cynically manipulative and corrupt regimes."[10]

The militant intellectuals that will take part in founding the Lebanese New Left in the mid-1960s were swept off their feet at a very young age by the tidal waves of Arab nationalisms and their promise of a united popular sovereignty on Arab lands after defeating colonialism, which had divided the Arab people into different state cantons. They grew up in that post–World War II age when the world, as Hourani observed in the early 1960s, had become one. The political, articulated ideologically, mainly between different nationalisms (say, Lebanese, Syrian, and Arab), appeared to have gained a greater autonomy from the social fabrics and cultural lifeworlds that previously articulated differences—what Hourani refers to as region, national character, and tradition. The postwar world that Hourani is describing is a time of modernity that, by abolishing the past of "westernization" and seemingly separating the political from the social and the cultural, especially in the form of Arab nationalism, acquires a higher degree of universality and renders political differences abstract and *commensurable.*

In what follows, I stitch together the biographical, political, and intellectual in a coming of age narrative that underscores the early pivotal events, particularly the high tides of Arab nationalism that marked these young soon to be militant intellectuals, and their own reconstructions of their distant pasts, before they founded the Lebanese New Left and became known as the 1960s generation.[11] "Recalling," in the chapter's title, is both an act of remembrance and a retrospective critical practice, as in requesting the return of a product already in use after the discovery of a manufacturing defect.[12] The products they are recalling are Arab nationalism and its promises of sovereignty and the modern, single ideological universe of political discourse they inhabited and that contributed so much to fashioning them into political subjects operating outside the boundaries of their own sectarian, regional, and kin communities.

This first chapter is also a "prehistory" of the New Left militant intellectuals who will for the most part found or join Socialist Lebanon (1964–70). I am using "prehistory" in four overlapping ways. First, it stands for the period that predates the time of their Marxist political engagement in underground political cells associated with practices of secrecy and anonymous publishing. Second, it also refers to the time before their deep immersion in Marxist theory: reading it, translating it, and producing it. I therefore mostly rely on their own reconstructions of their pasts in the interviews I conducted with them and in their memoirs to get a sense of the questions, hopes, and desires animating them there and then. Third, I use "prehistory" to refer to the times before the comrades' imaginations were captured by the movement of history whose milestones included such events as the Chinese, Cuban, and Vietnamese Revolutions. Finally, having been born in the first years of the Lebanese civil war (1975–90), a time when the Ba'th had already been in power in Syria and Iraq for more than a decade, I was not fully aware before I began conducting these interviews of the importance of Arab nationalism, and especially Ba'thist ideology and politics, to those militant intellectuals (such as Mahmoud Soueid, Abbas Beydoun, Azza Charara Beydoun, Fawwaz Traboulsi, Ahmad Beydoun, Waddah Charara, and Muhsin Ibrahim, among others) who would later form the backbone of the Lebanese New Left. The matter is not merely an empirical historical "lacuna" on my part. It is more than that. Having been born into times of "Really Existing Ba'thism," particularly in its Assadist incarnation, Arab nationalist politics and ideology was synonymous, from my own generational perspective, with authoritarian regimes and apparatuses of power masquerading as visions of national sovereignty against colonialism. For instance, revisiting the writings of Michel Aflaq, one of the founders and the ideologue of the Ba'th in and for our present, was never a question for me. The virulent debates between different strains of Arab nationalists—say, Nasserists and Ba'thists—were, as far as I was concerned, arcane historical materials. Despite their temporal proximity, they seemed light-years away from my own existential generational standpoint. They were a past past. On the other hand, coming of political age in the 1990s, after the interruption of the Lebanese civil war (1975–90) and in the wake of the hopes, projects, and mostly defeats of this generation of leftists, their past experiences, past projects, past hopes, and multiple political and intellectual transformations seemed alive and worthy of revisiting—enough at least to propel me to undertake this project.

Two caveats before I start narrating: writing about a generation of Lebanese leftist militant intellectuals coming of age in the aftermath of the 1948 Nakba and the rise of Abdel Nasser as the icon of Arab national liberation in the late 1950s requires taking stock of the particularities of Lebanese society's history and politics, namely, the shifting *articulations* of infranational familial, regional, and sectarian grounds with specific modern ideologies (Arab nationalism, communism, Lebanese nationalism) and supranational imaginaries and ties (Shi'i ties to Najaf, Maronites to Rome and France, for example). A word of caution is due here. In alluding to the articulation of infranational attachments, and supranational ones with modern ideologies such as Marxism, I could be misunderstood as going back to an older Orientalist literature on the area, which marginalized the importance of modern ideologies at work to explain all phenomena through the lens of an immutable Islamic civilizational whole. In an essay published in *Commentary* in January 1976, the British American historian Bernard Lewis wrote:

> For to admit that an entire civilization can have religion as its primary loyalty is too much. Even to suggest such a thing is regarded as offensive by liberal opinion, always ready to take protective umbrage on behalf of those whom it regards as its wards. This is reflected in the present inability, political, journalistic and scholarly alike, to recognize the importance of the factor of religion in the current affairs of the Muslim world and in the consequent recourse to the language of left-wing and right-wing, progressive and conservative, and the rest of the Western terminology, the use of which in explaining Muslim political phenomena is about as accurate and as enlightening as an account of a cricket match by a baseball correspondent.[13]

Edward Said's *Orientalism* (1978), in which this paragraph was cited, and the ensuing moment of postcolonial critique, has debunked the essentialist, ahistorical claims, on which such pronouncements on the Arab and Muslim world claiming its "exceptional" status are founded. In pointing to the peculiar *sociological* profile of these intellectuals and militants, such as the predominance of Shi'is among the ranks of the Lebanese Communist Party in the 1970s, or of Shi'i Beirut residents who hail from Lebanon's peripheries among the militant intellectuals of Socialist Lebanon in the mid-1960s, I do not highlight an ahistorical notion of religion, seeing in it the ultimate grid of explanation of an "exceptional" Arab politics.[14] Having said that, I also do not seek to erase the particular sociological profiles of these militants, which includes more than just an upbringing in a particular sectarian community, to engage in an "abstract" examination of theories and ideologies that does not account for the milieus in which these ideas found anchorage in particular times and places. Rather than isolating supposedly opposed first principles, "traditional" religious loyalty for the "Orientals" versus "modern" political ideologies for the "West," and either assert the distinction to prove the backwardness of the "Oriental" or negate it to assert the modernity of the non-Westerners and undo the "exception," it is more analytically fruitful, I think, to investigate how at different times and places, both in the West and in the non-West, different sociological distinctions and attachments based on, say, religion, region, family, gender, class, and race resonate and articulate with different political ideologies.

Second, after they disengaged from organized political activity, the intellectual militants who form the backbone of this project became distinguished social scientists, historians, and artists. There is no escape from engaging with their work, not only as the main body of material for this project but also to gain a thorough understanding of Lebanese history and its contemporary politics. As a result, in this chapter, and the rest of the work, I will follow Brinkley Messick's lead in using their texts *both* as "sources for analysis and objects of analysis."[15] There is no external detached body of texts that acts as a ground and is relied on to build a context in which these texts were intervening. I use these authors' oeuvre both to delineate the contours of a problem-space and to examine the interventions their texts were performing in a specific conjuncture.

Lebanon's Nations and Its One State

On September 1, 1920, French general Henri Gouraud proclaimed the state of Greater Lebanon, with Elias al-Huwayyik, the Maronite patriarch, standing to his right.[16] The new state was carved out by the French general, assuming the Mandate for Syria and Lebanon after defeating King Faysal's Arab forces and occupying Damascus, from territories formerly belonging to the Ottoman provinces of Syria and Beirut, which were annexed to the semiautonomous Mount Lebanon *Mutasarrifiyya* (provincial government). The new state, encompassing Sunni, Shiʻi, and Druze religious communities, eleven Christian ones, and a Jewish minority, was put together by the French around its long-term allies, the Maronite Christians, and *for them*.[17] The new arrangement was imposed on the land's Muslim communities, who had been torn away from the Syrian Arab hinterland, turning them "overnight from a millennium-old ruling majority into a 'minority.' They had become subject not only to the French themselves but to France's client, the Maronites."[18]

A weakened France, in the aftermath of its defeat during World War II, coupled with the Muslim elites' increasing adherence to the new state, produced a majority calling in 1943 for Lebanon's independence from the ailing imperial power. The fruit of this convergence was the National Pact, an unwritten agreement that founded independent Lebanon on a double negative: neither integration into Syria (the Muslims' Arab unionist demand) nor French protection (the Christians' demand). The double negation founding the nation defined Lebanon as a country "with an Arab face."[19] The new country would become part of the Arab world, taking part in the founding of the Arab League. It would also relinquish the West's protection, but not sever its ties with it, while pledging to become neither a sanctuary nor a passageway for colonialism, in the famous expression of Riad al-Sulh, Lebanon's preeminent Sunni leader and prime minister at the time. Lebanon, founded on a compromise between different infranational sectarian communities and their supranational (Arab and Western) imaginaries and loyalties, would continually fail to produce a hegemonic unifying narrative for what it means to be a Lebanese national.

Lebanon was, since its inception, and still is, a house of many mansions.[20] Not all of these mansions, though, would have equal stature in steering the Lebanese state, gaining access to resources, and articulating their vision of the nation. The division of political power since the country's first constitution, which was drafted in 1926 under French Mandate rule, would be allocated according to a system of *provisional* confessional representation. This system of inscribing religious identities as political ones was not entirely new. Mount Lebanon had witnessed different power-sharing agreements between the Maronite and Druze communities in 1845 and 1861, which were imposed by the European powers, "protectors" of Ottoman minorities, to quell sectarian tensions between the two groups. In a political game that was structured by quotas for the different constitutive religious communities of the nation, demographics are key.[21] The 1932 census was the last official census conducted in Lebanon. The 1990 amendments to the constitution, in the wake of the fifteen-year-long civil and regional wars, rectified the previous power imbalance by transferring some of the previous quasi-monarchic executive prerogatives of the Maronite president to the council of ministers and dividing parliamentary seats equally between Christians and Muslims. The country's open secret for a while now has been the retreat in the demographics of Christian inhabitants and the increase of its Muslim population, which forestalls conducting a new official census. The dangerous politics of sectarian population demographics is at the heart of Lebanese internal politics and its imbrications with regional and international ones.[22]

From the particularities of the infranational religious communities and the system of political representation that tied participation in the institutional political game to confessional denominations sprang the precarious Lebanese Republic. The division of the state institutions and resources between competing confessional blocs spared the Lebanese polity from the military coups and the grip of authoritarian rule that shook the neighboring countries in the wake of the 1948 Arab catastrophe. The Lebanese state, torn as it was, and still is, between the different constituencies that compose it and fight over it, did not manage to "rise above" these loyalties, or to articulate itself fully with one of the groups to subdue the others. The Maronite elite, in control of most key positions in the Lebanese state on the eve of independence, put forth a politically and economically (*laissez-faire*) pro-Western Lebanese nationalism that saw itself as part of the "free world."[23] Political movements and ideological currents would, when passing through the Lebanese prism, be predominantly refracted along the lines of the multiple components of the Lebanese polity, and be translated into the political game of sectarian balance. Anticolonial Arab nationalism, in its heyday, was therefore "perceived by some as a threat to the communitarian equilibrium, and by others as an instrument of mobilization against Maronite preeminence. Following from that, Arab nationalism's progress or its retreat became an *internal stake*, with civil war at its horizon."[24] As the late Samir Kassir, a sharp analyst of Lebanese history and politics, put it, "while in Syria, Jordan, or Iraq, the regional polarization had for effect to oppose the governments against society's vibrant forces, rather against the entire society, in Lebanon, it [regional polarization] came to be inscribed at the heart of society."[25] These modern ideological movements, such as Arab nationalism, Syrian nationalism, and communism, were *also* a means to oppose a politics centered around urban notables and rural feudal lords. Lebanon's French birth out of Ottoman ruins catering for an Eastern Christian community against the unionist wishes of its Muslim "national partners," the founding of a political system that divided the state along unequal confessional lines, and the failure to formulate a hegemonic vision of the nation resulted in the country's extreme susceptibility to regional and international developments.

The Palestinian Nakba and the Lebanese South

"If you go to 'Aitarun, you see Palestine . . . Israel, if you go to Marun al-Ras, you see the Hula Plains; and if you go to Rmaysh, you see Palestine," says Waddah Charara a little bit less than sixty years after the Palestinian Nakba of 1948, as he painstakingly describes to me the topography of the villages surrounding Bint Jbayl—the southern Lebanese town his father's family is originally from—and what they overlook on the other side of the border. "From Bint Jbayl," he adds, "you see Sa'sa'. . . a colony, a settlement, which is *mythic* in my family's stories. . . . I saw it before actually seeing it . . . both my paternal aunts used to talk to me about 1948. Theirs was not a political narration, and most probably their reports were fabricated."[26]

Palestine was not only geographically contiguous to southern Lebanese towns and villages from which one could spot the construction of settlements. The Lebanese bordering villages were integrated in more than one way into the economic, religious, medical, and administrative networks of pre-1948 Palestine. Traders would cross the borders from Yafa to sell their oranges and take wheat, barely, lentils, or corn in exchange, recalls Mahmoud Soueid, who as a child saw Palestinian currency before seeing the Lebanese one. Soueid was born in 1936 in Kfar Hamam, which is located at the southeastern tip of Lebanon, approximately at the intersection of the Syrian Golan Heights and northern Galilee. The village is part of the 'Urqub region, which became known as "Fatah Land" in the late 1960s after the Palestinian resistance established its bases there and used it as a launching pad for its guerrilla operations. His father, a Sunni cleric who studied in Damascus, established a school and a library at the beginning of the twentieth century and became the imam of the poor village, which survived mainly on agriculture. Its residents held Syrian papers before the establishment of Lebanon in 1920, papers they kept even after that date. If someone fell sick in the village they were taken to the Jewish doctor in Hula. No one used to go to Saida. Palestine was closer.[27] The commerce with Palestine was integral to the everyday lives of these southerners, who experienced the Nakba as a severely disruptive event. In his first work of social science, Charara registered how, in the wake of 1948, Bint Jbayl became increasingly incorporated into the commercial and administrative spheres of the recently independent Lebanese state (1943). Around the same time, modern political organizations—the Ba'th—also started attracting some of the town's inhabitants, particularly those who exited "the traditional life cycle such as: teachers, students and a small cohort of citizens."[28]

Born a few years before 1948, the soon to become militants were marked in their early years by the plight of the Palestinians in more than one way. As a result of the geographical contiguity of Palestine and Lebanon, around 100,000 Palestinians who were forcibly expelled by or fled Zionist and Israeli forces took refuge in Lebanon in the aftermath of 1948. The influx of refugees snatched some of these children from their private worlds and provided the impetus for some of their first public acts. Soueid, who was around twelve years old then, wrote a poem in his school bulletin. Fifty years later he can only remember its first verse: "Honor your guests O Lebanon generously."[29] Accompanied by other volunteers, he carried empty bags and knocked on people's doors in the coastal city of Saida. Residents gave them cans of food, batteries, and clothes that they stocked in one place for some organizations to pick up and distribute to the refugees. Soueid wasn't alone in taking part in gathering aid for the incoming refugees. Wajih Kawtharani (1941–), a member of Socialist Lebanon in the late 1960s and now a retired history professor at the Lebanese University, originally from the southern village of Ansar, was born and raised mostly in Beirut. Kawtharani was very young when the 1948 Palestinian Nakba took place:

> I remember Palestinian refugees coming and living in our neighborhood. I remember we used to gather aid for them at the time. I saw them in the neighborhood. I was six or seven years old. [I thought at the time] there is a problem, these people have been wronged, they have been evicted from their lands and they need help.[30]

Palestine was not a placeholder in their lives for a rightful anti-imperialist, nationalist cause mediated solely through passionate ideological rhetoric. Their geographic and generational position enabled them to see its plains, deal in its currency, visit Jewish doctors, and later on listen to the stories of exodus, write poems, and gather aid for the incoming refugees. During their teenage years, they were swept off their feet by the tidal waves of Arab nationalism that put the Palestine question at the heart of anticolonial struggles in the region. Two decades after the Nakba, they became main Lebanese allies of the Palestinian armed struggle for national liberation before some of them, like Waddah Charara—who theorized the alliance between the Palestinian revolution and the Lebanese Left—became staunch critics of it. That said, we are not there yet, and the militant intellectuals who founded Socialist Lebanon (1964) do not all originally come from southern Lebanon, which mediated an intimate relationship with Palestine.

Our Arab Brothers in Algeria, Egyptian Periodicals, and Iraqi Poets

Certain constitutive events of this generation's political coming of age and their repercussions no longer resonate in our present. Their echoes barely reached the shores of succeeding generations. Algeria's anticolonial star, which ignited passionate anticolonial sentiments, sunk with time. Today only scars remain.

As he unfolds the cardinal nodes of his political awakening that followed the Palestinian Nakba, Wajih Kawtharani highlights the Nasserite tides and the Algerian struggle for national liberation. He goes back in time to a demonstration he joined in support of the Algerian militant Djamila Bouhired, who was arrested, tortured, and sentenced to death on terrorism charges by French colonial authorities in 1957. It is very likely that it was the same demonstration during which Fawwaz Traboulsi (1941–) tried to climb up the wall of the French embassy, to be pulled down by a policeman and hit by a rifle butt on his forehead.

Traboulsi was heir to a different legacy than the southern and Shi'i one. The son of a Greek Catholic Christian hotel owner from Mashghara—a village in the Bekka Valley—he hails from a different sectarian, regional, and class background.[31] The family's famous hotel was a cosmopolitan microcosm that attracted prominent politicians—including Michel Aflaq, the founder and ideologue of the Ba'th Party that Traboulsi joined while studying in Manchester around 1959—illustrious artists, and members of the haute bourgeoisie from around the world. The hotel did more than that, though. It played a crucial role in developing Traboulsi's consciousness of social differences, through mixing with its workers, particularly an older communist cousin, who worked there during high season. What he shares though with some of his future comrades is descent from a lineage of intellectuals. Traboulsi is the grandson of 'Issa Iskandar al-Ma'luf (1886–1956), an eminent multifaceted scholar: historian, linguist, editor, and collector of original manuscripts. The scar, from the rifle butt blow, is still visible on Traboulsi's forehead. It acts as a reminder of a young man once captivated by Djamila's "pale, innocent face" and the country of a million martyrs. "I was madly in love with Djamila Bouhired," writes Traboulsi in his memoir. "I even drew a pencil portrait of her that remained on my bedroom's wall for a long time."[32] "And for truth's sake," he recalls, "Beirutis were never as giving toward an Arab cause as they were with the Algerian Revolution: in support, solidarity, and contributions. I remember scenes of Beirut's women taking off jewelry and bracelets to give them as donations."[33] Traboulsi's Algerian passion would lead many around him to mistake him for an Algerian national. Some years later, in 1961, when the "Evian negotiations" between the French colonizers and the FLN began, a delegation of Iraqi communists visited Traboulsi to congratulate him on his country's independence: "They wished me, in high militant seriousness, a quick and blessed return to the homeland."[34]

In one of our numerous interviews, Waddah Charara reacted to my proposition that a number of intellectuals, such as Edward Said (1935–2003), considered the 1967 defeat of Arab armies against Israel to be a watershed moment in their political consciousness by recounting the story of his first "political baptism."

The Algerian events had already begun when I was eleven years old. There were already some clashes before the first of November 1954.[35] The 1967 of others was in my case joining a demonstration under the rain probably in January 1953 . . . a demonstration I remember in great detail. . . . My parents had nothing to do with it at all.

We walked out of school and a young man,' who was three or four years older than us, stood on a small mound of sand in Burj al-Barajneh—under what is now called the Rasul al-A'zam Mosque that back then consisted of wide stretches of sand populated by goldfinch hunters where we used to go whenever we had a lira and quarter to buy a bird—anyways he stood there and said: "O Youth, O Arabs, O Nationalists, French colonialism is slaughtering our brothers in Algeria."

I understood [then] in the bodily sense of understanding, not merely in the discursive sense. Even though in 1952, when my dad used to come back from work . . . he used to bring home Egyptian newspapers. I remember I was ten years old when I started reading *al-Ithnayn* [Monday], which is similar to *Akhir Sa'a* [The Last Hour], *al-Musawwir* [The Photographer], but it had much more pictures in it. I remember very clearly Muhammad Naguib before Abdel Nasser . . . Abdel Nasser, of course, the smell of paper, ink, the hazy pictures of the [Suez] Canal battle [1956].

So even though there is a partial rupture between, on the one hand, home and its world, essentially my dad's world and the people you talk to there, and what they talk about and the magazines and school, on the other hand, which is a bunch of small kids learning dictation, grammar, "conjugaison" [conjugation of words in French], and a bit of math. . . . A certain translation, a certain investment of the atmosphere at home in this thing [the demonstration] took place that was surprising to me.

I remember this demonstration not only in its rain, the smell of wet clothes, my hair, and the thought that now my aunt is going to shout at me because I left myself under the rain and might catch a cold, and things of that sort, but also because there was some kind of implicit transmutation between these images, ideas, words, and emotions to something I was doing myself. I decided to walk out of school with the protest; some people did not go out. I was overwhelmed by great emotions. This was the baptism.[36]

Abdel Latif Charara, Waddah's father, an Arab nationalist, was a prolific author, linguist, and translator. His many works include volumes on classical and contemporary Arabic poetry, a book on George Bernard Shaw, another on Arab nationalism—*Ruh al-'Uruba* (The Spirit of Arabism) (1947) and republished later on—and translations (e.g., Herbert Marcuse). It was this Arab nationalist and anticolonial sensibility, cultivated through encounters with his father's Arab friends—such as the Syrian poet and statesman Badawi al-Jabal and the Iraqi poet Ahmad Safi al-Najafi—the reading of Egyptian periodicals, and the general atmosphere around the house, that was transmuted into Charara's participation in the demonstration of support to the Algerian national liberation struggle, generating tremendous emotions in the body of the eleven-year-old boy that transpire through the voice of the sixty-five-year-old man as he recounts with meticulous detail what he thought and how he felt on that rainy school day fifty-four years ago.[37] The intellectual hub that Waddah Charara grew up in transcended the frail borders of the Lebanese Republic and took part very early on in the fashioning of his Arab nationalist imaginary and sensibilities. Imagining the Arab nation, from Beirut, was made possible through the shared Arabic language, which tied these intellectuals together and circulated through mass media, such as Egyptian periodicals and, in the age of the transistor radio, through the fiery speeches of Gamal Abdel Nasser broadcast on Sawt al-'Arab (Voice of the Arabs).

Pan-Arab Passions: Politics, Sensibilities, and Institutions

The "Arab Cause," recalls Azza Charara Beydoun, "was more dominant [in our lives] than Lebanese concerns."[38] Charara Beydoun, a retired professor of social psychology at the Lebanese University and feminist thinker, joined Socialist Lebanon shortly after it was founded in the mid-1960s. Although they are siblings, Azza Charara Beydoun and Waddah Charara did not grow up together as a result of their parents' divorce. They also belong to different linguistic-intellectual universes. While he left for undergraduate studies in Lyon (1959) and then went back to France in the early 1970s to finish his doctorate, she enrolled in the American University of Beirut for an undergraduate degree in mathematics and shifted to social psychology after a number of years as a math teacher in Lebanese public high schools. Foreign languages, in the case of these siblings—as in the case of all these intellectual militants—is a crucial matter that provides insight into the readings, influences, and literary sensibilities and imaginaries out of which an intellectual's habitus is fashioned.

One of the instrumental mediums carrying "The Arab Cause" was Sawt al-'Arab (Voice of the Arabs), the Cairo-based radio station that broadcast a highly charged Arab nationalist rhetoric, the most effective of which were the speeches of Gamal Abdel Nasser. These speeches were a source of political education and induced a generalized popular mobilization in the Arab region.[39] Sawt al-'Arab was designed, according to Ahmad al-Sa'id, the radio station's best-known presenter and general manager,

> to explain to them [the Arab people] the ideals of the July Revolution, making them aware of the many plots they faced. The main aims of The Voice of the Arabs, therefore, were to liberate the Arab people; to unite the Arab countries; to liberate Arab resources from imperialism's grasp; and to encourage the use of those resources for the development of Arab civilization, science and culture.[40]

These were times, remembers Abbas Beydoun, when borders between Arab countries were thought to have been erased by the engulfing tidal wave of Arab nationalism:

> There was no sense of the borders at the time. This tide seemed as if it is one homogenous force, and it seemed as if there is a unified Arab history that was being made. There was no meaning to the [existing] borders. We were all part of this tide.... When communists in Iraq or in Syria talked about some borders, or the Ba'thists, after the failure of the union [after 1961], this talk seemed unintelligible.[41]

The resistance to recognize the borders and specific national affiliations of the different Arab countries during this time were evident in the discourses of Arab nationalist movements that "refused to say, for example, the Syrian people, the Lebanese people, the Egyptian people; they used to say the Arab people in Syria, the Arab people in Lebanon, the Arab people in Egypt."[42]

Arab nationalism is mostly remembered as a world saturated with strong political emotions. Its anticolonial sentiments and nationalist pride were perfectly conveyed by Nasser's demotic speeches; nationalist poems, novels, and songs; political pamphlets; and iconic photographs and portraits, such as those of Djamila Bouhired that Traboulsi hung on his wall. Charara recalled being overwhelmed by great emotions during the Algerian demonstration.[43] Azza Charara Beydoun recalls how as a twelve-year-old she strongly lived through Nasser's speech as he declared the nationalization of the Suez Canal on July 23, 1956. A few years later, the end of the short-lived union between the Egyptian and Syrian republics (1958–61) made her fall sick: "I had a fever," she recalls. "I took it somatically . . . just so that you know how emotional it was, and I was reading about how people were going to Damascus and talking about how handsome Abdel Nasser was. This is the emotional thing."[44]

The Arab nationalist fervor was not only diffused through the circulation of various media that young men and women read, listened to, and looked at. It also inhabited educational institutions. At some point in the 1950s al-Kulliyya al-'Amiliyya ('Amili College) in Beirut, which was dominated by Nasserists and members of the Arab Nationalist Movement, received a visit from Anwar al-Sadat to conclude an agreement between the Arab Republic of Egypt and the school whereby the Egyptian government would staff the college with Egyptian public school teachers.[45] Wajih Kawtharani was taught by these Egyptian school teachers who mainly taught Beiruti school children history, geography, and the Arabic language. These were subjects that, it need not be emphasized, easily lend themselves to being infused with the Arab nationalist zeitgeist.

Other schools were turned into quasi-political party centers where meetings and ideological education took place simultaneously with the school curriculum, especially during turbulent times, such as the short civil war that Lebanon witnessed in 1958. Recalling the atmosphere at al-Thanawyya al-Ja'fariyya, a Shi'i high school located in the southern city of Sur (Tyre), Abbas Beydoun tells the story of his first political engagements:

When I was thirteen, I was one of those who were politically active, because in al-Thanawiyya al- Ja'fariyya . . . one of the strange things about this era was that the school itself was a quasi center for the Ba'th Party, not only its teachers, but its administration—Ja'far Sharaf al-Din [the school's headmaster], who was an ally of the Ba'th at the time—and its students. We used to attend party meetings in the classroom, the unit of party meetings was the class/grade, and they were the centers of party talk. The teachers who were party members used to go in, and in the middle of class you could ask about the constitution of the Ba'th and the difference between Arab socialism and communist socialism. . . . There was no distinction between the school and the party center, and it was not thought to be strange—the swamping of all aspects of life with politics during that time used to make it seem normal.

During this period I was a Ba'thist. Since I was a precocious kid, they overlooked my age, and they promoted me especially that my young age was not correlated with how much I knew. Everyone in school was a

Ba'thist, but they had little interest in the theoretical side of the party, which consisted of a couple of pages, the constitution, and the [Michel] Aflaq readings. It did not take much time to read them, yet only a few had read them. So, at thirteen, fourteen, I was a reference about these things, a *hujja* [authority].[46]

Around 1961, when the union between Egypt and Syria came to an end, the Ba'th was one of the strongest parties in Lebanon, especially in Beirut, according to Mahmoud Soueid. As he was telling me the story behind his leaving the party when a significant group of Lebanese Ba'thists decided to split, protesting the leadership's position in Damascus that backed the dissolution of the Syrian union with Egypt in 1961, Soueid answered my interjection about why he thought the Ba'th was stronger than Nasserism:

> Yes, of course, it was stronger because the party was there before Nasserism came into being... and, second, it had an ideology. Nasserism was feeling its ideological way through Nasser's experience; he did not start from a pan-Arabist position. And, third, Nasserism may have become stronger later on the level of the masses but the Ba'th attracted intellectuals. It was either the Ba'th or the Arab Nationalist Movement. There was nothing else, or the Syrian Nationalists [if one decided to go] in another direction.... And, of course, we and the Syrian Nationalists were fighting. We had ideological fights, and discussions that spanned whole nights, [discussing] whether [we should aim for] Syrian unity or Arab unity... a Syrian nation or an Arab nation.[47]

Muhsin Ibrahim (1936–), who would much later in the 1970s occupy the post of secretary general of the Organization of Communist Action in Lebanon (OCAL)—among the many roles he played in Lebanese and Arab politics—was one of the leaders of the Arab Nationalist Movement at the age of twenty after its first conference in 1956. Ibrahim recalls his early years of engagement:

MI: In 1952–53, when I was around seventeen or eighteen [years] of age, I met the "Arab Nationalist Youth" that would become the kernel of the Arab Nationalist Movement. The first generation: George Habash, Hani el Hindi, and Ahmad al-Khatib.... I was considered, on the level of Lebanon, to be the symbol of the second generation. And despite what usually happens with students as part of growing up—you go into a party and then you get out of it—I did not.... The Palestinian question was very important for the Arab Nationalist Movement. We were just three years away from the Nakba; all of this generation grew up in this mood.

FB: And Abdel Nasser, what was your position vis-à-vis him?

MI: Abdel Nasser, he came later on. He was still on a trial period.[48]

Muhsin Ibrahim's early leadership experience with the Arab Nationalist Movement is indicative of how a difference of a few years between himself (born in 1936) and those born in the early 1940s—such as Traboulsi, Beydoun, and Charara—plays itself out vis-à-vis political engagement and the relation to Abdel Nasser. Ibrahim was already politically active when the Free Officers took hold of power in Egypt in 1952, and had already assumed leadership positions by the age of twenty when Nasser became the president of Egypt. His Arab nationalist sensibility was not fashioned by what was being broadcast, produced, and achieved in Cairo but, rather, what was taking place in Cairo was being closely monitored in order to formulate a position regarding these developments. The Arab Nationalist Movement later aligned itself with Nasserist politics and for a period of eight years Ibrahim developed, despite his young age, a close relationship with Abdel Nasser, traveling from Beirut to Cairo to meet him once a month on average. The relationship with Abdel Nasser deteriorated and eventually come to an end in the aftermath of the June 1967 defeat against Israel. The Lebanese branch of the Arab Nationalist Movement, with Ibrahim at its head, would undergo an auto-critique around 1968, reshape the organization internally, and adopt the name of Munazzamat al-Ishtirakiyyin al-Lubnaniyyin (Organization of Lebanese Socialists).[49]

The tidal waves of Arab nationalist sentiment did not engulf everything in their way. A majority of Lebanon's Christian population supported the pro-Western politics of President Camille Chamoun (1952–58). "Strengthened by foreign backing, the complicity of the bourgeoisie, and Maronites mobilization," Chamoun, Traboulsi notes, "exacerbated sectarian tensions as no other political leader had done before him. With the majority of the Muslim leaders outside parliament, the Muslim 'street' was massively attracted to the Nasserite and anti-colonialist discourse."[50] While growing up, some of these intellectuals straddled heterogeneous social worlds. At times, the political sensibilities developed at home—in the extended sense of family, neighborhood, and friends—clashed with the predominant atmosphere at school. Some of these intellectuals spent a part of their teenage years in schools where the mood was largely opposed to Arab nationalism. Waddah Charara spent three years in the mid-1950s as an intern in al-Ma'had al-Lubnani—Lebanese College—located in Bayt-Shabab, a Christian village in Mount Lebanon. His Shi'i southern origins from Bint Jbayl, the Arabism of his father, and the Egyptian periodicals lying around the house were very different from the new setting. When he moved there, Charara was already "armored with Arabism"; it was there

> that what we call Arabism . . . this world of ideas, feelings, opinions, reso-
> nances . . . found its formulation. The school's students were practically
> all children of Maronite immigrants and two or three Syrian National-
> ists. . . . And I was, along with two Shi'i sons of immigrants from Tyre, . . .
> in a certain sense, facing these people. . . . This year I started wearing the
> *Watani al-'Arabi* [My Arab Homeland] pin that Arab nationalists had
> made popular and was later adopted by the Ba'th. I also began contacting
> some relatives who were members of the Ba'th.[51]

Ahmad Beydoun also spent some years in schools with radically opposed politics. Between 1956 and 1958 he was enrolled in a school in Mashmusha—not far from the coastal town of Saida—that is affiliated with a Christian convent. The majority, he recalls, were pro-Chamoun and pro-Phalangists: "There was a hatred of Nasserism . . . this was the atmosphere [at the time]. . . . I used to write Arab nationalist poems on Algeria and Abdel Nasser."[52] Lebanese schools played a central role in fostering and sharpening the sense of belonging to the Arab nation. Whether these schools were receiving direct Egyptian aid, teachers, and visits by Anwar al-Sadat and becoming hubs of political party activity, in case they were pro-Arab nationalist, or whether they were Lebanese nationalist "haters" of Nasserism, they provided avenues to foster Arab nationalist rhetoric and emotions. Arab nationalist belonging gathered in the family and neighborhood surroundings could also be sharpened in the confrontations with Lebanese nationalists in school.

The 1958 "Revolution" and Operation Blue Bat

Camille Chamoun's alignment with Western powers during his presidency—indexed by the Lebanese government getting six million dollars' worth of US arms and economic aid in 1953 and allowing the US Air Force to use Lebanon's air space for reconnaissance missions in 1954—was exacerbated by his support of the Baghdad Pact signed in February 1955.[53] Although Lebanon did not join the pact signed by the pro-Western governments of Iraq, Pakistan, Turkey, and Iran, it nonetheless refused to take part in the Arab Defense Pact put together in response by Egypt, Syria, and Saudi Arabia. Chamoun's positions on Arab affairs had internal and regional repercussions. It soured the Lebanese government's relationship with Nasser's Egypt and Syria, and led to the resignation of Hamid Frangieh, Lebanon's minister of foreign affairs, in September 1955 after he "had assured 'Abd al-Nasir [Abdel Nasser] in the name of his government that Lebanon would oppose Western military pacts."[54] More importantly for our purposes was the mood of popular mobilization—mostly Muslim—against the president's foreign policy. The signing of the Baghdad Pact led to violent demonstrations across the country. In Beirut, a student was shot and killed and others were wounded when the police opened fire outside the American University of Beirut.

Chamoun's decisions not to sever diplomatic ties with France and England after the Suez crisis in 1956 resulted in the resignation of the Sunni prime minister, Abdallah al-Yafi, and minister Saeb Salam, both of them major Sunni political figures. Chamoun formed a new cabinet, handing the foreign affairs portfolio to Charles Malik, who was aligned with US foreign policy.[55] In April 1957, the Lebanese Parliament approved the country's adherence to the Eisenhower Doctrine. A couple of months later, the US-backed president organized national elections in which the major Sunni opposition leaders lost their seats.[56] By 1958, the president's politics managed not only to alienate Lebanese Muslims but also to divide the Christians who developed a "third force" to call for neutrality in Arab affairs. Moreover, Chamoun did not deny the circulating rumors about his intention to renew his presidential mandate—an unconstitutional act. The clashes began in the wake of the assassination of Nassib al-Matni, a journalist and editor strongly critical of the regime's foreign policy and corruption. The opposition controlled three quarters of Lebanon after two months of fighting. On July 14, 1958, while the fighting was still going on in Lebanon, the Iraqi monarchy was ousted.[57] On that same day, Chamoun "reiterated his request for a US military intervention within 48 hours, 'or else a second pro-western Arab regime will fall in its turn.'"[58] In less than twenty-four hours the US-initiated Operation "Blue Bat," which "included the landing of 15,000 American soldiers, backed by another 40,000 on the 70 warships of the US Navy's Sixth Fleet, in the first operation of its kind since the War."[59] The Americans ended up not defending Chamoun but choosing his successor, the Lebanese army general Fuad Chehab, elected on July 31, 1958, less than two weeks after the Marines had landed on Lebanese shores. Chehab's name was mentioned in the American-Egyptian negotiations that year and he "fulfilled the condition of Eisenhower, who wanted a military man."[60] By November 1958, the Blue Bat had decamped.

The summer of 1958 is an essential episode in modern Lebanese history and in the coming of "political" age of a generation growing up in the wake of the Palestinian Nakba and through the high tides of Arab nationalism. It witnessed the interlocking of local (sectarian tensions), regional (inter-Arab relations), and international (Cold War) political strands. Sixteen-year-old Charara was already the Ba'thist official of his high school in Beirut. His older relatives forged his papers to get him into the party. Mahmoud Soueid was posted at the party's radio station, also located in Charara's high school. Soueid was in charge of drafting the radio news bulletin and distributing pamphlets in the capital at night. Soueid and Charara missed each other during that summer. They met later on and took part in founding Socialist Lebanon in 1964.

When the violence erupted, Charara's parents sent him south to Saida, away from the bombings in Beirut. He did not fight in 1958, though he received some rudimentary military training in a public school at the hands of a Palestinian "commando, [this is] before the *fida'yi* label came about."[61] Charara would pass by the Makassed School in Saida, where Ma'ruf Sa'd, a local Arab nationalist political leader, surrounded by members of the Arab Nationalist Movement, established his headquarters. Among those around was Muhsin Ibrahim, "although I did not know him at the time," recalls Charara.[62] Ibrahim, who is approximately six years older than Charara, was already a high-ranking member of the Arab Nationalist Movement. Twelve years later, Waddah Charara and Muhsin Ibrahim would lead negotiations and decide to unify Socialist Lebanon and the Organization of Lebanese Socialists, giving birth to the Organization of Communist Action in Lebanon (1970).

Meanwhile, Fawwaz Traboulsi was an intern at Brummana High School. During his time at the boarding school, located in a Christian village of Mount Lebanon, he had, together with a bunch of his mates, formed a secret Arab nationalist leftist group in 1956 to face the Syrian Nationalists at school. "We went to Beirut in 1958," Traboulsi told me,

> and insulted the US Marines [in their own language] after they landed. We were in a high school that was mostly composed of Arabs and Muslims in Brummana. The atmosphere tensed up, we were accused by the village folk of having arms, and the Syrian Nationalists denounced us and began to conduct quasi-armed rounds around the schools with hunting rifles.[63]

Traboulsi spent the rest of the summer hiding in a northern Christian village. An arrest warrant was issued by a judge after one of the members of the Brummana High School pan-Arabist group was caught with a notebook containing the names of those who contributed money to support the "popular resistance," that is, the opposition forces. In the wake of the short civil war of 1958, the soon to be comrades continued their militancy under the banner of

Arab nationalism, mostly the Ba'th, before exiting and diving into a Marxist political and theoretical universe.

Arab nationalist thought and sentiments interpellated these young men and women in the first decade after Lebanon's independence from the French Mandate (1943). That said, they were also the products of Lebanese state institutions—public high schools, teachers' colleges, the Lebanese University—and their pedagogical practices, such as learning French and English. In varying degrees they shared the institutional spaces and the cultural and linguistic tools of the Lebanese nationalists they were opposing. This was not always the case for the generation of intellectuals preceding them.

"My father," recalls Waddah Charara, "was one of the first 'Amili writers who began writing in Lebanese newspapers, contemporary, modern newspapers such as *al-Adib* [The Writer] and *al-Adab* [Literatures]."[64] Abdel Latif Charara belonged to a generation of southern Shi'i writers who witnessed the withering away of a world, one where "the road to Najaf despite its length and its roughness was more congenial than the road to Beirut or Damascus."[65] The first, as Abbas Beydoun maintains, is

> a trip to a safe haven; where the sons follow in the footsteps of the fathers.... It is an internal immigration, while the second, despite its proximity, is a displacement and a journey that is not guided by the knowledge of forefathers and their memories.[66]

The story of transition from Najaf to Beirut is not only one of shifting directions from the centuries-old path to the site of religious learning toward the capital of an all too recent republic in contact with metropolitan fields of cultural production. It is also, for Beydoun, a narrative about the divergent cultural imaginaries of the constitutive communities of Lebanon. The Lebanese nationalist literature articulated by Western-facing—when not residing there—authors such as Khalil Gibran and his cohort, portraying and satirizing life in the mountains of Lebanon where they grew up, was a far cry from the world of the Najaf-trained clerics and their literatures. "My dad," says Abbas Beydoun,

> talked about Arab nationalism, but if you take the titles of his books, *they don't mean anything.* [He wrote a book on] Umm Salama, which is the name of one of the prophet's wives, who was close to Ali, and

another one on the biography of the prophet, most probably from a Shiʻi perspective.[67]

"They don't mean anything" means that there was no uptake for this type of literature in a national field whose hegemonic references, metropoles, and imaginaries were elsewhere. Their metropole, recalls Abbas Beydoun, was Egypt. "They were," he continues,

> Modernist, but from the other side, not à la Gibran [Khalil Gibran], Mikhail Naimy, and Maroun Abboud. This world was not familiar to them. The modernity of Egyptians . . . they could deal with it more. First, this modernity was an Islamic modernity, while here [in Lebanon] it was a Christian modernity in one sense or another . . . in all senses.[68]

Not only were their upbringings, intellectual references, cultural and literary imaginaries, and practices different from the budding nationalist field, but some of them did not possess any other languages than Arabic, which led to their increasing marginalization as they could not be à jour with what is happening in the world, that is, the metropoles. These ʻAmili authors also became separated, as Abbas Beydoun recalls, from their own progeny:

> When I began opening my eyes [to the world] and becoming a mature person, it seemed to me that my dad the writer and intellectual did not suit me. Very quickly I found myself in a different world, maybe one of Lebanese culture, and as a result *we had a problem of language.* In a novel I wrote and published called *Tahlil Damm* [Blood Test] . . . I talked about my dad. His voice used to sound strange to me. It is something that needs a psychoanalyst in order to make sense of. It was as if he was a person that is not there, *"inexistant"* strange and rare, or that he is not going to be repeated. . . . [He was] a person that used to write and read to me, and I never felt any sympathy with what he used to read to me. . . . I never had much connection with his writing, and it is difficult for me to consider myself a continuity to this writing.[69]

Abdel Latif Charara taught himself English and French, which he used to read but not speak, according to Beydoun, and "if you look at the titles of his books, there is one on Bernard Shaw, another one on al-Hajjaj—but then al-Hajjaj, there is something new in this, it is not a Shiʻi subject, it is wider—and a book on Arab nationalism. These three things put him in a different context, a Lebanese, regional, and international context."[70] Through contributing to new intellectual discussions that appeal to audiences beyond the Shiʻi community,

Abdel Latif Charara managed in these times of historical transition to escape the marginalization those intellectuals, like Beydoun's father, suffered. They became, Beydoun recalls, "'autochtone,' local." "They wrote," he adds, "without publishing and consumed what they produced in their own milieu. Their relationship with Lebanese culture was mainly weak."[71]

Communism also provided an alternative community of thought and practice for this generation of 'Amili intellectuals. Husayn Muruwwa (1910–87) is another important figure of that generation in the Lebanese political and intellectual field.[72] While he was studying and living in Najaf in preparation to assume clerical responsibilities in the footsteps of his father, Muruwwa became attracted to Marxist writings and the politics of the Iraqi Communist Party. Subsequently, Muruwwa, like the Iraqi poet Muhammad Mahdi al-Jawihiri, put an end to his religious career. He later became a member of the Lebanese Communist Party's Central Committee and a respected Marxist thinker who taught Islamic philosophy at Lebanese University. Muhammad Charara, Abdel Latif's brother, also got radicalized during the 1940s in Iraq and dropped his religious aspirations in order to become a communist militant and author.[73]

On February 17, 1987, during one of the bleak episodes of the Lebanese civil war, Husayn Muruwwa was shot dead, at the age of seventy-seven, in his home in Beirut. It is widely believed that a radical Shi'i Islamist faction carried out the assassination either by the orders, or under the auspices, of the Syrian Assadist regime. Four years before the collapse of the Soviet Union and eight years after the success of the Islamic Revolution in Iran, a long time had passed since Jawahiri's fiery poems on the Battle of Stalingrad and the Marxist radicalization of young clerics in Iraq. A long intergenerational journey: from Najaf to the central committees of communist parties in the anticolonial decades of the mid-twentieth century, and into the militant Shi'ism inspired by the Iranian Revolution in the last two decades of that century.

Coda: Then and Now

In his first work, *Transformation d'une Manifestation Religieuse dans un Village du Liban-Sud (Ashura)* (1968), Waddah Charara examined the changes in the ritual of 'Ashura in light of the structural transformations occurring in Bint Jbayl in the wake of the Palestinian Nakba. He notes the shifting of the location of the "religious manifestation" from the private sphere of the family to the public Husayni clubs, and the new participation of Ba'thist students, teachers, and traders in the festivities alongside the religious lector. These party members mapped the Palestinian Nakba on the religious story: the image of al-Imam

Husayn corresponded to that of Palestine, his murderers to "the enemies," his battle to that of survival and progress, and finally the justice of his cause to the political and social content carried by the modern political organization.[74] Charara, in the Arabic abstract to the French text, related its main problematic as follows:

> The confluence between a religious content and a political one in a historical period of transition from one mode of social organization to another is an issue that poses the question of the distinction between the layers of the social structure in "backwards" countries, their degrees of independence, and their evolution.[75]

It is the specific form *modernization* takes in "backwards"—placed between brackets in the original text—countries via the articulation between the religious and political levels that Charara was investigating.[76] In the mid-1950s the Ba'th, he observed, shifted the mythical understanding of the Nakba, which made sense of the event by attributing it to an "evil conspiracy against Arabs," in the direction of a "relative rationalization."[77]

Three years after the end of the long civil and regional Lebanese wars, Charara wrote a brief autobiographical piece "The Faltering Belonging: Segments from a (Pre-) Lebanese Autobiography."[78] In the twenty-five years that separate the two pieces, the beginning of the Lebanese wars in 1975 was a crucial turning point for Charara, witnessing his exit from radical politics and Marxist thought. The author begins by noting how his awakening to belonging to the Lebanese "homeland" took place at the beginning of the war in 1975. He wrote, "As much as I try to, I don't remember that a sense of belonging to Lebanon was a common or desirable thing among the people I grew up with. And these were Lebanese Shi'a, and of their two types: the Shi'a of the southern rural town, and those of the religiously mixed coastal town."[79] It is in this post–civil war context, which saw the fragmentation of the Lebanese polity mostly along sectarian lines, that Charara returned to his memories relating the absence of the Lebanese *national* referent and the predominance of infranational, familial, and regional solidarities in his childhood. The 1948 Nakba is recalled in order to reveal how the loss of the Palestinian homeland was narrated through provincial, self-sufficient (fabricated?) stories by the inhabitants of Bint Jbayl that put the town at the center of the action:

> And what is true of families, and kin, is also true of towns. Stories circulate, as well as storytellers, from one community to the other, without any alteration affecting the stories' structure. The meaning of the event

[whether related by family, kin, or townsfolk] does not need any action that was undertaken by others to be fully grasped. The town is deemed a unit, in case its inhabitants ... manage to narrate a story through which they recognize their town and themselves.[80]

From the story of a tentative modernization of a southern town in 1968, we move in 1994 to a story of the strength and parochialism of infranational communal loyalties and the absence of the national referent.

The war, and its aftermaths, triggered a revisionist history of the place of the national referent in the first years of the independent Lebanese Republic. The discovery, or rather the recovery, of Lebanon, and the rethinking of the "Lebanese question" in the wake of the country's implosion and after years of Arab nationalist and radical leftist militancy in support of the Palestinian resistance, is a common trope of this generation of disenchanted leftist militants—both Wajih Kawtharani and Azza Charara Beydoun, by way of example, mentioned it during our meetings. Charara found it, that is, Lebanon, absent among the more entrenched sectarian, familial, and regional solidarities of his own southern Shiʻi background, which he refers to as *ahli* loyalties.[81] The awakening to his belonging to the Lebanese homeland would not only be contrasted with the country's infranational communal solidarities but also with their supranational connections, namely, Arab nationalism. Charara, the former Baʻthist, who, in 1968, during the height of his Marxist militancy, interpreted the impact of the Baʻth as one of relative rationalization, inverted his analysis a quarter of a century later. Arab nationalism became the "religion [creed] of the *Ahl* [kin]."[82] Pan-Arab ideological politics were no longer part of a modernization story; they became in 1994 the supranational "religion" of the infranational loyalties whose articulation undermined the intermediary chain: the Lebanese nation. What Charara's post–civil war autobiographical piece elided was the specific articulation of the idea of Lebanese nationalism on the then dominant Christian Maronite pro-Western imaginary of Lebanon, and the peripheral position the Shiʻi community and southern Lebanon occupied in the new republic.

Charara's recollections do not only touch on the question of Palestine and Arab nationalist ideology. He also revisits the aftermaths of national liberation and the violent practices of the anticolonial movements he supported in his youth. The aftermaths of Algeria's liberation were marshaled to call into question the reified usage of Frantz Fanon's work in academic fields such as postcolonial and cultural studies. "Worlds, and hypotheses, are erected, while forgetting that Fanon wrote between 1957 and 1962–63 in the fold of the FLN [Front de Libération National]," he mentions during one of our meetings, "without giving any importance to the social and historical becoming of Algeria."[83] This comment about Fanon's contemporary usage in disciplinary settings was thrown in as an aside in the middle of a conversation where he expressed his reservation about a style of intellectual practice he dubbed "studding" (*tarsi'*). This style, a superficial theoretical rhetoric of sorts is premised on the appropriation of particular concepts and their use without paying attention to both their genealogy and how they articulate with, and relate to, unfolding sociohistorical processes. More importantly, Charara, nearly fifty years later, revisits the violent modalities of practice of the FLN and the internecine fights between Algerian nationalists at the time. After relocating to Lyon (1959), Charara got involved in the Algerian struggle for independence. The young Lebanese student joined the Réseau Francis Jeanson. The Réseau helped the Algerians via a network of couriers that used to transport weapons (though very few), money, and fake papers and direct militants to safe hideouts. "I got to know at the time from a French Algerian woman," he recalls, "that prostitution rings in France were in the hands of the Front de Libération."[84] It was also during that time that he became aware of the "FLN's assassinations of MNA [Algerian National Movement] militants, their forceful extraction of money, and liquidation of thieves."[85] These practices gave rise to intense feelings of "horror and real disgust" that were quenched by espousing a vision of "political practice as always containing a fundamental share of violence and dirt." This ideological justification, recalls the veteran militant intellectual, was inspired by Maurice Merleau-Ponty's *Humanisme et terreur* (Humanism and terror) (1947), which he read around that time. Charara recites from memory in French a line from the book: "It goes something like this," he says, "we don't have to choose between purity and impurity but between different kinds of impurities."[86] Around the same time, he began reading Karl Marx and Friedrich Engels, which shifted the terrain of questions he was preoccupied with. The question of violence in politics became sidelined. By immersing himself in the Marxist tradition, Charara began to be captivated by the movement of History.

2. DREAMS OF A DUAL BIRTH

Socialist Lebanon's Theoretical Imaginary

There is no royal road to science, and only those who do not dread the fatiguing climb of its steep paths have a chance of gaining its luminous summits.
—KARL MARX

Théorie: ce mot fit emblème. Non seulement pour une collection sévère d'ouvrages difficiles et exigeants, mais pour une génération. "La Théorie de Marx est toute-puissante parce qu'elle est vraie," répétions-nous avec Lénine.
—CHRISTIAN JAMBET

In the wake of the September 11, 2001, attacks, Susan Buck-Morss published a small book of essays, *Thinking Past Terror: Islamism and Critical Theory on the Left* (2003), in which she thinks through the possibility of a global leftist politics in the present. The book's main argument, Buck-Morss writes,

> is that Islamism as a political discourse can be considered together with Critical Theory as critiques of modernity in its western-developed form. It asks readers to suspend existing political identities and reconfigure the parameters of their discourse to recognize overlapping concerns. It does this performatively, analyzing the present through the work of contemporary Islamic rather than western theorists. Its touchstones are not Agamben, Žižek, Derrida, or Habermas, but rather, Taha, Gannouchi, Shariati, and Qutb.[1]

The essays call into question the supposed dominance of Western philosophical traditions, whose self-sufficiency is continually reinforced in the present by those thinkers who deem their conceptual resources enough to interpret the world. For instance, Buck-Morss draws attention to the renewed theoretical interest in Pauline Christianity: "By returning to the Western tradition, *yet again* 'putting on the mask of St Paul' (Marx!) in order to speak politically of the rupturing power of the event," she writes in a later piece, "the pragmatics of his [Alain Badiou's] action reinforces that tradition and obliterates change, weakening the messianic, political power of the present that he intends to affirm."[2]

In engaging Islamist political discourse, Buck-Morss's challenge is not only a theoretical one, which seeks to move beyond the consecrated canon of critical theory and Western philosophical traditions. It is also a politically courageous and generous intervention by a committed public intellectual who, amid the hostile political climate toward Muslims in the West, embarks on an engagement with Islamist political discourse to rethink "the entire project of politics within the changed conditions of a global public sphere" (TPT, 5). It's a task she undertakes through calling for translation between political languages, disrupting in the process the discourses of watertight distinctions between "us" and "them" predicated upon timeless cultural essences separating a Western civilization from an Islamic one. In doing so, Buck-Morss goes against the doxas associating Islamism with "dogmatic fundamentalism and terrorist violence that dominate in the Western press" (TPT, 49). She puts the accent on the multiplicity of positions taken in, and the vibrant character of, debates animating Islamist spaces of argument while also proposing that Islamism, like critical theory, "inaugurated an autonomous tradition of immanent critique in the Middle East" (TPT, 98). Without seeking to defend all positions or movements under the Islamist banner she underscores that Islamism "enables political discourses that are modern in their own terms, rather than as a failed mimicry of the West" (TPT, 51–52). Buck-Morss envisages her project as a challenge "to rediscover one's own commitments in a foreign political language, and to ask not only what is lost in translation but also what might be gained" (TPT, ix).

Buck-Morss's project of translation and rescue of the critical kernels of thinkers such as the Egyptian Sayyid Qutb (1906–66) and the Iranian Ali Shariati (1933–77) contrasts the new global Left, which she hopes will come about, with an older Marxist one. The picture she paints of Marxist thinkers and militants who were contemporaries of Qutb and Shariati is executed with broad brushstrokes. "A comparison informs us as to how the discourse of the new global Left will be different from the Marxist international one," Buck-Morss writes, "where translation occurred, but heavily in one direction" (TPT, 7). "Any Leftist," she continues, "who lived in or visited the 'undeveloped' world at that time will be aware of the degree to which the Marxist Left understood itself as an avant-garde in elite terms, rather than popular and democratic. Despite their radically critical stance Marxists embraced a vision of modernization that had in common with capitalism and imperialism a conception of the third world as inexorably backward and behind" (*TPT*, 7).

In "Can There Be a Global Left?," the book's final essay, Buck-Morss reiterates her critique of the Arab Marxist tradition as caught in the webs of modernization theory. "When Western critical discourse was adopted by Arabs in the Marxist mode, this absence of a double critique," Buck-Morss writes, "tended to be just as prevalent, as Arab Marxists were similarly adamant that their own societal and religious forms were vestiges of the feudal past" (*TPT*, 97–98). Why does Buck-Morss's admirable enterprise of translating Qutb and Shariati to Western audiences in the wake of the "War on Terror" has to be coupled by a schematic ahistorical critique of Arab Marxist thinkers and militants? Does her sketch of Sayyid Qutb as the immanent critic of Egyptian society necessitate painting his Arab Marxist contemporaries as adamant modernizers ensnared by Western concepts? Doesn't her sketch of Arab Marxists risk paralleling, and giving conceptual fodder to, nativist arguments attacking them for being vectors of a foreign, imported thought— failed mimics of the West?

I will now revisit the history of Socialist Lebanon (SL) with a focus on its labors of, and thoughts on, translation, as well as the uses and authority of its discourses. In doing so, I will touch on how the labors of theory as a mediator of political practice sheds light on the disciplinary uses of theoretical texts. Moreover, unearthing the long-neglected histories of the Arab Left—both as a discursive tradition and organized political practice—through reconstructing the international travels of militants, the global traffic in concepts, and the alliances of political parties, to pick just a few examples, brings to light a complex transnational story whose horizons transcend the frontiers of nation-states and the boundaries of religious traditions. It is also an argument against the easy dismissal of an entire tradition, which in the wake of postcolonial epistemology critique and the Islamic revival came to be characterized as plagued by crude modernizing Western assumptions or accused of foreignness. In recovering this history, my aim is not only to complicate Buck-Morss's sketch of Arab Marxism but more importantly to bypass looking at Arab thinkers as falling into one of two camps: either failed imitators of the West (call them self-Orientalizing if you want) or autochthonous—religious in this particular case—thinkers engaging in an immanent critique of their societies. I will return to Buck-Morss's work at the end of the chapter to think further with her about what she calls historical pragmatics, that is, "the practical implications of theory expressed within specific historical configurations" (*STF*, 72).

Traveling Student Militants: Beirut, Lyon,
Manchester

Fuad Chehab launched his presidential mandate in 1958 by meeting Gamal Abdel Nasser, the president of the United Arab Republic, on the Lebanese-Syrian border. The election of Chehab, the previous commander of the Lebanese Army (1946–58), to the presidency in the wake of the local, regional, and international 1958 crisis put a halt to the previous president's pro-Western and anti-Nasser policies. Chehab adopted a policy of neutrality in Arab affairs and collaboration with Nasser, and he worked in his first years on establishing a politics of national reconciliation. In a speech on November 21, 1960, the eve of Independence Day, Chehab laid out his modernization and welfare program: "He called for 'comprehensive social reform' and the 'building of a new society.' The message was clear: 'those who benefited from prosperity should take care of the deprived Lebanese . . . some should sacrifice and the others should be patient.'"[3] Chehabism came to denote policies of modernization and welfare. The president surrounded himself with a young generation of technocrats and "relied on new institutions: the Bureau of Planning, Bureau of Statistics, Office of Social Development, Water Services of Beirut, and even a Center for Scientific Research, which formed a sort of shadow ministry, all devoted to the president."[4] His statist and egalitarian social agenda, refracted through the Lebanese sectarian prism, would benefit the peripheral regions, as well as seek to redress Christian overrepresentation in state institutions.[5] It constituted a "partial response to the demands of sharing and participation by the insurgents of 1958."[6] The reverse of the developmentalist statist coin was the infiltration of state security agencies into the capillaries and major arteries of Lebanese political life. Chehab's project, Fawwaz Traboulsi writes, "sought to provide the country with an alternative political body by co-opting the armed protagonists of the events of 1958, using the army, the intelligence and the technocrats."[7] The president's mandate ended in 1964, but his personal clout persisted, and Chehabism "spread, continued and eventually ran out of steam under his disciple and successor as president, Charles Helou (1964–1970)."[8] It was in this post-1958 Chehabist national conjuncture that Socialist Lebanon was founded (1964). The two dynamos of the group, Waddah Charara and Fawwaz Traboulsi, already had some years of reading and political experience behind them as well as bouts of study in the West, the first in Lyon and the second in Manchester.

Charara's last two years of high school (1958–59) were reading intensive. His French had become solid enough to plow through theoretical texts and he had the chance to be taught by gifted teachers. Among those who taught him philosophy, discussed with him, and lent him his books was Hassan Ibrahim—Muhsin Ibrahim's brother—who had just come back from France. Ibrahim had studied with figures such as Jean Piaget, Maurice Merleau-Ponty, and Daniel Lagache, while working on a dissertation under the supervision of Vladémir Jankélévitch. Around this time, Charara read works by Albert Camus, Jean-Paul Sartre, Ferdinand Alquié, Henri Lefebvre, Merleau-Ponty, and Arthur Koestler's *Le Zéro et l'Infini* (*Darkness at Noon*). The readings were put to use by the seventeen-year-old in political discussions. He left the Ba'th in 1959, in his last year of high school, having spent a year and some months in the party, after engaging in intellectual discussions during which "my weapons were Sartre, Merleau-Ponty . . . and Lefebvre."[9] These "weapons" were wielded in numerous internal discussions about party structure, the relationship of the party to its base, taking state power, and the forms of socialism. These discussions were taking place against the backdrop of the formation of the United Arab Republic in February 1958, and the July 14, 1958, revolution in Iraq that ousted the Hashemite monarchy, bringing to power the Arab nationalist "free officers" six years after the Egyptian Free Officers assumed power in Cairo. On a scholarship in Lyon (1959), Charara collaborated with the Réseau Françis Jeanson and began reading Marx and Engels.[10] Charara ended up working with the Left's student syndicate and joining a workers' cell in the French Communist Party, while studying for a degree in philosophy and a diploma in *la psycho-pédagogie de l'enfance arriérée*—"psycho-pedagogy of retarded children"—on the basis of which he was granted a scholarship; a topic he had no particular interest in pursuing.

Unlike Charara, who quit the Ba'th before his travels, Traboulsi, who was very close to the Arab Nationalist Movement (ANM) in his school years, joined the Ba'th in 1958 while studying in Manchester. He had refused to officially join the ANM, whose right-wing agenda in the late 1950s centered on the primacy of Arab unity without making room for the social question.[11] "The Arab nation," in the ANM's ideological perspective, "had first to achieve a certain measure of political integration and freedom from Zionism and imperialism before it could turn its full attention to the process of building a democratic and socialist Arab society."[12] The ANM's stagism—union first, then socialism—was criticized by the Ba'th for its betrayal of the Arab masses in the interest of the bourgeoisie. It also did not convince the young man who, "obsessed with dialectics" at the time, engaged in long discussions with ANM cadres, such as King Hussein of Jordan's cousin, who later became prime minister of his country. "Of the questions I asked the latter [the king's cousin]:

Did the Algerian Revolution take place only for freedom, or for both freedom and bread? And he used to insist that bread was not related to Revolution, while I held on to my views about bread and freedom."[13] Traboulsi joined a Marxist wing of the Ba'th Party in Manchester, attracted by the leftist critiques of the ANM and of Nasser that centered on the necessity of tying socialism to the question of Arab unity.[14] Heading there to complete his GCES (General Certificate of Education) and study painting at night, Traboulsi was welcomed with a workers' demonstration, marching under the slogan "Bosses like tea, so do we!" that demanded a fifteen-minute daily tea break.[15] The young bourgeois man moving from the courtyards of his father's cosmopolitan hotel was shocked by Manchester's industrial misery: "Sugar was still rationed since wartime, and only varieties of brown sugar were available. Most houses lacked indoor restrooms. While workers on morning buses would smoke half a cigarette, keeping the second half for the ride back home."[16] Traboulsi soon dropped his artistic aspirations, studying a little, reading a lot, and militating even more: "I read a lot about plastic arts and economics, as well as socialist writings, from British Fabians to Marxists of all nationalities. In addition to whatever fell under my hands pertaining to the Arab world's politics, history and sociology. I was also especially captivated by the school of British realists in cinema and theater, bustling as it was with the anger and rebellion of the post-Suez war generation."[17] In addition to his Ba'thist duties and solidarity activities with the Algerian Revolution, Traboulsi inaugurated what would become a lifelong relation with, and attachment to, Yemen. He founded, alongside an Iraqi comrade, the kernel of what would become the Union of Yemeni Workers in the United Kingdom. "In the cold, humid houses, inside of which the sons of 'Happy Yemen' were packed by the dozen, I listened to many stories narrating the double tragedy of its sons' migrations: they flee the imamate's oppression through Aden to fall prey to industrial exploitation and English gangs' racist provocations."[18] Back in Beirut, after managing to stretch his A levels for two and a half years in England, Traboulsi enrolled as a student of political science at the American University of Beirut. He had his membership in the Ba'th frozen because he maintained contact with a group of Lebanese Ba'th cadres, which included Mahmoud Soueid, his future Socialist Lebanon comrade, who had left the party after Syria's secession from the United Arab Republic (1961).

Examining the travels, interests, and practices of Charara and Traboulsi reveals how the intellectual and political activities they took part in transgressed national, class, linguistic, ethnic, generational, and disciplinary boundaries: joining the French Communist Party; working with Yemeni immigrants in

Manchester; studying painting, philosophy, and psychology; engaging in student syndicate militancy; collaborating with the Réseau Jeanson; meeting Syrian, Iraqi, and Egyptian militants, party officials, and intellectuals. In engaging in these practices, these young militant intellectuals traversed a variety of social, political, and intellectual worlds that they were not necessarily groomed to inhabit. These travels and displacements helped fashion a political subjectivity that defied the logic of expertise and professionalization, one that was imbued with an internationalist sensibility and intently focused on its present (Arab unity, the Algerian anticolonial struggle, Yemeni immigrant workers, student syndicates). Modernization, backwardness, religion—the themes that will form the conceptual backbone of a retrospective epistemological critique of Arab Marxists—were not part of the constellations of questions that animated their pursuits. They were driven by political questions to which they sought answers in their numerous engagements, ideological conversions, and theoretical elaborations.

Early on, the readings of these future intellectuals were extensive and not circumscribed by disciplinary boundaries. These transdisciplinary readings—psychology, philosophy, psychoanalysis, Marxist theory, aesthetics, economics—were mobilized to both understand their present and to intervene politically either in internal party debates or on its fringes. Theory, particularly Marxist theory, in the late 1950s was the new "weapon" of choice they deployed against their own very recent past and against their Arab nationalist comrades. In a couple of years, by 1961, the theoretical weapon was no longer wielded individually and internally (the Ba'th's Marxist wing). Marxist theory occupied center stage of Arab nationalist debates in the wake of the first pan-Arab significant setback, nearly a decade after the Free Officers reached power in Egypt.

A Fateful Disunion

1961 constituted a critical year for the Arab unionist project. On September 28, 1961, a coup d'état in Syria dissolved the union with Egypt, which had been promulgated in 1958. The three-year union was a difficult time for the Ba'th. President Nasser insisted on "having parties in Syria agree to dissolve themselves as a condition for the unification of Egypt with Syria. The only organization Nasser would allow was the 'National Union,' to be copied from the Egyptian experience."[19] Nasser's high-handedness in controlling the National Union, and growing opposition inside the Ba'th Party to its agreement to dissolve itself, led to criticism of the United Arab Republic, which "intensified following the dismissal of party representatives and supporters from their government positions."[20] Prominent leaders of the Ba'th signed the manifesto in support of the dissolution of the union between Syria and Egypt in 1961. These were tense times for the Ba'th. Mahmoud Soueid was one of the Lebanese cadres who left in the wake of 1961.[21] "We left," says Soueid, "because the party in Damascus applauded the secession and we were unionists. How can an Arab nationalist party support the secession? There was a lot of shouting, screaming, and clashes. It was very harsh. We kept on meeting for some time while claiming that we are the party but they had everything, including the press, in their hands. Bit by bit, we dissolved and nothing remained."[22]

Military coups brought the Ba'th to power on February 8, 1963, in Iraq and a month later, March 8, 1963, in Syria. By that time Traboulsi's membership in the party had been renewed and he had established links with the emerging leftist trend, whose main ideologue at the time was the distinguished Syrian Marxist thinker Yasin al-Hafiz (1930–78), editor in chief of *al-Ba'th* newspaper. This trend adopted Marxist theoretical tools to call into question Aflaq's version of Arab socialism. Its manifesto, *Some Theoretical Principles,* was adopted in the party's Sixth Conference (1963). It denounced "the party's previous belief in the utility of private property and condemned it as a petty bourgeois socialism."[23] Arab socialism, according to the Sixth Conference's proceedings,

> was a negative and incomplete response to the challenge of local Communism. It warned that such an attempt might lead to a nationalist chauvinism, which rejects the universal intellectual heritage of socialist thought. Arab Socialism, the conference added, has remained, on the whole, partial and without any scientific content. Assessing the impact of the party's distorted image of socialism, the conference pointed to the dominance in the party organization of bourgeois elements and the prevalence of a petty bourgeois mentality in party ranks.[24]

Fawwaz Traboulsi was appointed to a committee to formulate the proceedings of the Sixth Conference, headed by the party founder, Michel Aflaq (1910–89), who "refused to sit on the same committee as the AUB student, who was supported by his leftist opponents in the Syrian and Iraqi regional leaderships."[25] Traboulsi was expelled from the party on the eve of the Seventh Conference (1964) after writing a "'Letter to the Comrades' protesting the party's relinquishing of the socialist option, and severely criticizing the Ba'thist coup in Iraq, especially the persecution of communists and the war against the Kurds."[26]

Socialist Lebanon was founded in 1964 by seven intellectuals in the folds of the Chehabist modernization experiment, which provided a time of internal stability, and out of a leftist opposition to it. The mid-1960s for members of Socialist Lebanon were times of intellectual ferment, of intense reading, discussions, and translations and writings. In the decade before the Lebanese civil war (1975), and prior to the radicalization of the ANM, which decried the postcolonial regimes as petty bourgeois after the 1967 defeat, and the beginnings of Palestinian armed struggle from the country's southern borders, Socialist Lebanon was an intellectual hub, which had no visibility on the national political radar. In its first years, the small group of militant engaged in intraleftist skirmishes whose favorite target was the Lebanese Communist Party (LCP). These skirmishes took place on the pages of the bulletin they began putting out in the fall of 1966 under their own name, Lubnan Ishtiraki (Socialist Lebanon). The bulletin was produced underground, without obtaining a license from the Lebanese state, and was reproduced using a Roneo machine.[27] The portable Roneo machine the group bought could be closed "like a suitcase" and was mostly kept in Traboulsi's apartment. Keeping the Roneo in a safe place and away from the Lebanese authorities was essential since the bulletins and tracts produced by the machine were the main "public face" of the emerging underground organization.[28] The bulletin was not produced in large numbers. At first probably a few dozens were produced and, according to Traboulsi, "later on a few hundred copies in its heydays and it was delivered by hand by members or partisans who made sure the 'contact' was 'secure' before they revealed themselves to him/her and started handing them the *nashra* [bulletin] which played the role of pretext for lengthy discussions supposed to prepare their joining a 'circle' of partisans."[29] The mimeographed bulletin was the medium through which Socialist Lebanon circulated its analyses and theories, as well as the main tool used in the recruitment of partisans.

Before I examine what those texts were about, and how they sought to interpellate their readers, in this chapter and the next, I will now look into the processes through which their militant intellectual habitus—reading, writing, translating—was fashioned. Fawwaz Traboulsi recalls the group's joy when Ahmad Beydoun and the late Hassan Kobeissi joined in the fall of 1966, a year and half after the beginning of the project:

FT: Work had started on Socialist Lebanon. The first newcomers were Waddah's colleagues Ahmad [Beydoun] and Hassan [Kobeissi]. . . . They were a great catch, "une grande revelation," and they were friends. . . . There was a "frenzy" of reading, and some competition. There was one that read more than the others. Waddah's distinction, which one has to acknowledge, resides in an exceptional, discipline that we had nothing to do with. . . . Reading *Le Monde* was a duty and taking notes from it.

FB: That's only him, or all of you?

FT: The whole atmosphere became like this. I was a bit of a deviant because of my Anglo-Saxon side, which is a bit more empirical.

FB: So they all used to buy *Le Monde*?

FT: Yes, yes, and there is always a book, always Maspero's publications, which were read in different degrees by different people.[30]

In conjunction with the reading of dailies, periodicals, *gauchiste* publications, and Third Worldist texts, Socialist Lebanon emphasized the reading of the primary texts of the Marxist tradition. "We did not really discuss a lot of secondary readings," Traboulsi recalls; "there was an idea: *how* should the mother texts—*ummahat*—of Marxism be read?"[31] The emphasis on establishing a direct affiliation with the main sources of the tradition, a *retour aux sources* of sorts, was a theoretical and political move to be understood in the context of the practices of Soviet-dependent communist parties, such as the Arab CPs including the Lebanese Communist Party and their "theoretical poverty" in the eyes of SL's intellectual militants. During our first meeting, Ahmad Beydoun fleshed out, in his poised manner and slow articulate speech, one aspect of the idea of the retour aux sources while providing a synopsis of the relationship of SL's relation to the Marxist corpus, emphasizing the cohabitation of different trends in the organization:

AB: In reality, Socialist Lebanon had many things. First there was a great sense of theoretical self-importance and a theoretical contempt of communists [LCP]. When I look at it now, I realize it was not built on such a solid base, we were not so advanced . . . but we used to consider ourselves light-years away from the LCP theoretically. So there was this thing, this sense of self-importance, with a lot of eclecticism. We did not force ourselves to choose, and this lasted for a while with an accent, an emphasis on a particular movement—each year or two maybe or every six months. I can't now delimit these periods for the five to six years spent in this experience.

We had a general Leninist heading, but we didn't say that we were a political party. We had read *What Is to Be Done?* well and discussed it, but we had certain issues, or problems, that were implicit with democratic centralism. We did not acknowledge its problems. Our way out was through saying that we are an organization and not a party and therefore it's not a problem if we did not apply all the criteria of democratic centralism in the Leninist formulation.

There was another heading, that we didn't name as such then, but you could call a *Marxisme Marxien*, a fundamental Marxism that used to be nourished through a direct relationship with the texts of Marx, and not fourth-degree people.

FB: [Such as] Soviet scientists?

AB: Not [Andrei] Zhdanov, or [Joseph] Stalin, or anyone of that sort. A direct affiliation to *Capital* and the *Manifesto*, this is the second point. We didn't hate Trotsky, we had a real sympathy towards him, especially because of his problems with Stalin, and of course a total enmity towards Stalin. From there onwards, there is something Cuban, Castro, Che, etc., something Maoist and something Italian . . .

FB: Was there a division of labor, say, between the "theoretician" and the "politician"?

AB: No, things didn't work this way. There was one [Waddah] who worked more than the others, and had an older relationship to this line of work than the others, because he had a tight relationship to the UNEF and the French Communist Party.[32] He was a Ba'thist beforehand too. . . . Fawwaz we used to consider the Leninist of the group, the class analysis guy, and the one with organizational conceptions. That's how things were.

The gist of what I want to tell you is that we did not feel the urgency, or the need of settling [on a trend]. We didn't even know how much we were with the Italians or the Cubans and how much we were against them; these were not clearly determined, and for Maoism it's the same. In reality, what we used to call theoretical superiority was a diversity of sources with a knowledge, as I was telling you, of these sources that is relative and with the selection determined by our subjects, the Lebanese and Arab ones.[33]

Socialist Lebanon was a loose space in both the organizational sense of not adhering to the strictures of democratic centralism and in the ideological sense of allowing multiple intellectual influences inside the group without declaring a full allegiance to any of the directions. This is how Beydoun put it during our second meeting, when I brought up again the issue of SL's intellectual interlocutors and ideological horizons:

AB: No one said I am Trotskyist, for example, or I am Maoist, or I am Guevarist.

FB: But how did Guevara, Castoriadis, and Lenin blend together?

AB: This is the issue. There was a presumption that we concentrate on our situation. Where are we? Where can we work? And at the same time understand what is happening beyond us, particularly in the Arab world with an emphasis on movements of political change, or insurrectionist movements; and, of course, with a concentration on what would necessarily make you gravitate towards it, because it constituted an event, such as the defeat of 1967. However, at the end of the day, how each one used to read the things he was working on was partially left to his own discretion. There was no real control of these things.... For example, Marx, OK Marx; Lenin, OK Lenin, but also Trotsky, Althusser, Foucault's early work, even [Jacques] Lacan....

FB: I was told that you used [Pierre] Bourdieu in writings against the [foreign language] failing grade?

AB: Even Bourdieu, of course ... *Les Héritiers*, for example. This book I discovered as soon as I arrived in France in 1963, it was published in 1964.... It shook me tremendously, and I felt as if something lit up.[34]

In "The Coming Battle of Secondary School Students," published in the fifth issue (April 1967), the anonymous SL writer argues that Lebanese schools are necessary institutions for the reproduction of social inequality in the country. The student protests, SL wrote, are the result of the internal rural-urban migration, and the clash between the new generation of students from destitute backgrounds, on the one hand, and the curriculum, which was put in place for different kinds of students, on the other. Eliminating students as a result of their low grades in foreign language examinations, continued the editorialist, was the *sieve* of the ruling classes "to bar the barbarian invasions of the sons of the petite bourgeoisie, some of the workers and the peasant classes," limiting them from reaching the echelons of the administration.[35]

The plethora of theoretical texts that SL members were reading found its way into their analysis of the situation, but were not all cited in the bulletin. Browsing through the issues, one will not stumble on citations of Fanon, Lacan, Foucault, Bourdieu, and Althusser, but on authors from the revolutionary tradition solely: mostly Lenin, as evidenced in the texts chosen and glossed over in the "theoretical education corner" of the bulletin, some Cuban references, and more Mao in the last years of the bulletin (1969–70) after the inauguration of Palestinian resistance operations from southern Lebanon (Fig. 2.1). Bourdieu was not mentioned in the text, nor was the essay signed. Our present academic culture would put the underground revolutionary organization on a plagiarism trial, since its members subscribed to a collectivist ethos. Bourdieu's critical sociology of the French educational establishment was translated into

العدد الخامس   نيسان ١٩٦٧

الافتتاحية

في وجه المناورات الطائفية

ليكن شعارنا : البرجوازي اخو البرجوازي، مهما كان دينه!
والنامي (العامل الفلاح الموظفه الحرفي ، ...) اخو
النامي، مهما كان دينه!

دلوال الشهر الماضي ، ثابت " المواد المتفجرة " في
السياسةاللبنانية عبارة عن سلسلة متصلة لم تنته بعد ، من
المناورات الطائفية ويمكن تلخيصا بما يلي :
١) خطاب البطريرك المعوشي في ٢٠ اذار المنصرم ،
عند " العناصر المخربة " معلنا ان لبنان (لبنانه هو) امة تؤمن
بالله وتنبذ الاشتراكية والشيوعية ، داعيا الذين لا يشاطرونه هذا
الايمان الى سلوك " طريق البحر المفتح امامهم " .
وسرعان ما تجاوب مع المديرين الثلاثي الرجعي (اده ، شمعون، جميل) ، فكانت مذكرة رئيس الكتائب
احتجاجا على " تدخل سفير ع.م.ع في الشؤون الداخليةاللبنانية " والعمل على انشاء جبهة برلمانية
معارضة من الكتلويين والكتائب والوطنيين الاحرار .
٢) تزايد نشاط " حزب النخبة الوطنية " الداعي الى ما يلي :
– تعديل الدستور .
– عدالة التوظيفة " نظرا لانه " لا يجوز ان تكون المراكز الرئيسية في الادارات العامة والمصالح
المستقلة من نصيب فئة دون غيرها " .
– الاحتجاج على " عدم التكافؤ في الحكم بين سائر الفئات اللبنانية " (اي سائر الفئات الطائفية) ،
وادعوة الى منح رئيس الوزراء سلطات كاملة " فلا تتجاوز بعد الاجهزة عليه ، ... " .
٣) الضجة التي اثيرت ، وما زالت تثار ، حول انتخاب الشيخ حسن خالد مفتي للجمهورية وحول زيارته
للقاهرة وتصريحاته العديدة هناك وعنا . وكل ذلك في محاولة لجعله با زريركا للمسلمين ، والمتحدث الرئيسي
باسمهم . ولعل خير دليل على هذه المحاولة البيان الذي اصدره " رؤساء الاحياء " البيروتية يعلنون فيهاالناء
زيارتهم التقليدية لنواب بيروت بمناسبة عيد الاضحى ، وتسليم كل قضاياهم للمفتي مباشرة .
٤) التصيد لعودة موسى الصدر من جولته بين المهاجرين اللبنانيين في افريقيا ، وبالمناسبة ، فان
الاحقاد الطائفية حول مقتل كامل مروة ، والثار ، مضبا ، فضلا عن الدعوة للحلف الاسلامي — تاليب
موسى الصدر ، علاقته المالية لتحويل كل مشكلات الجنوب (التي هي مشكلات تخلف واستغلال) الى مشكلات
طائفية حول " حقوق الشيعة " (في التوظيف خاصة) واقامة مجلس طي شيعي مستقل .
ان كل هذه المناورات على تنوعها وتمارسها ساحايا ، تلتقي عند قاسم مشترك بينها . وهو انها محاولات

Arabic three years after its publication, and put to work by militants to provide an analysis of how the Lebanese bourgeoisie uses foreign language grades to perpetuate its rule and to underscore the importance of supporting the student movement. Theory in practice in 1967 Beirut was put to use, unlike how we use it today in our academic worlds, without any reference to its creators.[36]

This double erasure of authorship was related to legal, political, and theoretical issues. Some of the members were public school teachers at the time, which made it legally difficult to write under their own names while calling for a revolution against the state, their employer. It also served them well politically because the veteran, and much larger, Lebanese Communist Party—founded in 1924—and the other parties they were subjecting to a ruthless critique on the pages of their bulletin could not assess the size of the new organization. The erasure of Bourdieu and company's names, on the other hand, was an integral part of the means of production of revolutionary authority. Charara mentioned during one of our conversations that his militant voice was partially a consequence of not wanting to be taken for a *farfelu* (eccentric, wacky) intellectual tinkering with culture, in contrast to a revolutionary grounding political practice in a Marxian theoretical analysis.[37] Their collectivist ethos permeated leftist political and artistic practices at the time.[38] At the heart of these collective endeavors was an attempt to transform the relations of production and to rearticulate intellectual and political practice away from the bourgeois notion of the individual author, the tortured romantic genius, and the fetish of the name of the master. In addition to reworking relations of production, these collectives strove to circulate their works outside of the market, by bringing them to the people in noncommercial venues such as factories, public spaces, and universities in order to circumscribe turning them into a commodity with an exchange value that would eventually overcome its use value. While Socialist Lebanon initially included prices on their underground bulletins, the organization ended up distributing it for free.

Winds from the South and Back

In *May '68 and Its Afterlives*, Kristin Ross notes that in the years directly before May 1968, those coinciding with events such as the bombing of Hanoi by the Americans in December 1966, "it was the North Vietnamese peasant, and not the auto-worker at Billancourt, who had become for many French militants, the figure of the working class. . . . [he] provided the transitional figure, the relay between the 'intimate' colonial other, the Algerian of the early 1960s, and the French worker during '68."[39] Ross then proceeds to investigate "the sites and discourses that allowed the geography of a vast international and distant struggle—the 'North/South axis'—to become transposed onto the lived geography, the daily itineraries of students and intellectuals in Paris in the early 1960s" (*May '68*, 82). François Maspero's bookstore La Joie de Lire in Paris and his publishing house were two such important relay sites. Maspero's bookstore, which opened its doors in 1956 and closed down in 1975, "coincides almost exactly with the rough twenty-year span—from Dien Bien Phu in 1954 and the Bandung conference in the following year to some time [*sic*] in 1975—the period during which the periphery became the center of interest to European, and particularly French, intellectuals" (*May '68*, 82). Maspero's publishing house began its activity in 1959 and stopped in 1982.[40] During the high tide of anticolonial struggle, François Maspero's publishing house was known, in Ross's words, as

> a "wind from the South": The press that tracked the ruin and collapse of Empire, that regularly gave voice to South American, African, and Asian political theorists and testimonies, the press that first published Fanon's *Les damnés de la terre*, with its preface by Sartre, as well as works by Ben Barka, Giap, Cabral, Che Guevara, Malcolm X and others.... It was largely because of the Editions Maspero, and because of the editorial direction followed by *Le Monde Diplomatique* and *Les Temps Modernes* during those years—these three publications shared many of the same authors—that one of the great *gauchiste* particularities of the time became palpably evident: theory itself was being generated not from Europe but from the third world. Not only was the figure of action, the militant peasant and freedom-fighter, a third world phenomenon—this, after all, was to be expected according to a standard international division of labor in which Europe and the West are the thinkers and the rest of the world doers, the men of action. But "the wretched of the earth"— Mao, Guevara, Fanon, Cabral and others—had become in this era of *gauchiste* reversal the thinkers as well. (*May '68*, 83–84)

Éditions Maspero also published continental theory works, notably Althusser's *Pour Marx* (For Marx) and *Lire Le Capital* (Reading Capital), which he coauthored with his students Étienne Balibar, Roger Establet, Pierre Macherey, and Jacques Rancière. Both volumes, which were published in 1965, were read, discussed, and put to use by Socialist Lebanon. These three gauchiste publications— books by Maspero, *Le Monde Diplomatique*, and *Les Temps Modernes*—were pivotal in the readings discussed in Beirut at that time.[41] Ahmad Beydoun complements the account provided by Traboulsi above, noting, "Fawwaz guided us to *New Left Review* and *Monthly Review* and until now I still have tens of these issues. . . . We were continuously following *Les Temps Modernes*, sometimes *Esprit* and *Critique. Le Monde Diplomatique* [we used to follow] with full diligence; we used to keep all the old issues."[42] The group's dominant Francophone imaginary, which followed the world's events through a close reading of *Le Monde* and *Le Monde Diplomatique* and sharpened its theoretical skills and political analysis via devouring Maspero and Le Seuil books and following *Les Temps Modernes*, was also enriched by Anglophone radical publications.

The peculiarity of the trilingual horizon (Arabic, French, and English) of Socialist Lebanon is predicated on the Lebanese educational system, which alongside Arabic teaches a second foreign language, or two, the most common during the 1950s being French, which was adopted as the main foreign language by Lebanese public schools at that time.[43] This trilingual imaginary would also prove to be crucial in expanding the range of available works for translation: Fawwaz Traboulsi on the Anglophone side, and Hassan Qobeissi and Waddah Charara on the Francophone, were among the most prolific translators of the group. The Parisian "wind from the South" traveled back to the South, to nourish sL's intellectual-political project. These Third Worldist metropolitan publishing houses were not only bringing the peripheries into the metropoles but also worked as a bridge, one that made the ideas and experiences of different militants from the South accessible to each other. French and English mediated between these different Third Worldist militants, who most probably would only have access to each other's writings through the former colonizer's language.

The Parisian publishing houses—Le Seuil, Maspero, and Minuit—also played an additional role when it came to the particularity of Arab politics. Socialist Lebanon, which emerged out of Arab nationalism's orbit, read and translated into Arabic the writings of Egyptian Marxist thinkers who put out systematic critiques of Nasser's regime from its Left. Anouar Abdel Malak (1924–2012), Hassan Riad (the pseudonym of Samir Amin, 1931–2018), and Mahmoud Hussein, the nom de plume of the duo Adel Rif'at (1938–) and Bahgat al-Nadi (1936–), wrote in French, published in Paris, and resorted to pseudonyms to escape retribution from Nasser's regime in the wake of the crackdown on the Egyptian Communist Party, which began on January 1, 1959.[44] These insurrectionary works highlighted how the caste of nationalist officers gave rise to a state bourgeoisie that exploits and dominates Egyptians while appropriating the social surplus for its own benefit, failing therefore to fulfill the necessary task of primitive accumulation needed for development. Abdel Malak's *Egypte, Société Militaire* (1962) was the first book Waddah Charara translated shortly after it came out, after he had returned from France (1963). It appeared in Arabic without the name of the translator and with a modified title coined by the publisher of the Beirut press Dar al-Tali'a—*Egypt, a New Society Built by the Military*—instead of *Egypt, Military Society,* to dampen the critical bite of Abdel Malek's title. French publishing houses in this particular case were a haven for Egyptian Marxist critics, enabling their work to escape Nasser's censorship and creating a bridge connecting them to their comrades in Beirut. What couldn't be published in Cairo in Arabic was published in France and translated back into Arabic in Beirut with the hope that it would circulate in the Arab world.

Diagnosing the Present, Acting Now

In its May 1969 issue, the journal *Dirasat ʿArabiyya* (Arab Studies), a vibrant forum for discussing contemporary Arab culture and politics published in Beirut, featured a forty-one-page essay titled "Madkhal li-Qira'at al-Bayan al-Shuyuʿi" (An Introduction to Reading *The Communist Manifesto,* hereafter IRCM).[45] Under the author's slot in the journal's table of contents, the editor wrote, "Prepared by 'Socialist Lebanon's' study circle." The "Introduction" counters economically determinist readings, authorizes antievolutionary positions, and develops SL's perspective on the centrality of translation for political practice. "The point of view adopted by the *Manifesto* regarding the succession of political stages," Socialist Lebanon writes, "is of crucial importance":

> It rids Marxism of the charge of evolutionism, which dominated Marxist writings for a long time, and is still prevalent in a number of works by communist parties. And perhaps the most significant position premised on evolutionism is the one that calls for the support of the national bourgeoisie because the history of the society in which the communist party is militating hasn't passed through all the required stages: . . . feudalism, capitalism, socialism. . . . And since this society hasn't passed through the capitalist phase, and its bourgeois political leadership, this means that the ambition of any group that belongs to the working class or the petite bourgeoisie to constitute the leadership of the period is illegitimate because its aim is not consistent with the [logic of] succession of stages. (IRCM, 47–48)

In an essay revisiting the history of Arab communist parties after the fall of the Soviet Union, the Iraqi social scientist Faleh A. Jabar writes that the five-stage Stalinist schema—"primitive communism, slavery, capitalism, and lastly communism, socialism being the first stage (or transitory phase of the latter)"—established the theoretical ground from which questions arose.[46] "What role could be found for the anti-colonialist nationalists?" communists were asking, and "what road should the 'revolution' follow: a capitalist path, a move toward socialism, or a third way that involved gradual change?"[47] The ideological battle lines of the 1960s, he continues, focused on whether communists ought to "burn stages" or adopt an "evolutionary" view of history in answering the following kinds of questions: "Was the national bourgeoisie, as a social class, capable of carrying out the required tasks? And, if so, to what extent should it be supported? Or if this class was impotent, should the working class step in as it had done in the October 1917 revolution to undertake both democratic (i.e., capitalist) and socialist tasks at one and the same time?"[48] It is as a response to this conjuncture that the militant intellectuals of Socialist Lebanon anchored their antievolutionary positions, which called for the autonomy of the working class and its capacity to "burn stages," in a retour aux sources to the *Manifesto*. In doing so they short-circuited Stalinist interpretations and undercut the official Soviet doxas of the time to announce that the positions calling for a historicist logic of stages, predicated on an economic reductionism, are not authorized by Marx's text. "If the forces of production, as well as their continuous development, lead to the shattering of the relations of production and to toppling the political regime that maintains them, then the fall of the regime also results in pushing the forces of production forward by removing all obstacles that were hindering their development," Socialist Lebanon observe, warning against a reductionism that does not pay attention to the fact that the "political structure plays an important role in the development of the forces of production" (IRCM, 48).

At the heart of SL's interpretation of the *Manifesto* is an argument against the historicist "not yet" that relinquishes the working class and the revolutionary act to the "waiting room" of history since the objective conditions of the moment are not ripe for its autonomous action.[49] In their refusal to wait for the revolution, they were insisting on the "now" as "the temporal horizon of political action," which the anticolonial nationalists had also done before them against the "not yet" of the colonizer. The difference was that in the late 1960s, more than a decade and a half after the Free Officers came to power in Egypt, and more than five years after the Ba'th Party established its rule in Syria, Socialist Lebanon's "now" was a postcolonial one par excellence. They refused to subordinate revolutionary politics to an alliance with, and support of, the national bourgeoisie, "traditional leaders" such as Kamal Jumblatt, the leader of the Druze community, who founded the

Lebanese Socialist Party, and to Arab nationalist regimes that also brandished the flag of socialism. In fact, the Lebanese organization made sure to draw their readers' attention to the "inaccuracy" of some of the widely circulated slogans of these actors. Socialism, they assert, is not "the society of sufficiency and justice. If dignified living and sufficiency and justice are some of the consequences of a socialist society, it is first and foremost the collective control of the producers over the means of production" (IRCM, 74–75). The unnamed author of this particular definition of socialism they are countering is no other than President Abdel Nasser.[50] This generation of militant intellectuals, who came of political age as Nasser's anticolonial star was rising in the 1950s and experienced the secession between Syria and Egypt in 1961 as a bitter personal blow, became by the late 1960s Marxist critics of the anticolonial nationalist regimes in power, the national bourgeoisie, and last but not least the pro-Soviet communist parties.

Socialist Lebanon's emphasis on the present moment also came across through inscribing their struggle in a globally shared contemporary horizon of the people's struggles from China to Cuba and by calling for a thorough diagnosis of the present's particularity. "What is the characteristic of our present era?" is a question that every communist has to ask, Socialist Lebanon assert, as they supply the direction of their answer: "[Starting] from here, a point which Marx, Engels, Lenin and Mao have recurrently come back to is clarified, and that is that the answer to this question cannot be general, and cannot be repeated, even if the circumstances preserved their general outline. Every Marxist work has to come back to this question with regards to its country and its circumstances, and to do so again with every transformation in its conditions and those of the rest of the world" (IRCM, 43). Communist politics in Socialist Lebanon's interpretation is given its coherence, overall general direction, and particular shape by an analysis that is attentive to the particularities of its present. The absence of this capacity for analysis, whose aims are simultaneously to rise above the particularities of disparate problems—say, in the syndicalist militancy of the student, worker, and peasant sectors—and unify them in a general political project that is grounded in the specificity of the situation, results in the disintegration of revolutionary practice. "The practice that pulls together all the isolated issues, and highlights the condition of their political realization," they affirm, "is theoretical practice or political analysis (we are momentarily using the two expressions interchangeably)" (IRCM, 71). If the analysis of the particular characteristics of the present are forgone, the party will be transformed into "splintered sectors, each working on its own without any relation to the others but attending central committee meetings and discussing the general 'line' that does not generalize anything but a bunch of slogans that should work in Bolivia and Sudan as well as in Lebanon, which means that they are not valid in any country" (IRCM, 71).

Transfiguration, Translation, Pragmatics

The emphasis on the diagnosis of the particularity of the present forecloses for Socialist Lebanon the possibility of a general and repeatable answer that cuts across times and spaces. In doing so, the Lebanese militant group was clearly arguing against viewing Marxism as a direct translation of a body of theory to disparate particular situations that are themselves not generative of theoretical elaborations, but passive recipients of a "revealed" universal discourse. Tackling head-on the question of translation in the Marxist tradition, Socialist Lebanon's critical posture is not one that emphasizes the unmasking of a particular parading in the guise of a universal, say, some of Marx's nineteenth-century Eurocentric formulations, even though they are not oblivious to them. As a matter of fact, they begin their "Introduction" with a reflexive move that stresses the spatiotemporal axis of difference separating their context of reading and interpretation from the time and place of the *Manifesto*'s writing:

> What is taken for granted is that *The Communist Manifesto* did not treat the problems we are suffering from nor did it "predict," as it is said, the enormity of the problems that colonized countries (those colonized by the West) would face. Rather those countries are only mentioned in the *Manifesto* in rare places, and with a name, which is not considerate at all: "The barbarian countries"! And it was not written on the eve of a national liberation revolution, but a month before the outbreak of the 1848 revolution in France, i.e., on the eve of the first workers' revolution that destroyed the bourgeois monarchy and laid the foundations for the Second Republic ... Moreover, the *Manifesto* was written in the mid-nineteenth century, i.e., in a period when European industry had not yet witnessed the biggest share of transformations, which would change the face of Europe and the globe in the second half of the nineteenth century. Besides, the workers' movement had not yet traversed the great number of experiences that it would endure during the next fifty years. (IRCM, 38)

In this opening paragraph, placed under the heading of "Why Do We Read *The Communist Manifesto*?," Socialist Lebanon firmly assert the difference separating the contours of their present from the *Manifesto*'s time and place of writing, deny any supposedly predictive quality to the Marx-Engels text, while ironically referencing and translating Marx's "barbarian countries" into the colonized ones. While they were certainly far from epistemologically naïve, subscribing to every letter of Marx's text, Socialist Lebanon's critical posture did not circumscribe itself to debunking the politics of theory. They did not throw the baby out with what they perceived as the Eurocentric bathwater because Marxist thought for them was more than a body of knowledge to be scrutinized for Eurocentric and Orientalist assumptions. For one it was a powerful analytical tool that helped them understand their colonial modernity and the class contradictions internal to their societies against other political forces such as Arab nationalists who were dealing with the meanderings of *The Arab Spirit*, and its resurrection—Ba'th means "Resurrection" in Arabic. More importantly, Marxism held a key to understand these societies, on the one hand, and a tool to effect their revolutionary transformation toward the horizon of social justice, on the other. It was a theory of political practice; Socialist Lebanon was fond of quoting Lenin's maxim, "Without revolutionary theory, there is no revolutionary practice." This is why the gist of their intervention does not lie in unmasking the particular hiding behind the universal, but in arguing that by not taking into consideration the spatiotemporal characteristics of Bolivia, Sudan, and Lebanon—the particular—one traffics in hollow universals that have no traction and are too general to be of any use.

Failure to translate is to transform Marx's oeuvre to a *lettre morte*. There is no way then of being a proper communist without engaging in a translation of Marx and Engels's works, one that does not constitute an inauthentic copy of the original, a particular distortion of the universal text, or a failed mimicry of the West. On the contrary, translations are generative and constitutive not only of Lebanese Marxism but of the communist tradition of thought and practice. "Innovative socialist revolutions," write Socialist Lebanon, "have been tied to novel theoretical thought: the Bolshevik revolution and Lenin, the Chinese revolution and Mao Tse-Tung, the Vietnamese revolution and Vo Nguyen Giap, the Cuban Revolution and Che Guevara" (IRCM, 71). In SL's interpretation, Marx's oeuvre constitutes the foundational text of the tradition, which *authorizes* socialist political practice and thought. It does not, however, stand as the untroubled transhistorical universal to the particular glosses that come in its wake. Rather, Marxism cannot be separated from the circulation and translations across time and space of Marxist works, including the numerous returns to Marx's oeuvre itself. The universality of Marxism is constituted through, and is a product of, the multiple acts of translations and does not precede them. Just think for a moment of Socialist Lebanon in late 1960s

Beirut going back to Marx after having just read Giap, Fanon, and Althusser, who himself was rereading Marx in the wake of such figures as Sigmund Freud, Jacques Lacan, Lenin, Gaston Bachelard, Mao, and Gramsci to get a sense of the distance we have traveled away from a view of Arab Marxists as ensnared by modernization theory and engaging in unidirectional acts of translation of Marxism characterized as a Western critical discourse.

At the heart of Socialist Lebanon's acts of translation lies the question of political practice, of providing new knowledges that authorize forms of revolutionary politics and participate in the formation of novel political consciousness and subjectivities. The "Introduction" was written for and used in theoretical education circles after the newly founded Democratic Front for the Liberation of Palestine (DFLP, 1969) approached Socialist Lebanon with a request for such a text. Marx, Lenin, Mao, Trotsky, Guevara, and others were read in French or English and translated into Arabic from these translations under the temporal pressure of political practice, sometimes comparing the translations in two different languages, or different translations in one of these languages while working on the Arabic text.[51] Their labors of translation from translations driven by the impediment of practice, whether working with Mao or Marx, bypassed the distinctions between original and copy, universal and particular. The question of linguistic difference, of fidelity to the original language, mattered less than the capacity of accessing, interpreting, and putting to practical use authoritative discourses about the analysis of class, imperialism, and guerrilla warfare.

These acts of translations and transfigurations, which were fueled by the impediment of revolutionary practice, were not mediations between a self and an other. Theirs was not an attempt that sought, as many anthropological works do, to render what seems unfamiliar at first glance familiar, or, going in the opposite direction, to denaturalize what we take for granted. Susan Buck-Morss's reading of Qutb and Shariati, which works toward a rediscovery of one's own commitments in a different theoretical language as well as revealing the contingency of Western norms when refracted through the prism of Muslim thinkers, is in line with this approach. That is because their world of the late 1960s and 1970s was neatly divided into the two camps of Left and Right, progressives and reactionaries, national liberation movements and colonialism. This was a time when young, militant intellectuals in Lebanon would debate national liberation movements in Latin America, as well as the minutiae of strikes and syndicates in some European factory, when the students of the American University of Beirut would demonstrate in protest against the war in Vietnam. This world, wrapped in one overarching *canvas* on which clear fault lines were drawn between Left and Right, has vanished. Theirs was a world that was eclipsed by the rise of the questions of community, by which I mean the resurgence of infranational sectarian, regional, ethnic, and familial solidarities, and the emergence of an array of militant political forces grouped under the banner of political Islam. Some of them, like Charara, were among the first to take note of the entanglement of political practice in the cobwebs of communal solidarities that relegated the march of the working classes toward brighter tomorrows into futures past (Fig. 2.2).

In the opening pages of *Thinking Past Terror: Islamism and Critical Theory on the Left* (2003), Susan Buck-Morss revisits her own trajectory as she pithily identifies the ebbing away of that old political world:

> In the 1970s when I was a student, Marxism in its multiple variants— Western Marxism, Marxist humanism, Trotskyism, Leninism, Maoism, Fanonism—provided the common discursive terrain in which critics of exploitation and domination could agree (often vehemently, even violently) to disagree. The secular Left throughout the Middle East was a vibrant part of that conversation.... Part of the postcolonial reality since the end of the Cold War has been the disintegration of the discursive unity provided by Marxism, for which some of us must confess feeling not a small bit of nostalgia. (*TPT*, 7)

Buck-Morss's translations take place in the wake of the disintegration of this common ground. Her project of translation takes place on a different plane than the one Socialist Lebanon undertook, whose unified world linked Hanoi to Cuba by way of Paris. Her translations are not actions that are undertaken under the urgent pressure of political practice, which seeks a revolutionary theory to ground and guide it. Translating Qutb and Shariati into English in New York produces very different kinds of analytical and political effects than translating Marx and Giap into Arabic in Beirut. I would like to think more with Buck-Morss about her crucial insight that "our forms of critique are actions that themselves affect history," which is central to her more recent essay, in which she returns to Qutb and Shariati (*STF*, 67). Buck-Morss writes:

> If we do *not* rescue the progressive moments in present-day religious writers—Qutb, Shariati, and so many others—whose political actions we have neglected even to see, but who belong objectively to *our* time and who are, in the uncomfortable sense our *contemporaries*, if we continue to ignore their highly influential work, abandoning them on the field of political imagination, then we allow their legacy to be taken

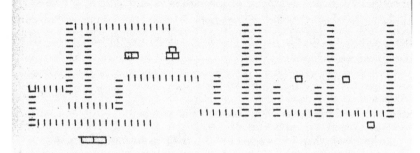

العـــدد الحـادى عشـــر   أيــار ١٩٦٨

في هذا العدد

FIGURE 2.2. *Socialist Lebanon*, Issue 11, May 1968.

over by those all too eager to appropriate it for their own hegemonic projects. A relevant anecdote: Nathan Coombs writes, 'When *Culture Wars* approached me to review a release from Verso's Radical Thinkers series, I responded "great give me Ali Shariati." But Shariati was not in the collection. (STF, 79)

Buck-Morss's call for engaging these intellectuals qua political theorists, and not merely as native, local intellectuals whose lives and works are framed through concepts and methods developed by the "theorists" of the Euro-American pantheon, is a necessary one. Her juxtaposition of the theoretical labors of Qutb and Shariati with those of Theodor Adorno and Walter Benjamin on the same page, in a montage of fragments from different intellectual traditions, produces salutary effects. Buck-Morss's textual montages jolt some readers out of complacent intellectual habits; despite the different theorists from the South that the Marxist tradition produced, some readers still expect "abstract," "universal" theory to be produced up North and "concrete," "particular" thinking to take place in what is now called the Global South. What concerns me is rather how Buck-Morss envisages the pragmatic effects of her rescue of those progressive moments in the corpus of religious thinkers. How would reading Shariati today by an American critical theorist, such as Buck-Morss, or his incorporation into Verso's Radical Thinkers series alongside Louis Althusser and Gillian Rose, help disarm those other readers who would like to appropriate his work for hegemonic, or other, ends? Shariati's oeuvre has been read, commented on, argued with, and mobilized in Iran and the Arab world for more than four decades now. Moreover, forms of critique, and their transnational travels, may produce multiple theoretical and political effects depending on the questions asked by those reading publics and the stakes animating their communities of argument. In saying "our rescue saves Shariati from appropriation by Iranian reactionaries as a tool of the ruling class," Buck-Morss is simultaneously attributing too much power to one reading of the work, which is isolated from the space of arguments in which this work has been discussed for a few decades now, and holding on to a too limited view regarding the potential pragmatic effects of traveling theories (STF, 80).

Coda: Here and Elsewhere

To raise the question, for example, of whether having a refrigerator, for American society, necessarily implies the destruction of another country and, after that, one's own destruction. "We start with Vietnam," he says, "in order to get to things that would be almost entirely French … to show, in the end, that it is clearly capitalism itself which is at stake."

These are the comments of a filmmaker from a discussion between a collective of filmmakers and the audience composed of workers at Rhodiaceta—a chemical factory—after the screening of *Loin du Vietnam* (Far from Vietnam) (1967). The director in question is Alain Resnais, the talented director who produced landmarks such as *Hiroshima Mon Amour* (1959) and *L'Année Dernière à Marienbad* (1961). The collective Société pour le Lancement des Oeuvres Nouvelles (SLON) included some of French cinema's well-known directors, such as Jean-Luc Godard, Agnès Varda, Claude Lelouch, Joris Ivens, and William Klein, in addition to Resnais and Chris Marker (*May '68*, 88–89). Kristin Ross notes that Vietnam and the Third World generally were viewed mostly in terms of class relations in France: "Global solutions to the problems of the third world could only be found in the radical transformation of the Capitalist world system and its replacement by a new economic order" (*May '68*, 89). "The third-worldist perspective Maspero had helped make available to French readers," she writes, "became the means, in his view, for reconceptualizing the French national situation" (*May '68*, 85). Maspero's views, like the comments uttered by Resnais of the film collective, take as their starting point that "'everything is linked' and that one cannot analyze Gaullism, capitalism, or syndicalism in the France of 1966 as though it were a phenomenon isolated from the rest of the world" (*May '68*, 86).

The idea that "everything is linked" undid the East/West distinction and nationalist imaginaries by providing one language to articulate the struggle of workers in French factories and Vietnamese fighters against American imperialism. In France, Maoism provided the "theoretical justification" for the merging of anticapitalist and anti-imperialist themes that Vietnam allowed by "loosening [the French Communist Party's] emphasis on the French proletariat by acknowledging the possibility of other political agents—peasants or farmers" and by emphasizing "the Third Worldist geopolitical organization of the World along a North/South axis—the one etched by the international division of labor" (80).

In Beirut, the "Chinification of Marxism" and the reading of Fanon as Waddah Charara recalled were spurring him and the group to think through a theoretical and political project that would "adapt" Marxism to Lebanese specificity: the Arabization of Marxism was on the table. Charara was asked if the intention behind the "Introduction to Reading *The Communist Manifesto*," which he had written, was to produce a Lebanese Communist Manifesto. "There was a dream that a number of people, including myself, had," he answered:

And it was a dream of a dual birth. The birth of a contemporary history from the womb of a local subjective history: Arabic Islamic [history] whose meaning was very different from the one it took later on and that this same history be born and at the same time from a general, common, universal human womb.... These two simultaneous births, and most likely we did not give ourselves the necessary tools to understand them, remained closer to a metaphor than to a concept. And even the metaphor remained foggy.[52]

Maoism and Vietnam enabled French students, intellectuals, and workers to realize that they were in the same fight against a common enemy and that they could not delink their domestic problems from the rest of the globe. Maoism and Vietnam in Beirut, especially after the June 1967 defeat of the Arab armies and regimes, provided a spur for the translation of Marxism to other southern contexts and for a popular guerrilla struggle against colonialism (Israel) and imperialist interests.

Looking at it retrospectively, the frenzy that captivated the members of Socialist Lebanon during their early revolutionary years of selfless immersion in reading, discussing, writing, and translating would prove pivotal for the fashioning of their intellectual habitus. The work ethic and discipline required to plow through dense theoretical texts and to follow the minutiae of global political developments from Prague, to Algeria, and Vietnam, as well as the labors of tying theoretical analysis to practical political situations, will help not only in the formation of a political subjectivity and a cultural capital but also a fostering of intellectual dispositions, which will remain long after the revolution's passing. Moreover, their intense focus on their political present, on reading whatever was useful in understanding it and revolutionizing it, widened their intellectual horizons toward transdisciplinary readings that escaped the logic of specialization and disciplinary boundaries.

The political defeat of a generation of revolutionaries produced a distinguished generation of intellectuals. The underground militants of the 1960s later became the distinguished professors, public commentators, and writers of the 1980s onward. The exit from organized political practice retained from the past the generalist's approach to reading and writing, dodging the logic of specialization. Ahmad Beydoun wrote poetry, a film script, and essays on linguistics and the sociology of culture in addition to his historiographical works. Waddah Charara wrote on themes ranging from popular culture, to cinema, Arab heritage, and Islamic studies, to translating French poetry, on top of his sociological and historical works. Abbas Beydoun became a distinguished poet, a novelist, and cultural critic. I asked the latter if it was clear to him that he would become a poet during the days of militancy:

> It was not clear to me what I would become. I was writing poetry. I wrote a collection, a lot. I started very early, but it wasn't clear to me what I was going to write. So at the same time, I would write poetry, stories, even theater, and it was all dependent on what I was reading at the time. . . .
>
> There were these varied options for someone who fundamentally needed a very long time before acknowledging that one has something that is *private*, before we even talk about specialization.[53]

After they quit organized political activity and found or developed their own individual interests, their period of militancy will be mostly recast as one of selfless political immersion, and the exit from it will be into a discovery or recovery of private passions.

But why today should we revisit SL's founding moment in the mid-1960s? Is it to argue for the saliency of their answers for our present? It is needless to point out that the national, regional, and global conjuncture they were working in half a century ago is not ours today. Their heated debates about whether the working class ought to "burn stages" or ally itself with the national bourgeoisie reach our shores as faint echoes from a lost world. So much has changed since then. So why return to Socialist Lebanon? Is it to denaturalize a present, permeated by communal discourses and attachments by excavating a past when politics was imagined and practiced differently? Sure, but my historical reconstruction is not fueled by a Left melancholy to a time when class-based politics had a thicker ontological density and when the lines were clearly drawn between the forces of progress and those of reaction.[54] I am trying to carve a path between a corrosive Left melancholy that disparages an uncertain present, on the one hand, and banishing this past's relevance to our present by dismissing this Marxist generation's critical labors and practice on the basis of their vanguardism or modernizing politics, on the other hand. What I am also after is a rescue of Socialist Lebanon's *ethos*, which shone through their indefatigable tracking of their global present, dodging the logics of professionalization and expertise, what Jacques Rancière calls the logic of the police. By following the minutiae of the secondary school student strikes in Lebanon while reading Bourdieu, analyzing at length the reasons for the defeat of the Arab armies in 1967, translating Fidel Castro's speeches on the defeatist line of the Venezuelan Communist Party, and publishing communiqués from a revolutionary Iraqi workers' organization, Socialist Lebanon's political imaginary was not locked on the tired East/West or South/North path. This ethos also shone through their sustained attention to the specificity of the conditions they were diagnosing and working in. For all their attention to the global unfolding of events, they were not frequent-flying international experts, or parachuted humanitarians on a mission, but committed translators and militants enmeshed in the fabric of their own societies, and accountable to them, whose theoretical acumen was part and parcel of their political project. The path Socialist Lebanon cleared half a decade ago is no longer recognizable to us today. Their dream of a dual birth, on the other hand, has certainly lost nothing of its luster.

3. JUNE 1967 AND ITS HISTORIOGRAPHICAL AFTERLIVES

> When the June war broke out I was still in Paris. . . . I felt something like a quake
> mixed with shame, which pushed me to quickly escape to Beirut. . . . And for months,
> in an atmosphere of depression and despair, I thought, every now and then,
> of committing suicide. But it was forestalled first by a sense of responsibility towards
> a wife and three children and some remainder of a metaphysical trust
> in the revolutionary potential of the Arab people.
> —YASIN AL-HAFIZ

> At the time the Vietnam peace movement was gaining momentum but
> for me the Palestine issue seemed more crucial.
> —MASAO ADACHI

There is no doubt that 1967, which marks the swift military defeat of Arab armies against Israel, has a ubiquitous historiographical presence. It is *the* turning point par excellence. You will find it referenced in Arabic newspaper articles, in Arab Human Development Reports from the United Nations Development Programme, and in the critical literature discussing artistic, intellectual, and political trends.[1] The use of the date of a military defeat as a marker for different genres, and not, for instance, the date of events that are internal to these fields of practice, is symptomatic of the saturation of Arab cultural scenes with politics, whether it is conceived as a national struggle against colonialism or a critique of discrimination based on sexuality, gender, and race. Artists and intellectuals often comment on the overbearing presence of political concerns. A few years ago, Hamed Sinno, the front man of the Lebanese pop band Mashrou' Leila, mentioned in an interview that it is very difficult to escape politics where he comes from.[2] Sinno echoed Jalal Khoury (1934–2017), the committed Lebanese theater director and playwright who more than four decades ago noted that "our world is asphyxiated by politics."[3] More than fifty years of age separate the two. Sinno was born in 1988, in the last years of the Lebanese civil war, a few years before the collapse of the Soviet Union, while

Khoury was at the vanguard of Lebanese political theater in the late 1960s. That said, both agree on the difficulty of artists escaping politics in our part of the world. Pierre Bourdieu's theories on the increasing autonomy of cultural fields away from sociopolitical contexts, and external constraints, find their limit in the neocolonial and postcolonial Arab world.[4]

Works on Arab intellectual history in English adopt post-1967 thought as a marker for contemporary Arab thought.[5] In Ibrahim Abu Rabiʿ's *Contemporary Arab Thought*, the post-1967 era is characterized by a variety of transformations that are hard to square with the historical event of the military defeat as their turning point.[6] In addition to mentioning the impact of 1967 on intellectual production, Abu Rabiʿ writes about "the Arab project of modernity [coming] to a standstill" (18); "most Arab states have experienced more not less authoritarianism since 1967"(22); "the social and economic transformations since 1967" (23); the "rise of the Gulf States to religious and economic prominence after 1967 mainly in the 1980's and 1990's"; the Islamic revival post-1967 (28); the "mode of production dominant in 1967 in the Gulf" (24); and capitalism after 1967. In this narrative post-1967 becomes the master key to unlock intellectual, political, social, and economic transformations in the Arab world. It's a master key that is without much heuristic value, one that plots structural transformations in societies and modes of production on the same plane as the event of a swift military defeat, without any distinction between different registers of analysis.

Suzanne Kassab's deployment of 1967 is much more focused. The intellectual and political crisis experienced in the wake of the military defeat, she argues, brought on two, increasingly bifurcated, responses:

> One the one hand, the search for totalizing doctrines, especially religious after the demise of the Left and of secular nationalism, and, on the other hand, the radicalization of critique. The first trend was the result of a deep yearning for a holistic vision that could offer an indigenous, non-alienating worldview and mobilize the necessary forces toward a way out of the humiliation and the oppression. The second was the outcome of a painful confrontation with the limitations and dangers of holistic views as well as of the growing realization of the vital need for critique in the face of multiple forms of oppression.[7]

Kassab has done an admirable excavation of critical strands in contemporary Arab thought. Her work reveals the multiplicity of critical positions—for example, Marxist, liberal, feminist, Islamist—in contemporary Arab thought, standing as a much-needed corrective to the reduction of this tradition's complexity to a stark ideological binary between secular nationalism and religious politics. Her comparative perspective, which ties in the motifs of Arab debates with global postcolonial conversations, undoes their exceptionalist treatment, which is so often their lot. It is also an invitation to carve new South-South intellectual paths that steer off the much trodden peripheries-metropole highway.

In the remainder of this chapter, I will revisit once more Socialist Lebanon's theoretical and political practice. In doing so, I have four aims. The first is to unearth a very early tradition of critique of the authoritarian regimes that pre-dates the 1967 defeat. Second, to complicate the historiography that crowns 1967 as the turning point, which generated a bifurcation between holistic doctrines and critique. I do so by underlining the radical hopes that accompanied the political rise of the New Left in the *direct* aftermath of 1967, which combined an adherence to thick ideological traditions, such as Marxism, an engagement alongside the Palestinian revolution, and a commitment to critique.[8] The dominant framing of 1967 as the double marker of transition and bifurcation, I argue, is less the result of the direct post-1967 conjuncture and more of the 1980s, when most of these militant intellectuals lost their political organizational moorings and their hope in the revolutionary masses to become detached, isolated critics squeezed between the Scylla of authoritarian regimes and the Charybdis of communal solidarities and Islamic militant movements. As the political-social questions of the 1960s focusing on the transfiguration of Marxism—its Arabization—to guide political practice gave way to the political-cultural questions of *asala* (authenticity) and *turath* (Arab-Islamic tradition), quite a few of the 1960s leftists rediscovered the heritage of the earlier generation of *Nahda* (Renaissance) liberal thinkers, such as Taha Husayn and 'Ali 'Abd al-Raziq.[9] The Arab liberal tradition, which they thought had been superseded by Marxism in the 1960s, proved to those former revolutionaries to be much more prescient in addressing the challenges they were facing from both state and society.

Third, unlike the most famous post-1967 self-criticisms, and here I have in mind the works of Sadik al-Azm and Adonis, which coupled the courageous ethical injunction of taking stock of one's own defeat with a culturalist critique that laid the blame on the "traditional" nature of Arabs, Socialist Lebanon focused on examining the social composition of these regimes, their ideologies, and more importantly the logics undergirding their technologies of rule and governing their political and military practices.[10] Critical diagnosis of actual practices of *power* is what they did.

Fourth, and to go back to our present, these very early Marxist critiques raise crucial questions regarding the question of minorities in the Arab world and the mobilization of the Palestinian question by the regimes to legitimize internal power struggles and repress political dissidents. These two questions—minorities and the struggle with Israel as necessitating a permanent state of emergency—will later be taken up by the Arab liberal critique against the leftist and Arab nationalist anti-imperialists. Socialist Lebanon's work does not only reveal how early and prescient their diagnosis of the regimes was but also how it was embedded in a Marxist project that combined it with a critique of imperialism. After the defeat of the Left, these external (imperialism) and internal (regimes) critiques bifurcated. Liberals, mostly democracy advocates and culturalist critics of their societies, opposed anti-imperialist nationalists and Islamists who focused only on the geopolitical game of nations and the regimes' place in it. The Arab revolutions (2011–), by reintroducing grassroots mass political mobilization, ignited, for a moment at least, the hope of transcending the impossible choice between national sovereignty under a tyrant and a hope for democracy brought about by foreign occupation. Collective political practice brought back the possibility of articulating an antiauthoritarian and anti-imperialist politics from one position, before the regimes, communal internal divisions, and the never ending interventions thwarted the possibility of emancipation. Even if the first wave of revolutions have now ebbed, post-1967 as a dominant historiographic trope can no longer stand as the undisputed marker of contemporary Arab thought. It is now a category of the past. Post-2011 also urges us to cast a fresh look on how the analytic and historiographical categories of historians reproduce the categories of practice of key intellectuals of the earlier generation who were marked by the 1967 military defeat.[11]

In excavating this alternative genealogy of contemporary Arab thought and politics, which does not assume 1967 as the cardinal and only historiographical turning point, I, of course, do not seek to deny the centrality of the defeat. In fact, I will discuss how it constituted a watershed moment for academics both at home and in the diaspora, such as Sadik al-Azm, Edward Said, and Talal Asad, jolting the first two out of their ivory towers and into an engagement alongside the Palestinian revolution. In doing so, I reclaim a different genealogy for 1967, one that argues that the political moment of 1967 was central, and constitutive, for diasporic strategies of criticism—Asad's and Said's—that ushered in the critiques of the entanglement of Western knowledges with power. What I am after is a double move that seeks to displace the monopoly of 1967 as the marker of contemporary Arab thought at home and to reinscribe it as a cardinal moment for the intellectual and political projects of diasporic intellectuals.

The end of the union between Egypt and Syria in 1961 is now largely forgotten. This event, which exists outside of the contradiction with colonialism and imperialism, was crucial for this generation of militants. It constitutes the first major setback of the anticolonial nationalist regimes, less than a decade after the 1952 Egyptian Revolution. This intra-Arab event ushered in the first immanent critiques of the regimes that pointed out the gap that separates their pan-Arab ideologies from their practices that could not sustain a union for more than three years. It inaugurated an early critical reflexive turn that found in Marxism a critical theory and a weapon of political transformation, which by conjugating together the internal class contradictions of these societies with an anti-imperialist agenda was more conceptually sophisticated than Arab nationalist ideologies.

Some of the comrades who founded Socialist Lebanon in the mid-1960s came from this cohort of disenchanted Arab nationalists. Ahmad Beydoun (1942–), who had lost the links he had with the Arab Nationalist Movement and was immersed in a Ba'thist atmosphere through his friends at Lebanese University, remembers the dissolution of the union as being a terrible and decisive event. Nearly fifty years after the establishment of the union in 1958, he draws my attention during one of our conversations to "something which the generation younger than us cannot imagine," most probably alluding to my generation's world, born during the Lebanese civil and regional wars (1975–90), a time of heightened Christian/Muslim sectarian tensions, Syrian military interventions, and Israeli invasions (1978 and 1982).[12] It seems light years away from the hopes of Arab unity that Abdel Nasser ignited in their hearts. "And that is," he adds, "how terrible the dissolution of the union was for us. It was a blow that changed the meaning of the world for us. The political history of the last three or four generations does not really stop sufficiently at that date. They stop more at 1967. For us, 1961 was decisive." It is this disenchantment "which gave rise to the desire and the need to know these societies that are called an *umma* [Arab nation]."

Turning their gazes inward from nation to class, these young intellectuals saw in Marxist theory and practice the answer to their desire to know and the appropriate tool to effect the revolutionary transformations of their societies. "The question of society," Beydoun presses on, "was the true and effective mediator of [Marxist revolutionary] theory." The year 1961 ushered in an early reflexive moment that turned away from nationalist rhetoric against external enemies toward criticizing the "progressive" regimes in power and diagnosing the internal political contestations lodged at the heart of these societies. It laid the first bricks of what would come to be known after 1967 as the New Left.

Muhsin Ibrahim's presence, demeanor, and speech are as close as possible to those of a godfather of the Lebanese New Left. He began our conversation by asserting:

> I am going to give it to you from the beginning. There is no New Left in Lebanon without a previous political foundation. Nothing fell on us called the New Left. The issue wasn't that the Lebanese students observed the French students's revolution [May 1968] and decided to do something similar. Its is that of the [Arab] nationalist movements... and some of the intellectuals of the Syrian Nationalist Socialist Party... the Ba'th Party and some of those who split from the Lebanese Communist Party. These are the birth pangs of the 1960s.[13]

By the time the comrades came together to found Socialist Lebanon they had radicalized their critique of the Arab nationalist movements and regimes. Early on, SL unmasked the Arab chauvinism of the Syrian Ba'th, which they knew from the inside, that was used against non-Arab minorities but cloaked itself in a progressive political rhetoric. The first issue of their bulletin—dated mid-September 1966—ends with an article entitled "Notes on the Last Agreement between the Kurdish Revolution and the Iraqi Government."[14] After enumerating some of the points of the agreement—recognizing the Kurdish nationality in the "temporary constitution," recognizing the language as an official one alongside Arabic in majority Kurdish areas, parity between Arabs and Kurds in educational delegations and scholarships, and so forth—SL assesses reactions to it, including the Ba'th's:

> Behind a leftist rhetoric that claims to take the unity of Arab toilers as its starting point, and considers all actions against it a service rendered to imperialist interests, lies the clear chauvinist position of the declaration: the Kurdish movement is a separatist one that distracts the Arab and Kurdish masses from their main enemies: imperialism, the forces of reaction, and the oil monopolies. It is therefore at their service. Moreover, the Kurdish movement is headed by "tribal and feudal and reactionary sectors" that are backed by international colonialism, the British petroleum companies, and the reactionary rule in Iran. All these accusations are put forth without a single piece of evidence to back them up.[15]

Socialist Lebanon, which supported Kurdish self-rule within Iraqi territory, denounced very early on the Syrian Ba'th's use of *takhwin*—to accuse someone or an entire group of treason or collaboration with imperialist or foreign powers, or both—one of the most commonly deployed tropes of political excommunication that was used mostly but not exclusively by Arab nationalist regimes and their acolytes. This political charge has had a long shelf life and even wider range of applications encompassing individuals, political parties, and entire communities. Arab communists were often the targets of Nasser's accusations of treason.[16] Ethnic or religious groups, such as the Kurdish movement in this case, were often accused of being the internal agents, or doing the work, of imperialism, seeking to divide and weaken the nation's body from within. For instance, Bashar al-Assad draws on this long tradition when he characterizes the Syrian revolutionaries as foreign-backed rebels, noting in the first months of the Syrian uprisings (2011–) that in the face of conspiracies that are multiplying like germs, the body's immune system has to be strengthened to resist them. The predominance of the national question then, during the global age of decolonization, and its persistence throughout the contemporary Arab world via the Arab-Israeli struggle and the direct foreign economic and military interventions in the post–Cold War era, provided fertile terrain for the regimes in power to appropriate the critical language of anticolonial emancipation in order to enhance their power, crack down on dissidents, undercut all forms of institutional political and civic life, and, of course, legitimize their own rule. In the case of minorities, as Socialist Lebanon argued vis-à-vis the Kurdish movement, anticolonial nationalism was a veil for an Arab nationalist chauvinism that sought to tie its own internal other with foreign imperialist agendas.

In addition to criticizing the politics of treason, Socialist Lebanon took issue with the obverse form that the predominance of the national question took, which is the mobilization for the liberation of Palestine and the fight against anti-imperialism to legitimize their own action, achieve or expand power, and interrupt revolutionary politics. "Concerning the slogan of 'liberating Palestine,'" they write,

> this is not a new one [slogan] for these movements [nationalists]. It was, and still is, the demagogic call that is brandished by all these movements to interpellate the masses to get to power or to keep it. The result has always been the suppression of the masses' consciousness and their movement as well as forbidding them from forming their revolutionary parties that truly represent their interests (this is what happened in Egypt, in Iraq, and what some fear might happen in Jordan).[17]

Socialist Lebanon engaged in acts of immanent critique that diagnosed the gap separating the regimes' progressive professions of faith regarding the two legs they stood on—the national question and the socioeconomic one—from their practices of rule. When it came to the latter, SL contrasted the promise of socialism with the privileges accrued to those in power. "The rule of the Ba'th in Syria is the rule of the rural segment of the petite bourgeoisie that appropriates surplus production through the army and the state apparatus."[18] These appropriations take the form of different kinds of income and privileges such as high salaries; army cooperatives that "provide them with everything they need—from the pin to the car—at cost value"; rent control and interest-free loans to buy apartments; automatic promotion of officers by one grade upon demobilization and receiving thereafter a monthly salary corresponding to their new rank while keeping all their previous privileges. To all of this should be added the additional incomes and privileges that come from being part of power, such as favors rendered to one's family and bribes received for facilitating transactions with the state.[19] The "military administrative bureaucracies" ruling Syria and Egypt foreclosed the possibility of political practice for the masses in their respective countries. Not only did they presume to speak for the entire nation, they also depoliticized the Palestinian cause by rendering it a military issue: an injustice that was caused by a military defeat and will be resolved by a military victory. This perspective provided the adequate ideological justification for "consolidating the army's role, which was considered the only force capable of resolving the Palestinian problem."[20] It was also used as the main excuse for the army's failure to resolve the predicaments of the national democratic revolution and for its taking the biggest share out of the national budget.

Socialist Lebanon also condemned the foreclosure of the masses from political practice by the top-down technological and economic development strategies. The development question, SL affirmed, cannot be resolved through these means and with foreign aid since it is a social problem. "Solving the question of backwardness—the Chinese model is clear on this front—cannot take place unless the wretched masses accept to make big sacrifices," they write, "which are accompanied by a consciousness of knowing that these will result in building factories and irrigating lands that will produce later on work, food, clothing, education, and health. It is obvious that these sacrifices and this consciousness cannot take place without the masses' popular organizations whose power is in contradiction with that of the military."[21] The regimes, whose raison d'être is the national question and to a lesser extent the development of their societies, banish the masses from the center of political practice by rendering the first a purely military affair to be undertaken by the army and the second a technocratic one to be solved by experts. Moreover, the regimes are characterized by an "enmity to popular organizations"[22] and strive to cancel their role in these two domains "while representing themselves as expressing the interests of the wretched masses by bringing into being organizations that are loyal to them."[23] The regimes' practice vis-à-vis "the new colonialism," on the other hand, is one characterized by wavering and an incapacity to exit from the capitalist market. "They are not able to break free from its hold and they are not able to ally themselves with it . . . [new colonialism] has more loyal allies represented by feudalism and the bourgeoisie and even the petite bourgeoisie that still retains right-wing organizations (the Muslim Brotherhood . . .)."[24]

Socialist Lebanon's verdict on these regimes is prescient and damning. They are a failure on the national, regional, and international fronts. The reason why they didn't fall after the swift and devastating defeat in June 1967 is because "the confrontation with colonialism still provides the advanced [al-mutaqaddima] (and even the backward) regimes an effective popular defense that refuses to let go of what nationalist forces have achieved in terms of independence. . . . This is exactly what these regimes understood and they began to call for restricting the battle to this aspect only."[25] A few years later, Anwar al-Sadat relinquished Nasser's statist economic policies and followed that with a visit to Jerusalem that buried the national question. The Assadist dynasty began its policies of economic liberalization in the 1990s, "followed by ambitious privatization initiatives in the mid-2000s."[26] It still seeks to draw its legitimacy from the national question.

1967: Personal Watersheds, Fellow Traveling, and Diasporic Institution Building

We owe the birth of two of the best known Arab public intellectuals of the 1960s generation to the 1967 defeat: Sadik Jalal al-Azm (1934–2016) and Edward Said (1935–2003). Unlike SL's militant intellectuals, who had nearly a decade of militant experience behind their backs in 1967, al-Azm and Said were detached academics for whom the defeat constituted a personal watershed moment. Said wrote:

> And 1967 brought more dislocations, whereas for me it seemed to embody the dislocation that subsumed all other losses, the disappeared worlds of my youth and upbringing, the unpolitical years of my education, the assumption of disengaged teaching and scholarship at Columbia, and so on. I was no longer the same person after 1967; the shock of that war drove me back to where it had all started, the struggle over Palestine. I subsequently entered the newly transformed Middle Eastern

landscape as a part of the Palestinian movement that emerged in Amman and then in Beirut in the late sixties through the seventies.[27]

Said, whose first and only attempt at political writing had been on the Suez crisis of 1956 submitted to the Princeton newspaper during his undergraduate years, wrote "The Arab Portrayed."[28] This piece was printed in a special issue of *Arab World*, "the Arab League monthly published in New York," guest edited by Said's close friend Ibrahim Abu-Lughod, the Palestinian academic and future member of the Palestine National Council (1977–91).[29] This special issue, Said noted, was "intended to look at the war from an Arab perspective. I used the occasion to look at the image of the Arabs in the media, popular literature, and cultural representations going back to the Middle Ages. This was the origin of my book *Orientalism*, which I dedicated to Janet and Ibrahim."[30]

The productivity of defeat did not only take the form of making public intellectuals out of detached diasporic academics. The defeat also produced new institutions, periodicals, and publications. In 1967–68, Arab American scholars wary of the founding in 1966 of the Middle East Studies Association "soon after the closure of the American Association for Middle Eastern Studies, and the overlap in the leadership of the two bodies" and fearing that "MESA was simply a continuation of the earlier pro-Washington and pro-Israel organization," established the Association of Arab-American University Graduates, "which organized a series of annual conferences and publications under the leadership of Ibrahim Abu-Lughod. For several years these were scheduled to conflict with the MESA meetings."[31] "The 1967 war had shocked" these diasporic intellectuals "into realizing that the scholars speaking about the Middle East in the United States, even the minority who seemed sympathetic to the Arab World, were not *from* the region, and did not speak *for* the region."[32] In the wake of the war they "began to challenge the style of academic detachment with which establishment scholars maintained both their status as experts and a silence about controversial issues, especially the Palestine question" as well as the construction of the Middle East as an area of study.[33] These diasporic intellectuals not only contested the styles of academic writing, and their flagrant elisions, but, more importantly, also turned their critical gaze toward a more fundamental level, to the politics inherent in the metropole's construction of its objects of knowledge, noting that the Middle East "was a colonial conception, which, by including Turkey and Iran with the Arab countries, minimized the much stronger common culture of the Arabic-speaking world."[34] Following up on "The Arab Portrayed," Said articulated a critique of Orientalist scholarship in 1974 at the Association of Arab-American University Graduates conference.

Sadik al-Azm, the Yale-trained philosopher, born to an upper-class Damascene family, was, like Said, a detached academic teaching at the American University of Beirut.[35] "If someone had predicted before the defeat of June 1967 that one day I would be producing the type of writing which I later did produce," al-Azm mentioned thirty years later, "I would have thought him mad."[36] al-Azm highlighted the gap between the "revolutionary" economic and political agendas of the Arab liberation movement and its "conservative" superstructural side, which did not tackle Islamic thought, characterizing it as reproducing "values of ignorance, myth-making, backwardness, dependency, and fatalism" and impeding "the propagation of scientific values, secularism, enlightenment, democracy, and humanism."[37] He went on to publish two of the most controversial and widely circulated works, even though officially banned by many countries in the aftermath of the 1967 defeat—*Al-Naqd al-Dhathi ba'd al-Hazima* [Self-Criticism after the Defeat] (1968) and *Naqd al-Fikr al-Dini* [Critique of Religious Reason] (1969).[38] These two books, now considered classics of post-1967 modern Arab political thought, are much indebted to the works of the Syrian Marxist thinker Yasin al-Hafiz, who early on focused on the analysis of culture and values in an effort to move criticism beyond the monopoly of the geopolitical grid. The year 1968 also witnessed al-Azm's expulsion from the American University of Beirut on the grounds of his writings and for signing a petition calling for the withdrawal of the American army from Vietnam.[39]

In the wake of 1967 Socialist Lebanon continued their critiques of the regimes in power while Said and al-Azm moved away from their disciplinary areas of expertise toward forging new modalities of public criticism. Intellectuals in the metropole, such as Said, intervened by calling into question the assumptions on which the West's knowledges of the non-Western world are built. This was a critical labor that, as Talal Asad put it, subjected these *Orientalist* works to the same scrutiny they used to subject "Oriental" peoples and languages to.[40] They turned the West's critical gaze on itself. The questions of colonialism that these diasporic thinkers tackled were tied to their experiences of everyday racism and the refusal of wide swathes of Western societies to understand the justness of Arab political causes, particularly when it came to the denial of solidarity to the Palestinians' struggle for national self-determination.

Things were inflected differently in the Arab world. The questions spurred by the defeat, there and then, were of course of a more direct political and military nature. Why were we defeated? How do we move forward from this point? What are the most suitable ideologies and organizational forms that should be adapted in reorganizing the struggle in the wake of the defeat? These were all hotly debated issues. The ideological and political problem-space was crowded with religious, Arab nationalist, and communist answers to these questions.[41] It was in this emotionally saturated, politically charged atmosphere that, Sadik Jalal al-Azm, influenced by al-Hafiz's work, steered away from widespread interpretations and prognoses that explained the defeat by external factors, blaming it on US imperialist conspiracies and the shortcomings of the Soviet Union, when not interpreting it as a divine punishment for having lost the proper Islamic way.

What is important to stress is how in both these problem-spaces—the metropolitan and the Arab—what was at stake was to isolate an internal cultural layer for critique. Diasporic thinkers called into question Western culture for its racialized portrayal of Arabs, while critical intellectuals at home isolated "traditional" Arab culture as the root of the defeat. It was a critique of culture that took the form of the problem of *race* and cultural imperialism in the supposedly enlightened metropoles of this world and the problem of *religion* and social conservatism in the supposedly socialist progressive Arab countries. What was also shared by both critical agendas was their *oppositional* character to hegemonic positions whether in Orientalist representations of the Arab world or in the widely circulated arguments in political literature after the defeat that blamed it on external factors. In both cases, these intellectuals saw their critical public interventions and staged them against prevalent cultural and political doxas of the time.

This is where their similarities end. al-Azm's critique was a jeremiad of sorts, a prophet lambasting his people for their traditional ways that brought this ignominious defeat upon them. Said's critique speaks back to the West that dehumanized Arabs through the cultural products of Western consciousness. For al-Azm—a vanguardist modernist critic—the Arab, a culprit of his own defeat, must change his own ways, while for Said, the diasporic oppositional intellectual speaking back to the white majority, the Arab is a victim of cultural imperialism that must resist and tear down the webs of Western racism.[42]

The critique of Arab cultures for their "lacks"—democracy, individual rights, women's rights—and the critique of "Western consciousness" for its webs of cultural imperialism that dehumanize the "Oriental" became increasingly widespread from the 1980s onward. While these two critiques where *theoretically* at odds with each other, the critics that produced them were politically in solidarity. Both Said and al-Azm became fellow travelers of the Palestinian revolution in the wake of 1967. The militant hopes initially generated by the Palestinian resistance in the late 1960s and the political solidarity with it would receive their first blow just a few years later when it clashed with the Jordanian army (September 1970). In the wake of the Iranian Revolution (1979) and the defeat of the Palestinian revolution in Lebanon (1982), which ushered in a wave of militant religious politics, the secular political space of anti-imperialist solidarity, premised on the presence of the feda'yi as the revolutionary subject, crumbled. The concept of anti-imperialism was stretched by Islamist militant movements to include cultural decolonization, while cultural critics in the metropoles increasingly called into question the colonial epistemological assumptions of modernist intellectuals. The defeat of the revolutionary subject, whose presence and institutions enabled political solidarity amid theoretical divergence, will result in an increased narrowing of the space separating theoretical critiques from political positions. Diasporic intellectuals and critical thinkers at home will increasingly part ways, but we are not there yet.

A Failed Arab Modernity or a Military Defeat of Postcolonial Regimes?

To get a sense of the distinct contours of SL's minoritarian critical labors, against the best sellers of contemporary Arabic thought, I will take a small detour via al-Azm's *Self-Criticism after the Defeat*. al-Azm dedicated a little bit more than a third of the volume to analyze samples of "the tendency of evading responsibility [for one's actions] and blaming it on others, which clearly manifested itself after the June 5th defeat."[43] The logics of justification, he underscored, are not only deficient analytical grids but also symptoms of deeper underlying traits permeating Arab culture. The revolutionary youth, he wrote, "are politically revolutionary, however, deep down, they are conservative socially, religiously, culturally, ethically and economically, except in rare cases."[44] The gap between the theory and practice of the Arab revolutionary reveals an incomplete, if not aborted, revolutionary transformation. al-Azm's strategy is wedded to a staunchly modernizing historical progressive agenda. Revolution means overcoming the "dark image of the past" and initiating a rebellion against past generations.[45]

When tackling the Arab progressive regimes, he emphasized their "ideological confusion" and their "centrism," as well as their ambiguity concerning the question of secularism and the scientific nature of their socialism. "There is no doubt," wrote al-Azm, "that the excuse for the existence of progressive and socialist regimes in the Arab world is the revolution against this weight of backwardness carried by the Arab human being . . . and not refraining from revolutionary socialist measures against it out of 'consideration for the people's religious feelings' . . . and the preservation of traditions."[46] In contrast to SL's diagnosis, which centers on power by analyzing the technologies of rule that substitute the people's political practice with top-down military and techno-cratic solutions, al-Azm's lament is precisely that the advanced regimes are fail-ing to adequately fulfill the promise of getting rid of their citizens' backward-ness. They are failing not because they are negating the political practice of the people (SL) but because they are conceding too much to their religious feelings and traditions.

al-Azm's culturalist diagnosis deploys all the binaries of modernization theory that are absent from Socialist Lebanon's political analysis: tradition/modernity, religion/science, superstition/reason, backwardness/progress. The two accounts differ not only in isolating different grounds for explanation—power and culture—and how this entails a divergent understanding of what con-stitutes progressive political practice and who is supposed to carry it out. It is also a difference between the deployment of rough and ready reifications, such as "the traditional characteristics of the Arab personality," and an empirically in-formed analysis of the many privileges of army officers, the mechanics of their co-optation of the political process, and their instrumentalist use of anticolo-nial sloganeering to consolidate their own internal powers.

Socialist Lebanon's analysis not only dodges the binaries of modernization theory, it also escapes another prevalent binary trap, which usually comes hand in hand with the former: internal versus external factors in the analysis of the 1967 defeat. al-Azm's inward turn toward culture (internal factors) is an ethical injunction to take responsibility for one's actions. His call, though, remains caught within the same nationalist matrix of the regimes—us/them—whose valences he inverts. Instead of blaming "imperialism" for the Arabs' defeat, he lays the blame on the "Arabs" themselves. The nationalist form of the ques-tion "why were we defeated?" takes its unified subject for granted—the Arab "we"—whatever the answer one gives. Socialist Lebanon's diagnosis of the re-gimes and the class composition of Arab societies displaces the nationalist sub-ject that delimits the possible answers in a binary matrix of us/them, internal causes/external ones to the political plane.

Socialist Lebanon was not preoccupied with questions of modernization, but with the coupling of the national and social questions on which an *autono-mous* left could be built—one that not only faced national issues but also the more covert economic domination of foreign capital and the local bourgeoisie. From their perspective, 1967 was not a failure of Arab modernity. It was a mili-tary defeat of the regimes that would come to constitute their own *historical chance*.

In the absence of masses, SL's theoretical virtuosity, which positioned itself to the left of Arab nationalist regimes and the Lebanese Left, managed to draw attention to them within these wider political circles. It will result in their merger with the radicalized Lebanese branch of the Arab Nationalist Movement led by Muhsin Ibrahim in the wake of the 1967 defeat. Before I address the union, I will now sketch the contours of SL's critique of the Lebanese Communist Party, which brings out early on the question of the autonomy of leftist political practice. This question will become increasingly significant as we move on into the 1970s and will go through different theoretical and political iterations, until Charara's final disenchantment in the first months of the civil war; but let's linger for a while in the hinge years of the late 1960s.

In June 1959, one of the historic leaders of the Lebanese Communist Party, Farajallah al-Helou, was arrested and tortured to death in Syria by the anticommunism department of the United Arab Republic; "the Lebanese communists considered Nasser to be merely a dictator and essentially a representative of the greedy Egyptian bourgeoisie."[47] The Syrian-Lebanese Communist Party had opposed the union between Egypt and Syria in 1958 and refused to disband after its establishment.[48] A couple of months before the killing of al-Helou, in March 1959, Nasser—in a similar vein to Aflaq's Ba'thist positions—declared Arab communists to be "[foreign] agents who neither believe in the liberty of their land or their nation, but only do the bidding of outsiders."[49] The anticolonial and anti-imperialist agenda of pan-Arab movements marginalized the communists by advocating socialist politics plus a nationalist agenda, in contrast to the communist parties, which could not escape the Soviet orbit. Even before the emergence of Third World and national liberation movements, Arab communist parties received what could possibly be their hardest hit when they followed Moscow in accepting the UN partition of Palestine in 1947. Their earlier anti-Zionist stances had to be forgotten after their acquiescence to Moscow's decision, which "not only pulled the figurative rug from under the Arab communists, but also reinforced their isolation in the Arab world and essentially forced them into the role of apologist for their prime support, the Soviet Union."[50]

The Palestine question, the relations with Arab nationalist liberation movements and the new national military regimes of the 1950s and 1960s, and the allegiance to the Soviet line were major issues plaguing the Lebanese Communist Party by the mid-1960s. Moreover, both the Syrian and Lebanese parties had been under the Stalinist command and the personality cult of the Syrian secretary general, Khalid Bikdash, who had ruled the party since the early 1930s.[51] By 1964,

> discontent was formalized with an explicit request that a party congress be convened to question the party's leadership. While the malcontents were purged from the party, dissension within party ranks continued, culminating in the party's fragmentation and the formation of a number of splinter groups.[52]

Not long after the founding of Socialist Lebanon in 1964, Waddah Charara and Christian Ghazi joined "the Leninist Movement," an opposition current inside the LCP.[53] This movement, Traboulsi recalls, "combined in a strange mix its renovating Italian communist influences critical of Stalinism and a loyalty to Khalid Bikdash's leadership and his continuing tutelage over the LCP.... These comrades [Charara and Ghazi] stayed there for a few months and came back disappointed."[54] After their attempt to work from the *inside* of the LCP, the comrades reunited again and began producing their bulletin.[55]

Socialist Lebanon, as we saw earlier, subjected the nationalist military regimes to a leftist critique, showing how their nationalizations failed to bring about a socialist revolution, producing rather a new state bourgeoisie of military officers and bureaucrats. The LCP, whose overall crisis became more acute in the wake of 1967, exacerbating the conflict between a senior pro-Bikdash old guard and a rising new generation of cadres, was subjected to a different strategy. The militant intellectuals' strategy focused on the old pro-Soviet party's *theoretical poverty* and its lack of autonomy.[56] In the first SL editorial, titled "Socialist Lebanon and the Left," they wrote:

> The theoretical aspect has to be given an important position that is being avoided by the current Left. Why is it avoiding it? Because it sheds light on its laziness and rashness, and on how it throws itself into the facile. And because it reveals its subscription to predominant ideological precepts which are those of the petite bourgeoisie, such as: reforms are a positive step and one ought to ally oneself with the nationalist wing in power.[57]

This editorial was a reply to early criticisms of the group that accused it of breaking the ranks of the Left and stigmatizing their intellectualism. The theoretically lazy Left dabbled in reformist petit bourgeois precepts, according to SL, which would keep it in a state of dependency. The only solution to rescue the Left from tailing behind nationalists, and to build an *autonomous* Left, was to give theoretical formulation its due, for it is supposed to guide political action. A little more than a year later, SL criticized the performance of the Front of National and Progressive Political Parties, Forces and Personalities two years after its inception.[58] The two feet on which leftist action stood, for SL, were the national question (anticolonialism and anti-imperialism) and the social question. While the front had succeeded in the first, it failed in the second. The front's national politics

> represented a wide current comprised of different sectors that refuse the direct domination of American Imperialism, or the humiliating, overt dependency to a force [the US] protecting Israel. . . . Within these limits the Front's actions were clear, positive and effective. This aspect, however, despite its importance, and while assuring that one ought to hold a solid position vis-à-vis its issues, is nothing but a nationalist position that rests on the refusal of direct domination or its manifestations. Moreover, the social groups that can adhere to such a position are relatively large; and their adherence does not at all lead to a specific social, or political, position regarding the confrontation of imperialist domination hiding in the economic sphere. Some of the groups that refuse to insure American capitals see no fault in drowning the Lebanese market in European commodities and having it suck up a wide share of Lebanese investments. . . .
>
> As soon as social problems emerge that are the result of the organization of Lebanese society and its deep problems, and therefore require a precise analysis and relatively isolated positions, the Front reveals another face, which is characterized by hesitancy, disintegration, and running away, unmasking the true character of this group. And it is clear that the greatest number of problems, and those that touch the most the establishment of a solid leftist action, are related to the second aspect, the social aspect.[59]

In both its critiques of the regimes and of the communists, Socialist Lebanon emphasized the project of auto-emancipation of the people, and of the autonomy of the Left, against the regimes' foreclosure of political practice and the Left parties' dependency on "nationalist forces" such as the Progressive Socialist Party, led by Kamal Jumblatt, the Druze leader and descendant of a political family of landowners. The anxiety the social question produced in the dependent and reformist Lebanese Left, which highlighted the national question and an antisectarian secular politics, will be revealed once more in its excision from the transitional program for reforms the Lebanese National Movement presented at the beginning of the Lebanese civil wars (1975). But for now, SL was fond of repeating that theoretical elaboration was an essential feature for building an autonomous leftist political practice. "The Theoretical Education Corner," an irregular rubric in their bulletin, was the ideal place to weave theoretical discussions into the analysis of a present political situation. "The corner" constituted a double intervention: didactic and political. It elucidated theoretical texts through shedding light on a specific political situation and in the process inserted a critical wedge between what it claimed the Marxist corpus truly said and how the LCP understood it—discrediting it.[60] Their theoretical critiques of the Nasserite regime, and the Left, which were inaugurated before the defeat, had a much greater political impact in an altered problem-space characterized by questions revolving around a theoretical renewal in the direction of more "solid" and "scientific" theories than Arab nationalist foggy rhetoric, a rethinking of the modalities of political struggle and the agents that will carry out the task of emancipation—popular war of liberation/Palestinian commando operations or conventional warfare conducted by the armies of Arab regimes. Socialist Lebanon's leftist critiques resonated with the disaffected Arab nationalists after the "fall of the regimes" who were in the process of severing their ties with Nasser, substituting Marxism-Leninism for their Arab nationalist socialism.[61]

State and Revolution

The second half of President Charles Helou's mandate (1964–70) witnessed a wave of Lebanese polarization around Arab regional issues. Lebanon, which did not fight in the 1967 war, dived straight into the conflict with the establishment of the Palestinian guerrilla resistance in its southern towns and the inauguration of military operations from its borders.[62] The Palestinian resistance post-1967 became a local player in Lebanese politics, putting on the table again the question of the content of Lebanon's national identity. In 1958, the question was posed as an alternative between the anticolonial national liberation pan-Arabism of Nasser and the pro-Western (Eisenhower Doctrine) Lebanese nationalism of the state and the majority of Lebanon's Christian population. After 1967, it revolved around Lebanon's involvement in the Arab-Israeli conflict and specifically whether the country ought to allow the Palestinian resistance to launch operations from its borders.

The masses rallying around the resistance, as witnessed in the tens of thousands marching in the funeral cortège of Khalil al-Jamal, its first Lebanese martyr who fell in Jordan (1968), constituted a moment of hope for the Left. The rallying was read as a sign of the Lebanese masses' radicalization around national ideological lines. Their embrace of the Palestinian resistance was an omen of transcending the politics of urban notables, ruling families, and rural landowners that dominated the Lebanese Parliament. There were other signs as well, such as the Lebanese southerners' welcome of the guerrillas' implantation in their villages, which challenged the authority of the landowning political families and the Lebanese army on its southern borders.[63] The 'Arqub area in the south was baptized the "Arafat trail," in comparison with Vietnam's Ho Chi Minh Trail.[64] It also became known as Fatah land.

State and revolution, and their ideological and sectarian constituencies, faced each other and clashed on a number of occasions from 1968 onward. Israel adopted a strategy of destabilization and disproportionate "retaliation" in the wake of Palestinian guerrilla action, exacerbating the country's internal polarization, in what would later be considered as the years leading to the 1975 war.[65] On December 28, 1968, an Israeli military unit destroyed on the ground thirteen Lebanese civilian aircrafts belonging to Middle East Airlines after Palestinian commandos hijacked an Israeli plane to Athens. In the summer preceding the airport raid, "Lebanese villages in the south came under heavy shelling. This led to the widespread destruction not only of homes but of crops and orchards which had served as the principal means of livelihood" for southerners who moved to safer areas in the suburbs of Beirut.[66] The repercussions of the attack on the air fleet exacerbated the polarizations, inaugurating a political crisis and the resignation of the government (January 16, 1969). Rashid Karami, the newly appointed prime minister, called on the Lebanese Parliament to recognize the right of the Palestinians to fight for the liberation of their homeland—a not uncontroversial statement amid the internal polarization.[67] The situation deteriorated on April 23, 1969, when "the army opened fire at a massive demonstration in solidarity with the Palestinian resistance in Saida and Beirut, leaving a number of dead and wounded. The violent reactions to the army's behavior—especially in his home town, Tripoli,—prompted Karami to resign."[68] Syria also became a player in the 1969 crisis. By the end of September, the army attempted to control the situation after a series of confrontations with the Palestinian resistance, as a result of which Syria closed its borders and imposed severe economic sanctions on Lebanon.[69]

On November 8, 1969, the Cairo Agreement was signed between the PLO and the Lebanese army under the auspices of President Nasser, temporarily relieving the tension, with Syria opening its borders, and the formation of a new cabinet on November 26. The agreement, ratified shortly afterward in the Lebanese Parliament, legitimized the resistance's actions on Lebanese territory.[70]

The Cairo Agreement would come to signify the national division on the Palestinian question even though most Lebanese parties accepted it. A solution of last resort, it generated political resentment, which led to clashes between Christian Phalangist militants and the resistance.[71] After 1971, Lebanon became the *only* vital space for the resistance, in the aftermath of its clashes with the Jordanian army (1970–71), resulting in its defeat and the relocation of the PLO's command to Beirut. Around the same time, the Syrian regime also shut its borders to Palestinian guerrilla activity.

Around forty years later, Waddah Charara recalled these times:

[The years] 1968–69 constituted the peak of mythification and religiosity in Socialist Lebanon. We began working [in 1964] with Fawwaz [Traboulsi] and others on the issue of renewal of [Lebanese president] Chehab's mandate. For four or five years we were fishing for syndicates, workers, and student demonstrations as well as tackling problems of the National Front and the LCP. These were our problems.

In 1969, we entered a different epoch. It is important that this different epoch be looked at from its internal side, i.e., how we were seeing it and experiencing it. At this time one was twenty-six or twenty-seven years old, not an old man, but with already ten to twelve years of "militantisme," part of them in the French Communist Party, in contact with European Marxism.... And then there was this tremendous internal shock, where it was revealed to us, after what was called "the defeat of the regimes," i.e., Nasserism, that *this was our historical chance*.[72]

Two Resistances: The Palestinian and the Lebanese

"The ruling Lebanese interests cannot acknowledge the links that tie its farmhouse, Lebanon, to the region's causes," wrote the anonymous author—Waddah Charara—of "The Two Resistances: The Palestinian and the Lebanese," a central piece from 1969 that captures the height of Socialist Lebanon's activist fervor (Fig. 3.1).[73] The long and scathing article against the Lebanese authorities located the Palestinian resistance as the external revolutionary agent that will detonate the contradictions of the system. "The Lebanese position," wrote Charara, "i.e., the authorities' position, is clear, Lebanon is of the Arab region: its economy and the prosperity of its financiers and merchants rise on the role they play in that region. Lebanon, however, is on the margin of the Arab region when it comes to political problems threatening to destabilize those who rule it" (1). "*The Lebanese entity*," continued SL's major theorist contemptuously, "is

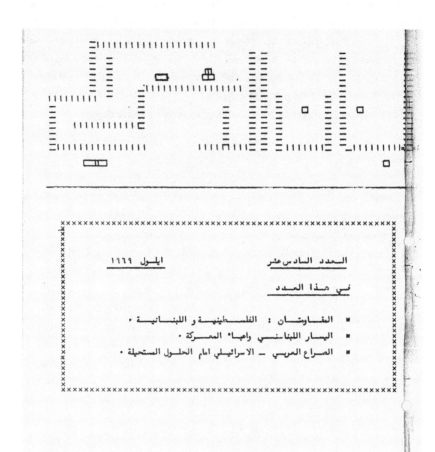

FIGURE 3.1. *Socialist Lebanon*, Issue 16, September 1969.

the fortified haven for the domination of a banking-commercial bourgeoisie that would not have existed if not for the role it plays in the imperialist pillage operation of the Arab region. This is Lebanese independence. And this is the unique position that God under his sun did not create anything like" (2).[74]

The main diagnosis constituted a strong indictment of the Lebanese state's politics of neutrality in the Arab-Israeli conflict and of the country's laissez-faire capitalist system. It was into this situation—characterized by Lebanese economic integration into, and political isolation from, the Arab world—that the Palestinian resistance made its entrance. It unmasked the real face of the Lebanese regime, for "how can a regime that plays the role of the watchdog of imperialist dependence agitate an entire people for a national battle? And how can the Lebanese system, which survives on the remains of imperial interests, go through this battle that will put its banks, agents, and summer resorts in danger?" (5).

At the heart of this theorization is a view of the Lebanese sectarian political system as devised by French imperialism. This system is what preempts the elaboration of a class-interest driven political practice. Charara writes:

> The sectarian formation, which was made the geographic and political basis of Lebanon, is able to stifle every form of political maturity that carries the masses to fuse with the Arab region's battle against imperialism. This is not only because it puts every political discord to the test of civil war, but because it stifles every disagreement by annulling its true political aspect—a conflict of interests within the framework of power—by making it subservient to the sectarian conflict that conceals and fragments the issues pertaining to power. This makes political opposition, whether it wants to or not, acquire a sectarian dimension. In this situation, there is no "national" party that "covers" the Lebanese territory and no Lebanese ideology and no Lebanese history. (2)

The homogenizing force of capitalist expansion, which is supposed to drown the ecstasies of religious fervor and of chivalrous enthusiasm in the icy water of egotistical calculation, stopped at the gate of Lebanon's sectarian political fort.[75] "Sectarian and regional distinctions," SL writes, "bring to the attribute of the 'citizen' . . . other attributes that dominate it: the Sunni from Beirut, the Maronite from the Mountain, the Shi'i from the South or Baalbeck"(2–3). The coming into being of the abstract Lebanese citizen that would follow an interest-based politics was prevented by the political system that produced a "hybrid citizen; organized political practice stops at his door without being able to pass its threshold" (3). In brief, the commensurability and political equality between abstract citizens that is supposed to come into being with the generalization of exchange in a capitalist mode of production is thwarted by a political system assembled by imperial interests.

The effect of the presence of the Palestinian resistance in Lebanon was not merely quantitative, that is, not just another item on the agenda of the Lebanese Left. Rather, it is the anti-imperialist detonator that is working toward overcoming the imperial legacy of disjunction between capitalist economic integration and sectarian political isolation. "The public that fought the battle in 1958," wrote Socialist Lebanon in the second article of the same issue,

> fought it with loyalty to the feudal lords, [and] a sectarian, familial, local loyalty that was enhanced by their representing a Nasserite, Arabist tendency. While the [current] rallying around the Palestinian Resistance rises on the remains of that loyalty.
>
> The event in itself carries a potential that allows, and this has been proven, the breaking of traditional sectarian loyalties, transforming them into national loyalties, that will fragment the base of the sectarian right whatever the sect it belongs to. Does the fact that the main transformation is happening among Muslims lessen its value? Not at all. The sectarian knot is not solved in one go, and if the entry point to its dissolution is revealing the conflict [i.e., its political nature] on the Muslim level the next level would certainly reveal its true nature when the Muslim Right finds its natural ally in the Christian Right.[76]

In the large demonstrations in support of the Palestinians on April 23, 1969, during which the Lebanese army opened fire, killing and wounding a number of protestors, it became clear that Muslim public opinion had turned, embracing the resistance and insulting traditional political leaders (Abdallah el-Yafi and Adnan al-Hakim) and the grand mufti of Lebanon, Hassan Khaled. The Palestinian agent, which acted as a solvent of sectarian loyalties, contributing to rearticulating politics along national lines, was enhanced by a second factor:

> The conflict does not take place on the closed internal level. The factor that is detonating it is not "Lebanese." ... It is far more reaching, and it shall extract the conflict from its "Lebaneseness"—i.e., from its specificity, and hence its sectarian nature—to posit it on the level of the whole region. And therefore the poles of the ruling alliances can no longer contain it within the sectarian frame because it reveals their common positions despite their different sects. And this position is not only in contradiction with the continuity of Palestinian Resistance in Lebanon but also with

> the rest of the Arab people (qua people) on which the Lebanese bourgeoisie relies to assure its continuity by living off them and cashing commissions on their account.[77] (16)

The revolution would neutralize the bourgeoisie's sectarian tricks and defenses, revealing that the heart of its politics is "interest based and political and can no longer veil itself with sectarianism (7)." Revolutionizing the Lebanese polity and the solidarity with the Palestinian resistance were not envisaged as a bloodless undertaking. Yet the impact of the revolution, SL predicted, would transform the clashes "from a sectarian conflict into a civil war" (17). "If democratic national rule cannot be reached without a civil war," they wrote, "the 'real coordination' with fida'yi action cannot [also] take place without exposing the southern region to an Israeli invasion" (17). Socialist Lebanon's, and Charara's, 1969 prognosis was right in predicting the coming conflict and wrong in predicting its nature. Six years later, a civil war erupted, splitting the country along sectarian lines. Israel invaded in 1978 and pushed the PLO and leftist militants away from the borders.

The fall of 1969 was a long way from the theoretical and ideological skirmishes of the mid-1960s between Socialist Lebanon and the Lebanese Communist Party on the proper understanding of the Marxist canon and its diverse political translations. In the years leading to the civil war, the revolution altered the Lebanese political landscape and the Left's role in it. A year later, in 1970, Socialist Lebanon would fuse with the much larger Organization of Lebanese Socialists, establishing a unified organization that became known as the Marxist-Leninist Organization of Communist Action in Lebanon (OCAL).[78] The years leading to the civil war witnessed a number of splits from the young OCAL, which played a pivotal role in the Lebanese National Movement when the fighting broke out in the spring of 1975.

Sitting in his office in *al-Safir* daily in July 2008, Abbas Beydoun reminisces about the beginnings of the collaboration in 1969 between the Organization of Lebanese Socialists (OLS), which he belonged to, and Socialist Lebanon, before their union. Around this time, "I founded a Lebanese [rubric] in *al-Hurriyya*, which did not exist earlier. I wrote it through an understanding and alliance with Socialist Lebanon, and predominantly with Waddah, with whom we had a developed relationship."[79] And around the same time, he adds,

> I wrote a theoretical text that is similar, parallel, to a Socialist Lebanon text called "The Two Resistances," mine was called a look at the Palestinian resistance and the Lebanese reality, something of that sort. The theorization was the same. They were both based on a frightening idea: it was

the theorization of the civil war. [It ran along the lines] that this was a prosperous country, which can't generate a revolution for a number of reasons . . . because it has benefited from Arab defeats and it has a certain level of economic leisure, etc. . . . No true revolution was possible here unless it comes from the outside.[80]

In a similar vein, Muhsin Ibrahim, who was at the head of the OLS, dubbed the Palestinian resistance the lever that will lift the Arab national liberation movement.[81] On the fortieth day commemorating the assassination of George Hawi, the former secretary general of the LCP, which took place in Beirut on June 21, 2005, Muhsin Ibrahim issued an auto-critique of the Lebanese National Movement's involvement in the 1975 war, which centered on two major points, or faults as he called them. The first consisted in Ibrahim's acknowledgment that in supporting the Palestinian struggle, the Left went too far in burdening Lebanon with the military weight of the Palestinian cause. And the second was that the Left "deemed it easy to board the civil war's ship, under the illusion of cutting short the road to democratic change."[82] A major figure of Socialist Lebanon commented on Ibrahim's auto-critique. Ibrahim, he said, uses the same idea found in "Two Resistances," but flips its valence. In the late 1960s the resistance was the detonator, the lever, the catalyst that in alliance with the Left would explode the system. In 2005, Ibrahim, the major political leader of the Lebanese New Left, observed that the Left went over the top by overburdening the country with its support of Palestinian militancy.

1967's Historiography Redux

To get a sense of how SL's revolutionary high hopes, carried by the tidal waves of the Palestinian revolution, were framed in the scholarship of the time before 1967, which came to be read as symptomatic of the bifurcation of critique from ideology, let's revisit Anouar Abdel Malak's introduction to his edited volume *Contemporary Arab Political Thought*, originally published in French in 1970.

> Everything accentuated despair. . . . And then, from the heart of the night, there came a gleam of hope. The people of the tents, the anonymous men and women, children and old people of Palestine embarked upon the only valid course open to a nation stripped of its homeland and faced with that ethnic, cultural and political racism which lies at the core of all imperialism. The people of Palestine endowed themselves with resistance

organizations charged with the co-ordination, definition, and pursuit of a campaign of armed national liberation.[83]

The coming into being of the New Left and the Palestinian resistance, and the revolutionary hope they generated in the wake of 1967, gets excised from the smooth narratives that associate 1967 with the end of Arab modernity, or the hinge moment between nationalism and Islamism, when ideology bifurcated from critique. Even if one discounts the covert critical work of revolutionary organizations like Socialist Lebanon, a number of the critical public intellectuals at the time were either militants, like Yasin al-Hafiz, or fellow travelers of Marxist and Palestinian political parties. In the wake of the defeat, al-Azm joined the Democratic Front for the Liberation of Palestine and had a brief political experience. The vital need for critique was not detached from a political engagement for Palestinian emancipation and a subscription to thick ideological traditions such as Marxism, but in a lot of cases was wedded to them. In fact, Samir Kassir compared the defeat of 1967, which acted as a catalyst to leftist thought and practice, to the cultural desolation in the aftermath of the 1982 Israeli invasion. He rereads the same history through the hegemonic religious/secular binary of his present. Post-1967 is split into two: 1967–1982 corresponds to the efflorescence of socialist and secular thought generally, while the rise of religious politics takes over after 1982, which Kassir dubs the endpoint of the Arab Nahda.[84]

The historiography around the 1967 defeat is a magnet for the deployment of the mythological language of Nahda (Renaissance) and Nakba (Catastrophe)—Arab impotence, stagnation, and defeat, which bestows meaning and provides a certain frame of reference to understand the event but not necessarily to diagnose it. Different authors dubbed the military defeat a second Nakba and the endpoint of the second Nahda.[85] "The June 1967 war was the most serious event in modern Arab history," wrote Faysal Darraj, the Palestinian literary critic, in 1989:[86] "Israel's establishment was an expression of the defeat of the Palestinian people and the impotence of the Arab regimes in a certain historical period when they were dependent on colonial forces. But the June defeat was an expression of the defeat of the Arab revolution as a whole."[87] Other thinkers posited 1967 as the second event, in the wake of colonization, that led to a collective Arab neurosis. "It is important to understand well the two historical stages of what I call the neurosis of the Arab world," Georges Tarabishi writes:

First, there was colonization, the shock with the West constituted by the arrival and victory of Napoleonic troops that shook the Arab street for the first time. Later, the encounter with Israel, and the totally unexpected defeat of 1967, led to a second collective neurosis. The Arab world, the Arab street, were completely undone and the culture became entirely Salafi.[88]

In a more recent text, Darraj underscores that 1967 "resumed in different circumstances the defeat of Muhammad Ali Pasha in the nineteenth century."[89] The year 1967 is taken as a singular event, a turning point on all levels, but also a contemporary expression of a deeper structure of defeat that has been plaguing the Arab world since the Napoleonic invasions. Structure and event are both present in the historiography of 1967, which is simultaneously the most serious event in modern Arab history and a resumption of Muhammad Ali's defeat. What this mythological language forecloses is alternative historical and social scientific inquiries that diagnose and attempt to articulate the past's relationship to the present.

A similar evacuation of history takes place in the work of postcolonial scholars who criticize Arab modernist thought from the Nahda to the present for being trapped in a colonial epistemology of progress. The secular modernist intellectual and the postcolonial academic are both trapped within the progress/backwardness (defeat) binary. If the former laments the backwardness of the Arab social structure and its production of a successive string of defeats, the later laments the attachment of the former to ideologies of progress and civilization and their critique of backwardness:

> Sadik al-Azm criticized, in his book *Self-Criticism after the Defeat*, the Arab social structure, which is invariable in its defeats: for it was defeated in the Ottoman period, and it was defeated in the period preceding independence, and it was defeated even more in the period of "independence states."[90]
>
> . . .
>
> The proper question is the following: What makes Arab intellectuals, from Najib Azuri to Taha Hussein, and from Constantine Zurayk to Yasin al-Hafiz and from Mahdi Amil to Fawzi Mansour and Saadallah Wannous, confront a society that firmly combines defeat and backwardness?[91]

The critic of epistemology, on the other hand, puts some of the same names together to show how these intellectuals share colonial epistemological assumptions with US discourses about the backwardness of their own societies:

> In reality, post-1967 Arab intellectuals quite visibly have struggled with the "failure," of their own societies and states, often implicitly agreeing

with the developmental discourse found in the assessments of *Bootstrap* [a 1953 United Nations Jordan valley development project pamphlet]. The editorial in English-language dailies such as the *Daily Star*, *Kuwait Times*, *Arab News*, or, *al-Ahram Weekly*, written by mainstream indigenous intellectuals, analysts, journalists, and activists, confirm such an observation. In fact, the discomforting verisimilitude between Arab and American criticism reveals the double colonizing move performed by the very epistemology that will be under examination in this book. Like in *Bootstrap*, intellectuals from Constantine Zurayk, Sadiq Jalal al-Azm, and Nadim Bitar to Hisham Sharabi and Hazim Saghiyah might agree that the disempowerment of the Arabs cannot be separated from their cultural and political illiteracy.[92]

To recapitulate, I excavated in this chapter a minoritarian tradition of critical diagnostic Arab thought that focused on actually existing relations of power. Socialist Lebanon's heterodox Marxism, revolving outside the Soviet orbit, examined the ideologies, logics, and practices of rule of the progressive regimes. The history of this minoritarian tradition calls into question the historiographical molds that take June 1967 as their sole anchor. The diagnostic thought that Socialist Lebanon produced provides us with an alternative conceptual universe from the prevalent ideological jargon of "remedies" and "deficits," and the mythological one of collective neurosis, a multiplicity of catastrophes (Nakba) and endpoints of successive Renaissances (Nahda). Having said that, Socialist Lebanon did not only produce a critical diagnosis of the regimes in power. In the aftermath of the 1967 defeat, the critical and theoretical work they were producing gained in ideological power. It interpellated the Arab nationalists who were increasingly steering toward Marxism as Palestinian armed struggle took over the mantle of anti-imperialist confrontation from the discredited "progressive regimes." With the formation of the Organization for Communist Action in Lebanon (1970), SL's militant intellectuals were catapulted into a different modality of political practice at a time when the resistance was increasingly becoming a key player in the tense years leading to the outbreak of the civil and regional wars.

Historiographical accounts, which anchor the bifurcation of Arab thought into holistic doctrines and reflexive critiques in 1967, skip the revolutionary high tides that directly followed the defeat. These high tides conjugated—not always easily, as we will soon see—the thick Marxist ideologies that hailed the Palestinian fida'yi as the new revolutionary subject with a commitment to critique. The bifurcation, I suggested, is better read as a product of the conjuncture produced in the wake of the Lebanese wars (1975–90), the Islamic revival and the Iranian Revolution (1979), and the defeat of the Palestinian revolution (1982). That is when the mediation between revolutionary theory and political practice was finally severed. The much-coveted revolutionary subject was either mired in the webs of communal solidarities, converted into a militant Islamist universe, or defeated. No one was left to carry out the project of emancipation. Critique was all that was left on the table. History, it seemed, had exited its own stage.

PART II.
TIMES OF
THE SOCIO-
CULTURAL

The war was a total social fact as much as it was
a political one, and may be more so.
—WADDAH CHARARA

The passage to Islam was a putting
into practice of Maoist principles.
I went into Islam, like some go to the factory.
But here in Lebanon, no one goes to the factory.
There are no factories, or so few of them.
—ROGER ASSAF

4. PARADOXES OF EMANCIPATION

Revolution and Power in Light of Mao

Organization is the form of mediation between theory and practice.
—GEORG LUKÁCS

There are two ways of making investigations,
one is to look at flowers on horseback
and the other is to get off your horse and look at them.
—MAO TSE-TUNG

The turn to Marxist theory and practice came in the wake of a political failure—the scission of Syria from the United Arab Republic (1961)—and a military defeat (1967). Marxism constituted a powerful critique of both Arab nationalist ideology and the practice of the "progressive" regimes. It was the tool that enabled disenchanted Arab nationalist militants to turn their critical gaze inward to dissect both their society's class composition and the modus operandi of the regimes. Moreover, Marxism worked. The successes of the Chinese, Cuban, and Vietnamese Revolutions fueled the hopes of the militants who joined the Palestinian Resistance or oscillated in its orbit. Socialist Lebanon was critical in theory of communist stages of development, modernization theories, and the top-down development projects of the national liberation regimes. Having said that, their theoretical virtuosity, which led to their political visibility and merger with the Organization of Lebanese Socialists, reinscribed in practice a vanguardist pedagogical mode of politics.[1] They brought the gift of theory to the much more numerous and veteran militant Lebanese branch of the Arab Nationalist Movement. The Organization of Communist Action in Lebanon (1970–) would be plagued by splits and expulsions from the beginning. The party members could not agree on internal organizational questions and on external ones concerning the modalities of political practice they ought to engage in. Questions of autonomy and discipline as well as what constitutes political practice, where it should take place, with whom, to what end, and in whose name shook the young organization from the start. The union brought together militants with different organizational legacies, theoretical genealogies, styles of political practice, and sensibilities toward party discipline and hierarchy who clashed along these lines. The early splits from the OCAL (1971–73) turned the critical gaze inward for a second time, this time to subject Marxist theory and politics to an auto-critique. In this chapter, and the next, I move from the reconstruction of a collective project of emancipation (SL and OCAL), in which Charara played a significant part, to the in-depth examination of his own militant trajectory and critical work.

A couple of years after the foundation of the OCAL, at the height of the social, political, and military polarization that preceded the outbreak of the fighting, Charara subjected the three main components—organization, theory, and political practice—of the revolutionary machine to critique. The people were still, for the time being, the revolutionary subject of History, but they too showed increasing complications. This critique was formulated in a translated and transfigured Maoist idiom when Mao Tse-Tung's thought was, in the wake of the Chinese Cultural Revolution, at the apex of its global influence. The Maoist critique of the party, theory, and practice rearticulated the meanings of power and emancipation as it addressed the political and epistemic dimensions of the question of representation. The vicissitudes of political practice opened up questions that bear a family resemblance to those that would later be taken theoretically in the academy by the labors of critique grouped under the umbrella of postcolonial studies. For now, questions of power, emancipation, and representation were articulated from militant grounds as an auto-critique and a political critique of the OCAL. Charara's Maoist episode put forth a "postcolonial" Marxism that attempted to conjugate the salience of communal solidarities—sectarian, regional, and kin—with class struggle and the possibility of revolutionary militant political practice.

The reflexive, auto-critical dimension and its prescient postcolonial tenor reveal once more a minor tradition of contemporary Arab thought that was forged by militant theorists whose distinctive interventions stand outside the canonized figures and thematics of contemporary Arab thought. The character of the Maoist auto-critique, while highlighting the resilience of communal solidarities, escapes the culturalism of figures like Sadik al-Azm. Moreover, this minor Marxist tradition, which sought to incorporate communal relations into class struggle, was not interested in restricting its intervention to criticizing Marxism for its Eurocentric discourses. It did that, but it was more invested in attempting to forge a theoretical idiom that enables the pursuit of militancy in the wake of realizing the saliency of communal contradictions internal to the masses that complicate revolutionary practice. Retrospectively, Charara's Maoist interlude constitutes the first episode of a very early unraveling of leftist political practice as it stumbles upon both the top-down modalities of practice of leftist parties and the recalcitrance and reproduction of communal relations. Charara's militant experiences, particularly his observation of the failure of the worker and teacher-student movements at the time, as well as his dissertation research on modern Arab intellectual thought, revealed to him the complexity of Arab histories and the multiple solidarities at work in Arab societies in comparison to the poverty of theoretical languages that attempt to subsume them by a few concepts. Maoism was the theoretical idiom through which he articulated his early disenchantment with the belief in the political powers of theory and accounted for the multiple logics, temporalities, and solidarities at work in Lebanese society that foreclose the possibility of a revolutionary teleology while retaining the militant's hope in emancipatory political practice.

The Workers' Sector and the Blue Pamphlet Splits

Soon after the unification between the Organization of Lebanese Socialists and Socialist Lebanon, and after adopting a loose organizational structure for a short while, the nascent organization shifted to a Marxist-Leninist form: democratic centralism.[2] In 1971 a major scission—that of the workers' sector—shook the OCAL. The split took with it a substantial number of militant intellectuals who came from Socialist Lebanon who were ill at ease with the strictures of organizational forms associated with official pro-Soviet communist parties. "What was left was an organization whose true effective body was constituted by the Organization of Lebanese Socialists," recalls Abbas Beydoun, a member of the Politburo at the time. Moreover, those who left, Beydoun adds, were "of the same weight as Waddah [Charara], Ahmad [Beydoun], Fawwaz [Traboulsi], and Muhsin [Ibrahim]; you are not talking about us, who were the 'little ones' of the Politburo."[3] The adoption of democratic centralism soon erupted in disputes over decision-making and prerogatives. "The first dispute," wrote Traboulsi, who was a proponent of democratic centralism,

> took place between the rapporteur of the "Workers Sector," a member of the Politburo, and the committee responsible for the sector mostly composed of the intellectual cadres of Socialist Lebanon. It revolved around their mutual prerogatives: Is the committee's power superior to that of the rapporteur or vice-versa? The Politburo settled the matter by supporting the rapporteur as a representative of the higher committee

[the Politburo] over the lower one. And after going back and forth it was decided that either the Workers Sector committee abides by the Politburo's decision or be subject to an organizational sentence. The committee unanimously refused to follow the Politburo's decision, which then issued a resolution to freeze the membership of its constituents.[4]

What exacerbated matters was the fact that the Politburo member, an OLS member initially and more of an "on the ground militant," did not come from the same theoretically imbued context as SL's militant intellectuals. Enmeshed in the organizational dispute, and highlighted through it, were the heterogeneity of the two recently unified groups: the democratic heritage and very loose organizational structure of militant intellectuals and the "disciplined traditions" of the Organization of Lebanese Socialists, "which were inherited from the Arab Nationalist Movement."[5] The split brought out the question of the place theoretical abilities ought to play in assuming leadership positions. In a thick ideological political practice such as Marxism—where theoretical virtuosity endows its bearer with political authority—it was difficult for intellectual cadres to bow down to the decisions not only of a politburo member but also of one who wasn't perceived to be of the same theoretical caliber. This was especially the case since it seemed "as if there was a promise to hand over the unified organization to the cadres of Socialist Lebanon to educate it since they were accomplished and superior in this domain."[6] This first split was followed up with a great amount of labor around the four corners of Lebanon to recuperate the OCAL's energy in its wake.[7]

The split of the majority of Socialist Lebanon's constituency a short time after the fusion left its marks on Charara: "They went out in the spring-summer of 1971 and I traveled right after. My travels were partially motivated by this."[8] A fellow member of the Politburo recalls the surprise provoked by Charara's decision to leave directly after the split to pursue a PhD in France, despite the fact that he was at the forefront of upholding the Politburo directives against the worker's sector: "I don't know what was the reason behind it. No one told him no. Although this thing was very 'frappant' [striking], not only surprising. . . . Waddah was not one of those people you say to, what are you going to do. So he went."[9] "He came back a very different person," the comrade adds, "adopting things similar [to the positions of the] Gauche Prolétarienne against democratic centralism, and with a position exactly opposed to the one that led to the organizational crisis."[10] Charara finished his dissertation, entitled "Le Discours Arabe sur L'Histoire" (The Arab discourse on history), in 1972, came back, and headed an opposition movement inside the organization that would split in 1973, two years before the beginning of the Lebanese civil war. After a number of meetings with the dissenting comrades, Charara formulated the opposition's political, organizational, and theoretical positions in a lengthy document (ninety-six pages), which came to be known as *al-Kirras al-Azraq* [*The Blue Pamphlet*,] that declared the group's independence from the OCAL. *Al-Hurriyya*, the weekly political magazine and mouthpiece of the OCAL at the time, published a four-page article on July 16, 1973, entitled "A Communiqué from the Politburo of the OCAL Announcing the Expulsion of the Boyish Leftist Band of Apostates [*al-Murtadda*] of Marxism-Leninism."[11] The dissenting group, which called for direct action among the masses and not through institutions, such as syndicates or Marxist-Leninist parties, and for "fusion [*iltiham*] with the Palestinian Resistance,"[12] did not survive long after the split and its members went in different directions. Some comrades adhered to the Lebanese Communist Party, some joined Fatah, while others went home.[13] The scattering of a substantive number of OCAL dissenters between different factions of the Palestinian resistance and the Lebanese Communist Party can be understood in light of Traboulsi's retrospective assessment: "While the first split [of the Workers Sector] brought up issues pertaining to organizational structure, and the second [*The Blue Pamphlet*] focused on the modes of militancy, they were also, and especially, bringing out the question of the raison of d'être of the organization in comparison to two references: pan-Arab [*qawmi*] and leftist, i.e., in reference to the Palestinian resistance and to the Lebanese Communist Party."[14]

Some of the dissenters, he added, "deemed that the Lebanese situation does not warrant an additional new communist organization to the left of the Communist Party, so they directly adhered to the Palestinian resistance."[15] Others "realized the weight and popularity of the Communist Party and its importance in the life of the working class,"[16] therefore canceling the justification for the OCAL's existence. The two stronger forces eroded the national and socioeconomic feet on which the OCAL stood.

The prewar years were not exclusively marked by the polarization around the Palestinian resistance. They were also years of mobilizations around socioeconomic questions in the privileged sectors of leftist militancy: peasants, workers, and students.[17] November 1972 witnessed the strike of Ghandour's biscuits and chocolate factory workers. The twelve-hundred-strong workforce at Ghandour's, the largest nonunionized force in Lebanese industry, Traboulsi relates, demanded "a wage increase, equal pay for men and women workers, the recognition of the shop floor committee, and their right to trade union organization" (167). Police opened fire at the workers' demonstration, killing

"Yusuf al-'Attar, a militant of the OCA's Workers' Committees, and Fatima al-Khawaja, a member of the LCP, and wounding 14 others" (168).[18] Approximately a month after the demonstration, Ghandour fired all his workers. He later opened shop again, reemploying all of them except for a hundred whom he considered to be at the head of the protest. "The outcome of the Ghandour battle," Traboulsi, the historian, writes, "left only frustration and resentment. The trade union attaché at the US embassy noted that the demonstration and the general strike had been a 'moderate success' for the Left, which had managed to go on the offensive and win the 'propaganda war.' However, he concluded that neither the Left nor the trade unions had secured any gains for the workers" (168). The Ghandour strike was followed by the strikes of tobacco farmers in the south and a number of strikes in the educational sector, notably by public school teachers, which included violence between the state apparatus and the protesters, in what would prove to be the last months of a struggle conceived along the lines of an *opposition* to the state before the outbreak of the fifteen-year-long civil and regional wars. The year 1972 saw the strike of sixteen thousand public school teachers, "demanding a wage increase, the right of trade union organization and retirement after twenty-five years of service" (170). The strike lasted two months, and ended when the government stopped paying their salaries. It picked up again from January to July 1973. While 324 teachers lost their jobs, the network of solidarity with the teachers covered all of Lebanon, as "their sit-ins and hunger strikes became a rallying point for all social movements" (170). In January 1973, "a procession of thousands of tobacco planters occupied the offices of the Régie in Nabatiyeh, demanding a 20 percent increase in the purchase price of their products. The following day, the army shot at the demonstrators and killed two peasants" (166).[19]

Waddah Charara wrote *The Blue Pamphlet* in the spring of 1973, in the wake of all of these events, weaving a reexamination of what was called for on the theoretical, political, and organizational levels, the causes for failure as well as the direction for future political action (Fig. 4.1). Charara observed these mobilizations closely. At times, he took a more active part in them, such as attending the public meetings held by the striking Ghandour workers, until he was forbidden by the OCAL to do so.[20] "Why weren't the largest demands-based mass movements," he wrote, that represent "the interests of the main popular classes able to snatch one partial benefit from the authorities? Why could the authorities resort to violent oppression without falling apart, or at least leading to a change in the government?"[21] Two years before his exit from Marxism, Charara engaged in an auto-critique from within the boundaries of

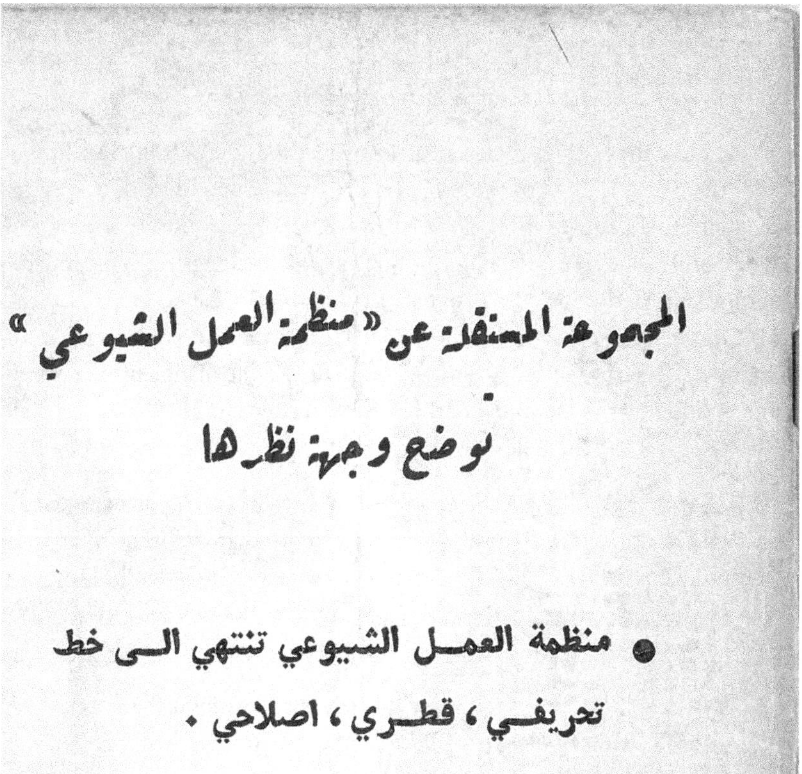

المجموعة المستقلة عن «منظمة العمل الشيوعي»

توضح وجهة نظرها

● منظمة العمـل الشيوعي تنتهي الـى خط تحريفـي ، قطـري ، اصلاحي .

● الخـط الديمقراطي والمسألة الوطنية .

● في سبيل خط وطنـي جماهيري .

FIGURE 4.1. Front cover of *The Blue Pamphlet*.

the tradition, repositioning himself in an ultraleftist, fervently pro-Palestinian Maoist position.[22]

The Twilight of the Organizational Idol

In the wake of the 1967 Arab defeat against Israel, and the ensuing reexamination of the causes leading to the defeat of the Arab armies by political parties and intellectuals, the Arab Nationalist Movement previously gravitating in Nasser's orbit proposed resorting to popular armed struggle to fight imperialism in Arab lands. Socialist Lebanon participated in the argument regarding the direction of the Arab liberation movement. After emphasizing that for Marxists the question ought not to rest on the principle of violent confrontation but rather on the suitability of this form of struggle for the present, Socialist Lebanon reached the following conclusion:

> We asked a question about the meaning of proposing the slogan of armed struggle in the current period. Now is the time to answer that what is meant by it is the deferral of the primary task of Arab struggle: the building of Marxist-Leninist parties, which history has not devised any alternative to, for leading the liberation of oppressed masses to victory![23]

Socialist Lebanon, which was still loosely organized, distinguished itself from the calls for "armed popular struggle" positing the Marxist-Leninist party as the sole agent of emancipation of the masses. Three years after the small group of intellectuals merged with the Organization of Lebanese Socialists, the opposition inside OCAL came to perceive organizational practices as a means of oppression. The organization's leadership, Charara wrote, "sees in every act of political accountability a risk with uncertain consequences. And this has been consolidated after the 1971 split: since the leadership has seen it a result of some comrades' desire to discuss with no limits!" (*The Blue Pamphlet*, hereafter cited as *TBP*, 4). In this veiled auto-critique Charara accused the leadership of evading the discussion of important political events such as Anwar al-Sadat's decision to expel all Soviet experts from Egypt, the issues of contention in the Syrian Communist Party, and the Ghandour workers' strike.[24] Additionally, the splinter group accused the Politburo of "suspending the internal regulations, interfering in the details of organizational issues, establishing special relations with specific members, in addition to using arguments of safety, security, and secrecy for no valid reasons." "In one word," Charara summarizes, "the organizational relationships have become a means of authoritarianism, abuse, and isolation" (*TBP*, 6).

Charara and his comrades reproached the OCAL's leadership not only for their internal authoritarianism but also for adopting a certain form of political action that went hand in hand with the organizational dimensions of the crisis. The organization, whose primary objective was to lay the foundations of the working class's leadership for emancipation, had reduced its struggle, according to the splinter group, to a politics "from above." The OCAL's contribution in the "Rally of National Parties and Forces" had begun to monopolize all of the organization's political activity.[25] The leadership began to increasingly think that "the only 'struggle' is the one that takes place in meetings of leaders and 'generals' while the main work which takes place in the midst of the masses diminishes" (TBP, 15). "The disdain for mass struggle" produced internal repercussions as well, since the leadership started to think that it is the organization and "what it sees is correct," forgoing discussion, political confrontation, and "the rules of organizational relations that permit the comrades to present their views and differ from those of the leadership" (TBP, 15). In the summer of 2008, Charara remembered the state of the OCAL when he returned from France:

> When I came back I didn't have any idea of what had happened to our work, to the organization. I came back and found out that Muhsin Ibrahim had made a "bande à part" [separated himself] in a complete way, with a personal link to Arafat and Kamal Jumblatt. And what is called the organization is practically living off this relationship, to which it had no link, and over which it had no control. No one knew what was said, what was happening, and all the attempts to move the OCAL from its student base to popular, workers, rural bases were either stopped, or no longer had any political echo.[26]

Charara's substitionist critique underscored that the organization had been reduced to its leadership, while mass struggle and militancy had been reduced to private meetings with the "generals" of progressive political parties.[27]

The telos of the organization's practices had long forsaken emancipation. This form of politics from above was driven by the increase in the organization's institutional share of power. "When the organization reaches syndicate positions," Charara wrote, "its pretense of democracy ends, and it begins fearing the students' interference in issues that concern them" (TBP, 34). Moreover, these political strategies of reaching power, which begin by alienating and fearing those the party seeks to represent, are refracted internally by an increasing stratification of relationships. "Members of cells are not supposed to distribute communiqués," Charara writes, "a task that is delegated to the 'lightweights,' as someone describes the members of assemblies and circles" (*TBP*, 33). This political practice, which was predicated

> on reaching power—externally—and on an increasing importance of ranks and relations of power internally, renders the talk about the point of view of the working class, the popular masses, and the national battle empty. And it enables, behind the mask of Marxist jargon, a petite bourgeoisie whose horizon of ambition is constituted by the state apparatus to move forward; a bourgeoisie that glorifies in talk workers and peasants while it does its best [in practice] to retain the differences between itself and them. (*TBP*, 35)

Charara's harsh critique underscored how particular—petit bourgeois—interests had occupied the party, turning Marxism into an ideology that is deployed to serve its own interests. In doing so, it reproduced in practice the relations of power it claims to eradicate in theory. It is not hard to see a continuity between Charara's critique of the OCAL and Socialist Lebanon's earlier critique of the "military-administrative-bureaucratic" regimes during the mid-1960s as apparatuses of power that foreclose the masses' political practice while speaking in their name.

The question of autonomy, of taking part in putting together a movement of auto-emancipation, that is neither dependent on nor subjugated to parties outside of it, whether they are state bureaucracies, nationalist parties, or sectarian formations, has been at the heart of Charara's thought since the 1960s. Decades later, he drew a retrospective distinction between Socialist Lebanon's critical theoretical labor and its political practice: "We didn't have a problem with the critical aspect of things. . . . Tracking inconsistencies, contradictions, ignorance, and deviations from Marxism and Leninism. This was work we had fun doing." Having said that, the political task of building "an autonomous sociopolitical force," Charara continued, "proved to be an astronomical task, particularly that the work was being done by thirty to forty people maximum including about ten of them in cells, and the rest were students, and some were teachers."[28] The expansion of the small and loose group of militant intellectuals into a wider organization in the turbulent years leading to war witnessed the fall of the "organizational" idol, once theoretically assumed to constitute the transparent vector of people's emancipation. It became the vector of a "petite bourgeoisie" in its bid for power with the other constituents of Lebanese society rendering Marxist ideological positions its Trojan horse.

Today, in the wake of the defeat and sclerosis of Arab leftist parties, it is not difficult to be swayed by *The Blue Pamphlet*'s prescient critique of instrumental and top-down politics and leadership unaccountability, which turned progressive parties into the means of production of new elites. Muhsin Ibrahim remains till today the secretary-general of the practically nonexistent OCAL, nearly fifty years after it came into being. Having said that, if one brackets the seductive reading of the 1970s from the present perspective of a Left in ruins, we get a more nuanced picture of the conditions of possibility of political action in a particular conjuncture. These very tense pre–civil war years, whether on the Palestinian front or on the socioeconomic one, and the mobilizations that ensued polarized the Lebanese polity. Fawwaz Traboulsi, one of the very few SL militants who did not leave the OCAL in the early years after the union, and stayed on as the number two in command after Muhsin Ibrahim till the mid-1980s, recalled the beginnings of their emergence on the "official" national political field. "The battle of Ghandour [fall 1972] opened up a new period in the life of the organization," wrote Traboulsi, "during which we had to cooperate with the other leftist parties in a mobilization that took larger dimensions than the [usual] factory ones and which surpassed our capacities to carry it by ourselves."[29] "As a result," he continued, "our relationship to Kamal Jumblatt and the LCP improved after a period of boycott, estrangement and mutual accusations that reached the extent of student fights between us and the latter, which were not devoid of violence" (PYMR, 134). It was in this context that the OCAL emerged on the national political scene when it was invited to the meeting held by the Rally of National and Progressive Parties—the precursor of the Lebanese National Movement—to protest the severe draft law limiting the freedoms of political parties.

Traboulsi gestured in his memoir to his ambivalence during this hinge moment (1973): "We entered the Left's front [the Rally of National and Progressive Parties] from the door of our militancy at the level of the base. But, is there a possibility of reconciling base-militancy and participation in action 'from above' and public political life?" "This was the question," Traboulsi recalled, "that would trouble us, or rather trouble me personally, and characterize my positions and behavior with much wobbling and hesitancy" (PYMR, 135). Muhsin Ibrahim, the veteran of official Nasserite politics, on the other hand, called for the "political fructification" of theoretical analysis.[30] Ibrahim is less concerned with questions regarding the modalities of political practice and its autonomy that troubled Charara and Traboulsi, Socialist Lebanon's founding dynamos, and divided them on the cusp of the war. Rather, Ibrahim's position is articulated as double avoidance: of the endless discussions of intellectuals (theory without a practice), on the one hand, and political opportunism (practice without theory), on the other hand. With the beginning of the Lebanese civil war, Muhsin Ibrahim became, alongside Kamal Jumblatt and George Hawi (the assistant to the secretary general of the LCP), one of the main leaders of the Lebanese National Movement, the coalition of leftist and pan-Arab parties that were allied with the Palestinian Resistance.

Power and Emancipation along Maoist Lines

As Marxist political parties became—alongside the bourgeoisie and imperialism—the targets of critique from within the tradition, the meaning of emancipation and power were also rethought. The nodal shift in the rethinking of emancipation and power according to Maoist lines was related to the crisis in political and epistemic representation. If the Marxist-Leninist political party was no longer the representative of the working classes, its reaching power no longer constituted a revolution; it was merely a substitution of one ruling class by another, retaining the "differences" between itself and the masses. Maoism, wrote Charara, meant that

> conflict between the masses and their enemies, takes place in inter-penetrating, camouflaged, or overt forms in *all* of society's cells and its institutions. The masses taking the reins of power is not therefore an unforeseen rupture that puts the leadership of the masses' movement in charge of state power, giving it suddenly the task of eradicating from above the relations of oppression and exploitation. Rather, the mass line is present in the conflict in all positions of social power from the narrowest to the widest. (TBP, 91)

Power was no longer a thing that was solely concentrated in institutions of rule and at the nodes of capitalist production. Charara's Maoist critique, by extending the domain of conflict between the masses and their enemies into all corners of society and making it internal to all institutions, rearticulated the horizon of emancipation away from the mere fact of seizing power. The political question was clearly no longer monopolized by who was in power. The extension of power and struggle to all cells of society and the stress on the insufficiency of increasing one's share of power in institutions to constitute emancipation was translated in *The Blue Pamphlet* by an emphasis on new forms of struggle that put the masses' practice as the mainspring of political action. Maoism meant "the foregrounding of the masses' own struggle on any pretense of leadership that builds itself outside of its own movement" (TBP, 89). The organization that put its own interest before that of the masses and outside of their movement was to be overcome by the masses' formulation of their own political project in light of their own practice. For this practice, wrote Charara, in a direct echo of Mao, "always contains a true kernel, behind all phenomena, that ought to be deduced and returned to the masses," (*TBP*, 90).[31] Foregrounding the masses' own practice also entailed a rethinking of the role of intellectual vanguards. "An illusion that has always flirted with professional 'intellectuals,'" Charara wrote, "is to try and spare the masses any experience, or to take their place in digesting their own experience" (*TBP*, 74). The intellectuals were to become the editors/formulators that take in the word of the masses, reformulate it, and give it back to them—and not to be the originators of thought.[32]

Estranged Intellectuals

Maoism's emphasis on the logics of political practice and the relations of production cleared the path for questioning the powers of political and epistemic representation. Charara's critique of the OCAL's internal organizational structure and its relationship with the masses brought out Maoism's critique of the politics of delegation, and of expertise, premised on the distinction between those who have knowledge and those who lack it.[33] I now turn to his auto-critique of how leftist militancy articulated the relationship of theory to practice and his reflexive account of why it did so, which is driven by two fundamental ideas. The first is Charara's critique of the imputed power of theory, that is, its performative political powers. If Lenin said "without revolutionary theory there can be no revolutionary movement," Charara, who spent about a decade immersed in militancy and in practices of reading, translating, and writing, particularly during the intellectually fervent years of Socialist Lebanon, came to the realization that revolutionary theory does not necessarily guarantee the coming into being of a revolutionary movement. What may seem to some today like an obvious realization is not exactly so. The theoretical and political conjuncture of the times placed a lot of weight on the political value of theory. Louis Althusser for one, whom Charara had read carefully and put to use, wanted "to guarantee an autonomy for theory that would make it capable of investing Marxism with the theoretical edge to generate political renewal."[34] The radical post-1967 conjuncture in the Arab world was characterized by a turn away from Arab nationalism to Marxism that was fueled partly by the latter's theoretical sophistication. Even today, critical scholars who warn of the ontological and epistemological violence of discourses still subscribe to a strong belief in the powers of theory that supposedly, and without much friction, will produce predictable effects in the world.

The second is Charara's observation regarding the ruggedness of the social terrain and the complexity of practices and political events in comparison to the poverty of theoretical languages that attempt to subsume them. He came to this deduction via several routes. It was the result of his close observation of mass movements, the consequence of leftist militant practice, and his Maoist turn, which highlighted the focus on practices and the empirical idea of investigation.[35] It was also the result of his close reading of Abd al-Rahman al-Jabarti, the Egyptian historian who chronicled Napoleon's invasion of Egypt, for his dissertation work (1972). What al-Jabarti revealed to him was the gap between the richness, complications, and contradictory aspects of historical events and the poverty of the ideological discourses that came to dominate Arab discourses on history and politics.[36] The gap between theory and practices was now wide open in both directions: by severing the direct highway that tied theoretical virtuosity to revolutionary practice, and by highlighting the complexity of practices that cannot be adequately captured by mastering a few big concepts. Charara's political experiences, his theoretical persuasion, and his historical excavations led him away from theoretical abstractions and into much more empirically inclined sociological and ethnographic modes of analysis that he will develop fully in the wake of the Lebanese civil and regional wars. Having said that, he noticed very early on the gap separating the revolutionary ideological political line—its anti-imperial *content*—and its practices, modes of operation, and communal *forms* of mobilization. Just a few months before the founding of the OCAL, in a sequel to "The Two Resistances," he had a moment of doubt regarding the revolutionary potential of the Palestinian resistance, which he had theorized a few months earlier. Charara underscored "the rupture" between the resistance's supposed role as a detonator of Lebanese contradictions and its material fostering of "traditional political actors," whose base rises on personal, familial, and regional loyalties.[37]

He put these two ideas to work in his auto-critique of the political practice of militant intellectuals, starting from the founding of Socialist Lebanon. The cornerstone of the account given for the "disease that has infiltrated all parts of the organization" was the origins of its constitutive members, who were for the most part "marginal intellectuals" (*TBP*, 17). In this first reexamination of Socialist Lebanon—and the Organization of Lebanese Socialists—Charara remarked that the former's practice "did not coincide with work to extend militant roots in the ranks of the popular movement" (*TBP*, 17). Socialist Lebanon's work mostly grew "in the cracks of [other] political parties' positions, that is their contradictions. . . . What 'Socialist Lebanon' did not realize, and it is also the case for the 'Organization of Lebanese Socialists,' is that the correctness of political critique does not constitute a foundation to build a militant organization and to form militants" (*TBP*, 17). In other words, drawing attention to the LCP's theoretical poverty via the intertextual theoretical practice that Socialist Lebanon engaged in, as we saw all along, was no longer a guarantee for building an autonomous popular movement. To get an idea of the strength of the idea tying theoretical prowess (or the political line) to political efficacy, it is worth revisiting the interview Fawwaz Traboulsi gave to the Middle East Research and Information Project (MERIP) in October 1977, in which he affirmed that "the correctness of our [OCAL] political line accounts for our influence on the masses and within the front [the LNM], disproportional to our numerical situation."[38] In Traboulsi's vanguardist reasoning, good theory accounts for political influence on both the masses and other leftist parties despite the organization's small size.

Charara extended his auto-critique of militant intellectuals beyond the reduction of political practice to political critique, noting that their relative privileges compared to peasants resulted in an increased *distance* between them—inhabiting the "language and culture of professional party member politicians"—and the effective everyday issues and struggles of the masses (*TBP*, 18). "The organization's ranks and before it those of Socialist Lebanon and the Organization of Lebanese Socialists," wrote the fresh PhD graduate from France in an accusatory tone, "are swarming with those pursuing a university education in order to improve their social and economic conditions of living. And this [situation] results in distancing them from the masses' ranks where they aspire to militate" (*TBP*, 17). This distance between the intellectuals and the masses resulted in the former's engagement in a "cultural" critique of the dominant political practice that "veiled itself with Leninism." "And there is no doubt," added Charara, "that our cultural critique is a result of the weak relation that linked us to the real struggles taking place in our society" (*TBP*, 18).

Charara argued that they were held captive by an "imaginary image" of workers that in fact carries "the features that are really those of intellectuals, but transposed into the factory" (*TBP*, 23). Workers were seen only as workers, that is, as a homogenous group produced by factory relations, not only because of the bookish character of these intellectuals' knowledge of workers but more importantly because of their sociological profile. These militant intellectuals broke their relations with their villages, their families, and the parliamentarians of their areas. Moreover, they accessed their jobs by passing an exam or holding a degree "independent of traditional relations," and joined a "homogenous milieu composed of employees who like them have left the countryside and their relationships with their families" (*TBP*, 23). The estranged militant intellectual who speaks in the name of the masses is a product of an internal migration to the city whose means of livelihood were mediated by abstract, institutional means that broke away from the regional, kinship, and sectarian forms of solidarity that mediate the Lebanese citizens' relationship with the state and the market. Yet "when these traditional relationships still play a role in the intellectuals' conditions," Charara wrote, "they [the intellectuals] make efforts to hide it so that it does not devalue them and their merits" (*TBP*, 23). Briefly put, the image of the "abstract worker" is a consequence of the intellectual's abstraction from multiple attachments and mediations, whose haunting presence is capable of generating streams of anxiety.

Charara also put his critique of the estrangement of militants from the masses into practice. He followed Mao Tse-Tung's recommendation that "since [intellectuals] are to serve the masses of workers and peasants, intellectuals must, first and foremost, know them and be familiar with their life, work and ideas."[39] He relocated in the spring of 1973 to Burj Hammud—a multiethnic, multinational, working-class suburb northeast of Beirut—and lived there until the outbreak of the fighting in 1975 made it impossible for him to stay there. Charara's établissement in Burj Hammud took the form of making connections and working with groups of rural migrant workers from 'Irsal, a northeastern Lebanese town on the border with Syria, as well as with a number of factory workers in the surrounding area during this time. Charara's Maoist period, and his établissement, was premised on his own physical displacement into a working-class neighborhood where he engaged in everyday investigations and political practices with the people living and working there. It was an effort to learn from them and to overcome the gap between intellectual and manual labor. In contrast to Socialist Lebanon's textualist phase, when the emphasis was on the translation and transfiguration of texts to produce an adequate theory of one's political present, the militant intellectual during this last period of militancy, not the texts, traveled with the hope of both reconfiguring himself and the masses. "After all," Kristin Ross writes in her discussion of the établissement of French Maoists, "as Mao was fond of asking, how can you catch a tiger cub without entering the tiger's lair?"[40]

Revisiting Sectarianism

In the spirit of Maoist self-criticism, *The Blue Pamphlet* revisits in a postcolonial mode Socialist Lebanon's theoretical premises on which their political analysis and practice were built:

The political axis of analysis was, and still is, the presupposition of a European-like capitalism that eradicates all inherited relations from the precapitalist formations, such as family ones and relations of political "feudalism" . . . and this main presupposition is bolstered by another one in conjunction with it, [revolving] around a working class which as soon as it enters the factory gains a class homogeneity [and] gets rid of its clan solidarities [al-'asha'iriyya]. (TBP, 19)

In the moment of auto-critique Charara irons out Socialist Lebanon's intricate theoretical work, as well as his own emphasis on the necessity of translation and transfiguration of Marxism. Nonetheless, he draws our attention to the increasing salience of the question of sectarian-regional-kinship solidarities and the Marxist metanarrative that tried to take stock of the problem of communal ties that divided the masses and hindered their practice according to their own economic interests. Charara's target at the height of his populist glorification of the masses is to show how the Marxist metanarrative, which predicated revolutionary practice on overcoming the different forms of social solidarities, was the product of estranged intellectuals. He continues:

And the persistence of this imaginary image has transformed it into a fixed political mode that we try to transpose to all phenomena, squeezing into it all important events. So we understood the national movement, and its kernel the Palestinian Resistance, as the realization of what capitalism could not achieve in the sphere of social relations. We were under the illusion that the Resistance's main role was to eradicate the fragmentation of the popular masses by the sectarian, regional, and kinship relations, i.e., we practically put the resistance in the place of the Lebanese capitalism we dream of! (TBP, 19)

Charara is referring to "The Two Resistances" (1969), his key text, which was built on a series of dualities that sought to account for the blockage of revolutionary practice by noting the disjunction between the economic infrastructure and the political superstructure. Lebanon, he had argued, is characterized both by the propagation of the universal laws of capitalist expansion in the economic sphere (commensurability) and the sectarian political brakes of the political system that were devised by French imperialism, which impede the birth of the interest-based politics of citizens (incommensurability). This duality is also inscribed at the heart of Lebanon's exploitative relationship with its Arab neighbors. Lebanon is economically integrated into the Arab world, thriving on the investment of Palestinian capital after the 1948 Nakba and exports to the Gulf countries while being politically isolated from Palestine, via its politics of neutrality in the Arab-Israeli conflict. The ruling alliance itself reproduces this duality since it is conceived as the partnership between the banking and commercial bourgeoisie of the coast and the landowning families of the mountains. The hybrid Lebanese citizen—for example, Sunni from Beirut, Maronite from the mountains—is also the outcome of this dual structure, which combines the universality of the bourgeois notion of citizenship and the particularity of sectarian and regional affiliations.

Sectarianism, in "The Two Resistances," plays a very different role whether we are talking about the Lebanese ruling alliance or the people. Sectarianism, by splitting the Lebanese citizen, is responsible for stifling class-based politics. The split needs to be overcome for a "mature," interest-based political practice to take place. If we shift our analytical gaze to the composition of the Lebanese regime, we get a different picture. The split between universality and particularity is not internalized in its "hybrid" subjects. Rather, it becomes a sociological feature of the two groups—the bourgeoisie of the coast and the landowning lords of the mountains—that constitute it. Socialist Lebanon does not attach a sectarian attribute—Christian or Muslim—to the Lebanese bourgeoisie. Sectarianism is not treated as an essential component of the Lebanese bourgeois identity but as a veil that masks its defense of its privileges. During his militant days, Charara's analysis had to provide an account of the particularity of Lebanese sectarian politics and loyalties on a Marxian ground that takes class politics and exploitation as the universal underlying realities that explain the Lebanese social formation. He was faced with a puzzle of how to square the proliferation and multiplicity of apparent infranational loyalties and political divisions with a notion of politics that is predicated on the contradiction between Labor and Capital. The differential distribution of his universal/particular binaries (economic integration, commensurability, banking-commercial bourgeoisie; and political isolation, incommensurability, political feudalism, hybrid citizens) and the different meanings sectarianism acquires are his answers to the conundrum of explaining along class lines the multiple sectarian allegiances and divisions within the frame of one exploitative system.

Sectarianism has different ontological weights and plays a variety of roles in "The Two Resistances." It is at the same time the backbone of the Lebanese political structure, one of the main sources of identification of Lebanese citizens, and a mask covering class exploitation. Sectarianism is both a form of political power that fashions hybrid citizens and paralyzes their political practice and a veil that covers up the interest-driven politics of the banking-commercial bourgeoisie. The Palestinian resistance, the anti-imperial Arab agent par excellence after it made its entrance into Lebanese politics, will contribute to the overcoming of the system's duality. Its intrusion into Lebanese politics unmasked the bourgeoisie's exploitation, which can no longer veil itself with sectarianism, and refashioned the sectarian subject into a revolutionary one.[41]

Two years before the war, Charara, under Mao's sign, recodes his previous theoretical and political quests to be on the lookout for the external agent that will overcome the fragmentation of the masses along nonclass lines, as an act of estranged intellectuals. Charara inverted his previous analysis, noting:

> We have neglected a key issue, which is that clan, family, neighborhood, and sectarian relations are relations of class struggle that are no less acute than exploitation relations in the factory, even if their forms veil themselves and differ. Since those who play the role of middlemen do not only receive a concrete material price for their roles, they often join the ranks of the commercial and financial bourgeoisie: since it allocates to them positions, jobs and supports their notability and their power. So that the fusion becomes complete between the "upper" middlemen (members of Parliament, important electoral keys, and high-ranking employees) and the bourgeoisie itself. . . . Working to reveal the forms of this struggle and investigate the issues it revolves around is a hard task that is awaiting our initiation, because it has long remained, and still is, on the margin of intellectuals' interests, especially those who are party-members. (*TBP*, 81–82)

Charara's widening of the definition of struggle to engulf social, institutional, and political dimensions beyond the exploitation of labor enabled what was previously seen as an obstacle to class struggle to be repositioned as part of it. Expanding the notion of class struggle to encompass the multiple communal forms of solidarity, though, is not merely a numerical addition of clan, family, neighborhood, and sectarian components to class. The forms of communal solidarity are politically *polyvalent*. They can constitute a "vital agent in curbing resistance against exploitation and oppression" (*TBP*, 81) without being

> fully geared to the advantage of the agents [between the bourgeoisie and the working class] and through them to the bourgeoisie and its power. For the masses, with their "class instinct" as Lenin says, use this weapon to their advantage. In a number of factories, the familial and local solidarity is overturned against the factory owner and the agent, and workers use it as a strong pressuring measure on the factory owner to retract a dismissal decision, a wage deduction penalty, or to consolidate a strike. . . .

> To rely on these relations of solidarity, and to work such as the masses
> will benefit from them against the agents, against the commercial and
> financial bourgeoisie and against the authorities, is a line we should not
> deviate from in expanding the people's struggle. (*TBP*, 82)

Two years before the war, Charara the militant, noting the growing opacity of
the masses, and the growing complications lodged at the heart of the revolutionary subject, recast the scope and modality of political militancy away from
its restriction to workers qua workers, seeing in the "traditional relations of
solidarity" a potential to be exploited and mobilized in the struggle of the masses
against both the bourgeoisie and the political authorities. "This is the revolutionary content of 'dealing with reality as it is,'" Charara wrote, "and of dealing with
the exploited and the toilers first, and not from the perspective of the petite
bourgeoisie only" (*TBP*, 82). This expansion of the domain of class struggle
underlined the equivocal and political polyvalence of these communal forms.
They are at the same time an integral part of class struggle, a form of its manifestation outside of labor exploitation, *and* a weapon that can be mobilized
either by or against those who hold economic and political power. The political polyvalence of the masses-as-they-are, so to speak, complicates revolutionary teleology.

In the wake of realizing the false prophecies of his previous theoretical
analyses and political lines regarding the historical *forces* that would deliver
the Lebanese working class of its fragmentation, Charara revised his analyses
of Lebanese capitalism, subjected the OCAL and the Lebanese Left to a scathing critique, and radicalized his political position, calling for a "people's war."[42]
Before the outbreak of "real" violence, resulting in his crisis and disenchantment, Charara wallowed in the glorification of the masses' violence:

> The people's war is not an armed struggle launched by an isolated or ad-
> venturous "vanguard." It is the eruption of the violence carried by the
> masses who throw it in the face of its enemies, in various forms inside all
> the spaces of the social order. It finds its unity and reaches its prime form
> in the direct confrontation with the imperial-classist domination and the
> political power that embodies it on a general level. (*TBP*, 90)

The Blue Pamphlet, a couple of years before the official beginning of the war,
bears the marks of the tension between the critic's scalpel, which dissects
the internal contradictions of the masses, and the remainder of the revolutionary's hope in them as the subjects of emancipation, which glorifies their
violence.

Coda: The Origins of Sectarian Lebanon—
The Right-Wing's Mass Line

During his établissement in Burj Hammud, Charara pursued his investigations of the disjunction between theory and practice, the politics of representation, and the paradoxes of emancipation. In March 1975, a month before the official date of the beginning of the Lebanese civil and regional wars (April 13, 1975), he published *Origins of Sectarian Lebanon: The Right-Wing's Mass Line*.[43] This brilliant, polemical, and long-neglected book is an intervention against the theorization of sectarianism by liberal, technocratic, secular, and Marxist politicians and intellectuals. Charara develops his earlier auto-critique and confronts head on the different theories that deploy secularism as an ideological mask and an instrument that will soon be vanquished by an external agent. He writes, "Employment, science, technology . . . sectarianism dies in the same way old empires did under the hooves of barbarian invaders . . . and sectarianism's barbarians come from Europe, a new 'land between two rivers' that exports the epidemic that decimates the ancient man, making him into a colorless employee, an intellectual that has dusted off the mountain's residues, and a technician with the passions of a calculator" (*Origins of Sectarian Lebanon*, hereafter *OSL*, 7). All these accounts of sectarianism are premised on a historicism—the European barbarians—that Marxist accounts partake in: "This "outside," Charara writes, "shares with the modes that preceded it and follow it, the fact that it forms the necessary direction of History's movement. It also shares with them history's apparition fully armed and in full gear from Jupiter's head, the god of gods in selected quotes from Hegel and Engels" (*OSL*, 8). The Left iterations of these theories make sectarianism an ideological mask that falsifies the underlying "real" social conflict. Sectarianism is then conceptualized as an instrument of sedition and division by you name it—landowners, Ottoman interests, the fighting imperial powers, and the local bourgeoisie. "In the beginning was unity and innocence," Charara writes ironically about the theoretical tropes organizing the accounts of sectarianism as the weapon of choice exploited by outsiders to divide the nation's citizens, and wielded by both outsiders and insiders to weaken working-class solidarity.[44]

Charara's book does not only criticize these dominant accounts of sectarianism that see it as a top-down phenomenon that was "created" by foreigners and elites to delude and divide the masses and that will soon vanish. It revisits the nineteenth-century Maronite peasant movements in Mount Lebanon against the sheikhs and lords—*muqata'ji*—mediated through his own reading of Mao and Gramsci to propose that sectarianism was constituted from below through the political practice of the peasants. Charara's compressed history charts the movement of Lebanon's Maronites from the position of subalternity to dominance (OSL, 40) through the formation of a Maronite social and political force, a historical bloc, composed of peasants and led by traders, artisans, and clergymen (OSL, 74).

Amid the resistance to the lords, Charara writes,

> new relations were forged. Those relations made Europe, Capitalism, the Church, and the commoner's political and military organizational forms intertwined threads which are tied together at the juncture of the peasant's movement. This is how a deep-rooted mass line, which was tightly connected to popular struggle then, was constituted. This mass line carried the Lebanese political formation with its fixed features, namely sectarianism. This means that sectarianism is historically concomitant to the Mass Line that founded present-day Lebanon and not an incidental that can be cast off. This highlights the contradiction that can be designated as "The Right-Wing's Mass Line," which is at the heart of continuing political contradictions whose network form the superstructure of the Lebanese formation. (OSL, 97)

Charara's narrative charts how, in a very complex historical conjuncture characterized by capitalist penetration, European imperial interventions, Ottoman reforms, and Egyptian campaigns, the Maronite peasants' revolutionary practice against their lords fashioned Maronite political sectarian solidarities.

Charara's book is a very early constructionist argument that underscores the modernity of the phenomenon of political sectarianism against the widely circulated culturalist arguments that repeat ad nauseam the trope about essentialist, primordial loyalties that supposedly overdetermine Arab politics. The US-based historian of the Middle East Ussama Makdisi will make a similar argument about the modernity of sectarianism twenty-five years later.[45] Despite the similar conclusions Makdisi reaches about the modernity of sectarian relations of political solidarity, the character of the two interventions are very different. The post-*Orientalism* antiessentialism of Makdisi's work deploys a constructionist approach against Orientalist culturalist tropes that de-rationalize, look down on, and make an exception of Arab politics by highlighting the fatalism of "tribes" fueled by their atavistic passions. His is a culturally progressive move that marshals historical transformations and breaks to undo the imputed timelessness of a "traditional culture" that produces repetitive bloody episodes that are out of sync with an imputed civilized "modernity." In brief, Makdisi's postcolonial antiessentialist move marshals historical discontinuities against timeless culture—modernity against tradition—to undo a particular colonial logic that singles out Arabs to classify them according to what makes them different, in this case sectarianism.

The character of Charara's much older intervention is very different. *Origins of Sectarian Lebanon* was written on the eve of the Lebanese civil war, after a decade and a half long parenthesis of political militancy that would soon be closed off for good. "The theoretical and political urgency of these questions," he writes in the last sentence of the book, "are fostered by the harshness of defeat and the determination of struggle" (125). It is a rethinking, born out of militancy, that underscores that sectarianism is neither a mask nor a tool that is contingent on a "pure social struggle" that is imposed on it from above by powerful players. Sectarianism, Charara argues, in a remarkably counterintuitive move, is not external to revolutionary practice, nor is it an impediment to it; rather, it is the result of it. The modernity of the phenomenon in Charara's account is not all that there is to the story. Rather, what is important is the fact that sectarian solidarities are not the result of false consciousness and top-down ideological imposition. Charara's and Makdisi's work on the same historical period, which underscores the modernity of sectarianism, constitute very different interventions. Makdisi marshals history to make a theoretical point against Orientalists and Western pundits that underlines that sectarianism is not a fatality. Charara, in contrast, is not concerned with the dichotomies of essence/construction and culture/history. The deep popular roots of sectarianism are highlighted to show not only the thinness of leftist accounts but also, in the wake of political losses, the recalcitrance of sectarianism in practice in contrast to its critique in theory.

Charara's account of practice and theory in nineteenth-century Mount Lebanon is written as a mirror image of his own auto-critique of militant experience a century later in *The Blue Pamphlet*. In contrast to the top-down modalities of leftist militancy, which seek to represent the masses—epistemically and politically—and end up hijacking their initiatives and reproducing the modalities of power they sought to overcome, we are presented with an account of grassroots practice that breaks free from the old relations of subjugation to fashion new modes of practice, organization, and relationships. For instance, instead of leftist parties' practice, which is premised on gaining power through increasing its institutional share of power, we are presented with an account of the Maronite Church as reworking existing relations. The Maronite Church's historical transformation made it into an institution with deep organic roots with its peasant base, which made it the only party that fulfilled "organizational, military, ideological and economic functions" (OSL, 107). "The Church didn't undertake its political role," Charara writes in a direct echo of his critique of the Lebanese Left, "by taking over a centralized power that has fully formed and autonomous apparatuses. Rather, it worked on creating these apparatuses, or worked on readjusting the existing ones to the demands of the current tasks" (OSL, 108). The nineteenth-century Maronite Church, which was the major source for intellectuals then, looked at through the Mao-Gramsci prism is the mirror image of the twentieth-century Leninist vanguardist party. Last but not least, Charara underlines the feeble character of Lebanese nationalist ideology—in contrast, say, to Marxist theory—that was the offspring of the constitution of Maronite sectarian identity, despite the fact that the Christian bourgeoisie had long separated itself from its nineteenth-century peasant base. The theoretical thinness of this ideology, which wavers between an economic integration with the Arab world and a political isolation from it, with its dependency on Western powers, does not impede its practical effects. "To refute Lebanese ideology based on its 'incoherence,' its 'crudeness,' its 'feebleness,'" Charara writes, "does not rob it of its effective and practical source that nourishes it, even if its tongues are Michel Chiha, Sa'id Akl, Charles Malik, and Kamal al-Haj" (OSL, 121). Lebanese nationalist ideology is the mirror image of Marxist theory. A theoretically thin and incoherent ideology is much more practically effective than a thick Marxist theory and political analysis that he once thought held the key to a successful emancipatory practice. The evolution of the Lebanese formation, argued Charara, reproduces the sectarian line:

> Each time intellectuals of a certain sect (in the wide Gramscian sense), regardless of their inclinations, meet with its toilers—peasants and workers—the sectarian form plays the role of the unifying reference. This is practically always true regarding the Druze, whose peasants' conditions have not stopped deteriorating. It is also the case with the Shi'a during their last "demands movements" in 1974. The "progressive content" [of the demands] is neither an exception nor a new feature. We have seen that the Maronite movement had a content, and was based on practices, that both carried an effective revolutionary potential that surpassed, in its political practices and its organizational forms, what the other movements have achieved till today. (OSL, 114)

Charara's Maoist episode stretched his Marxist analysis to its limits by revealing the paradoxes of emancipation, the impossibility of teleology, as well as the disjuncture between theory and practice. *Origins of Sectarian Lebanon* showed how peasant emancipatory political practice in the nineteenth century that contested the dominant order managed to rework the relations of production, the political and military modalities of organization and ideologies, and paradoxically give rise to a right-wing sectarian political formation. Nineteenth-century Maronite peasants' practice was revolutionary, but it ended up producing a sectarian formation and a right-wing ideology and politics. The mid-1970s Left, as we will soon see, reversed the equation—revolutionary and anti-imperial ideological demands were articulated on, or did not manage to break free from, sectarian constituencies.

5. EXIT MARX/ENTER IBN KHALDUN
Wartime Disenchantment and Critique

When the community no longer raises objections, there is an end, too, to the suppression of evil passions, and men perpetrate deeds of cruelty, fraud, treachery and barbarity so incompatible with their level of civilization that one could have thought them impossible.
—SIGMUND FREUD

Le désespoir est une forme supérieure de la critique.
—LÉO FERRÉ

In *Left-Wing Melancholia: Marxism, History, and Memory*, Enzo Traverso observes that the significant defeats the Left has suffered in the past did not break the tradition's spine. The hope in a revolutionary utopia, which provided both a historical perspective and a shared horizon of expectation, sustained the tradition through its many defeats. Traverso dates the exhaustion of the tradition's stock of revolutionary hope and the exit of History from the stage with the downfall of the communism:

> When communism fell apart, the utopia that for almost two centuries had supported it as a Promethean impetus or consolatory justification was no longer available; it had become an exhausted spiritual resource. The "structure of feelings" of the left disappeared and the melancholy born from defeat could not find anything to transcend it; it remained alone in front of a vacuum. The coming neoliberal wave—as individualistic as it was cynical—fulfilled it.[1]

Traverso's canvassing of global political transformations, from Left internationalism to the neoliberal wave, reinscribes the disaggregation of the Left's "structure of feelings" with the end of the Cold War. Similar historiographical markers are also put to use by keen observers of ideological transformations in the Arab world. "The fall of the Soviet Union," Michaelle Browers writes, "was a decisive event for socialist forces throughout the world and certainly

Arab socialism is no exception. Much of the political discourse of 'popular' democracy, the revolutionary party and Frontal politics, has given way to a more 'liberal' discourse of pluralism, human rights and civil society."[2] Browers, who is writing more than a decade before Traverso and is focusing on the transformations of political languages in the Arab world, highlights how the problematic of liberal democracy displaced the exhausted family of progressive languages that were preoccupied with revolution. This state of exhaustion not only affected the Marxist tradition as a grid of analysis and a set of conceptual tools but also had a detrimental effect on Marxist-grounded politics. Marxist-Leninist organizations such as Arab communist parties, but not exclusively so, were by the early 1990s shaken by debates revolving around questions ranging from whether they ought to change their names to the relevance of "the dictatorship of the proletariat" in the party's political agenda as well as measures of democratization internal to the organizations.[3]

Waddah Charara's trajectory is doubly contrapuntal vis-à-vis Traverso's and Browers's accounts. It presents a very early unraveling, with the beginning of the Lebanese civil and regional wars (1975–90), of the hope generated by the historical perspective of revolutionary utopias. It is also an exit from Marxist militancy and ideology that displaced the question of the political away from the centrality of class politics toward the investigation of the socio-logics and modalities of power of infranational solidarities as he observed the division of the Lebanese masses into their different Christian and Muslim sectarian constituencies. Charara did not substitute one ideology (Marxism) for another (liberalism). Rather, as we will soon see, he examined how the political could not extricate itself from, and carve out, an autonomous sphere outside of communal relations of solidarity. It is not the collapse of communism that eclipsed the faith in History, but the fragmentation of the revolutionary subject along communal lines that foreclosed the possibility of autonomous political practice.

The critical distance Charara took from the warring camps was a very rare move at the time. He was probably the first of his cohort of leftist militants to pay attention to, and theorize, the communal logics—predominantly sectarian, but also regional and kinship based—and the modalities of power at work in the Lebanese civil war and their impact on thick ideological politics. Reinserting his intervention into the problem-space of the 1970s Left before the ebbing away of revolutionary tides reveals to us how divergent his solitary and farsighted diagnosis of the war was from the positions of leftist political parties and former comrades. Charara was a bellwether of sorts for the waves of disenchantment to come of leftist intellectuals around a decade and a half before the fall of the Soviet Union. With the waning power of the Left in the following years of the war—the Syrian military intervention in 1976, the assassination of Kamal Jumblatt in 1977, the withdrawal of the PLO after the Israeli invasion of 1982, the increasingly inter- and intrasectarian nature of the war, as well as the rise of Islamist political forces—a number of leftist militants would experience successive waves of disenchantment. During his Maoist interlude (1972–75), which witnessed mobilizations and military clashes between the Palestinian resistance and the Lebanese authorities (May 1973), omens of the devastations to come, Charara took stock of a decade of Marxist militancy. His corrosive auto-critique targeted the building blocks on which he, alongside his comrades, sought to inaugurate a revolutionary political project. In brief, the political party he cofounded was no longer the collective agent of emancipation; his militant intellectual comrades no longer constituted a revolutionary vanguard; and revolutionary theory was no longer the royal road to effective practice. Disenchanted with the party, militant intellectuals, and revolutionary theory, Charara turned to Maoism, placing his ultimate militant wager on the masses. Despite the acknowledgment of the difficulty of holding on to a teleology of emancipation, his militant catechesis took the form of a romantic mythologization of the masses, whose revolutionary violence makes History unmediated by the authoritarian apparatuses of the party. Retrospectively, one could map the salient objects of Charara's revolutionary trajectory before disenchantment and their accompanying practices along the following lines: *revolutionary theory* (Socialist Lebanon, 1964–68, translation/transfiguration); *revolutionary organization* (Socialist Lebanon/OCAL, 1969–71, political union); *revolutionary masses* (*Blue Pamphlet* movement/solo militancy, 1972–75, établissement). Waddah Charara, who is of Shi'i descent, was in the first months of the fighting still living on and off in Burj Hammud where he had relocated in 1973 for his établissement.

In a country where national consensus is a rare currency, April 13, 1975, stands in for the beginning of the civil and regional wars that lasted until the end of 1990. On that day a car fired shots at a congregation of Phalange partisans in front of a church in 'Ayn al-Rummana, a Christian suburb east of Beirut. The shootings wounded a number of people, "to which the Phalangist militiamen reacted a few hours later by machine-gunning a bus heading for the Tall al-Za'tar refugee camp, killing 21 Palestinians. Fighting broke out throughout the southeastern suburb of Beirut between the Phalange and the Palestinian resistance and their Lebanese allies."[4] Charara continued to commute between Beirut and Burj Hammud until September 1975. Around the end of the month, on either September 24 or 25, Charara took a cab to Beirut with Fares, his flatmate at the time, leaving everything as is in their apartment.[5] This proved to be his last day in Burj Hammud. "Things exploded a bit after that," he recalls, and "Black Saturday happened . . . and I never saw the apartment again and the books of course. Everything was gone. This [établissement in Burj Hammud] was the last attempt to contact people and to call for something."[6] The "Black Saturday" massacre took place on December 6, 1975, when, after discovering the bodies of four young men associated with the right-wing nationalist Phalange Party, Christian militiamen established checkpoints in Beirut, stopping cars, lining up and murdering "some 200 innocent Muslims, mostly port workers."[7] On January 18, 1976, the Christian forces attacked Karantina, a northeastern multiethnic (Kurds, Armenians), multinational (Palestinians, Syrians, and Lebanese), predominantly Muslim working-class suburb under the control of the Palestine Liberation Organization, which is contiguous to Burj Hammud. After conquering Karantina, the militias massacred hundreds of civilians. Two days later, the Lebanese National Movement and Palestinian forces attacked the Christian coastal town of Damur south of Beirut, and committed a massacre against its inhabitants. The outbreak of the civil war in the spring of 1975 closed off for good Charara's nearly two decades of militant life (1958–75): seventeen years of militancy inaugurated on the eve of the 1958 clashes, a stint of radical activism bracketed by two civil wars.

Charara, who was stunned by the sectarian forms of the killing, destruction, and pillaging, began to take stock of the logics governing the wartime practice. In the opening paragraphs of "Hurub al-Istitba'" (Wars of Subjugation) the opening chapter of a book of essays carrying the same title, (February 1976, hereafter cited as *ws*), he wrote,

> Numerous phenomena have come to dominate the surface of our lives in the past ten months, phenomena where blood mixed with cut limbs, and hot ashes with spilled viscera from pierced bellies. . . . Spectators used to close their eyes in horror at the movie theaters whenever [Luis] Buñuel and [Salvador] Dalí's blade would cut through a cinematic eye in *"An Andalusian Dog."* We now began tallying sliced eyes. And between one round and another, laughter filled the theaters showing "action movies" with pity: *Bloody Mama* is evil because she killed three or four policemen![8]

Charara compared the violence, pillaging, and battles in Lebanon from April 1975 to February 1976 with the differential responses of moviegoers to violent scenes in Luis Buñuel's *An Andalusian Dog* (1929) before the war and Roger Corman's *Bloody Mama* (1970), shown during the war. They had an audience whose everyday lives had become so exposed to bloodshed that the meaning of violent scenes in movies was experienced as comic relief. Inasmuch as the radical change in the everyday life of moviegoers had led to their recoding of the movies' original messages, the war would also have a great effect on Charara's theoretical and political positions, his authorial voice, and the location from which he wrote. The sectarian form the violence took in the first few months of the war brought a very early and final disenchantment with the masses as the subjects of History and with emancipation as a horizon of political practice. Charara also radicalized and extended his earlier critique of the OCAL to encompass the Lebanese National Movement (LNM), the front of leftist and Arab nationalist parties, led by Kamal Jumblatt, who fought alongside the Palestinian resistance against the Lebanese nationalist, overwhelmingly Christian, parties.

The Lebanese National Movement: Parties of Rule or Parties of Revolution?

In the fall of 1977, a MERIP writer asked Traboulsi, "Could you give an overview of the Lebanese National Movement?" The LNM, he answered,

> seems unique in the Arab world, in that it's the first time any Arab people has come to the defense of the Palestinian resistance. We believe we are unique in that sense, but the defense of the Palestinian revolution is a Lebanese patriotic duty. We have been struggling for years to have Lebanon play its role, and pay its share in the Arab liberation movement and its anti-Zionist struggle. One characteristic of the Lebanese regime prior to the war was a very flagrant contradiction between its economic integration in the Arab world and its political and cultural isolation from the Arab world. We have struggled to put an end to this. The term "isolationist" is scientific, denoting those currents, groups and political forces that believe they can live for the rest of their lives depending economically on the Arab world while isolating themselves politically and culturally.[9] This isolation has always meant a policy not of independence but of subjugation to Western imperialists.[10]

Traboulsi leaned on Socialist Lebanon/Charara's theoretical heritage in reformulating the critique of the Lebanese system put forward in "The Two Resistances" (1969), which now became a centerpiece of the Left's wartime ideological arsenal. He also touched upon the transitional program for reforms proposed by the LNM, which "gives priority to the setting up a secular state and abolishing confessionalism in political representation. This is the most essential democratic achievement to be struggled for because it affects the interests of the wide Lebanese masses."[11] The transitional program put forward by the Left did not address the socioeconomic question.

Much later Traboulsi provides an explanation in his memoir: "Jumblatt did not want to scare the bourgeoisie, and especially its Muslim wing, since he was predicting to win it over to his program of political change; he ended up being disappointed."[12] Socialist Lebanon's early analysis of the anxiety generated by the social question in a Lebanese Left dependent on an alliance with powerful political leaders with a sectarian constituency, like Kamal Jumblatt, was, and still is, prescient.

Waddah Charara lambasted the LNM's proposal for reforming the Lebanese system. In "Reform from the Center" (November 1975), he wrote:

> If the masses are supposed to be the water that the militants ought to circulate in with the happiness of the swimming fish, in this case the "masses" in the text are the water that drowns the fish, i.e., the problem. Of what masses is the text talking about? If the question was posed before the last civil war, and notably the last two months (since mid-September), it would have seemed an exaggeration that need not be investigated. But the program seeks to mobilize masses that are sundered by a sectarian civil war as wide as the masses themselves. (*WS*, 117)

Charara in this passage borrowed Mao's exhortation to militants to relate to the people like a "fish to water" to highlight the gap separating the Left's ideological languages of representation of a unified revolutionary subject—the masses—and their sectarian divisions. "When the program talks about the 'Lebanese' masses' that are looking forward to a 'national progressive regime,'" he wrote, "it is in general talking about one group, or one direction within this *Muslim* group" (*WS*, 119). Charara reiterated in this essay his long-standing critique of top-down reform programs, instrumental modes of militancy, and external ones that kept the political outside of, and separate from, the social formation. These external modes of political party militancy, he noted, focused on seizing a share of power "without tackling its foundations, forms, and functions or concentrated on widening power in sectors that the state could not dominate" (*WS*, 132). These political parties, concluded the disenchanted Marxist, are "'political' parties, in the narrow sense of the word, i.e., **parties of rule** and not parties of **social revolution**" (*WS*, 132).[13]

Charara's harsh and minoritarian critique not only separated him politically from Fawwaz Traboulsi and Muhsin Ibrahim, who held leadership positions during the war, it also distanced him intellectually from former comrades like

Aziz al-Azmeh, the Syrian historiographer and Islamic studies scholar, who of-fered a contrasting interpretation of the events.[14] al-Azmeh offers an account that recapitulates again Charara's "The Two Resistances," the theoretical text with multiple political and academic afterlives in both Arabic and English, while arguing against the prominence of sectarian solidarities. "Through the Palestinians," he writes, "the Lebanese entity was reinserted into its Arab context and deprived of that artificial isolation which had hitherto served to maintain the political safeguards necessary for its international economic role."[15] "Attempts to set up sectarian Shi'i organizations were very short lived," al-Azmeh notes:

> The "Movement of the Disinherited" of the Imam Musa as-Sadr, as well as his military organization, Fityan Ali, had hardly got beyond a few mass rallies when the Shi'is decided they did not want to star in a bad melodrama and opted for the leadership of men like George Hawi of the CP, a Greek Orthodox from the Matn, or Fawwaz Trab[o]ulsi, of the OCAL, a Catholic from the Southern Biqaa (PF, 62).

Political radicalization did not only occur among the Shi'a but was also at the heart of the transformation of the Sunni community. "Yet it should be noted," al-Azmeh asserts, "that not all of the largely Sunni organizations took this leftward secular and radical trend" (PF, 66). That said, he continues, "such residues of traditional confessionalism are unimportant in any effective sense today yet such movements have participated emotionally and, in some cases, militarily, with the left-wing forces which are grouped around what has been termed the cause of the Palestinians" (PF, 66–7). al-Azmeh's analysis, like Charara's, takes the Lebanese sectarian communities as the units of analysis but draws the opposite conclusion by giving prominence to the ideological factor over the sectarian and to the presence of Christians at the head of communist parties whose body is considerably Shi'i.

The Breakdown of a Common World

In the introduction to *Wars of Subjugation* (1979), Charara writes, echoing Émile Durkheim, that "the war [Lebanese civil war] was a total *social fact* as much as it was a political one, and maybe more so" (WS, 10). The essays that are assembled in the book abstracted themselves from the course of events and the political divisions in order to examine "the social dimension (or the socio-historical as Castoriadis says) [which] reveals the unity of the implicit rules that govern the warring parties and tear Lebanese society apart. . . . for it was not a civil-communal [ahliyya] battle in vain, and it did not lead to a relative fusion of the different forces into two sectarian groups randomly" (ws, 11). The outbreak of the fighting revealed to Charara the close intertwining of the domain of the political with the logics of communal—sectarian, regional, familial—solidarities, which makes the labors of conceptual subsumption and ideological generalization difficult.

The "war," he observes, was in fact a multiplicity of small, local wars that cannot be subsumed under one general category. In a small country, where the citizens' sect and place of birth are inscribed on their state IDs, the act of killing, the former militant observes, is a direct unmediated act that targets for the most part "faces, names and belongings" that are well known (ws, 231). The fighting that erupted in the different parts of the country did not constitute "one, common war, rather there were as many wars as there were fronts: the war of 'Ayn al-Rummana-al-Shiyah, the war of Dikwana-Tall al-Za'tar, the war of Miryata-Irdi, the war of Tripoli-al-Qibba" (ws, 231). "If there is no doubt," Charara affirmed, "that these local wars are nurtured by common political elements, what is sure is that these common factors did not replace the local enmities and did not eliminate the harshness of revenge" (ws, 231). "Wars of Subjugation," will proceed to diagnose the multiple modalities of operation of the communal relations of solidarity, which undermine the possibilities of a politics that rests on a common, unified ideological criteria.

Charara's diagnosis of the entanglement of the political in the multiple webs of the social fabric leads him to rethink the operations of power in dialogue with Gramsci, whose work he translated, and by reactivating concepts from Ibn Khaldun's work. The Lebanese civil wars, he registers, reveal that the politics of sects, families, regions, professions, political parties, and Arab regional politics carry heterogeneous, and independent, "codes of internal relations and rules of internal hierarchy" (ws, 233). "The difference of criteria and their variety (despite the intertwinement of some of them)," he notes, "raises difficult obstacles in the face of power as hegemony and not as dominance" (ws, 233). Power qua hegemony presupposes a political leadership that generalizes an encompassing set of criteria that covers multiple professional and administrative spheres, concealing in the process the basis of its power, while dominance is content with an "an external possession of instruments of power: armed forces, administrative apparatuses, a share of production" (ws, 233). In his deployment of Gramsci to make sense of wartime practices, Charara is far from positing a stark either-or scenario, where in a particular social formation power either solely operates as hegemony or as dominance. Power operates differently depending on the different articulations of hegemony/dominance. At the deep end of the spectrum, when hegemony's capacity to generate a "common sense" is at its weakest, and the necessity of direct domination is at its apex, "power takes a form that Ibn Khaldun knew perfectly that of *iltiham* [fusion] and *istitba'* [subjugation]" (*WS*, 233).[16]

Gramsci's elaboration of his conceptual arsenal—such as hegemony, historical bloc, war of position, war of maneuver—that Charara drew on during his militant phase took place in the wake of the failure of socialist revolutions in Western Europe in the 1920s. His critique of "economism," by turning his analytical gaze to the political and ideological terrains and investigating the relationship between hegemony (consent) and domination (force), was an attempt to understand capitalist societies' sources of resilience.[17] Gramsci and Charara were both forging new concepts in the wake of political events that challenged an older theoretical understanding. That said, the Lebanese civil wars, which resulted in the fragmentation of Lebanese society into its infranational—sectarian, regional, kin—components and the breakdown of the Lebanese state, was the obverse of capitalist society's resilience against revolutionary transformation as a result of the moral and intellectual leadership of its dominant class. The external modality of power at work in Lebanese society, a formal dominance, as Charara dubbed it, does not target the internal social bonds of dominated groups. The subjugating power does not seek to fashion new subjectivities. It is content with subjugating a group or a community while leaving their internal relations, hierarchies, and codes intact.

The Lebanese civil wars were attempts at mutual subjugation while none of the warring sides engaged in attempts at interpellating actors from the opposite side of the trenches. Charara proceeds to diagnose the fighters' practices as they relate to land, bodies, and commodities with the foundational trinity of political economy in mind. It is the "deep nature" of the conflict, Charara writes, in reference to its social dimension, that accounts for its "barbarism" (*WS*, 235). In the battle for subjugation, the destruction of the adversary's material and moral forces—primarily its bodies and properties—tops the list of missions to accomplish. "The political body, when dominance [in distinction to hegemony] is in effect," Charara notes, "is not a general abstract labor power that has been emptied of its individuality, its desires, its attachments and had its power to symbolize excised, before turning it into a disciplined tool of production and consumption" (*WS*, 235). Rather, it is "a body in 'solidarity,'" a carrier of both attachments to and detachments from family, sect, and neighborhood (*WS*, 235–36). The personal body, the point of intersections of multiple attachments and detachments, then becomes the site of a semiotic interrogation with the aim of revealing the side it belongs to. In becoming a symbol, it also becomes a body for defacement and mutilation, since what the killers are after in liquidating an individual is his belonging to his sect. Defacement "is a summoning of the sect's large body" (*WS*, 236).

Concrete communal belongings that mark bodies and property mediate all relationships in a wartorn capitalist society where liquidated individuals are stabbed multiple times and property destroyed. When the body is a stand-in for communal belongings, commodities become part of "the owner's body (the owner = the sectarian group). The owner is therefore not addressed from the perspective of his position vis-à-vis power and production, and their relations" (*WS*, 236). As for land, it acquired in the conflict a "mythological 'place'" that took the form, more predominant on the Christian side, of cleansing it from "the 'foreign' patches that contaminate the pure metal" (*WS*, 237). Here, too, Charara emphasizes, that what was at work in the sectarianization of geography was not solely interest driven, functional, and pragmatic practices that are part and parcel of winning a battle. "Expulsion," he writes, "comes hand in hand with all forms of abuse, and humiliation, and the symbol regains its power and efficacy: bulldozers are used so that there is not a single wall—not even a tin wall—left standing, and empty, fissured houses are burned down by a purifying fire so that no trace of impurity is left" (*WS*, 237).

Charara's interpretations of wartime violence, which combined ideology, politics, and economics with magical and ritualistic behaviors—killing and defacing; looting and destroying; evicting and burning down to purify—led him to call into question the distinctions of social theory that are built on separating these spheres from each other. Charara noted that these distinctions—say, between magic/ritual and capitalist economies/ideological politics—are not suitable to analyzing the situation. "We were summoning up capitalist distinctions," he added, "without any critique or differentiation (even if they reached us through Marxism)" (*WS*, 238). Note that in this passage he did not refer to these distinctions as Western, modern, or Enlightenment, but as capitalist, ones. The form of Charara's critiques of Eurocentrism, like his earlier one in *Origins*, is less to show how the "universal" categories of history, social theory, and political economy cannot escape their European origins.[18] Rather, faced with the urgent question of how to interpret wartime violence, he begins by criticizing social theory's binary distinctions before turning to forging a new conceptual universe.

Charara reactivated Ibn Khaldun's concepts to account for how power operates during the Lebanese civil wars, but it was Marx that predominantly supplied the theoretical ground for why it did so. His account of the multiple and heterogeneous foci of power at work in Lebanon that foreclose the possibility of articulating a political project that abstracts itself from these sites, generalizing in the process a set of common criteria, was not a return of sorts to a theory of the essentialist culturalist attributes of Arab societies, or a historicist move emphasizing the persistence of precapitalist remainders in the present. "Is capitalism's metal (and its parliamentary democracy) different from the one the people of the backwards country, their relationships, and their world, are made [of]?" "The matter is not sure," he answers (*WS*, 239). The entanglement of the political in the social was not an account of a failed, or backward, modernity but the form modernity took in Lebanon:

> Sectarianism, familialism, and regionalism were not the "remainders" of precapitalist social relations. And while all of them were based on elements that predate capitalism, they only rose to prominence in organizing social and political life inside the movement of capitalist expansion on the one hand, and inside the formation of the Lebanese state with its frontiers, administration and hierarchies on the other hand. (*WS*, 250)

The former Marxist militant elaborated an account of the working of Lebanese capitalism that underlined the relative autonomy of small-time producers and the processes of formal subsumption of labor that boosted communal relations of solidarity by incorporating them into the relations of production. Capitalist production in Lebanon was wary of "uprooting the artisan or the peasant from their relations [of production] and from 'liberating' these producers from them" (*WS*, 239). The reason why capitalism did not eliminate the world of artisan labor and small and family-owned farming by transforming them into wage laborers "was not, of course, [because of] the sentiments of capital and its compassion." Rather, it was because the artisan and the peasant "own an effective tool of pressure on the landowner and through him on the apparatuses of rule and its politics" (*WS*, 239). If the landlord's family wishes to play any political role, it has to "grant, even if partially, peasants' demands, whether related to leasing the land or taking charge of its crops" (*WS*, 240). "Moreover, the bourgeoisie," wrote Charara, moving from the peasant-landlord relation into analyzing the constitutive features of Lebanese capitalism, "resorts to expand its sphere of exchange and to break the link that ties production to local consumption (through developing commercial capital) without resorting to stripping the peasant and the artisan of their means of production, and without paying an exorbitant political and ideological price for it, which is the formulation of a sharp class consciousness" (*WS*, 240).[19] The Lebanese commercial bourgeoisie therefore did not extract its surplus at the point of production, which was done by "autonomous" producers, but in the sphere of circulation and marketing under its control, such as by exporting to neighboring Arab countries. In the case of both the landlord-peasant relation and the bourgeois-worker relation, capital's Lebanese path did not "free" the laborers from everything but selling their labor power. Lebanese peasants and artisans retained some degree of control over their means of production, which therefore preempted the development of class consciousness.

Moreover, production units are characterized by "a weak division of labor," which means that the "labor of abstraction that capitalism performs on social relations and on labor power specifically is still preliminary" (*WS*, 243). Labor still relied on an artisanal unit of production and "the worker, in this case," added Charara, "is not transformed into an 'appendage' to the machine or production" (*WS*, 243). Therefore, inherited skill still plays its role and "the village (and kinship generally) has retained its function in professional preparation" (*WS*, 243). The dominant social relations, Charara wrote, have moved from society into the units of production, as in the cases when Lebanese capitalists make use of family hierarchies by "appointing a small-time notable in his family or village as a foreman in the factory supervising one of its divisions. And the small notable will participate in choosing some of his divisions' workers from his family or clan" (*WS*, 245). This resulted in controlling worker absenteeism and confrontations with factory owners through family relations. Moreover, the Lebanese bourgeoisie makes use of sectarianism to pit workers against each other, as when "using certain workers [from a different sect] as supervisors over others . . . and distributing wage benefits along sectarian lines; increasing wages along sectarian belonging . . . and this way, part of the workers is controlled and the other subjugated" (*WS*, 245). Therefore, "the (Lebanese) bourgeois organization of labor" concluded Charara, "consolidates at the end of the day the relations of solidarity that it seeks to subjugate" (*WS*, 245). And "if this subjugation is an essential element in its [bourgeois organization of labor] strategy, it is also simultaneously," Charara wrote, "an essential element in the workers' resistance to capitalist relations of production. And this is because subjugation preserves the familial and sectarian relations of solidarity" (*WS*, 245). While Charara noted how these relations of solidarity, which are used to control and divide workers by the bourgeoisie, work also in the opposite direction to resist the latter, recapitulating his analysis in *The Blue Pamphlet* (1973), he did so in the wake of the civil war as a detached social scientist in a constative manner. The days of militancy are over.

In the following section, entitled "Solidarity Relations against Capitalism and the State," the author wrote as if he had just realized that his analysis—springing from a Marxist ground and addressing privileged political economy themes—was entangled in what he was in the process of leaving behind. He wrote: "These phenomena [relations of solidarity] are not restricted to the domain of production (and if we emphasized their effectiveness in this particular domain, it is because this domain is privileged in the official leftist analysis, fostering deep-seated political illusions). Rather, they surpass it [the domain of production] to [affect] the different aspects of social life" (*ws*, 246).[20] That done, Charara proceeded to explore the other manifestation of these strengths and transformations of the relations of solidarity, such as in Lebanese modern cities that rearticulated the function of *iltiham* (fusion) that keeps family, and group units, cohesive, by inscribing it within a market, "which is not only different by its extension from the past one, but also in the tendency of economic values to dominate, and in its internal hierarchization depending on the relation with imperial centers, and by its inscription within state relations" (*ws*, 247).

Charara's diagnosis of the Lebanese state paralleled the one he put forward about capitalist production. The loyalty to the state remained a "formal" one that does "not touch the internal relations of these groupings, and does not work on changing their forms and logics, despite the transformations it effects on their general function" (*ws*, 251). This "formal adherence" had serious consequences for the state, which had to share its citizens' loyalty and its sovereignty on its own territory with

> the leaders of family-regional-sectarian groups and their blocs, with the *millet* blocs and their councils and institutions (hospitals, property and schools), with the armed wings of these blocs (armed clans, armed strongmen, militias), in addition to the rule's retinue, and the agents or friends of civilian and military apparatuses that are concerned with "general" security, i.e., the sharing of allegiances leads to the sharing of organized and legitimate violence with the state—which is the one that "should" monopolize this violence, in a legal framework that generalizes the European experience. (*ws*, 251–52)

It was in opposition to this *common* modality of power that governs and divides Lebanese society and reaches its maximal limits in times of civil war that Charara proposed, fleetingly, without much elaboration, the *logic* of the state:

"and one cannot transition from the logic of subjugation to the logic of the state but through a different socio-historical foundation" (*WS*, 12). The former Maoist militant retains his apprehension of top-down politics, however. Transitioning to the logic of the state cannot be the result of a political imposition from above. The problem is that this sentence does not designate a subject that could potentially lay this new foundation.

Charara's formulation of the question of the social fabric primarily in the guise of sectarianism in the beginning of the civil war not only entailed the acknowledgment of the primacy of these communal solidarities in the face of ideological programs. More importantly, it attempted to underscore how these forms of solidarity were transformed historically and produced and reproduced in the present. "Killing, pillaging, defacing, and destroying," Charara underscored, "are at the heart of our contemporary 'traditions and habits' . . . and are not remainders from the past but are constitutive of the present we build every day" (*WS*, 230). *Wars of Subjugation* was a hard-hitting intervention against the attempts of the Right and the Left to evade responsibility for sectarian violence that drew on nationalist/culturalist and historicist registers, such as these acts are not part of "our traditions"; these are "mistakes" on the way to building bright futures; these are a consequence of "precapitalist remainders" that will soon melt into thin air.

In *Origins* (1975), the Lebanese sectarian structure was the paradoxical outcome of the masses' political practice, while in *Wars of Subjugation* the political could not escape the communal—sectarian, regional, and family—structure.[21] In order to avoid falling back on a metaphysical cultural essentialism that reifies sectarianism, Charara, as we just saw, emphasizes the modernity of these relations and grounds his account in a Marxian account of Lebanese capitalism's trajectory—formal subsumption—and the formation of Lebanon's sectarian state, as well as the rearticulation of these forms of solidarity in the wake of rural-urban migrations and their insertion in a capitalist economy. The arguments of the two books can be schematically represented in the following way. *Origins*: masses/hegemony/diachrony/history, and *Wars of Subjugation*: social fabric/dominance-subjugation/synchrony/structure.

Charara's works right before and right after the war articulate two notions of the political that are in tension with each other. The first is a celebration of the masses' autonomous political practice that remakes their world as it refashions their own subjectivities. It is a romantic, populist notion that highlights the primacy, autonomy, and creativity of political practice from below. It is anchored in a critique of the division between manual and intellectual labor and of top-down and instrumental politics, whether carried out by states, leftist parties, organizations, or experts. The second notion, which is implicitly articulated in *Wars of Subjugation*, pits the logic of the state against the civil war's logic of subjugation. It reasserts the need for a politics that is grounded in common criteria that rise above the particularities of infranational communal solidarities. Ahmad Beydoun captured Charara's oscillation between a militant celebration of the autonomy of the political against the instrumental top-down practice of organizations and a disenchanted observation of its entanglement in the social fabric in the title of his review of *Wars of Subjugation*: "Waddah Charara: 'The Democracy' of the State or 'The Depth' of Freedom?"[22] Beydoun returned to, and rearticulated, Charara's oscillation as one between *"la politique-expression"* (a politics-as-expression) of the revolutionary subjects' practice and *"la politique-maîtrise"* (politics-as-mastery) of the murderous infranational divisions of the social fabric by a transcendent state.[23]

From Zahi Cherfan to Waddah Charara: Death of an Organic Intellectual, Birth of a Ṣuʿlūk

The opening passage of *Wars of Subjugation*, in its literary tone, its references to Buñuel, Dalí, and *Bloody Mama*, bears witness to a departure in form, content—the artistic references—and the locus of enunciation in the writings of one of the most influential New Left Marxist militant intellectuals of his generation. In October 1974, seven months before the outbreak of the civil wars, Zahi Cherfan—Waddah Charara's pseudonym—wrote the following:

> Just from enumerating some of the new phenomena [one can realize] the extent of actual victories that the student movement achieved in facing the authorities. Some of its elements, in Beirut, Baalbek, Saida, Tyre, Nabatieh and Tripoli no longer bother with the democratic legality and its interior minister. These elements no longer stand vulnerable in the face of oppression forces trained by the authorities to exert direct bodily violence, and no longer believe that violence is a monopoly of the reactionary authorities in the service of stability, the hotels, and the factory owners. (*WS*, 147)[24]

In this passage, Charara evaluated a certain line of action undertaken by the student movement, while taking it "upon himself to rectify 'deviations'" in its path.[25] Less than a year before the outbreak of the war, his coordinates on the political plane are precise. Charara/Cherfan is writing from a militant leftist position, critically assessing the movement so that its actions may yield more fruitful results in the future. The militant imagined his community of readers and the role his written interventions were predicated to play. Ahmad Beydoun outlined the contours of the militant position Cherfan/Charara occupied: "There is a good thing that is starting and we have to make sure to put it on the right track.... Obstacles on the way are numerous, and the errors we committed and those we may commit are likely not the product of chance.... But it is unacceptable that our efforts come to an end ... or to put it briefly 'there is always something that can be done' (Sartre)."[26] Beydoun, who also withdrew from leftist practice at the beginning of the war, alluded to how Charara's militant position "exacts from the text a heavy theoretical price," noting that it "seems forced to 'pave' the ground under the feet of the student movement to the extent of surprising whoever reads 'Wars of Subjugation.'"[27]

Charara's earlier prewar essays, either unsigned or written under his pseudonym, were activist interventions. They were analyses of specific situations geared toward either evaluating a certain line of action or formulating political positions, and at times they were used as theoretical education texts. When writing was in the direct service of the people's cause, it de facto excluded certain subjects and forms that might detract from the pressing and primordial political task. It left no room for the militant writer to dabble in analogies, artistic references, and a prose that might eat away at its political yield by distracting the reader. Linguistic "flourish" may detract from the seriousness of the matter, relegating the militant to the status of an intellectual who tinkers with culture in distinction to a revolutionary who formulates political positions. Moreover, Charara adds, "Why use these metaphors when you were convinced that analysis that takes for its base economics and grand transformations is self-sufficient? Its intelligibility is within it. So why borrow and use analogies from other fields like cinema, theater, poetry?"[28]

One of the first pieces Charara wrote after he put an end to militancy was a text in two parts relating his experience as a public school teacher. It weaves together autobiographical threads, an analysis of the Lebanese educational system, and a close observation of the minutiae of power relations inside schools as well as insightful comparisons between schools and political parties.[29] We have come a long way from the unsigned articles of Socialist Lebanon. Not only did Charara's prose become denser with analogies, casting a much wider net of references, but he also moved from not signing texts at all and using a pseudonym to writing autobiographical pieces. Engaging in this genre of writing would have been unimaginable, or, if that is too strong, unlikely only a few months earlier, when he was still one foot soldier of History, albeit a distinguished one, among others.[30] Wartime disenchantment established the conditions of possibility of thinking and writing about his personal and collective pasts, distilling experiences into texts as well as venturing into new registers of political analysis, subjects, and styles of writing.[31]

In "Marxism and Form," a review essay mostly addressing *Spectrum*, a collection of texts by Perry Anderson, Stefan Collini observes how in the 1960s and 1970s, when "it was possible for Anderson and his collaborators to believe that history was on their side, that the proper union of intellectual labor and working class militancy would help bring about the socialist supersession of capitalism," Anderson's writing "did not feel the need to make any concessions to those who were uninitiated theoretically or unsympathetic politically."[32] "The task was too urgent," he adds, "the stakes too high, and in any case the 'bourgeois' media were too complicit with capitalism and its political outriders."[33] While these essays retain their brilliance today, Collini continues, "one cannot help noticing how the whiff of sectarianism, of laying down the 'correct' line *now* hangs about some of these articles like stale cigarette smoke."[34] In going over Anderson's trajectory, Collini, the intellectual historian, notes that with the changes in the political landscape taking place in the 1980s and 1990s, a time when it became much less convincing to think that history was on one's side, Anderson "appears to have undergone something of a political or intellectual crisis . . . leading not just to reassess the prospects of the left in a world dominated by neo-liberalism but also, one may infer, to reconsider the function of his own writing."[35] He then asks, "Yet to what readership, so much of the world having changed, does Anderson now address himself, and from what vantage point, so many of the old doctrinal certainties having shriveled, does he now write?" Collini answers, "Olympian universalism," a designation that he sees fitting Anderson's commitment to Enlightenment reason and the scope of his work. Anderson is a "universalist in the geographical as well as philosophical sense, attending impartially to developments in all parts of the world."[36]

Collini's review reminds us that transformations in intellectual labor accompanying the ebbing away of the 1960s revolutionary tides are not an exclusively Arab affair. Having said that, if Anderson reinvented himself as an Olympian universalist, for whom and from where was Charara writing after his disenchantment? The first person plural Charara uses throughout *Wars of Subjugation* is, to say the least, problematic. Who does this fictitious "we" refer to? It cannot refer to the Lebanese Left since he is overtly critical of it. Moreover, his exit from the Left was not accompanied by a right-wing conversion. To put this loss of identification in the words of Ahmad Beydoun, whose ties to Charara were strong at the time, "we were forced," he recalls, "as a result of the *diagnosis* to take a great distance from the National and Palestinian camp, and of course [regarding] the other camp [the right-wing and Christian parties] it was taken for granted. So, we found ourselves . . . against all sides. Very early on, there was an impossibility of identification with any of the sides in the war, because of the war itself."[37]

The shift from class-based investigations into the conceptualization of communal relations of solidarity led to a reconfiguration of Charara's style of critical analysis, his theoretical universe, his horizon of expectation, and his redefinition of the function of intellectuals. It dislocated power from its previous possessors, the dominant classes and the state, to lodge it in the logic of the social fabric. The Lebanese civil war ended the militants' wagers on designating a revolutionary subject that will carry out the task of emancipation. The acknowledgment of the incapacity to a carry out an autonomous, common political project that is not enmeshed in the logics of communal solidarity signaled the unraveling of a utopian future of emancipation as the horizon of expectation of political practice.[38] Consequently, Charara developed a form of immanent critique and rearticulated the role of the intellectual in congruence with the substitution of class by community. The critic is the one who took up the role of "unmasking subjugation whenever it is cloaked with 'modern' ideologies or *asala* [authenticity]" (*WS*, 12). This rearticulation of the role of intellectuals as unmaskers of the logics of practice that lie beneath the surface of political discourse, regardless of its ideological colors, led to a stance of "permanent critique." This is not, he asserts, because of an incapacity "to be 'positive,' but because it is hard to articulate division and contradiction in the language of *belonging* that shortly after will turn into multiple oratory arts: laudation, eulogy and satire" (*WS*, 12). "The war," recalls Ahmad Beydoun, "very early on revealed itself to be a new situation, a new story, a new logic. It was over [for us]. We could not work in this situation, so we started to become 'individuals' (*afrad*), we disbanded, and each of us, approximately, became by himself."[39]

In the opening paragraph of his review of *Wars of Subjugation*, Beydoun highlighted the minoritarian position occupied by Charara who "stands alone in a desolate tight spot," who does not abide by the rules of production of Lebanese political discourses. "For amongst the protocols of competition in this field—cluttered with dullness," adds Beydoun sarcastically, "is that the valiant knight does not stand aside, but always in a *known group*, never reaching the battleground having forgotten his father's name, because he has to declare his linage before attacks and retreats: 'I am Ali son of Hussein son of Ali. . . .' And Waddah Charara has no lineage . . . or at least he declares that what he is saying cannot be spoken in the 'language of affiliation.'"[40] Beydoun's text brought out the solitary and impossible position Charara occupied by writing from a nonaffiliated position in the first years of the war, noting the refusal of engagement with his work. Lebanese political languages, he wrote "are fences, and no one is interested in getting closer to another—through dialogue—or bringing him closer. . . . And Zayd's son and 'Amr's son may fight and later become like brothers again. However, neither fighting nor fraternizing owes anything to the rhymes [ahajiz] they exchange between them."[41] Beydoun reactivated the vocabulary of Arab patrilineal lineages to describe the fragmentation of shared spaces and idioms of public discourse, when in times of war texts like a coat of arms bear the insignia of the "tribe." The passing of the "masses" went hand in hand with those who seek to represent them, the family of organic and vanguardist intellectuals. The organic intellectual was dead and replaced by the tribe's poet singing his kin's glories. Charara and Ahmad Beydoun were among the first of this cohort of militant intellectuals to become "individualized" in reference to their double dissent from their leftist political parties and their communities. They refused, after their disenchantment with the Left, to retreat into the fold of sectarian identities, which would have entailed for both of them to start writing as Shi'i intellectuals, not necessarily from within the religious Shi'i tradition but from within the sectarian perspective of the community's interests.

In his historiographical magnum opus, Beydoun associated the standpoint of the critical historian who does not seek to write Lebanese history from the standpoint of his own community with that of the sa'alik in the pre-Islamic and early Islamic era. If Charara's sociological immanent critique took the form of unmasking the logics of subjugation that are cloaked in a multiplicity of ideological languages, whether secular or religious, Beydoun's develops a historical form. The critical historian in his reading is the one who steers away from writing a history whose matrix is the "ego-ideal" of the community. Immanent historical critique is another name for the disjunction between the community's own narrative of itself and the historian's account. This disjunction, writes Beydoun, "transforms the historian into an individual; that is, into a su'luk, in the old tribal terminology. We prefer the term su'luk to 'citizen,' which was invented by the French Revolution." This is because in Beydoun's account the labor of abstraction that produces the "citizen" through abstracting him from his attachments, and inserting him in a world of interchangeable citizens, did not take place. This individual qua historian is the exception and not the norm, which makes him a su'luk. That said, continues Beydoun, "he did not fall from a cloud. He finds his place of birth in a relatively recent social sphere; this lumpen-State (the actual State) that is at the crossroads of the communitarian lines of struggle, and that tends, in reality or ideally, to separate itself from these lines. The communitarian historian weaves a totally smooth, total myth. The individual-historian is led by his methodology to put his finger on the fault lines of communitarian myths."[42]

Beydoun provides an alternative genealogy of the critical, dissenting "individual-historian" away from an account of modernity that emphasizes the coming into being of a society characterized by abstraction, commensurability, and interchangeability whose political form entails equality between citizens. The shape of Lebanon's postcolonial modernity renders the "individual-historian," who is the product of the modern "Lumpen State," closer to the pre-Islamic sa'alik, outcasts who, either by choice or expulsion, were no longer members of their tribes. Beydoun's association of the critic with the individual qua su'luk, in the wake of Marxist disenchantment, is the Lebanese answer to Anderson's "Olympian universalism." It urges us to inquire into the political, social, and economic conditions of possibility of adopting an "Olympian universalism." Another way of putting this is to ask, from where can you adopt an Olympian position? And to whom? The critic as su'luk is another acknowledgment of the difficulty of articulating a critical discourse that could assume a hegemonic function in a wartorn, communally divided country, where there are no "citizens" and no common political community.

In Charara's case as well, the acknowledgment of the multiplicity of criteria of power, which work according to the logic of subjugation and preempt the formation of a hegemonic political Left, steered his critical project in new directions and into new forms of articulating critique. In the wake of his observation of the failure of political abstraction and commensurability, and the incongruity of wartime practices with the categories of social and political theory, Charara relinquished the labors of theoretical abstraction that seek to conceptually subsume the discourses and practices it studies. This new modality of critique builds on Charara's Maoist phase, during which he also discovered the empirical richness of al-Jabarti's historical works, which clearly revealed to him the poverty of the theoretical discourses of towering contemporary Arab thinkers—such as Abdallah Laroui—and scholars of the Arab world who sought to subsume a very rich, contingent, and contradictory history under a few concepts.[43] In the wake of the war and his exit from militantism, he leaned on his Jabartian-Maoist heritage to fashion a form of immanent critique that confronted the coherence of the self-proclaimed discourses of political parties and communities with the contingency and multiplicity of historical events, discourses, logics, and practices that fashioned them. This form of immanent critique, as it is put to use, for instance, in Charara's detailed work of historical sociology on the formation and rise of Hizbullah, the Lebanese Shi'i militant party, and its ensuing clout over its community bears a number of traits in common with Nietzschean/Foucauldian genealogies.[44] It seeks to disrupt the coherence of the account the group, in this case the Shiʻi Islamist military party, gives of itself, emphasizing contingent events that led to its formation, destabilizing the certainties of the group's own version of its rise and subsequent achievements. In brief, it seeks to emphasize the contingent, historical, prosaic elements in contrast to the heroic and epic dimensions in the Islamist political party's own self-image.

Charara's texts are notoriously difficult partly because of the author's methodological dictate to stay as close as possible to the thickness and dispersion of the materials he is working with. It is a reflexive method that strives toward finding the most adequate form to represent the modern transformations and fragmentations of societies divided by communal solidarities. If political universals, in the form of hegemonic projects, are preempted by proliferating logics of subjugation that tear states, societies, and institutions apart, preventing the formation of a totality, then it would be difficult to apprehend the state of division through a set of abstract universal concepts that pretend to subsume these incommensurable multiplicities. The end product is a chameleonic language that is differently colored by the language and internal references of the materials it is working through. Ibn ʻArabi's precept "Know your God, the Knowledge of a Chameleon" became one of Charara's methodological guiding lights.[45]

Orphans of the revolution, Charara and Beydoun became Lebanese citizens in a wartorn polis and "public intellectuals," without a public at the beginning of the war. Their early disenchantment and articulation of the centrality of communal solidarities during the civil war raises historiographical, theoretical, and political questions. First, it calls into question the predominant historiographical signposts that are deployed in writing histories of the international and Arab Left that seek to ground their narratives in landmarks that supposedly parallel the internationalism of the tradition and those events that are elevated to the rank of global events—the implosion of the Soviet Union. These sweeping narratives associated their global historiographical markers with grand ideological shifts as well: Marxism to liberal democracy or to neoliberalism.

Second, it raises the theoretical question of where do you fashion a critical project from, and how you do it, once you acknowledge that community is the problem, so to speak, without becoming a liberal, like some of their former comrades. The sociological and historical immanent critiques they formulated retained at their core Marx's commitment to the formulation of a reflexive critique. Unlike liberalism's grounds of persuasion, which rest on a belief in the context-less universalism of reason, the Marxian tradition emphasized that the persuasiveness of ideas "depended on historical and situational factors like *class*."[46] It is the Marxian tradition's "emphasis on the social mediation of rational plausibility" that generates its deep theoretical engagement with the question of translation, which, through its theoretical mapping of a society's mode of production, social structure, and so on, ought to guide emancipatory political practice.[47] In noting that community displaced class as the main category of social mediation, they inhabited the difficult position where they couldn't fall back on a liberal celebration of context-less reason, while their own theorization also foreclosed the possibility of Marxist emancipatory political practice. It is this attachment to reflexivity after the passing of revolutionary hopes that makes them, to me at least, more sophisticated and interesting than Arab and non-Arab Marxists who, like Perry Anderson, retreated to an Olympian universalism and a defense of abstract, context-less reason against authoritarianism and religious politics.

In becoming critics of communal relations of subjugation and the mytho-histories Lebanese communities spin about themselves, their reflexive critical practices, which took stock of their diagnosis of the difficulty of economic and political abstraction, moved away from critical theory's powers of conceptual subsumption. Their critiques became increasingly distant from the critical theory that they spent the past two decades of their lives reading, translating, and writing. Paradoxically, it is their commitment to reflexivity and to diagnosing the contours of their present, which they developed during Socialist Lebanon's days, that contributed to marginalizing them from the cosmopolitan world of traveling theory, as they increasingly articulated critique in a sociological and historical mode. This is why I focused on *Wars of Subjugation* and Beydoun's sharp reading of it. This volume marks Charara's initial movement away from Marxist concepts and into his Khaldunian-inspired analysis of the logics of operation of communal solidarities. In it one detects the movement of thought at critical hinge-moments, when the labor of beginnings, of clearing the conceptual ground, and making the case for a new interpretive idiom is performed on the ground of, and by engaging, the earlier—Marxian—one. The traces of these labors would soon vanish from view, erasing the historicity of the problem-space from what would become a normalized paradigm had initially emerged.

Last but not least, their diagnosis raises questions that still plague Lebanese political practice. If community is the main category of social mediation, and the logics of subjugation are still at work to varying degrees depending on the local, regional, and international conjunctures between the different communities, then engaging in politics always entails deciding whether practice ought to be articulated from within these communities' boundaries while relying on their solidarities, or outside of them, like the 1960s Left half attempted to do. I say half because its autonomy was compromised with its alliance with the more powerful Kamal Jumblatt, who had a double life, one inside and the other outside the Lebanese sectarian system. Jumblatt's duality was nicely captured by a distinguished representative of the prewar establishment's political club. In the aftermath of the last parliamentary elections before the war (1972), Saeb Salam, four-time prime minister of Lebanon, said of Jumblatt, who was awarded the Lenin Peace Prize by the Soviet Union (1972): "We welcome Kamal Jumblatt, the son of the noble Lebanese house and the leader of the esteemed sect [the Druze]. We, however, utterly refuse to deal with him as a promoter of strikes and sabotage and the protector of the Left and communism, and the exploiter of popular causes."[48]

Coda—Marxism in Crisis: Antitotalitarianism, Nationalism, and Post-Marxism

The first years of the Lebanese civil war in 1975 coincided with the antitotalitarian moment in the French intellectual field that cut short the leftist and Third Worldist militancy of the 1960s' shifting intellectual and political preoccupations to the support of dissenters from the Soviet Union and issues of human rights. In *Wars of Subjugation* Charara digressed a little from the diagnosis of wartime violence to ironically note that if the capitalist metropoles practiced their "barbarism in 'Sun My' or 'My Lai', that's imperialism. . . . The Archipelagoes of political concentration on the other hand do not concern us, for we are in the national democratic phase, and we befriend those who befriend us, like Vietnam" (*WS*, 227).[49] I was intrigued by the use of "Archipelagoes" in this fleeting critique of the Left's silence on the violence perpetrated by its own camp, and whether it was a reference to Alexander Solzhenitsyn's *The Gulag Archipelago*. Charara, it turned out, had read the book on his rooftop in Burj Hammud as soon as it came out in French, during his years of Maoist militancy (June 1974).[50] The publication of *The Gulag Archipelago* had a tremendous effect on France's intellectual field:

> Unable to ignore so unimpeachable a source, Dreyfus and Dostoevsky in one, non-Communist intellectuals underwent a Damascene conversion. The scales fell from their eyes, exposing them not only to the true

enormity of "real socialism," but to the realization that the worm was in the bud. Not Stalin or Lenin, but Marx—and, in a flight backwards, Hegel and Rousseau (possibly Plato)—was the progenitor of the *univers concentrationnaire*. Contra Sartre, [Raymond] Aron, Camus and Castoriadis had been right all along.[51]

The "gulag effect" was spearheaded by former militant intellectuals of different generations. Both Claude Lefort (1924–2010), a student of Merleau-Ponty's and cofounder with the Greek polymath and revolutionary Cornelius Castoriadis of Socialisme ou Barbarie (1949–65), and the younger André Glucksmann (1937–2015), member of La Gauche Prolétarienne (1968–73), produced book-long essays on Solzhenitsyn.[52] The two commentaries "reprimanding other intellectuals for not listening to Solzhenitsyn, and developing political philosophies proclaimed in his name . . . were highly influential in the developing critique of totalitarianism."[53] The Solzhenitsyn years, from the mid- to late 1970s, left their mark on newspapers (*Le Nouvel Observateur*), journals (*Esprit*), and scholarly works such as that of the anthropologist Pierre Clastres and on François Furet's influential *Penser La Révolution Française* (1978).[54] Michel Foucault's oeuvre also stands witness to the mood of the age. The first edition of Foucault's *Discipline and Punish* (1975) "compares the Gulag and the West's disciplinary institutions, which he describes as an 'archipel carcéral.'"[55] The new media "stars," a number of whom were former '68ers, of this anti-Marxist intellectual movement who became known as "les nouveaux philosophes" made the cover story of *Time Magazine* in the autumn of 1977 with the title "Marx Is Dead," the international press "betraying evident pleasure at the discovery (at long last!) of a group of young, handsome and militantly anti-Marxist French intellectuals."[56]

Back in Beirut, the circuits of traveling revolutionary theory and militants were also interrupted, although it was less as a result of theoretico-political waves. The fragmentation of the subject and agent of revolution along communal lines and the resurgence of identitarian binaries in the wake of the Iranian Revolution foreclosed both the politics of internationalist solidarity and the mediation between theory and practice that the earlier practices of translation and transfiguration had enabled. A decade had passed since the Marxist and anticolonial publications published by Maspero were read, discussed, and translated by eager twenty-something men and women in Socialist Lebanon circles. In the early 1980s, François Maspero ended up selling his publishing house, which became Éditions la Découverte, after he stipulated that the name be changed. The internationalist circuit of Left traveling militants also came to a halt. The Dziga Vertov Group, which included the Swiss-French director Jean-Luc Godard, spent three months in 1970 shooting in Palestinian refugee camps in Syria, Jordan, and Lebanon in preparation for a film in support of the revolution that was to be titled "Til Victory: Thinking and Working Methods of the Palestinian Revolution." It was commissioned, and partially funded, by the Information Service Bureau of Fatah. In mid-1980s Beirut, after the Iranian Revolution in 1979, the defeat of the Palestinian resistance (1982), and the increasing inter- and intracommunal divisions, circulating was fraught with many more dangers for westerners, including potential kidnappings by the newly formed Islamist groups.

These political transformations, which had started to bring the earlier decades of Marxist internationalist militancy to an end, were not confined to the Arab or Muslim worlds. In the first lines of *Imagined Communities* (1983), Benedict Anderson, working from another part of the world, revealed how nationalism, one of the perennial thorns in Marxism's side, had made another cut in the leftist internationalist fabric:

> Perhaps without being much noticed yet, a fundamental transformation in the history of Marxism and Marxist movements is upon us. Its most visible signs are the recent wars between Vietnam, Cambodia and China. These wars are of world-historical importance because they are the first to occur between regimes whose independence and revolutionary credentials are undeniable, and because none of the belligerents has made more than the most perfunctory attempts to justify the bloodshed in terms of a recognizable *Marxist* theoretical perspective.[57]

The globally interconnected world, united by the ideological coordinates of emancipation from capitalism and imperialism and fashioned by the internationalist solidarity networks of militants and the labors of conceptual transfiguration, had begun its disintegration from different corners.

Charara's wartime theory of the difficulty of achieving hegemony in societies that are deeply divided along communal lines, where it is difficult to separate political practice from the social foundations on which it rises, reveals the limits of post-Marxist theories that, in the mid-1980s, supplemented the last great Marxist debates of the 1970s. These theories, and here I have in mind Ernesto Laclau and Chantal Mouffe's distinguished contributions, sought to move beyond a class essentialism by deconstructing and reactivating Marxist categories and dissociating the notion of antagonism from its class referent.[58] As a result, the political actors and social movements that can potentially carry out emancipatory struggles have been multiplied, beyond the contradiction between Labor and Capital and the proletariat as the presupposed universal subject of revolution. Laclau and Mouffe's theoretical project rested on asserting the autonomy of political activity and a hegemony that constituted a politically specific universality as a result of a contingent articulating practice:

> As we argue, only one particularity whose body is split, for without ceasing to be its own particularity, it transforms its body in the representation of a universality transcending it (that of the equivalential chain). This relation, by which a certain particularity assumes the representation of a universality entirely incommensurable with it, is what we call a hegemonic relation. As a result, its universality is a contaminated universality: (1) it lives in this unresolvable tension between universality and particularity; (2) its function of hegemonic universality is not acquired for good but is, on the contrary, always reversible. Although we are no doubt radicalizing the Gramscian intuition in several respects, we think that something of the sort is implicit in Gramsci's distinction between corporative and hegemonic class.[59]

Charara's analysis signaled the difficulty of a hegemonic articulation in a political terrain saturated by communal solidarities that form an integral part of capitalist relations of production and of the modus operandi of the workings of the Lebanese state. *Origins of Sectarianism* signaled the difficulty of the Maronites in the twentieth century both to represent their own interests and to craft a hegemonic pro-Western Lebanese nationalism that is economically integrated into, and politically separated from, its Arab surroundings. The clashes of 1958 and the wars that began in the mid-1970s bear witness to that. More recently, Hizbullah, the militant Shi'i Islamist political party and militia, attempted to articulate a hegemonic vision of Lebanon along the lines of its own agenda of a "Culture of Resistance," in alignment with the Syrian and Iranian regimes, against the Israeli breaches of Lebanese sovereignty and the dictates of US foreign policy. In all of these cases, the condition that Laclau and Mouffe describe, in which a "particular social force assumes the representation of a totality that is radically incommensurable with it" to form a "hegemonic universality," failed. The divisions of the Lebanese state along its confessional lines, by enmeshing political practice in the multiple webs of the social fabric, ensured the prevalence of multiple countervailing powers that has till now foreclosed the emergence of dictatorial or authoritarian regimes, such as the ones ruling neighboring Arab countries. The obverse of that coin is that those same countervailing powers, whether they are represented in the state apparatus or not, have, through their mutual attempts at subjugating each other, produced a constant oscillation between civil wars and "cold civil-communal peace"—and thus have so far preempted the formation of a totality that could be represented by a particular political force.[60]

6. TRAVELING THEORY AND POLITICAL PRACTICE

Orientalism in the Age of the Islamic Revolution

> I speak of "occidentosis" as of tuberculosis. But perhaps it more closely resembles an infestation of weevils. Have you seen how they attack wheat? From the inside. The bran remains intact, but it is just a shell, like a cocoon left behind on a tree.
> —JALAL AL-E AHMAD

> Our culture was felt to be of a lower grade.
> —EDWARD SAID

> My dear friends, you should know that the danger from the communist powers is not less than America. . . . Both superpowers have risen for the obliteration of the oppressed nations and we should support the oppressed people of the world.
> —AYATOLLAH RUHOLLAH KHOMEINI

In the span of a few years (1972–76), as he confronted organizational crises at the heart of the OCAL he helped found (1970–), militant setbacks (1972–73), and the eruption of fighting (1975–), Waddah Charara attempted to take stock of the fast-paced unfolding of events he took part in, and observed, in a politically saturated, polarized society. Leaning on theoretical resources from the Marxist tradition Charara's works from that period called into question the Left's theories of the workings of capitalism and sectarianism in Lebanon. In his late militant years (1973–75) Charara's populist Maoism first turned "backwardness into an advantage" by celebrating the revolutionary potential of the masses as they are, enmeshed in their communal forms of solidarity in their neighborhoods, outside of an imaginary idea of the "factory worker" devoid of attachments.[1] He attempted to resolve the militant's conundrum by stretching the notion of class struggle so that it encompasses communal solidarities while acknowledging how including these forms redefines the notion, foreclosing the possibility of emancipatory teleology. Second, it showed the founding paradox at the heart of modern Lebanon, by underscoring how sectarianism is a modern outcome of nineteenth-century Maronite peasants' struggle against their lords.

Both these accounts celebrate and highlight the primacy of political practice from below and, in *Origins of Sectarian Lebanon*, its capacity to fashion subjectivities and new military, economic, and political forms of organization. The autonomy of the political, and of the masses' own initiatives, were advanced as an internal, minoritarian, oppositional argument against top-down organizational forms, and against vanguardist and instrumental political practices. It also targeted a common Marxist theoretical trope that takes the form of designating the agent, for example, capitalism or the Palestinian revolution, that will get rid of difference—sectarianism as a brake on revolutionary politics—and pave the way for a "difference-free" emancipatory political practice. After the outbreak of the fighting, he underlined again the poverty of social and political theory in accounting for the logics of power, and the forms of violence, at work during civil wars.[2] Ibn Khaldun's accounts of fusion and subjugation supplemented Mao's and Gramsci's emphasis on the political and the operations of hegemony. Charara moved from a celebration of the autonomy of the political will of the masses against a vanguardist Marxism to the practical realization of the structural primacy of the social fabric over the political and the ideological. This last move foreclosed the hope of an emancipation-to-come. Political practice no longer made History. It became hostage of the social fabric's structural times of repetition.

Charara inhabited an impossible position that did not easily align itself with the axes of theoretical and political positioning either in Arab cultural spheres or in the Western academy. It was an anti-anti-imperialist political position that articulated an immanent critique of communal politics—and adopted a genealogical approach to the history of Arab societies and discourses while leaning on their own theoretical resources—coupled with a muted attachment to a horizon of emancipation from the communal logics of subjugation. It was, at one and the same time, *politically* critical of the Left and subsequent Islamist militant anti-imperialist forces, *theoretically* Arab-Islamic, and *normatively* attached to an overcoming of the permanent civil wars produced by the logics of subjugation. Charara's impossible position will be at odds with the anti-imperialism of diasporic thinkers, like Edward Said, who subjected the West's knowledges of the non-West to critical scrutiny, revealing their entanglement with power, and of the majority of his former comrades at home who splintered in different political directions in the wake of the fragmentation of the revolutionary subject into its infranational communal solidarities and the high tides of militant Islamist political practices after the Iranian Revolution in 1979.

This chapter takes the critical reception of Said's *Orientalism* as its focal point, to chart the theoretical and political divergences that separated Left militant intellectuals at home from diasporic critics who were initially brought together by their support of, and engagement with, the Palestinian revolution in the wake of the 1967 defeat. In doing so, I also highlight Charara's solitary position along these cardinal axes that came to delimit the different positions of thinkers and intellectuals. Charara's critiques of Eurocentrism, and the modernizing distinctions of social theory that separate myth and ritual from politics and economics in the face of the salience of communal forms of solidarity, have much in common with Arab diasporic modalities of criticism and with the South Asian ones that will inaugurate the field of postcolonial studies in the Anglophone academies. Having said that, these agendas of criticism, operating in different problem-spaces and arising from different personal and political experiences and sensibilities, will become increasingly at odds with each other. For instance, both Charara and Ranajit Guha, the inspiration behind the Subaltern Studies collective, who were also influenced by Gramsci's and Mao's thought, used the same expression, "dominance without hegemony," to diagnose their respective postcolonial modernities. Having said that, this term does different labors for these two thinkers. For Guha, "dominance without hegemony" is imbricated within a historical project critical of the postcolonial state that reveals the continuities between the rule of colonial and national elites. Charara's argument in *Wars of Subjugation* about the imbrication of the political in the social was formulated in the aftermath of the state's breakdown and the acknowledgment of the impossibility of revolutionary practice during a sectarian civil war. As the subaltern historians posited the subaltern as the new revolutionary subject, Charara was affirming the impossibility of identification with any of the warring parties.[3]

Charara's critique of the Lebanese and Palestinian anti-imperialist Left, and his focus on the logics of subjugation and the mutating resilience of forms of social solidarity, will come to clash with the anti-imperialist critique of Eurocentrism that singled out the epistemological layer for criticism, catching like wildfire in the wake of Said's *Orientalism* (1978). This critique unmasked how Western concepts, artworks, traditions, and disciplines reified non-Western difference and marked it as inferior and backward. It revealed the entanglement of representations of non-Europeans in the colonial enterprise. These critical strategies also showed how modern "universal" categories could never escape their own European particular origins. Therefore, their deployment across the globe by Westerners and non-Westerners was not part and parcel of a universal process of modernization but an imperial act of epistemological and ontological violence. To put it briefly, they injected history into the culturalist reifications of Orientalists to undo the exceptionalism of the "Orient" and foregrounded the culturalism of unmarked universal categories. Both these strategies are acts of theoretical anti-imperialism—they are defensive vis-à-vis non-Western societies and extend the critique of Western imperialism beyond the economic and the political to the discursive.

The critical works of Said and Charara, who were both writing in the mid- to late 1970s, shared an important feature. They both sidelined the ideological dimension of the political by uncovering deeper and more fundamental planes than the ideological one that organizes the difference between Left and Right, progressives and reactionaries. They did it from different angles, though. The first showed how, in practice, the political could not extricate itself from the *social fabric*, while the second argued in theory how it could not extricate itself from *discourse*. The primacy of the social fabric, and of the discursive, sidelined the political and rendered the ideological more or less epiphenomenal to what came to be posited as a deeper structural ground. Moreover, both authors posited that modalities of operation of the social fabric, and of Orientalist discourses, managed to both transform themselves historically while reproducing themselves. The communal forms of solidarities are modernity's offspring, whose articulation is transformed with the modern state, capitalist penetration, and urbanization, while retaining their function. *Orientalism*, in Said's text, can digest and incorporate works by different traditions and authors—for example, Oswald Spengler, Darwinism, the Freudian tradition—and transform itself from textual hermeneutics to area studies modernization theories while retaining its structural knowledge-power features.

This is where similarities end. At a time when diasporic intellectuals were theoretically criticizing their disciplines for their culturalist reifications, militants and intellectuals at home were discovering, and confronting politically, the problem of the social fabric. To put it somewhat crudely, when the Manchester anthropologist Emrys Peters was dealing with genealogies of Shi'i families, equilibrium models, and trying to account for historical change and reproduction, Socialist Lebanon's militant intellectuals, many of whom came from southern Shi'i villages—the same area Peters was doing fieldwork in— were reading Marx, Althusser, Gramsci, and Foucault to formulate a revolutionary project.[4] Anglophone metropolitan academic fields, as I have noted earlier, were theoretically "belated" vis-à-vis the readings of Lebanese New Left militant intellectuals. That said, belatedness is not only an "abstract" temporal marker that connotes a before and an after. It is a function of power that inscribes itself temporally. When anthropologists and literary critics drew on these same theoretical resources in the mid- to late 1970s to subject their disciplines to critique, these by now disenchanted militants had already left these theories behind to home in on understanding the communal violence that was tearing the country apart.

In the wake of the Iranian Revolution, the politics of culture will come to occupy center stage, adding further complications to the multiple communal politics at work. Diasporic oppositional intellectuals had to increasingly face the problem of the politics of representation of Islam. This took the form of opposing increased racialization and discrimination where they lived, and an anti-imperialist, anti-interventionist stance against multiple strands of imperial liberalism, feminism, and so on. Whether on the internal front or the external one, the diasporic oppositional position could be articulated within a theoretico-political jargon of binary opposition: colonizer/colonized; empire/resistance, self/other; majority/minority; secular liberalism/Islam. Things were not nearly as clear-cut and easy in the Arab world. For instance, the aftermaths of the Iranian Revolution witnessed the formation of militant Islamist parties that confronted the anti-imperialist Left. By the late 1980s the Lebanese Left had lost its ideological, political, and military confrontations with the nascent Islamist groups. Militants and thinkers had to confront a host of political and military powers—foreign interventions, Arab regimes, militant Islamist political parties, and infranational communal forces—that could not fit neatly into the anti-imperialist binary matrix.

With every intra-Arab major event that will take place, starting with Lebanese civil war or even the Jordanian Black September until the Arab revolutions, without forgetting the Iraqi invasion of Kuwait, the pan-Arab political consensus around "Empire" as the main contradiction, which reached its zenith during Nasser's reign, will slowly erode. The Syrian revolution will reveal the moral and political bankruptcy of the Arab and international anti-imperialist discourse that denied its solidarity to Syrian revolutionaries from the beginning on the basis of a geopolitical support of a "progressive," "anti-imperialist," "secular" regime. All of these events, forces, and powers could hardly be squeezed within the binary matrix of diasporic intellectuals who have developed the *theoretical* critique of Empire at the time when leftist and secular nationalist *political* anti-imperialist forces were being sidelined by Israeli invasions, authoritarian regimes, communal forces, and militant Islamists who took from them the anti-imperialist mantle.

Even when oppositional diasporic intellectuals such as Said were critical of the authoritarianism of regimes and of communal infranational politics, these practices did not constitute for them an *event in theory* that steered them toward a conceptual investigation of the modalities of power at work. Their criticisms remained ideological ones that condemned the abuses of power and corruption of authoritarian rule, or called for upholding values such as freedom of speech and human rights, but did not displace Empire as the main object of their political and theoretical cathexis.

In other words, this is a story of the dispersion and fragmentation of a generation of intellectuals, both at home and in the diaspora, who were brought together by, and became political allies and fellow travelers, of the Palestinian revolution in the late 1960s. The military defeat of 1967 snatched academics at home and in the diaspora, like Edward Said and Sadik al-Azm, from their professional lives and threw them into the political fray.[5] The meteoric rise of the Palestinian revolution, as the alternative revolutionary force in the wake of the defeat of the "progressive regimes," brought together the new political converts, as well as the militant intellectuals of Socialist Lebanon. It won't take much time before the two academics and the militant intellectual (Said, al-Azm, and Charara), who were united in the wake of 1967 by their solidarity with the Palestinian revolution, will go their separate political and theoretical ways. The relationship of al-Azm, a fellow traveler of the Palestinian New Left, with the revolution deteriorated after the events of Black September in 1970, during which it clashed with the Jordanian army. al-Azm wrote a book lambasting the failure of the Palestinian experience in Jordan.[6] It caused him several problems. He lost his job with the PLO's Research Center (Markaz al-Abhath al-Filastini) in Beirut, which he took part in founding, after Arafat considered him persona non grata, and he was forced to use a pseudonym whenever he published pieces in *Shu'un Filastiniyya* (Palestinian Affairs).[7] Very early on, Charara theorized the revolutionary potential of the Palestinian resistance, dubbing it the detonator of Lebanese contradictions in 1969, calling a few years later on the masses to fuse with it at the height of his Maoist phase of militancy (1973). In the wake of the civil and regional wars, he would grow increasingly distant from and severely critical of the military and political practices of the Palestinian resistance in Lebanon. Unlike al-Azm and Charara, whose critique of the Palestinian revolution pertained to its intra-Arab practices in Jordan and Lebanon, Said will resign from the Palestinian National Council much later (1991) in protest over the terms the PLO agreed to for going to the Madrid conference, before becoming a vocal critic of the Oslo accords (1993) and their legacies.

Fragmentation and Conversion of the Revolutionary Subject

In the wake of the Lebanese civil and regional wars, the posited Arab revolutionary subject began its division into its infranational, regional, familial, and sectarian components. A couple of years later, the Iranian Revolution of 1979 and its regional aftershocks brought to a close the anticolonial age of national liberation inaugurated by the Egyptian Free Officers in 1952, nearly thirty years earlier. What took place in Iran proved that Islam, to the chagrin of a couple of generations of modernization theorists, could be an endogenous revolutionary force. Why go to Marx, a nineteenth-century European thinker, when you could politically mobilize the masses through their own autochthonous tradition? Moreover, a decade and a half after its rise, the Palestinian revolution was defeated in the wake of the brutal Israeli invasion of Lebanon (1982).

These thirty years, from the Egyptian Revolution of July 1952 to the June 1982 invasion, would constitute the thick ideological interlude during which political questions, namely, anticolonial ones, were negotiated for the most part on a common discursive ground, which began its splintering by the late 1970s. It was this age of thick ideological politics that produced the demand for intellectual labor and theories to guide political practice toward achieving socialism, Arab unity, and national liberation, as well as arguments about the appropriate organizational forms this practice ought to take: Would it be a loose collective leadership? A Marxist-Leninist democratic centralism? Or a more a Maoist inspired mass line? The most appropriate modes of militant struggle were also debated: Should it be conventional warfare by the regular armies of the nation-states? Or should one adopt a national popular liberation war, and follow the foco theory of revolution? Whether they understood themselves as a Leninist vanguard, Gramscian organic intellectuals, or swimming like a fish in the masses' waters following Mao Tse-Tung's aphorism, the labors of militant intellectuals were predicated on the presence of the people, a universal subject and agent of emancipation. This fragmentation not only destroyed the societal and discursive ground from which their theories rose but also dispensed with the role of the progressive committed intellectual and the revolutionary militant intellectual: Where does he speak from? And to whom does he address himself after the fissuring of the masses—the revolutionary subject—into a multiplicity of regional, familial, sectarian, and religious loyalties?

From the 1980s onward, the stark secular/religious and modernity/authenticity binaries would come to replace the earlier multiplicity of ideological shades. The vigorous arguments in the 1960s and early 1970s on the most appropriate forms of socialism would soon be perceived as faint echoes of a vanished world. One can get a glimpse of these larger historical transformations in following the successive theoretical and political turns of Georges Tarabishi, the prolific Syrian thinker (1939–2016). Tarabishi, who started out as an Arab nationalist and a member of the Ba'th Party, later steered toward Sartre and Marxism, the title of his first book (1964).[8] Sartre's positions in the wake of the

June 1967 war, which did not express solidarity with the Arabs' cause, shocked the Sartrean Arab intelligentsia. "In a few days," Tarabishi recalls, "his [Sartre] aura crumbled."[9] With the beginning of the Lebanese civil and regional wars in 1975, Tarabishi took refuge in Freudian psychoanalysis: "He [Freud] helped me to stay alive intellectually and psychically, he was a protecting father against all this barbarian auto-destruction."[10] In the 1980s Tarabishi began reading and commenting on the Islamic tradition (turath), engaging in a "struggle against Islamism," and founding, in 2007, a decade before his death, the League of Arab Rationalists.[11] Dwelling in the ruins of the Left and having lost their revolutionary organizational moorings, some of these former revolutionaries would retreat to guard the Enlightenment's temple.

If militant intellectuals of the late 1960s attacked the Arab regimes and revolutionaries for not being radical enough, three decades later some would withdraw to a defense of liberal and democratic ideals. "Don't you agree with me that some old Marxists have taken off their cloaks and put on secularist and sometimes fundamentalist ones?" al-Azm was asked in 2007. "This is true," he replied, affirming that with the failure of socialist experiences, a majority of Marxists have "retreated to the second line of defense."[12] In a retrospective gesture, al-Azm tells his interviewer that his generation of Marxists thought they were defending "a more advanced set of values" than "human rights, social justice, democracy and the rotation of power," which were brought forth by the French Revolution and the "liberal revolution."[13] al-Azm then points out that a substantial number of Marxist intellectuals staged a defense of these values "in the face of a 'Medieval Talibani' march . . . we are now faced either by the emergency and martial laws [of the postcolonial regimes] or the Taliban model."[14] Unlike Charara's immanent sociological diagnostic critique, al-Azm's description of the political situation is an ideological lament mapped on a secular/religious Enlightenment grid. al-Azm sees in the retreat to liberalism—a historicism in reverse—an insurrectionary ideological language that calls for the defense of the "values" that are threatened by state authoritarianism and the forces of "medieval" religious forces. His diagnosis was not uncommon in the years preceding the Arab uprisings. Samir Kassir, who defined himself as a secular, westernized, Levantine Arab, wrote the following:

> If it is primarily a consequence of the democratic deficit, the rise of political Islam could not constitute an answer to the impasse of Arab states and societies. While it is a resistance to oppression, it [the rise] is also born from the failure of the modern state and the ideologies of progress

and in this sense it has a resemblance to the rise of fascisms in Europe. Actually, the social conduct of Islamist movements reveals a number of analogies with fascist dictatorships once the religious veil that envelops them is uncovered.[15]

While al-Azm (1934–2016) and Kassir (1960–2005) belonged to two different generations, separated by a quarter of a century, these two intellectuals were bound by a common affiliation to a defeated leftist tradition and the vision of total emancipation it sustained.

Shifting the analytical gaze inward toward the culture of these societies, inaugurated as a minoritarian position in the wake of 1967 and propelled then by the ethical impulse to take responsibility for one's defeat, became more and more normalized, and at times acrimonious, among some disenchanted leftists. Some, such as the Tunisian ex-Marxist al-Afif al-Akhdar (1934–2013), welcomed foreign military operations during the US invasion of Iraq (2003) as the solution to the deadlock of "unenlightened religious culture" and authoritarian rule.[16] In 1965, three years after Algeria's independence, al-Akhdar took part in the meeting between Che Guevara and Abu Jihad at the Hotel Elité in Algiers.[17] Forty years separate the victory of the Algerians against French colonialism (1962) and the American occupation of Iraq (2003). Forty years also separate the meeting of Al-Akhdar with Guevara in Algiers from his celebration of the US missiles on, and the invasion of, Iraq. The harsh prose of this veteran of national liberation struggles, Marxist ideologue, and militant alongside the Palestinian resistance from 1962 until he left Beirut for Paris in the first years of the Lebanese civil war (1975–90) is not his alone.

Facing those disenchanted leftists who had elected the question of culture and modernity as "the main contradiction" were their ex-comrades who remained attached to the question of politics and empire as the central contradiction, critically aligning themselves at points, as fellow travelers, with nascent militant Islamist parties, such as Hizbullah and Hamas, who took on board the national question. The fracturing of the Marxist ground of total emancipation from colonialism and imperialism, economic exploitation, and tradition split the inheritors into those coalescing around the first leg of the tripod, focusing on geopolitical analysis (game of nations), the balance of powers, and imperial intervention (external causes), and those emphasizing culture, sectarianism, and religion as the internal impediments to progress (internal causes). In the splitting of the Marxist inheritance between culture and geopolitics, the socioeconomic question found no heirs. The calls of the very few who claimed it were muffled in a setting saturated by questions of authenticity/modernity, authoritarian rule and civil wars, and relentless imperial interventions.

Reading Orientalism in the Wake of the Iranian Revolution

If Said published "The Arab Portrayed" in the wake of the 1967 defeat with a focus on the Arabs, by 1981 he would put out *Covering Islam*, which tackled the image of Islam in the West, particularly in the US, and the different uses it is put to.[18] From 1979 onward, a string of events, including the Iranian Revolution, the assassination of Egyptian president Anwar al-Sadat (1981) in the wake of the Camp David Accords between Israel and Egypt (1978), and the aftermaths of the Soviet invasion of Afghanistan (1979), will increasingly put "Islam" at the center of media, policy, and scholarly attention. Said noted in *Covering Islam* the "critical absence of expert opinion on Islam" (18), highlighting in the process the experts' failure to understand that "much of what truly mattered about postcolonial states could not be easily herded under the rubric of 'stability'" (22) and how the area programs that house modern scholars of Islam are "affiliated to the mechanism by which national policy is set" (19). Around the same time, "Islam," long the preserve of Orientalists, emerged as an object of anthropological inquiry. Talal Asad opens "The Idea of an Anthropology of Islam," an essay that realigned the coordinates of the field, by saying that "in recent years, there has been increasing interest in something called the anthropology of Islam. Publications by Western anthropologists containing the word 'Islam' or 'Muslim' in the title multiply at a remarkable rate. The political reasons for this great industry are perhaps too evident to deserve much comment."[19]

The 1980s inaugurated the battle for the representation of Islam that took place on several fronts: the academy, the media, and policy centers. Ayatollah Khomeini is the icon par excellence of this decade, which heralded the post–Cold War politics of culture. A few months before his death in 1989, Khomeini addressed both the Eastern and Western camps. On January 1, he sent a long letter to Mikhail Gorbachev, the general secretary of the Soviet Communist Party, which he concluded by noting that "the Islamic Republic of Iran as the greatest and most powerful base of the Islamic world can easily fill the vacuum religious faith in your society."[20] A few weeks later, on February 14, 1989, he issued his famous death sentence against Salman Rushdie, which alongside the burning of *The Satanic Verses* in Bradford, England, a month earlier, increased the hostility toward Muslim immigrants and saw the proliferation of discourses about Muslim "fundamentalism," "violence," and "integration" into the "host" society.[21] By the end of the 1980s, the battle for the representation of Islam was a no longer a matter of "how we see the rest of the world," as Said's subtitle to *Covering Islam* had it. It gradually became an integral part of internal politics in Europe and increasingly in the US after the September 11, 2001, attacks.

"Maybe the biggest catastrophe that befell Arabs is Marxism as a set of foreign templates," said Maroun Baghdadi (1950–93), the young and talented Lebanese movie director in February 1979, to his interviewer Hazem Saghieh (1951–), a journalist at the Beirut-based *al-Safir* daily. "Until now, Marxism did not manage to find a place for itself in the Arab world."[22] The Lebanese Communist Party (LCP), which was founded in 1924, had been around for more than half a century when Baghdadi underscored Marxism's exogenous status. Having said that, this statement was not really an affront to the longevity of the LCP. Its shock effect, so to speak, comes from the fact that it was asserted only a decade after the birth of the New Left by one of its members. Both intellectuals, Baghdadi the movie director, and Saghieh the journalist, were previously associated with the OCAL.

As a result of a historical contingency, Said's US-based critique of Marx and contemporary Third World radicals was contemporaneous with the rise of the question of culture, one symptom of which was a wave of conversion of Marxist militants into supporters of political Islam in the wake of the Iranian Revolution. This conversion was particularly prominent among Lebanese and Palestinian Maoist militants and intellectuals, for whom swimming in the waters of the masses entailed this time around an exit from Marxism into the authenticity of the masses' creed. Roger Assaf, the prominent Lebanese theater director, who did his Maoist établissement in the Palestinian camps in the 1970s, was one of the converts. Assaf told his interviewer: "The passage to Islam was a putting into practice of Maoist principles. I went into Islam, like others go to the factory. But here in Lebanon, no one goes to the factory. There are no factories, or so few of them."[23] Nicolas Dot-Pouillard draws our attention to the fact that "the intellectuals of Fatah's Student Brigade began integrating a non-Marxist intellectual corpus: Ali Shariati, and particularly Ibn Khaldoun" before the Iranian Revolution.[24] I quote at length from Dot-Pouillard's interview with Nazir Jahel, a member of the brigades, who taught at the Lebanese University:

> For us, what did Maoism and the passage to Islamism entail: it was reading our history, in order to transform it; reading our culture, our history, through apparatuses and conceptual tools that we could fashion ourselves through a return to traditions (turath), to history, to Islamic thought. We read Mao, Lenin, Gramsci, all the Marxists, but we also began reading Ibn Khaldun.... We reinvented a vocabulary with *Ghalaba*

[predominance], *'Assabiyya*, *Mumana'a* (resistance, refusal), Hadara (civilization).... All of this led us bit by bit to Khomeini, to Islam. Because Khomeini constituted an effective mass discourse, a popular discourse that articulated the intellectual dimension with the popular aspect.[25]

The conversion from Marxism into a Khomeinist militant Islam via Maoism's vector retained its Third Worldist anti-imperialism, but rearticulated it through Arab-Islamic conceptual tools. The conversion was both a personal and theoretical act of cultural decolonization as well as a political alignment with the Islamic masses, under the leadership of Khomeini, as the new revolutionary subject.

Souheil al-Kache, another member of the brigades who was swept by the tidal waves of the Iranian Revolution, criticized modernist Arab thinkers for reproducing the classifications of Orientalists, while underlining how for Islamists these two groups share the same theoretical framework and are associated with foreign political, ideological, and cultural interests.[26] In opposition to the sapping of Islam by colonialism and its internal agents, the Islamist discourse asserts, according to al-Kache, the continuity of the Arab and Islamic Self throughout history, refusing the narrative of its defeat by the West. This emphasis on the historical continuity of the self enables a politics of cohesion in the face of the central issue: "that of foreign domination, particularly on the cultural level."[27] The discourse of the Islamic Awakening, al-Kache argues, constitutes the resolution of the West's cultural domination since it affirms the Muslim Self, as a discourse of the master that escapes the resentment of the dominated. This discourse, he writes, stands for the end of the contradiction with "Orientalism and its shadow, the modernist Arab intellectual." Its fundamental concern in its hostility to Orientalism, he adds, is a political one, but it also leaves its marks on the methods and hermeneutics of Arab political thought. In advocating an affirmation of Muslim identity as a voluntary action, the "Muslim Self" is resuscitated "while ignoring the Other (the West). This Other then sees the universalism of its culture contested. Al-Khomeini is the best illustration of this discourse."[28] The revolutionary fervor of some of the converts to and fellow travelers of militant Khomeinist political Islam will subside in the wake of the Iran-Iraq War, and Khomeini's "quasi-total elimination of the Marxist Left and the Islamo-Marxist one in Iran."[29]

Marxists like al-Azm, who did not exit the tradition like Charara and Beydoun, or were not swayed by the Iranian Revolution, will increasingly become on the defensive. "Former radicals, ex-communists, unorthodox Marxists, and disillusioned nationalists" have come to form, in the wake of the Iranian

Revolution, "a revisionist Arab line of political thought," wrote al-Azm in his review of *Orientalism*.[30] "Their central thesis may be summarized as follows: 'The national salvation so eagerly sought by the Arabs since the Napoleonic occupation of Egypt is to be found neither in secular nationalism (be it radical, conservative, or liberal) nor in revolutionary communism, socialism or what have you, but in a return to the authenticity of what they call 'popular political Islam'" (234). The set of conditions that confronted *Orientalism*'s eastern travels couldn't have been more fraught. At a time when Marxists were being politically and ideologically attacked from their eastern flank, so to speak, came an additional theoretical blow, this time, though, from New York. In his afterword to *Orientalism*, written in 1994, Said wrote the following on the reception of his book in the Arab world:

> Moreover, the actuality I described in the book's last pages, of one powerful discursive system maintaining hegemony over another, was intended as the opening salvo in a debate that might stir Arab readers and critics to engage more determinedly with the system of Orientalism. I was either upbraided for not having paid closer attention to Marx—the passages on Marx's own Orientalism in my book were the most singled out by dogmatic critics in the Arab world and India, for instance—whose system of thought was claimed to have risen above his obvious prejudices, or I was criticized for not appreciating the great achievements of Orientalism, the West, etc. As with the defenses of Islam, recourse to Marxism or the "West" as a coherent total system seems to me to have been a case of using one orthodoxy to shoot down another.[31]

Indeed, al-Azm and Mahdi 'Amil spent a lot of intellectual energy on these few pages of Said's book, strenuously attempting to extricate the moor (Marx) from the charge of Orientalism. Marx's views on British rule in India in Said's work were put to work to reveal how a non-Orientalist's writings on Asia first reveal his "humanity" and "fellow feeling" for the suffering inflicted by colonialism to be shortly hijacked thereafter by Orientalist discourses when Marx posits that the British destroyer is also the creator of a new modern society. "The idea of regenerating a fundamentally lifeless Asia," wrote Said, "is a piece of pure Romantic Orientalism." Marx's humanity has succumbed in Said's reading to the "unshakable definitions built up by Orientalist science."[32] al-Azm's tone in his defense of Marx is harsh:

> I think that this account of Marx's views and analyses of highly complex historical processes and situations is a travesty. . . . Marx's manner of

analyzing British rule in India in terms of an unconscious tool of history—which is making possible a real social revolution by destroying the old India and laying the foundations of a new order—cannot be ascribed under any circumstances to the usurpation of Marx's mind by conventional Orientalistic verbiage. Marx's explanation (regardless of whether one agrees or disagrees with it) testifies to his theoretical consistency in general. . . . Like the European capitalist class, British rule in India was its own grave digger. There is nothing particularly "Orientalistic" about this explanation. Furthermore, Marx's call for revolution in Asia is more historically realistic and promising than any noble sentiments that he could have lavished on necessarily vanishing socioeconomic formations. (226–27)

al-Azm's strategy of defense lay in reinscribing Marx's views on Asia within his overall progressive historicist framework, undoing in the process any essentialization of East and West as a product of Orientalism's "ahistorical bourgeois bent of mind" (228). Marx, wrote al-Azm, "like anyone else, knew of the superiority of modern Europe over the Orient. But to accuse a radically historicist thinker such as Marx of turning this contingent fact into a necessary reality for all time is simply absurd" (228).

Said was most probably referring to al-Azm and Aijaz Ahmad, and maybe others, regarding the defense of Marx.[33] He may have not been mistaken in pointing out the dogmatic character of some of their defenses. Nevertheless, their harsh responses, al-Azm's at least, are not adequately and fully captured by just dubbing them dogmatic critics defending their guru and guarding the orthodoxy. They may be doing so, but what Said's reading overlooks is the character of the intervention Marx performed for these militant intellectuals in their respective fields, and how an epistemological critique of Marx's Orientalist discourses came hand in hand with, and could possibly be mobilized in, the intellectual and political battles they were fighting in the difficult conjuncture of the late 1970s and early 1980s. At a point when Marxism was attacked by the purveyors of authenticity for its foreignness, Said's critique, which repositioned Marx from the thinker of emancipation to one who is discursively complicit with Orientalists, could, to say the least, not be warmly received by cornered Arab Marxists. The discursive ground, on which ideological differences were organized, was being called into question simultaneously by the political heralds of authenticity calling for nativist solutions and the theoretical critics of Eurocentric epistemology.

Said, who never tired of calling for secular criticism and of drawing attention to the domestication of radical theories, and whose hypersensitivity to closed systems and dogmas needs no further exploration, was as far as possible from nativists of all ilk in the East as well as poststructuralist pieties in the North American academy.[34] He, in fact, had much more in common with Marxists, such as al-Azm and 'Amil, than the fraught reception of *Orientalism* reveals. To say the least, they were in agreement on the question of secularism and religious politics. Here, however, I am less concerned with pointing to convergences and divergences than in fleshing out how political and theoretical developments led to the emergence of a fork in critical agendas between thinkers at home, who were attached to an emancipatory theory of politics under attack, and diasporic oppositional intellectuals in the metropole, who inverted those terms to focus on the politics of revolutionary theory and its entanglement with power. What I am after is an examination of the different analytical and political effects produced by traveling theories hopping from Paris to New York to eventually land in Beirut.

In the years following the Israeli invasion (1982), Mahdi 'Amil (1936–87) wrote a hundred-page-plus polemic against Said's book entitled *Does the Heart Belong to the Orient and the Mind to the West? Marx in Edward Said's Orientalism* (1985).[35] Hassan Hamdan, who was academically trained as a philosopher in France and wrote under the pseudonym of Mahdi 'Amil (the Laboring Mahdi), was, and still is, regarded as the most prominent theoretician of the Lebanese Communist Party. 'Amil, who had joined the party in 1960, was later elected to its central committee in 1987, the year of his tragic assassination. 'Amil's ambitious theoretical project ran counter to al-Azm's Marxist historicism. He had "meshed Althusserian influences with conceptualizations of the periphery inspired from dependency theory" in an effort to break away from historicist readings of Marx through his theoretical development of the characteristics of a colonial mode of production.[36] 'Amil's conceptual labors were as far as possible from epistemological naïveté. He sums up the overall argument of his *Theoretical Prolegomena* in the introduction to the third edition of the two volumes (1980) as an attempt to produce a "scientific knowledge of the mechanism of capitalism's colonial development in Arab societies" and of the national liberation movement, which is the peculiar form class struggle takes in this case, as well as "the tools of production of this knowledge."[37] Reflexivity was at the heart of 'Amil's project, which sought to produce a theory that thinks the conditions of possibility of its own conceptual building blocks as it is thinking its object. 'Amil's lengthy and at points repetitive Marxist critique of *Orientalism* begins by pointing to Said's idealist move, which affiliates Orientalism to Western thought in general rather than rooting it in the particularity of its historical class character. The title of the first chapter says it all: "The

Nation's Thought or That of the Dominant Class?" 'Amil's defense of Marx, in a similar vein to al-Azm's, is keen on shifting the terms of the debate from Said's categories of Orientalist Western thought to those of bourgeois thought. The exclusion of the historical class character of this body of knowledge, in 'Amil's reading, "banishes the possibility of existence of its opposite, which gives it a totalitarian aspect by which it occupies the whole cultural space."[38] In doing so, he seeks to steer back the conversation from one that rests on common discursive formation of European knowledges to one grounded in opposed ideologies.

More importantly for our purposes, 'Amil points to how *Orientalism*'s critique of Marx and contemporary Marxists is in line with the positions of his nativist political opponents in the Arab world. "The main ideological weapon used by counterrevolutionary forces in their counterattack on the advanced positions they began to occupy in the strategic historical horizon," wrote 'Amil in his characteristic tortuous theoretical prose, "is to portray this thought [Marxism] on the basis of the Self/Other binary, or that of East and West. As if it [Marxism] is bourgeois imperialist thought, since it is, like its class antithesis, Western thought."[39] Again, Said, of course, would have protested, as he did later on, that he didn't hold nativist views, of the Western thought is only valid for the West and Eastern thought for the East, but what I am after is less Said's retrospective views and more the political and theoretical stakes animating the problem-space into which *Orientalism* landed at a particular time and place. Not any time and place, for that matter, but the place to which its author is intimately related, and a time when he was becoming more and more immersed in public political and intellectual interventions.

Nearly five years after al-Azm's observation on the resurgence of a politics of authenticity, 'Amil criticizes Said in the wake of the progress of what he dubbed the "counterrevolutionary forces." On May 18, 1987, during one of the bleak episodes of the Lebanese civil wars, 'Amil was shot dead on the street. Like Husayn Muruwwa, who was assassinated on February 17, 1987, it is widely believed that 'Amil too was shot by Shi'i Islamist militants. Under the biographical details corner of the book's third edition (2006), published by the LCP's printing house, the publisher wrote that 'Amil was assassinated for "his commitment to the struggle for a unified, secular and democratic Lebanon." "He was called," the blurb continues, "the Arabs' Gramsci, since he was the only one in the Arab world who tried to construct a comprehensive scientific theory of the Arab revolution, and perhaps, of the revolution of underdeveloped countries, more generally."

In the wake of *Orientalism*, Marxists and liberals in the Arab world continue to be critically targeted by the rise of postcolonial studies in the North American metropoles, which would collapse the question of the political into its episte-mology critique. What these quarreling critics shared, and what constituted the condition of possibility of a postcolonial critique, was an attachment to, and an interpretation of, a body of theory drawn primarily from the corpus of European thinkers. Their difference was located in how they both conjugated the relationship of theory to politics. If the age of national liberation (1952–82) was characterized by a high demand on theory as a guide for political practice, as the biographical blurb on the back of 'Amil's book tells us, the eclipse of the revolutionary subject and the rise of postcolonial studies would inaugurate the age of the politics of theory. It is not because they are dogmatic critics, although some may well be, that these thinkers singled out the passages on Marx in *Orientalism*; it is rather because, as Said would surely agree, traveling theories dis-able certain critical paths and open up new ones, stifling political projects while potentially boosting others, despite the best intentions of the secular critic.

Ending the story of *Orientalism*'s Marxist reception at this point will only reveal a set of resistances to the text. There is more to its travels than that. In the second section of his review of *Orientalism*, al-Azm productively and stra-tegically puts Said's insights to use to debunk the claims of Arab nationalists and of, mostly ex-Marxist, "Islamanic" intellectuals who had fallen under the spell of the Iranian Revolution. In this section, which is expanded from the five pages of the text's initial English version to twenty-six pages in the later Arabic iteration, al-Azm mobilized Said as an ally to counter antihistorical and nativist anti-Western pronouncements of Arab intellectuals.[40] "One of the most prominent and interesting accomplishments of Said's book," he wrote, is its critique of

> Orientalism's persistent belief that there exists a radical ontological dif-ference between the natures of the Orient and the Occident.... This ontological difference entails immediately an epistemological one which holds that the sort of conceptual instruments, scientific categories, so-ciological concepts, political descriptions and ideological distinctions employed to understand and deal with Western societies remain, in principle, irrelevant and inapplicable to Eastern ones.... This ahistori-cal, antihuman, and even antihistorical "Orientalist" doctrine I shall call *Ontological Orientalism*.... This image has left its profound imprint on the Orient's modern and contemporary consciousness of itself. Hence Said's important warning against the dangers and temptations of apply-ing the readily available structures, styles, and ontological biases of Ori-entalism upon themselves and upon others.[41]

al-Azm's *Ontological Orientalism* shares with Said the analytical and political worry of always pointing to the "Oriental" exception, eliding history, politics, and economics altogether to reproduce tautologies such as "Islam is Islam, the Orient is the Orient."[42] Said and al-Azm worried about the elision of historical transformations, which mask the contemporaneity of social dynamics, of the vast social, political, and economic shifts that did and still work on and in the area. Said's concern to get rid of Arab exceptionalism and to put Arabs back in history was applauded in *Ontological Orientalism* by al-Azm, who sought to uncover the claims of those who have fallen "in the temptations against which Said has warned," engendering "what may be called *Orientalism in Reverse*" (231).

al-Azm's reading of Said's work as fundamentally an antiessentialist critique enabled him to use it to counter Arab nationalist Ba'thist thinkers who "proposed to study 'basic' words in the Arabic language as a means to attaining 'genuine knowledge' of some of the essential characteristics of the primordial 'Arab mentality' underlying those very words" (231). It also enabled him to take a stab at the post–Iranian Revolution revisionists, such as the famous Syrian poet Adonis who, in the wake of 1967, like al-Azm, professed culturalist critiques of Arab backwardness. Adonis wrote after the Iranian Revolution that the "Western essence is 'technologism and not orginality'" and that "'the peculiarity of the Orient' 'lies in originality' and this is why its nature cannot be captured except through 'the prophetic, the visionary, the magical, the miraculous, the infinite, the inner, the beyond, the fanciful, the ecstatic', etc." (236). al-Azm concluded his review by alluding to recent debates on whether the "Islamic Republic" can be qualified as democratic, citing "the conservative 'Orientalistic' logic" of the prevailing argument that "Islam cannot accept any additional qualifiers since it cannot be but Islam" (236). As Ayatollah Khomeini, quoted by al-Azm in the last sentences of his review, put it, "the term *Islam* is perfect, and having to put another word right next to it is, indeed, a source of sorrow" (237).

Orientalism in reverse put the accent on the unmasking of essentialist assumptions in Arab thought and Islamic thought that point toward its self-sufficiency and its implicit and sometimes explicit superiority to its Western counterpart. al-Azm mobilized Said to shift the lens of critique from imperial discourses on the "Orientals" to the latter's own knowledge of themselves. These Arab thinkers share the same essentializing traits and methods of Orientalist scholars while reversing the normative value judgment to the benefit of the Orient, which comes out triumphant in its face-off with its materialist, decadent Western counterpart. *Orientalism in Reverse* is then not the self-

Orientalizing that Said warns against, and that al-Azm, with his critique of the backwardness of Arab society, can easily fall into, and is not merely Occidentalism, which is the reification of the West.

al-Azm's resistance to *Orientalism*'s treatment of Marxism, as well as his productive use of some its insights, are, of course, part and parcel of the same response to the newly emerging political conjuncture. On the one hand he was attempting to leave a breathing space for his historicist Marxist critique (of "backwardness," "religious obscurantist thought," and "tradition") by disentangling Marx from Orientalism, and implicitly himself from the charge of self-Orientalization—one that could too easily be used against him by the postrevolutionary currents. On the other hand, he uncoupled Said's epistemological and ontological critique from the West's will to dominate and reversed the terms to undo the antihistorical and self-congratulatory currents in Arabic thought of both the earlier nationalist and more recent Iranophile strands. *Orientalism in Reverse*, by inverting the terms of Said's work, from a criticism of the West's knowledge of the non-West to the internal criticism of the then current politics of authenticity in the Arab world, reveals clearly the emerging fork in critical agendas—that will solidify subsequently—between al-Azm and Said, whose births as public committed intellectuals we owe to the 1967 defeat and who were brought together personally and politically by their engagement alongside the Palestinian revolution in the late 1960s.

Coda: Culture and Imperialism

There are more interesting critical readings of Said's work that are not theoretical attempts to salvage Marx or Enlightenment thought from the charge of Orientalism, or to show how his binary divisions between East and West reinscribe in practice a certain nationalist logic. These readings underscored how Said's binaries, which focus on imperialism and the resistances to it, do not take into account the different modalities of power at work in colonized and postcolonial societies.[43] In the last pages of *Orientalism*'s introduction, under the subheading "The Personal Dimension," Said borrows Gramsci's words about the importance of "knowing oneself" through compiling an inventory of the historical processes that have deposited an infinity of traces on the self as a starting point for a critical elaboration. *Orientalism*, Said then notes, is an attempt to "inventory the traces upon me, the Oriental subject, of the culture whose domination has been so powerful a factor in the life of all Orientals."[44] This practice of self-knowledge, like Freudian psychoanalysis, has an emancipatory aspect. The critical awareness of colonialism's constitutive traces is a first step toward neutralizing their grip on the self.

Said's pathbreaking work, and this is not unrelated to its appeal, is a theoretical work with a therapeutic edge. By diving into the multiple sedimented layers of the inexhaustible Orientalist archive, while making a strong case for its repetition in the present, and rendering visible the patterns of its entanglements with power, Said's text contributes to undoing their hold not only over disciplines but also on colonial and postcolonial subjects. Postcolonial theory has a therapeutic dimension, particularly for diasporic subjects who experience everyday and institutional racism in their metropolitan homes. Said's theoretical practice, like psychoanalysis again, is not a normative one. The Lebanese and Palestinian Maoists who converted to Islamist politics in the wake of the Iranian Revolution—and for some, such as Roger Assaf and Munir Shafiq, who were born into Christian families, this entailed a religious conversion—were also critical of the cultural domination of the West. Their critique of the multifaceted dimensions of imperialism entailed a personal and political conversion that inscribed them in a nativist ideological universe.

Both Said and the Maoist converts to Islamism retain Western imperialism at the heart of their attachments. Said fought it through acts of theoretical deconstruction of its hegemony and a political alignment with the Palestinian national liberation movement. He held the tension alive between his critical theoretical practices and his national liberation politics. The Maoists, on the other hand, underwent a process of conversion to militant Islam that came to form the unified ideological and political, and at times personal, ground of their anti-imperialism.

al-Azm and 'Amil retained Marxism at the heart of their attachments. They attempted to salvage it from Said's critique and its association by Islamists with Western Orientalism and forms of cultural domination. They tried hard, in desperate political times, via different theoretical strategies to defend Marxism's promise of universal emancipation. They clashed with Said theoretically and Islamists politically. 'Amil was assassinated by Islamist militants. al-Azm retreated in subsequent years to a defense of Enlightenment values, holding very critical views of Islamist politics. In the last years of his life, he supported the Syrian revolution against the brutal Assad regime, steering away from his earlier hardline critiques of religious politics.

In the wake of his very early disenchantment with revolutionary politics, Charara turned into a harsh critic of leftist and anti-imperialist politics. This was compounded by his observation of how these emancipatory discourses were put to use by political parties, national liberation movements, and regimes to strengthen their hold on power and silence their opponents. His early observation on the difficulty of establishing hegemony in a country divided by multiple communal solidarities put him at odds with Said's views on two main points. The first was Said's emphasis on the strength and effectivity of the webs of imperial power-knowledge discourses. The second was Said's theoretical silence on the multiple modalities of power and rule at work in these societies that are not part of the matrix of Empire. Charara called into question very early on the poverty of the categories of Western social theory to account for non-Western forms of power. Unlike the Maoists, whose nativist *ideological* concerns led them to fashion a political vocabulary from the resources of the Arab-Islamic tradition, Charara turned to some of the same resources, but for heuristic and *theoretical* reasons. His turn to Ibn Khaldun was coupled with an implicit normative horizon that saw in the logic of the state—which he didn't articulate—and more broadly in the logic of the autonomous functioning of institutions an antidote to the pervasive logic of subjugation. Unlike al-Azm, his immanent critique of the societies was never articulated in the reified stock phrases of modernist intellectuals that posit "religion" and "culture" as a problem and the Enlightenment or "democracy" as the panacea.

I illustrate some of these points, and bring this chapter to a close, with Ahmad Beydoun's generous review of Said's *Culture and Imperialism*.[45] After lauding the comprehensiveness of the work, and some of its brilliant readings, Beydoun notes that Said's defensive position, especially that he lives in the West, is very precise in its diagnosis of the different manifestations of Western racism.[46] Having said that, Said's work, Beydoun continues, is less precise when it comes to looking into, and analyzing, the suffering the dominated underwent at the hands of their rulers and fellows. Not taking the modalities of power at work in these societies and their cultures, alongside imperial ones, Beydoun writes, leads to "theoretical disasters in understanding historical catastrophes. This is the case in [Said's] dubbing Saddam Hussein no more than an 'appalling figure.'"[47] Beydoun's critique shows the limits of Said's binary matrix—colonizer/colonized, oppressor/oppressed, imperialism/resistance—to diagnostically apprehend the complexities and catastrophes of postcolonial Arab history. Beydoun notes how the theoretical emphasis on showing how Orientalists invent their Other, to assert the superiority of their own self-image, is an easy inversion of the racist position that locks the colonized in ahistorical essences. Difference in a larger scale is neither an ahistorical essence nor an invention of colonizers. He finds theoretically wanting the confinement of the critique of power to imperialism. Toward the end of his review, Beydoun remarks that the vital question is whether there is a possibility for a critique of the practices of the colonized and the oppressed that finds its sources in their own culture—and not in the acts of imperialists—that both escapes essentialization and would not be dubbed an act of racism or self-racism.

There is no theory of subversion that cannot also serve the cause of oppression.
—JACQUES RANÇIÈRE

What gets from the territory onto the map?
—GREGORY BATESON

Authority of Theory

Attempts to think the relationship of theory to the world have suffered from a priori fetishization of its political performative powers. This hegemonic image of theory's a priori powers in, and on, the world is shared by critics who occupy divergent ideological positions: anxious reactionaries who fret about the decline of the West, epistemology critics who think that the discourses of Arab intellectuals make them complicit with, or vectors of, imperial epistemological and ontological violence, and those calling for abandoning critical theory after it became a weapon in the hands of conspiracy theorists and climate-change deniers. Bruno Latour, for instance, paints a picture of a world, a West to be more accurate, turned upside down, a world where danger no longer comes from ideology posturing as fact, but "from an excessive *distrust* of good matters of fact disguised as bad ideological biases!"[1] The conspiracy theorists may be deforming the critics' arguments, but Latour, drawing on a military analogy, notes that they are appropriating "our weapons."[2] The weapons have moved into the hands of the wrong party and are now aimed at wrong targets. It is time to stop manufacturing them.

Constructionist skepticism, after all, was not initially devised by critical social scientists to undo reifications and essentialized and naturalized accounts, and later on moved into the world. Syrian Ba'thist ideologues and officials refused to recognize Lebanon's sovereignty by marshaling constructionist arguments. Lebanon's borders, they claimed, were artificially designed by imperial powers, which carved it out of greater Syria. The Ba'th condensed its constructionism into two mantras repeated ad nauseam: "One people in two countries" and "Unity of path and destiny." The Iraqi Baʿth marshaled similar constructionist arguments to prepare and legitimize its invasion of Kuwait. Constructionist skepticism is one of the oldest tricks in the book of Arab nationalists, which, rest assured, they did not appropriate from Bourdieu's critical sociology. Needless to assert, there was nothing emancipatory in the Baʿthist breed of skepticism. It was not, in essence, an antiessentialist move against the fabulations and invented traditions of Lebanese and Kuwaiti nationalist ideologues. It was an ideological tool of political power that was marshaled by much larger and powerful countries (Syria and Iraq) to call into question the right to sovereignty of their much smaller neighbors (Lebanon and Kuwait).

Latour's calls, and those of the epistemological critics of Arab intellectuals, are not entirely new. They share similar structural features, and anxieties, with earlier debates about relativism, which an older generation of critics like Allan Bloom dubbed a disease carried by philosophy that has infected politics.[3] "The practical efficacy attributed to academic philosophy and social science— both to destroy and save its object of analysis—quite belies its actual power and role," John Gunnell writes.[4] Holding critical theory's corrosive skepticism responsible for the increasingly precarious and friable world we inhabit, whether it is done from the Left or the Right, partakes of the same short-circuiting of thinking the relationship of theoretical discourses with the world that forgoes an investigation of the former's authority in its zones of deployment and intervention.

Doing fieldwork in theory calls into question the assumptions of scholars, who simultaneously give too much and too little practical efficacy to theory. They give it too much by attributing radical transformations in the world— whether it is the breakdown of a common world or the ontological violence that threatens life forms—to its own internal workings and discursive assumptions. And they give it too little, because they do not investigate how, in particular conjunctures, theory may be appropriated, transfigured, and embedded in various political projects, endowing it with ideological force and authorizing practices. Granting critical theory both too much and too little are the result of adhering to a metaphysical image of theory that assumes that the practical effects it will produce in the world are contained a priori in its epistemology. Theory, then, is cast in either the heroic role of saving the world or the bad one of destroying it. I hope I am not understood as calling for abandoning the reading practices of epistemological critics altogether and for reverting back to a celebration of universals such as human rights as the harbingers of emancipation. This would be to revert to the same metaphysical thinking that mistakes theoretical questions that are contested politically for philosophical ones that can be settled a priori once and for all by a "better theory."[5]

Difference in Theory

Earlier generations of Orientalists and anthropologists, who mapped Christianity and Judaism onto the West and Islam onto the Middle East, elided, as a consequence, the discussion of Judaism and Christianity in the region.[6] They saw Sephardic Judaism and Eastern Christianity as being in the area but not of it, their histories being tied to European history. Today, the plurality of intra-Arab and intra-Islamic religious, ethnic, and communal differences remain invisible and cannot constitute the matter of theoretical reflection for a binary grid that sifts people through a mesh that separates the westernized native from the nonwesternized one and the secular-liberal Muslim from the pious one. What counts as difference and what does not? Whose lives, discourses, and practices are interesting and subject to the minutiae of anthropological understanding and translation? And who is incorporated into (by Orientalists), or criticized for being an agent of (by epistemological critics), the West?

The overdetermination of critical scholarly works on the Middle East by the injunction of speaking back to hegemonic Western discourses is clearly revealed in the different theoretical engagements with the question of difference. Roughly speaking, there is a form of difference—Islam—that one seeks to understand, via ethnographic close-ups and a deep engagement with the complexities of that tradition, and understandably so, in Islamophobic times, when Muslims are increasingly targeted and racialized.[7] And then there is that other form of difference—community, mostly sectarian, but also ethnic, regional, or kinship based—that one seeks to deconstruct and explain away by zooming out to shed light on the structural forces (imperialism, capitalism, modern states) that construct it. In the first case, the discourse of the critical scholar is close to the discourse of the subjects of study. In the second, it takes its distances.[8]

Both of these contrasting theoretical treatments of difference highlight the modernity of the phenomena they are investigating. One form that imperial discourses of power take is asserting that one cannot be a practicing Muslim and a modern subject, that the process of reaching the much coveted shores of modernity necessitates jumping ship and converting out of Islam into secularism.[9] Critical scholarly works counter these discourses of power by contending that one can be both a Muslim and modern. Alternatively, they show how the Islamic tradition is inside-outside modernity, by making a case for how

Muslims have been conscripted by the powers of Western civilization, to draw on Talal Asad's felicitous phrase, without eradicating difference.[10] Another form that discourses of power take is asserting that conflicts in the Arab and Muslim worlds are fueled by atavistic religious, ethnic, and sectarian hatred that are as far as possible from a modern world that overcame its wars of religion centuries ago. Against these discourses, oppositional scholarship highlights the modernity of communal solidarities, but this time around not to highlight that a subject can be both attached to his community and modern since this literature rarely bestows its ethnographic, charitable understanding on those subjects. It is worth quoting at length Lara Deeb's courageous reflexive consideration of how writing in, and for, a US audience on the Middle East impacts the objects of study, the scale of analysis, and the methods and theories at work. "For the most part," Deeb writes,

> this critical scholarship addresses sectarianism in its political, institutional, or legal registers rather than in the social or interpersonal realms. Why is there so little attention to the latter? Perhaps, as scholars of the region, we hope that we can move beyond the category by demonstrating that sectarianism is socially and historically constructed and maintained through institutional and political-economic processes. Perhaps acknowledging that people care about sect feels a bit like airing a family secret, or venturing into the messiness of discrimination and prejudice that we wish didn't exist, or a betrayal of activist efforts that we support. Perhaps we fear that writing about how sect matters at an interpersonal or affective level will contribute to those seemingly intransigent assumptions that sectarianism is unchanging or primordial. But much as we want to escape or deny it, the fact remains that *sect matters* to a lot of people in their daily lives, not only in relation to politics, networks, legal status, or the material realm but in their interpersonal interactions.[11]

Deeb's rich panoply of possible explanations for the neglect of work on sectarian subjects are instances of psychic disavowal, which operates according to the formula: "I know very well, but still . . ."[12] I know very well that sectarianism matters, but still I can't write about it because it is a thorny issue and I want to wish it away, or I am afraid that in doing so I will be betraying my own politics. More importantly, the disavowal of sectarian matters is related to the fear of consolidating an already impressive archive of Orientalist discourses, and the anxiety generated by the potential of having one's critical work *appropriated* by imperial policies that lean on such discourses in setting out their agendas. These anxieties about consolidation and appropriation of scholarly discourses produced and circulated in imperial centers about a major area of Western military intervention result in what Deeb called "representational paralysis."[13] The critical metropolitan scholar of the Middle East is split and endowed with a form of double consciousness, which can be mapped onto the binary spatial-temporal structure of fieldwork and writing. He knows, for instance, from his own everyday encounters during fieldwork that sectarianism matters. And he also knows very well that writing about these issues in English for a Euro-American audience is a potential minefield. Double consciousness results in a disavowal that itself results in representational paralysis or theoretical diversion.

This same double consciousness, conjured by the justifiable anxieties of consolidation and appropriation, and which results in disavowal when it comes to one's work, is also responsible for the drive to censor, which takes the form of critique, the discourses of those intellectuals, militants, and artists in the Arab world who steer away from the critique of empire to address those same issues of authoritarianism, sectarianism, and gender inequality.[14] If the Muslim subjects and discourses are understood, sectarian ones are disavowed, and the liberal/leftist/feminist/queer/secular varieties are subject to criticism or critique. In this theoretical economy of handling difference, those who are seen to bear the least coefficient of difference do not get understood or redeemed as modern, or deconstructed as modern, but get hailed as accomplices of Empire. In splitting these subjects into two—"westernized natives," "liberal Muslims"—they conjure back into being specters of "culture" that are used to adjudicate on the representative nature, and therefore the validity and political import, of these discourses.[15]

If we shift our attention for a minute from geopolitical notions of Empire and the idealist predication of the subject as consciousness to the materialist predication of the subject as labor power, we get a very different picture of how what is constituted as difference relates to power.[16] Julia Elyachar's brilliant ethnography *Markets of Dispossession* shows how, by the late twentieth century, international organizations, the Egyptian state, and nongovernmental organizations attempted to produce new economic value by transforming the social networks and culture of Cairo craftsmen into value.[17] Nineteenth-century British colonial rulers such as Lord Cromer, twentieth-century modernizers, and historians of labor, Elyachar argues, put the indigenous cultural practices on the side of tradition, backwardness, and impediments to progress and development. Culture, which was thought to be an obstacle to modernity, was later incorporated into the market as a new source of economic value.[18]

Coda

For as long as I can remember, I have witnessed intellectuals and critical theorists slide from critique to loss and melancholia after having witnessed a political defeat or experienced a regression in the state of affairs of the world. Some Arab Marxists criticized liberalism, or thought that they had transcended it, as the revolution was just an arm's length away, before they suffered a string of defeats. In their wake, they rediscovered the works of nineteenth-century Arab liberals and mourned the margins of freedom that the prenationalist regimes enabled. Pierre Bourdieu spent a good deal of time as he was chiseling out his theoretical cathedral from the body of classical social theory, critically analyzing how the institutions of the welfare state reproduce social inequalities, before emerging from his theoretical workshop into the world of politics and strikes to staunchly defend those same institutions. Wendy Brown eloquently issued an appeal to resist left melancholy in the late 1990s before ringing the alarm about neoliberalism's hollowing out of liberal democracy a couple of years ago.[19] I can go on and on about critics of liberal multiculturalism mourning its loss, or potential loss, as chauvinist nationalism cast its ominous shadow over large parts of capitalist liberal democracies. What is common to these theoretical moves is a retreat to a second line of defense, in the wake of political setbacks, not theoretical critiques. This retreat seeks to defend what one took for granted and criticized earlier for its enmeshment in grids of power—domination, exploitation, exclusion, you name it. They index a regression in practice from the promises of a dignified life and equality, as well as a radical tightening, and fencing off, of the boundaries of political communities.

This retreat is in tension with the positions of some of these same thinkers—Bourdieu and Brown—against the collapse of the space of intellectual inquiry to that of political engagement and for preserving the autonomy of thought and the unexpected paths it may lead one toward.[20] This call is a generous and sensible one. I am also mindful that this call to separate thought from politics has certain political, economic, and institutional conditions, mainly that it is much more amenable to be achieved in liberal capitalist societies—for now at least—that have more stable political governance (not as prone to coups, civil wars, occupations), relatively autonomous educational institutions, more legal guarantees for freedom of expression, and economic conditions, such as salaries, grants, prizes, that allow some intellectuals to lead a more or less comfortable middle-class life. As Bourdieu reminded us in *Pascalian Meditations*, his last major work, *skholè* (leisure in Greek and the etymological root of school and scholastic) is the condition of existence of all scholarly fields.[21]

Thinking in politically saturated and precarious conditions, in a police state, during civil wars, in underfunded, failing educational institutions under the weight of bureaucratic inflation and political interferences—when speaking your mind, and parrhesiastic speech, can cost you anything from a mild phone call by a security officer to your life—is a different game altogether. The uncharitable readings, condemning tone, and accusations of unoriginality that contemporary Arab intellectuals are subjected to by epistemic critics could be partly understood as a result of the latter's embarrassment because of their "theoretical unsophistication"—read, they still believe in progress or that liberal democracy is a good thing—and "old fashioned" Enlightenment positions.[22] This, as I mentioned earlier, reproduces a historicist progressive logic in practice as it criticizes it in theory, contributing to reinforcing the trope of a "belated" Arab world. More importantly, though, its conflates the labors of the situated and accountable critic with what it takes to be the most updated version of critical theory, whose cognitive superiority enables it to be parachuted into Buenos Aires, Seoul, and Beirut to become operational in capturing these societies as soon it hits the ground.

Acknowledgments

From the time the idea of this book germinated till its completion, a little bit more than a decade passed. Researching, and writing about, the 1960s New Left and its becomings in the times that span the aftermath of the US invasion of Iraq and the Arab revolutions (2011–) was punctuated by a seesawing of intense political moods. Despair was washed away by revolutionary tides before receding, leaving in their wake those fortunate enough to survive the counter-revolutionary ordeal scattered and bereft. Revolutionary passion and political disenchantment moved out of the archive of theoretical texts and experiences I was writing about to lay claim on the present, mandating in the process a modulation of the major keys in which this past was cast and recast. I could not have kept on working and completing this book without the many gifts received along the way.

I am deeply grateful for the intellectual generosity of all the members of the 1960s generation of leftist militant intellectuals who took the time to share their own political experiences, answer my questions, and in the process help me work through the intergenerational blind spots that cropped up during our exchanges over the years. I would like to thank a few of them in person without whose offerings this work would not have been possible. I had very generative exchanges with Azza Charara Beydoun, Muhsin Ibrahim, Wajih Kawtharani, and Mahmoud Soueid. Reading Fawwaz Traboulsi's works and articles in the mid- to late 1990s was an integral part of my own political education. I later learned from him in person when he served as an external examiner on my master's thesis and have been in close, and enriching, conversation with him ever since. Ahmad Beydoun granted me full access to his personal Socialist Lebanon archive; without his trust and generosity, this book could not have been written. Abbas Beydoun's dialogues with Husayn Muruwwa were a source of inspiration. Reading the dialogues, it was hard to shake off the sense that as he sat down with the old man a few months before his assassination, he was very much aware of being a scribe to a vanishing world, as he came to terms with a share of his own inheritance. Beydoun's vivid, detailed recollections and the uncompromising honesty with which he revisited his own militant past were a gift to this project. In the autumn of a life of intellectual sparring, a time of treason of many "secular" bishops of Arab culture, the late Sadik al-Azm stood up for the Syrian revolution. His fiery public writings were matched in private by a gentle and dialogic sensibility.

I have been in conversation with Hazem Saghieh for nearly two decades now. Those exchanges have seeped in more than one way into the veins nourishing this book. From Hazem I also learned how to sustain warmth and cordiality amid heated political exchanges and intellectual differences. The initial ideas for what years later became this book emerged in conversation with the late Joseph Samaha. I learned from him in more ways than I can now remember since we first met in the late 1990s. Joseph's sharp analytical prose, his ethico-political disposition to not sell short his opponent's positions, and the sheer conceptual firepower of his arguments took the art of political editorials to unmatched heights: ephemeral sculptures of the "here" and "now." Waddah Charara concluded our initial interview by saying that he is less interested in future meetings in making speeches on "intellectuals" and "revolutions" than he is in being "questioned" and "shaken"—playfully borrowing Henri Calet's words "do not shake me, I am full of tears" before swiftly adding, "not ideological tears, though." These words capture something of Charara's intellectual dispositions that are difficult to discern if one is only acquainted with his complex scholarly works and trenchant political commentaries. In the numerous exchanges I had with him, I experienced firsthand an openness to critical dialogue and a deep ethnographic attunement to listening to, and mulling over, his interlocutors' words. I cannot help thinking that these deep antihierarchical dispositions are carryovers from his Maoist past. I cannot thank him enough for his generosity, which enabled a string of exchanges that began more than a decade ago as an expression of a desire for questions.

This book began as a dissertation in the Department of Anthropology at Columbia University, under the supervision of Brinkley Messick, who exuded a tranquil confidence in the potential of the project, which kept me going as I was feeling my way around my materials. I also learned from him how to go through texts with a fine-tooth comb looking for the worlds they construct, the practices they authorize, and the devices planted inside of them to preempt potential criticisms. Timothy Mitchell was generous enough to join my dissertation committee, and offer valuable feedback, in its last stages. I was fortunate to benefit from Rashid Khalidi's encyclopedic historical knowledge, close reading, and generosity with his time and suggestions. Meetings with Rashid always left me energized and recharged to resume the solitary labors of writing. Taking a graduate seminar with Talal Asad on "re-thinking the idea of tradition" and working as a teaching assistant in Elizabeth Povinelli's large lecture class on "the interpretation of cultures" were indelible formative experiences.

Nadia Abu el-Haj offered invaluable guidance, incisive comments that always tested the limits of my own argumentation, and friendship. I have learned so much about close reading and immanent criticism from her razor-sharp mind, and am forever in her debt. Ghassan Hage has accompanied all my projects from very early on. For the past two decades, he has offered a treasured friendship and an uncompromising critical eye with a talent for dismantling hurdles of all kind. I encountered David Scott's critical thought shortly after moving from Beirut to New York. Its resonance was immediate and its purchase incontrovertible. This book took shape in conversation with his work. Over the years, David offered unflinching support, criticism, generosity, and friendship, which were pivotal to carry out my work.

I later on held a postdoctoral fellowship at the Europe in the Middle East– The Middle East in Europe program (EUME), where I was affiliated with the Center for Middle Eastern and North African Politics at the Otto Suhr Institute for Political Science at the Freie Universität Berlin. I cannot thank Georges Khalil enough for his ongoing hospitality, interest in, and critical engagement with my work. The year I spent at EUME, which made Berlin a hub for critical work on the Middle East, was memorable on so many fronts, not least because it coincided with the seismic event of the Arab revolutions. I was also fortunate to be part of a vibrant cohort of EUME and Wissenschaftskolleg zu Berlin fellows that year. My thanks especially to Elias Khoury, who read a chapter of this book, provided valuable comments, and generously shared elements of his militant and intellectual trajectory, as well as to Toufoul Abou-Hodeib, Kamran Asdar Ali, Gülhan Erkaya Balsoy, Behrouz Ghamari-Tabrizi, Hannan Hammad, Tamer el-Leithy, and Zeynep Türkyılmaz. Cilja Harders ensured that I felt at home at the Center for Middle Eastern Politics, and immediately integrated me into its intellectual life, where I worked on my book, and shared many ideas and meals with Naoual BelAkhdar, Malika Bouziane, Anja Hoffman, and Katharina Lenner.

My time as a Harper Fellow at the Society of Fellows at the University of Chicago was one of intellectual effervescence, a collegiality bordering on solidarity, and warm friendships. This wouldn't have been possible without Hussain Agrama, Orit Bashkin, Greg Beckett, Fred Donner, Noha AboulMagd Foster, Roxana Galusca, Daragh Grant, Haytham Ibrahim, Reha Kedakal, Julia Klein, Satyel Larson, Mark Loeffler, Birte Loeschenkohl, William Mazzerella, Benjamin McKean, Yasmeen Mekkawi, Elham Miresheghi, Deb Neibel, Don Reneau, Geneviève Rousselière, Lauren Silvers, Karl Swinehart, Zhivka Valiavicharska,

Audrey Wasser, and Junko Yamazaki. Whether in Chicago or Berlin, Bettina Stoetzer read many drafts and provided numerous suggestions to realign and refine arguments. Lisa Wedeen offered infinite hospitality, quickly turning Hyde Park into home, and the gift of close, critical reading. The late Moishe Postone's piercing and passionate interpretation of Marx's concepts, and the tenacity with which he made the case for their relevance for our present, are simply unforgettable.

At the University of North Carolina–Chapel Hill I had the good fortune of working with, and learning from, many colleagues and students. My thanks especially to Jean Denison, Mark Driscoll, Carl Ernst, Juliane Hammer, Lori Harris, Emma Harver, Julia Haslet, Didem Havlioglu, Micah Hughes, Ji-Yeon Jo, Charles Kurzman, Townsend Middleton, Christopher Nelson, Robin Visser, Nadia Yaqub, and Gang Yue. Zeina Halabi was a daily interlocutor on all matters—intellectual, pedagogical and political—who made UNC feel like home. Treasured long walks with Cemil Aydin fine-tuned many ideas. Dispensing invaluable insights, which improved both form and content, came so naturally to Peter Redfield.

During my memorable year at the Institute for Advanced Studies, Joan Scott provided invaluable guidance, made sure I finished the manuscript before the end of my time there, and read it in its entirety. This book is so much better for Joan's generous and detailed insights. I cannot thank her enough. I also benefited greatly from the comments of my companions in the writing group Joan assembled: David Kazanjian, Massimiliano (Max) Tomba, and Linda Zerilli. I also learned a lot from my interlocutors in the informal reading groups we put together throughout the year, particularly from Amy Borovoy, Andrew Dilts, Reuben Miller, and Max, who was also my daily conversation partner. Our year-long reading seminar on rethinking critique in and for our present, steered by Didier Fassin and Bernard Harcourt, was a collegial and vibrant space of intellectual exchange made so by the contributions of Lori Allen, Nick Cheesman, Andrew Dilts, Karen Engle, Vanja Hamzic, David Kazanjian, Allegra McLeod, Juan Obarrio, Ayse Parla, Peter Redfield, and Linda Zerilli. The Historical Studies–Social Science Library was a formidable workspace, in large part due to its formidable staff; a special thanks to Erica Mosner, Marcia Tucker, and Kirstie Venanzi. I also shared many ideas with Lalaie Ameeriar, Céline Bessière, and Anne-Claire Defossez. Thomas Dodman has been a close intellectual interlocutor since our time together at the Institute. Pascal Marichalar read the entire manuscript and among other things provided crucial insight on the narrative arc of the book. Jaeeun Kim was an exemplary work companion who also made sure to hold me accountable to my self-imposed deadlines. Conversations with Christian Lentz continued in Durham and became part of the fabric of our lives. Didier Fassin offered encouragement and critical insights throughout the year. His generosity, and Donne Petito's and Laura McCune's hospitality, quickly made the school of social science a convivial environment in which to write, share ideas, and nurture friendships.

The Committee on Globalization and Social Change (CGSC) at the City University of New York's Graduate Center is an exceptionally vibrant space of intellectual exchange. I would like to thank all the participants in the 2017–18 seminar on populism for the conversations; in particular Susan Buck-Morss, Grace Davie, Linsey Ly, and Julie Skurski. Uday Mehta commented on a chapter and provided an insightful comparative perspective. Gary Wilder offered a warm welcome to the committee, incisive comments, and inspiring conversations.

Some parts of this book have been adapted from previously printed materials. An earlier version of chapter 2 appeared as "Dreams of a Dual Birth: Socialist Lebanon's World and Ours," *boundary 2* 43, no. 3 (2016): 313–35. Sections from chapter 3 appeared in "The Inward Turn and Its Vicissitudes: Culture, Society and Politics in Post-1967 Leftist Critiques," in *Local Politics and Contemporary Transformations in the Arab World: Governance beyond the Centre*, edited by Cilja Harders, Anja Hoffman, and Malika Bouziane (London: Palgrave, 2013), 91–109. Sections from chapters 5 and 6 appeared in "Sidelining Ideology: Arab Theory in the Metropole and Periphery, c. 1977," in *Transformations of Modern Arabic Thought: Intellectual Culture after the Liberal Age*, edited by Jens Hanssen and Max Weiss (Cambridge: Cambridge University Press, 2018), 163–80. My research and writing were supported by Columbia University's Anthropology Department and Middle East Institute, the Fulbright Program, Europe in the Middle East—The Middle East in Europe program (EUME), the Asian Studies Department at the University of North Carolina–Chapel Hill, and the Institute for Advanced Studies.

I would also like to thank my colleagues, the librarians, and staff at the Institut Français du Proche Orient with which I was affiliated during parts of my research: special thanks are due to Miriam Ababsa, Jalal al-Husseini, and Pénélope Larzillière. The Center for Behavioral Research at the American University of Beirut, in particular its administrator, Leila Jbara, welcomed me back as a predoctoral fellow in 2007–8. My thanks to Samir Khalaf, my teacher and the center's director, for his support and generosity over the years and for sustaining a vibrant space of interdisciplinary intellectual exchange for over a decade.

I owe an immeasurable debt to all the musicians/friends I learned from, and played with, over the years and who in their own way sustained me and enabled this project to be carried out: Tareq Abboushi, Huda Asfour, Tawfik Ben Amor, Issa Boulos, Nicholas Chbat, Jennifer Curtis, Johnny Farraj, Megan

Gould, Laura Grimaldi, Robbie Link, AJ Racy, Simon Shaheen, Zafer al-Tawil, and George Ziadeh. A special mention is reserved for Rachid Abu Hassan, my fellow conspirator in the New York Arab Orchestra, and for Wanees Zaarour, who welcomed me with open arms to the Middle East Music Ensemble at the University of Chicago. From Bassam Saba, an extraordinary mentor and musician, I learned the most.

I owe much to friends and colleagues who each in their own way helped shape this book. They include Saleh Agha, Sara Ajlyakin, Raghda Allouche, Lama Bashour, Rosie Bsheer, Jon Carter, John Chalcraft, Yasmeen Daifallah, Leila Dakhli, Hoda El Shakry, Omnia El Shakry, Nergis Ertürk, May Ghaibeh, Sari Hanafi, Amin Hannoun, Jens Hanssen, Sune Haugbolle, Ghenwa Hayek, Angie Heo, Alia Karame, Elizabeth Suzanne Kassab, Laleh Khalili, Adriane Lentz-Smith, Claudio Lomnitz, Lamia Moughnieh, Nada Moumtaz, Martha Mundy, Michelle Obeid, Zeynep Oz, Karim Nader, Friederike Pannewick, Karim Sadek, Nisrine Salti, Rasha Salti, Richard Saumarez-Smith, Kirsten Scheid, Ozge Serin, Zainab Saleh, Mayssoun Sukarieh, Jana Traboulsi, Ana Vinea, and Max Weiss.

At different stages, Alireza Doostdar, Samer Frangie, and Khaled Saghieh sat with me the longest in the engine room of this book. They offered unbounded solace, helpful suggestions and much-needed criticism that kept me going. Zouheir Aniss Rahhal accompanied this book during its various stages. Consumed early on by the fires of political passion, Zouheir crossed many borders and generations, lived in different regions, and inhabited a variety of social worlds. Zouheir, the anthropologist extraordinaire of the Lebanese Left, dispensed invaluable ethnographic, historical, and personal advice along the way in his characteristically off-the-cuff manner. I learned so much from him without him ever pretending to teach anything.

I had the good luck of being born into a family of unconditional love, boundless generosity, and unwavering trust. I was also fortunate to grow up in a buzzing open-door home, so to speak. My parents, Abdo Bardawil and Gisèle Araman-Bardawil, welcomed people from all walks of life, dissolving in the process the social hierarchies that divide people and ideologies, which pit them against each other, as civil and regional wars tore things down around us. This was not done out of ideological reasons. My parents never spoke about it. And they certainly never thought they were more "progressive" than others. I am infinitely grateful for growing up in a sea of difference suffused with a generous ethos, which always nurtured and never directed. Special thanks are due to Nadia Araman, Ziad Bardawil, Nicolas Araman, Sahab Bardawil, Bechara Bardawil, Tarek Bardawil, and Elie and Nicolas Geahchan. I am grateful for the many family members who sustained me with love and encouragement along the way.

Notes

NOTES TO PROLOGUE

1. For recent scholarship that similarly takes note of the overlooked status of the Arab Marxist archive, see Omnia el Shakry, "'History without Documents': The Vexed Archives of Decolonization in the Middle East," *American Historical Review* 120, no. 3 (2015): 920–34; and Sune Haugbolle, "The New Arab Left and 1967," *British Journal of Middle Eastern Studies* 44, no. 4 (2017): 497–512.

2. For a contemporary concern with mobilization across difference, see Anna Tsing, "Is There a Progressive Politics after Progress?" *Cultural Anthropology* website, accessed June 26, 2018, https://culanth.org/fieldsights/1133-is-there-a-progressive-politics-after -progress.

3. Reinhart Kosselleck, *Futures Past*, trans. Keith Tribe (New York: Columbia University Press, [1979] 2004. See also David Scott's rearticulation of Kosselleck's pivotal concepts—"spaces of experience" and "horizon of expectation"—to think the temporalities of texts in *Conscripts of Modernity: The Tragedy of Colonial Enlightenment* (Durham, NC: Duke University Press, 2004).

4. I borrow the notion of post-postcolonial from Charles Piot, *Nostalgia for the Future: West Africa after the Cold War* (Chicago: University of Chicago Press, 2010), 16.

5. Edward Said, *Culture and Imperialism* (New York: Vintage, 1993).

6. I engage the failures of the metropolitan anti-imperialist Left in "Forsaking the Syrian Revolution: An Anti-Imperialist Handbook," *al-Jumhuriya*, December 22, 2016, https://www.aljumhuriya.net/en/content/forsaking-syrian-revolution-anti-imperialist -handbook.

7. Rey Chow, *The Age of the World Target: Self-Referentiality in War, Theory, and Comparative Work* (Durham, NC: Duke University Press, 2006), 41. Hereafter cited in the body of the text.

8. Achille Mbembe, *Critique of Black Reason*, trans. Laurent Dubois (Durham, NC: Duke University Press, 2017), 1. See Ghassan Hage, *Alter-Politics: Critical Anthropology and the Radical Imagination* (Melbourne: Melbourne University Press, 2015) for an intellectually courageous and imaginative theoretical work that seeks to steer the radical critical imagination away from an exclusive investment in oppositional politics (antipolitics) and toward opening up new spaces for thought to reimagine our futures together (alter-politics).

1. Their occupations at the time: Fawwaz Traboulsi (student), Waddah Charara (school teacher), Wadad Chakhtoura (school teacher), Ahmad al-Zein (lawyer), Christian Ghazi (film director), Madonna Ghazi (school teacher), and Mahmoud Soueid (lawyer).

2. Partha Chatterjee, *Lineages of Political Society: Studies in Postcolonial Democracy* (New York: Columbia University Press, 2011).

3. Nicolas Dot-Pouillard, "De Pékin à Téhéran en regardant vers Jérusalem: La singulière conversion à L'Islamisme des 'Maos du Fatah'" [From Peking to Teheran while looking toward Jerusalem: The Singular Conversion to Islamism of "Fatah's Maoists"], *Cahiers de l'Institut Religioscope*, no. 2 (December 2008): 1–37.

4. I borrow the notion of "transversality of knowledges"—*la transversalité des savoirs*—from the French thinker Christine Buci-Glucksmann. https://www.franceculture.fr/emissions/voix-nue/christine-buci-glucksmann-15.

5. Homi Bhabha, *The Location of Culture* (New York: Routledge, 1994), and Jean Comaroff and John L. Comaroff, *Theory from the South: Or How Euro-America Is Evolving towards Africa* (New York: Routledge, [2012] 2016).

6. See Kristin Ross's insightful *May '68 and Its Afterlives* (Chicago: University of Chicago Press, 2002) for a discussion of the Third Worldist parenthesis when theory was generated from the South, and Gavin Walker's *The Sublime Perversion of Capital: Marxist Theory and the Politics of History in Modern Japan* (Durham, NC: Duke University Press, 2016) for a similar point regarding the invisibility of Japanese Marxist theorists.

7. See, for instance, Susan Buck-Morss, *Thinking Past Terror: Islamism and Critical Theory on the Left* (London: Verso, [2003] 2006). I offer an appreciative and critical engagement of Buck-Morss's work in chapter 2.

8. For a history of early generations of left-wing radicals in the region, which embeds it in global transformations, see Ilham Khuri-Makdisi, *The Eastern Mediterranean and the Making of Global Radicalism, 1860–1914* (Berkeley: University of California Press, 2013).

9. For a kindred critique of binaries, see Leyla Dakhli, "The Autumn of the Nahda in Light of the Arab Spring: Some Figures in the Carpet," in *Arabic Thought beyond the Liberal Age: Towards an Intellectual History of the Nahda*, edited by Jens Hanssen and Max Weiss (Cambridge: Cambridge University Press, 2016), 353.

10. For a discussion on the practice of contemporary Arab intellectual history, see Max Weiss and Jens Hanssen, "Introduction: Arabic Intellectual History Between the Postwar and the Postcolonial," in *Arabic Thought against the Authoritarian Age: Towards an Intellectual History of the Present*, ed. Jens Hanssen and Max Weiss (Cambridge: Cambridge University Press, 2018), 1–35.

11. Volumes dealing with contemporary thinkers and trends in Arab thought do not include Edward Said among the authors they discuss. See, for example, Ibrahim Abu Rabi', *Contemporary Arab Thought: Studies in Post-1967 Arab Intellectual History* (London: Pluto, 2004); Suzanne Elizabeth Kassab, *Contemporary Arab Thought: Cultural Critique in Comparative Perspective* (New York: Columbia University Press, 2009).

12. See Walter Benjamin, "Left-Wing Melancholy (On Erich Kästner's New Book of Poems)," *Screen* 15, no. 2 (1974): 28–32; and Wendy Brown, "Resisting Left Melancholy," *boundary 2* 26, no. 3 (1999): 19–27. Enzo Traverso's *Left-Wing Melancholy: Marxism, Mem-*

ory, Culture (New York: Columbia University Press, 2016), offers a more appreciative reading of the potential of Left melancholy than Brown, who interprets it as "Benjamin's name for a mournful, conservative, backward-looking attachment to a feeling, analysis, or relationship that has been rendered thinglike and frozen in the heart of the putative left," 22. I am deploying Left melancholy in Brown's sense to point to a structure of feeling among leftists in Lebanon of different generations, who mourn the good old days of the 1960s and 1970s. Having lived through these times is of course not necessary to be afflicted by Left melancholy. See Nicolas Dot-Pouillard, "Boire à Hamra: Une jeunesse nostalgique à Beyrouth?" [Drinking in Hamra: A Nostalgic Youth in Beirut?], in *Jeunesses Arabe—Du Maroc au Yémen: Loisirs, Cultures et Politiques* [Arab Youth—From Morocco to Yemen: Entertainments, Cultures and Politics], ed. Laurent Bonnefoy and Miriam Catusse (Paris: La Découverte, 2013), 125–33.

13. Talal Asad's early work is exemplary in this respect, and so are the reflexive writings in the 1980s, such as James Clifford and George Marcus, eds., *Writing Culture: The Poetics and Politics of Ethnography* (Berkeley: University of California Press, 1986), and James Clifford, *The Predicament of Culture* (Cambridge, MA: Harvard University Press, 1988).

14. Middle East anthropology has been exploring research veins that transcend the earlier theoretical metonyms for the study of the region—tribalism, religion, gender—as well as the frontiers of nation-states and the boundaries of religious traditions. These works explore lives, ideas, practices, and institutions in the Arab world through situating them within transnational streams of capital, art, politics, and mass media. See Julia Elyachar, *Markets of Dispossession, NGOs, Economic Development, and the State* (Durham, NC: Duke University Press, 2005); Jessica Winegar, *Creative Reckonings: The Politics of Art and Culture in Contemporary Egypt* (Stanford: Stanford University Press, 2006); Lori Allen, *The Rise and Fall of Human Rights: Cynicism and Politics in Occupied Palestine* (Stanford: Stanford University Press, 2013); Amahl Bishara, *Back Stories: US News Production and Palestinian Politics* (Stanford: Stanford University Press, 2012).

15. For a recent reflexive work that turns its ethnographic gaze inward to investigate the practice of Middle East anthropology in the US academy, see Lara Deeb and Jessica Winegar, *Anthropology's Politics: Disciplining the Middle East* (Stanford: Stanford University Press, 2016).

16. Jean Comaroff and John Comaroff call attention to a recent "retreat from theory" in the social sciences at large and in anthropology, in "Theory from the South: A Rejoinder," "Theorizing the Contemporary," *Cultural Anthropology* website, February 25, 2012, https://culanth.org/fieldsights/273-theory-from-the-south-a-rejoinder.

17. Robert A. Fernea and James M. Malakey, "Anthropology of the Middle East: A Critical Assessment," *Annual Review of Anthropology* 4 (1975): 183–206.

18. Lila Abu-Lughod, "Zones of Theory of Theory in the Anthropology of the Arab World," *Annual Review of Anthropology* 18 (1989): 267–306. For a more recent review of the literature on the region, see Lara Deeb and Jessica Winegar, "Anthropologies of Arab-Majority Societies," *Annual Review of Anthropology* 41 (2012): 537–58.

19. "What we call our data," as Clifford Geertz put it in his memorable phrase, "are really our own constructions of other people's constructions of what they and their compatriots are up to." Clifford Geertz, *The Interpretation of Cultures* (New York: Basic Books, 1973), 9.

20. See Vincent Crapanzano's *Tuhami: Portrait of a Moroccan* (Chicago: University of Chicago Press, 1980) for an early methodological reflection on the consequences of the effacement of the anthropologist's mark in both of these two moments.

21. See Talal Asad's "Ethnographic Representation, Statistics and Modern Power," *Social Research* 61, no. 1 (1994): 55–88, for an incisive discussion of the empiricist distinction between "observation" and "theorization" in ethnography and his plea, also briefly discussed in the introduction to *Formations of the Secular* (Stanford: Stanford University Press, 2003), not to collapse anthropology as a discipline of intellectual inquiry into its predominant method, fieldwork-based ethnography.

22. Cited, and critically engaged, in Talal Asad, "Anthropology and the Analysis of Ideology," *Man* 14, no. 4 (1979): 622.

23. Michael Jackson, "Ajàlá's Heads: Reflections on Anthropology and Philosophy in a West African Setting," in *The Ground Between: Anthropologists Engage Philosophy*, ed. Veena Das, Michael Jackson, Arthur Kleinman, and Bhrigupati Singh (Durham, NC: Duke University Press, 2014), 41.

24. Jackson, "Ajàlá's Heads," 42.

25. Jackson, "Ajàlá's Heads," 28.

26. João Biehl and Peter Locke, "Deleuze and the Anthropology of Becoming," *Current Anthropology* 51, no.3 (2010): 348.

27. Giovanni Da Col and David Graeber, "Foreword: The Return of Ethnographic Theory," *HAU: Journal of Ethnographic Theory* 1, no. 1 (2011): vi–xxxv.

28. Da Col and Graeber, "Foreword," xii.

29. Asad, "Anthropology and the Analysis of Ideology," 614.

30. Émile Durkheim opened his magisterial *The Elementary Forms of Religious Life* (New York: Free Press, [1912] 1995) by asserting the social origins of the categories of human thought, targeting both philosophical empiricists and a priorists. Pierre Bourdieu makes a homologous move that grounds aesthetic perception and consumption in social space in *Distinction: A Social Critique of the Judgment of Taste*, trans. Richard Nice (Cambridge, MA: Harvard University Press, [1979] 1984). For an early critique of Bourdieu's sociology, see Jacques Rancière, *The Philosopher and His Poor*, trans. John Drury, Corinne Oster, and Andrew Parker (Durham, NC: Duke University Press, [1983] 2004).

31. David Scott, *Stuart Hall's Voice: Intimations of an Ethics of Receptive Generosity* (Durham, NC: Duke University Press, 2017), 132.

32. See Bruno Perreau, *Queer Theory: The French Response* (Stanford: Stanford University Press, 2016). "Thus, when the category 'queer' travels from one shore of the Atlantic to the other," Perreau writes, "it retains the same terms, but its meaning is literally distorted.... I bring to light the numerous modulations of queer theory, showing how sexuality, nation, and community are conceptually and politically interwoven," 9.

33. For works that share similar concerns on how to approach the archive of Arab contemporary thought, see Samer Frangie, "Theorizing from the Periphery: The Intellectual Project of Mahdi 'Amil," *International Journal of Middle East Studies* 44, no. 3 (2012): 465–82, and Omnia El Shakry, *The Arabic Freud: Psychoanalysis and Islam in Modern Egypt* (Princeton, NJ: Princeton University Press, 2017).

34. For a divergent position that argues for forging critical theory for historical narrative in the study of contemporary Arab thought, see Yoav Di-Capua, *No Exit: Arab Existentialism, Jean-Paul Sartre, and Decolonization* (Chicago: University of Chicago Press, 2018), 20–23.

35. Among the key political events and structural economic, legal, and educational transformations that have destroyed certain ways of being in the world and brought forth new ones are Napoleon's invasion of Egypt (1798); the Ottoman Tanzimat (1839–76), which included the codification of parts of the Shari'a put forth in the Mecelle since 1869; the integration of Mount Lebanon's silk-centered production into the world economy; dense missionary activity and competition; the French Mandate in Syria and Lebanon since 1918; the declaration of the Lebanese Republic by French colonial powers in 1926; and its independence in 1943.

36. The relationship to France is part of a long and complex history, whose multiple episodes include the French Mandate in Syria and Lebanon (1920–43), missionary activity, and centuries-old privileged commercial, political, and religious ties with the Christian Maronites. See Iliya Harik, *Politics and Change in a Traditional Society: Lebanon, 1711–1845* (Princeton, NJ: Princeton University Press, 1968).

37. Dense missionary activities and competition resulted in the founding of the Syrian Protestant College (1866) by American Protestants, which later became the American University of Beirut (1920), and the Université Saint-Joseph (1875) by Catholic Jesuits. These two elite private institutions of higher learning founded by missionaries in the nineteenth century are still active today. Currently, their predominant languages of instruction are English and French, respectively.

38. In their teaching career at the Lebanese University, Charara and Beydoun relied a lot on existing translations in Arabic or translated the material they wanted to teach from French into Arabic themselves. This was a labor that Traboulsi, teaching in English in the private elite universities, was spared.

39. For a recent exploration of the dislodging of the image of the public intellectual as a prophetic figure and a national icon from the 1990s onward, see Zeina G. Halabi, *The Unmaking of the Arab Intellectual: Prophecy, Exile and the Nation* (Edinburgh: Edinburgh University Press, 2017).

40. They translated writings by authors from the revolutionary tradition such as Karl Marx, Isaac Deutscher, V. I. Lenin, Leon Trotsky, Antonio Gramsci, John Berger, Mao Tse-Tung, and Cornelius Castoriadis; anthropological authors such as Claude Lévi-Strauss and Evans Pritchard; poets such as René Char, Pierre Tardieu, and Yannis Ritsos. In the past two decades, Fawwaz Traboulsi translated some of Edward Said's later works including his autobiography, *Out of Place: A Memoir* (New York: Knopf, 1999). Waddah Charara, who was for a number of years the editor of *Sahafat al-'Alam* (the World Press supplement) of the Saudi-owned Arab daily *al-Hayat*, translated a number of newspaper, magazine, and journal articles that were published every Wednesday.

41. "The migration to the metropolis," Robert Malley wrote, "resulted in contact with Third World exiles," whose solidarity can be viewed as the "diaspora's offspring." Robert Malley, *The Call from Algeria: Third Worldism, Revolution, and the Turn to Islam* (Los Angeles: University of California Press, 1996), 22–23.

42. "Focusing on transfiguration," Dilip Parameshwar Gaonkar and Elizabeth Povinelli write, "rather than translation—the refunctioning of a text as such for different demanding-sites—orients our analysis toward the calibration of vectors of power rather than vectors of meaning-value. We will care more about the distribution of power than of meaning, more about institutions of intelligibility, livability, and viability than about translation." Dilip Parameshwar Gaonkar and Elizabeth A. Povinelli, "Technologies of Public Forms: Circulation, Transfiguration, Recognition," *Public Culture* 15, no. 3 (2003): 396.

43. Talal Asad, "A Comment on Translation, Critique, and Subversion," in *Between Languages and Cultures: Translation and Cross-cultural Texts*, ed. Anuradha Dingwaney and Carol Maier (Pittsburgh: University of Pittsburgh Press, 1995), 330. Take, for instance, the Algerian journalist and writer Kamel Daoud, whose novel *The Meursault Investigation* (Meursault, contre-enquête), written in French, was crowned with three prestigious French literary prizes: the Prix François Mauriac and Prix des Cinq Continents de la Francophonie in 2014 and the Prix Goncourt in 2015. After consecration, the writer's culturalist statements—"Is the refugee a 'savage'?" he asked—about the sexual misery of the Arab world, its sick relationship to women, bodies, and desire that he professed in *Le Monde* (January 29, 2016) in the wake of New Year's Eve's sexual assaults on women in Cologne circulated globally (the article was also published in the *New York Times*), spawning discourses pointing out the author's racist and colonial account, while others came to his defense. http://www.bbc.com/news/world-europe-35653496.

44. Rosalind Morris, "Introduction," in *Can the Subaltern Speak? Reflections on the History of an Idea*, ed. Rosalind Morris (New York: Columbia University Press, 2010), 14.

45. For a critical reading of Marxism in India and a cogent discussion of the different grounds of persuasion in the history of ideas, see Sudipta Kaviraj, "Marxism in Translation: Critical Reflections on Indian Radical Thought," in *Political Judgement: Essays for John Dunn*, ed. Richard Bourke and Raymond Guess (Cambridge: Cambridge University Press, 2009), 172–99.

46. For a series of dialogues on translation and the constitution of universality, see Judith Butler, Ernesto Laclau, and Slavoj Žižek, *Contingency, Universality, Hegemony: Contemporary Dialogues on the Left* (London: Verso, 2000), 91–107.

47. Faleh A. Jabar, "The Arab Communist Parties in Search of an Identity," in *Post-Marxism and the Middle East*, ed. Faleh A. Jabar (London: Saqi Books, 1997).

48. For traditional anthropological work on Lebanon that was later criticized by Talal Asad in passing for its failure to account for structural transformations and political power that was contemporaneous with, and seems "belated" from the perspective of the Marxist theory and practice of Socialist Lebanon, see Emrys L. Peters, "Aspects of Rank and Status amongst Muslims in a Lebanese Village," in *Mediterranean Countrymen*, ed. Julian Pitt-Rivers (The Hague: Mouton, 1963), 159–200, and Emrys L. Peters, "Shifts in Power in a Lebanese Village," in *Rural Politics and Social Change in the Middle East*, ed. Richard Antoun and Iliya Harik (Bloomington: Indiana University Press, 1972), 165–97. For Asad's critique, see Talal Asad, "Anthropological Texts and Ideological Problems: An Analysis of Cohen on Arab Villages in Israel," *Economy and Society* 4, no. 3 (1975): 276.

49. Jean-François Lyotard, *The Postmodern Condition: A Report on Knowledge* (Minneapolis: University of Minnesota Press, [1979] 1984).

50. Edward Said, *Orientalism* (New York: Vintage Books, [1978] 1994), 325.

51. Said, *Orientalism*, 325.

52. David Scott, *Refashioning Futures: Criticism after Postcoloniality* (Princeton, NJ: Princeton University Press, 1999).

53. See Charles Hirschkind and Saba Mahmood, "Feminism, the Taliban, and the Politics of Counter-Insurgency," *Anthropological Quarterly* 75, no. 2 (2002): 107–22.

54. See Nadia Abu El-Haj, "Edward Said and the Political Present," *American Ethnologist* 32, no. 4 (2005): 538–55, for an insightful reading of the scholarly and political relevance of Said's oeuvre in the aftermaths of the US wars in Afghanistan and Iraq.

55. Said, *Orientalism*, 27.

56. Leila Ahmed, *Women and Gender in Islam: Historical Roots of a Modern Debate* (New Haven, CT: Yale University Press, 1992), 162–63.

57. See Joseph A. Massad, *Desiring Arabs* (Chicago: University of Chicago Press, 2007), 17, for a reading practice that underscores "the continuing influence of Orientalist and colonial taxonomies on Arab intellectual production." See also Saba Mahmood, "Secularism, Hermeneutics, and Empire: The Politics of Islamic Reformation," *Public Culture* 18, no. 2 (2006): 323–47, and the subsequent exchange between Mahmood and Stathis Gourgouris on the pages of *Public Culture*. Stathis Gourgouris, "Detranscendentalizing the Secular," *Public Culture* 20, no. 3 (2008): 437–45; Saba Mahmood, "Is Critique Secular? A Symposium at UC Berkeley," *Public Culture* 20, no. 3 (2008): 447–52; Stathis Gourgouris, "Antisecularist Failures: A Counterresponse to Saba Mahmood," *Public Culture* 20, no. 3 (2008): 453–59; and Saba Mahmood, "Secular Imperatives?," *Public Culture* 20, no. 3 (2008): 461–65.

58. For an insightful discussion of the authority of discourses in the societies anthropologists study and of anthropological—and theoretical—discourses, see Asad, "Anthropology and the Analysis of Ideology," and David Scott, "Criticism and Culture: Theory and Post-Colonial Claims on Anthropological Disciplinarity," *Critique of Anthropology* 12, no. 4 (1992): 371–94.

59. See Gayatri Chakravorty Spivak's discussion of the two meanings of representation in "Can the Subaltern Speak?" in *The Post-Colonial Studies Reader*, ed. Bill Ashcroft, Gareth Griffiths, and Helen Tiffin (New York: Routledge, 1995), 28–37.

60. Kuan-Hsing Chen, *Asia as Method: Toward Deimperialization* (Durham, NC: Duke University Press, 2010), 2.

61. Albert Hourani, *Arabic Thought in the Liberal Age, 1798–1939* (Cambridge: Cambridge University Press, [1962] 1983). See Rashid Khalidi, "The Legacies of *Arabic Thought in the Liberal Age*," in *Arabic Thought beyond the Liberal Age: Towards an Intellectual History of the Nahda*, ed. Jens Hanssen and Max Weiss (Cambridge: Cambridge University Press, 2016), 375–86.

62. Hourani, *Arabic Thought*, v.

63. Gary Wilder, *Freedom Time: Decolonization and the Future of the World* (Durham, NC: Duke University Press, 2015), 11.

64. For two different critiques of how difference is configured as a site of resistance against universal homogenizing forces that engages Dipesh Chakrabarty's *Provincializing Europe: Postcolonial Thought and Historical Difference* (Princeton, NJ: Princeton University Press, 2007), see Zahid R. Chaudhary, "Subjects in Difference: Walter Benjamin, Frantz

Fanon, and Postcolonial Theory," *Differences* 23, no. 1 (2012): 151–83, and Viren Murthy, "Looking for Resistance in All the Wrong Places? Chibber, Chakrabarty, and a Tale of Two Histories," *Critical Historical Studies* 2, no. 1 (2015): 113–53.

65. See James Tully, *Meaning and Context: Quentin Skinner and His Critics* (Princeton, NJ: Princeton University Press, 1989), for a collection of Skinner's methodological writings, a valuable introduction to his work by Tully and a series of engagements with it.

66. In addition to countering the anachronistic readings of texts, this method also bypasses causal explanation by attempting understanding through a redescription of the linguistic action in terms of its ideological point and not "in terms of an independently specifiable condition." Tully, *Meaning and Context*, 10.

67. Skinner's historical method, centering as it does on the figure of the author and the contrast-effect her intervention creates in a field of arguments, operates at a different level of analysis than Michel Foucault's archaeologies, which dilute the author in a deep episteme, and the Foucauldian-inspired critique of discursive assumptions. See Michel Foucault, *Les mots et les choses: Une archéologie des sciences humaines* [The Order of Things: An Archeology of the Human Sciences] (Paris: Gallimard, 1966).

68. Quentin Skinner, "An Interview with Quentin Skinner," *Cogito* 11, no. 2 (1997): 71.

69. Skinner, "Interview with Quentin Skinner," 73.

70. David Scott, "David Scott by Stuart Hall," *Bomb* 90 (Winter 2005), https://bombmagazine.org/articles/david-scott/.

71. Scott, *Conscripts of Modernity*, 4.

72. Scott, *Conscripts of Modernity*, 4.

73. Scott, "David Scott by Stuart Hall."

74. Scott, *Conscripts of Modernity*, 54.

75. Part of the differences between Scott and Skinner on the uses of historical inquiry can be understood in light of their different intellectual projects and objects of inquiry. Skinner, the historian of early modern political thought, seeks to unearth traditions of political argument that have faded from view in the past five centuries, and therefore destabilize the current liberal idioms through which political thinking proceeds in the present. While Scott's interest in *Conscripts of Modernity* is in a much more recent mid-twentieth century anticolonial history, and his project is not to rehabilitate lost treasures, as Skinner would put it, but to escape antiessentialist presentism that dismisses the older generation's work, through reconstituting their intervention in their context and to interrogate whether our present demands of us a different kind of intervention and different practices of criticism. While both thinkers engage in a historical reconstruction, their objects, periods of inquiry, and projects are different: Skinner's past has long ago faded from view, while Scott's past is still active in the present, and therefore the uses historical reconstruction are put to are of a different order.

76. Scott, *Conscripts of Modernity*, 55.

77. For an insightful reconstruction of the problem-space of French political anthropology, and its comparison with the US, which ends with a call for a critical French political anthropology, see Didier Fassin, "La politique des anthropologues: Une histoire

Française" [The Politics of Anthropologists: A French History], *L'Homme* 185–86 (2008): 165–86.

78. See Linda M. G. Zerilli, "Feminism, Critique, and the Realistic Spirit," *Philosophy & Rhetoric* 50, no. 4 (2017): 589–611.

NOTES TO CHAPTER 1

1. Hourani, *Arabic Thought*, vii.
2. Hourani, *Arabic Thought*, viii.
3. Hourani, *Arabic Thought*, vii–ix.
4. Albert Hourani, "Albert Hourani," in *Approaches to the History of the Middle East: Interviews with Leading Middle East Historians*, ed. Nancy Gallagher (Reading, UK: Ithaca Press, 1994), 33.
5. Hourani, *Arabic Thought*, ix.
6. Hourani, *Arabic Thought*, ix.
7. Hourani, *Arabic Thought*, 348.
8. Hourani, *Arabic Thought*, 348.
9. Hourani, *Arabic Thought*, 349.
10. 'Partha Chatterjee, "Anderson's Utopia," *Diacritics* 29, no. 4 (Winter 1999): 130.
11. For those of them who are of Shi'i descent, they are lodged between the "religion to modern secular ideologies" generation of Husayn Muruwwa (1910–87), who moved from being a Shi'i cleric to a central committee member of the Lebanese Communist Party, and the militant Islamic revival generation that came in the aftermath of the Iranian Revolution—Hassan Nasrallah, the secretary general of Hizbullah, was born in 1960.
12. See Bruno Latour, "The Recall of Modernity: Anthropological Approaches," trans. Stephen Muecke, *Cultural Studies Review* 13, no. 1 (March 2007): 11–30.
13. Cited in Said, *Orientalism*, 318.
14. See Roschanak Shaery-Eisenlohr, *Shi'ite Lebanon: Transnational Religion and the Making of National Identities* (New York: Columbia University Press, 2008), 24, and Waddah Charara, "al-Rifaq" [The Comrades], in *Isti'naf al-Badi': Muhawalat fi al-'Ilaqa Ma Bayn al-Tarikh wa-l-Falsafa* [The Resumption of Beginnings: Attempts at an Encounter between History and Philosophy] (Beirut: Dar al-Hadatha, 1981), 11–55.
15. Brinkley Messick, *The Calligraphic State: Textual Domination and History in a Muslim Society* (Berkeley: University of California Press, 1993), 5.
16. The Maronites, an indigenous Christian sect in communion with the Roman Catholic Church, are Lebanon's largest Christian community.
17. Samir Kassir, *La Guerre du Liban: De la dissension nationale au conflit régional 1975–82* [The Lebanon War: From National Strife to a Regional Conflict 1975–82] (Paris: Karthala, 1994), 33.
18. Walid Khalidi, *Conflict and Violence in Lebanon: Confrontation in the Middle East* (Cambridge, MA: Center for International Affairs Harvard University, 1979), 35.
19. Borrowed from the famous 1949 quip of George Naccache, the Lebanese Francophone journalist and editor, "Deux négations ne font pas une nation" [Two negations do not make a nation].

20. See Kamal Salibi, *A House of Many Mansions: The History of Lebanon Reconsidered* (Berkeley: University of California Press, 1990).

21. In the aftermath of independence, the Lebanese elites agreed on "the distribution of the chief political and administrative responsibilities, among the six largest communities: Maronite, Greek Orthodox, Greek Catholic, Sunni, Shi'i, and Druze. At the suggestion of General Spears, the British delegate in Beirut, the number of parliamentary seats proportionally assigned according to data from the 1932 census was to be a multiple of eleven: for each six Christian deputies, the chamber would include five Muslim and Druze deputies. In the government and civil service, the ratio accepted was 50:50, but according to a hierarchy in which the Maronites still held the top positions: the presidency and the command of the army. The office of prime minister went to the Sunnis, the presidency of the parliament to the Shi'is, and the vice presidency to the Greek Orthodox. Thus, on the pretext of securing an "equitable" distribution of power and its prerequisites, the criterion of communitarianism took precedence over that of competence at every level of the political hierarchy: the administration, the judicial apparatus, the municipal councils, the army, and even the banking sector." Elizabeth Picard, *Lebanon, a Shattered Country: Myths and Realities of the Wars in Lebanon*, trans. Franklin Philip (New York: Holmes and Meier, 1996), 70. The literature on Lebanon uses communitarianism, confessionalism and sectarianism interchangeably to denote the system of political representation based on quotas for the different religious minorities constitutive of Lebanon, as well as for the form of sectarian loyalty that hinders allegiance to the nation.

22. For instance, a substantial number of Christian Palestinian refugees were granted Lebanese citizenship under the regime of President Camille Chamoun in the 1950s. In the aftermath of the Syrian revolution (2011), Lebanon received more than one million, predominantly Sunni, Syrian refugees. They are living in extremely precarious conditions under constant threat of xenophobic attacks and police and army roundups, as well as the overtly racist discourses circulating in the public sphere by some government officials, politicians, and the media.

23. Some of its ideologues sought to bypass Arab history and identity by anchoring the Lebanese nation in Phoenician times, and calling in its extreme right-wing versions to drop the Arabic script and classical Arabic and adopt a Latinized alphabet to write the Lebanese dialect.

24. Kassir, *La Guerre du Liban*, 55.

25. Kassir, *La Guerre du Liban*, 55. Samir Kassir, a professor of history at the Université Saint-Joseph in Beirut, was a distinguished and courageous leftist political editorialist. He was assassinated on June 2, 2005, in Beirut, in the turbulent times that followed the assassination of Prime Minister Rafic al-Hariri on February 14, 2005, and the subsequent withdrawal of Syrian troops from the country under substantial internal and international pressure in April of the same year. Kassir in the last years of his tragically interrupted life wrote fiery articles against the Syrian Ba'th regime and its domineering influence in Lebanon, and was politically involved in the political movement (March 14th) calling for reclaiming Lebanese sovereignty from Syrian tutelage in a very tense regional and international conjuncture, characterized by the US occupation of Iraq in 2003, the worsening of its relations with Syria, and direct UN interference (UNSC 1559), which called

"upon all remaining foreign forces [i.e., Syria] to withdraw from Lebanon" and "for the disbanding and disarmament of all Lebanese and non-Lebanese militias," referring mainly to Hizbullah's guerrilla force. It is widely believed that the Syrian regime or its local allies and acolytes are behind Kassir's assassination.

26. Waddah Charara, interview by author, June 9, 2007, Beirut, Lebanon.

27. Mahmoud Soueid, interview by author, July 7, 2008, Beirut, Lebanon.

28. Waddah Charara, *Transformations d'une manifestation religieuse dans un village du Liban-Sud, Ashura* [Transformations of a Religious Manifestation in a Village of Southern Lebanon ('Ashura)] (Beirut: Publications du Centre de Recherches de L'Institut des Sciences Sociales, 1968), 3.

29. Mahmoud Soueid, interview by author, July 7, 2008, Beirut, Lebanon.

30. Wajih Kawtharani, interview by author, July 15, 2008, Beirut, Lebanon.

31. Kawtharani's father owned a grocery store in Beirut while Soueid's father was a Sunni cleric in a poor southern village. Charara's father, a prolific author, worked at the Bibliothèque Nationale Libanaise, and Abbas Beydoun's father was a school teacher and local intellectual. Ahmad Beydoun's case is different. He is the son of Abdel Latif Beydoun, a notable from Bint Jbayl who was twice elected to the Lebanese Parliament.

32. Fawwaz Traboulsi, *Surat al-Fata bi-l-Ahmar: Ayyam fi al-Silm wa-l-Harb* [Portrait of the Young Man in Red: Days of Peace and War] (Beirut: Riad el-Rayyes Books, 1997), 45. Bouhired, the twenty-year-old militant, quickly became an icon in the Arab world of the Algerian anticolonial struggle against the French. Iraqi, Syrian, Egyptian, and Algerian poets, among others, would depict her struggle. The Egyptian director Youssef Chahin directed a movie entitled *Djamila* in 1958 and the Lebanese diva Fairuz sang a "Letter to Djamila" in 1962. Hereafter cited in its English translation.

33. Traboulsi, *Portrait of the Young Man in Red,* 45.

34. Traboulsi, *Portrait of the Young Man in Red,* 45.

35. November 1, 1954, is the date of the first radio appeal to the Algerian people broadcast by the Front de Libération Nationale and is used to mark the beginning of the war of independence.

36. Waddah Charara, interview by author, June, 9, 2007, Beirut, Lebanon.

37. See Salma Khadra Jayusi, *Modern Arabic Poetry: An Anthology* (New York: Columbia University Press, 1987), for biographical entries on both poets.

38. Azza Charara Beydoun, interview by author, July 23, 2007, Beirut, Lebanon.

39. Wajih Kawtharani, interview by author, July 15, 2008, Beirut, Lebanon. See Laura M. James, "Whose Voice? Nasser, the Arabs, and 'Sawt al-Arab' Radio," *Transnational Broadcasting Studies*, no. 16 (June–December 2006), accessed July 21, 2010, http://www.tbsjournal.com/James.html.

40. James, "Whose Voice?"

41. Abbas Beydoun, interview by author, July 31, 2008, Beirut, Lebanon.

42. Muhsin Ibrahim, interview by author, August 4, 2008, Beirut, Lebanon.

43. Charara's second baptism was traveling with his father to Damascus in 1954 on the day the newspapers were discussing Czech arms deals, and being present among family, politician, and poet friends of his father who were discussing the implications of this

important event. He dubs listening to Nasser's entire speech on the day of the national-ization of the canal his third baptism.

44. Azza Charara Beydoun, interview by author, July 23, 2007, Beirut, Lebanon.

45. "Established in 1929," the school, which was created "because of the discrimination and socioeconomic difficulties confronting rural and poor Shi'ite migrants to Beirut," also doubled in its beginnings as a "socioreligious center for many Shi'ites" where the new migrants commemorated 'Ashura. Shaery-Eisenlohr, *Shi'ite Lebanon*, 56.

46. Abbas Beydoun, interview by author, July 31, 2008, Beirut, Lebanon.

47. Mahmoud Soueid, interview by author, July 7, 2008, Beirut, Lebanon. For Olivier Carré, the French political sociologist, Nasserism was characterized more by an attach-ment to a charismatic leader than it was to a doctrine. Carré mentions the diatribes between Nasser and the Ba'th in the aftermath of the union's rupture. Numerous writings by the Ba'th, from 1961 to 1965, accused Nasser of Arab inauthenticity, while Nasser replied, accusing it of being a fascist and atheist party in 1963. The question of Palestine and the Arab-Israeli struggle was at the heart of these quarrels. To Nasser's position in 1964–65, that the battle against Israel was not possible until Arab unity was attained, the Ba'th replied, naming Nasser the Pétain of the Arab Nation, and that the champion of the Battle of Suez (1956) was a traitor to Israel, and would be punished by the Arab people. See Oliver Carré, *Le nationalisme Arabe* (Paris: Payot, [1993] 1996), 105–8.

48. Muhsin Ibrahim, interview by author, August 4, 2008, Beirut, Lebanon.

49. The documents and arguments for dropping the earlier version of Arab national-ism and espousing Marxism-Leninism were published under the title *Limadha Munaz-zamat al-Ishtirakiyyn al-Lubnaniyyin (Harakat al-Qawmiyyin al-'Arab min al-Fashiyya ila al-Nassiriyya): Tahlil wa Naqd* [The Organization of Lebanese Socialists, What For? (The Arab Nationalist Movement from Fascism to Nasserism): An Analysis and a Critique] (Beirut: Dar al-Tali'a, 1970).

50. Fawwaz Traboulsi, *A History of Modern Lebanon* (London: Pluto Press, 2007), 130.

51. Waddah Charara, interview by author, June 9, 2007, Beirut, Lebanon.

52. Ahmad Beydoun, interview by author, July 11, 2007, Beirut, Lebanon. The Pha-langes are a right-wing Christian Lebanese nationalist party founded in 1936. They were one of the major political and military players in the first years of the Lebanese civil and regional war, facing the predominantly Muslim Lebanese National Movement (LNM), a pro-Palestinian coalition of leftist and Arab nationalist parties.

53. The historical background supplied in this section relies on Fawwaz Traboulsi's *History of Modern Lebanon*.

54. Traboulsi, *History of Modern Lebanon*, 131.

55. Charles Malik (1906–89)—the new foreign minister—was a philosopher by training, graduating from Harvard in 1937 after a period of study in Germany in the early 1930s. Malik was one of the drafters of the Universal Declaration of Human Rights at the United Nations and succeeded Eleanor Roosevelt in chairing the commission for human rights in 1951, after her retirement. Later on, Malik was also Lebanon's representative at the nonaligned conference in Bandung that took place in April 1955, a few months after the signing of the Baghdad Pact, where he pushed for the acknowledgment of the Universal Declaration of Human Rights in the confer-

ence's final statement. Malik's active political life at the time lends itself to be read retrospectively as encapsulating some of the features that came to define the political conjuncture after World War II, from the Universal Declaration of Human Rights to Bandung, via the Eisenhower Doctrine. Much later, in the mid-1970s, Malik became one of the ideologues of the anti-Palestinian, Christian right-wing National Front, which fought against the predominantly Muslim, pro-Palestinian Lebanese National Movement.

56. As the CIA's main operative in Beirut at the time, Wilbur Crane Eveland wrote, "Throughout the elections I traveled regularly to the presidential palace with a briefcase of Lebanese pounds, then returned late at night to the embassy with an empty twin case." Traboulsi, *History of Modern Lebanon*, 132.

57. For a historical reassessment of the fighting and tensions in 1958 in Syria, Lebanon, and Jordan that argues that they resulted in state-formation surges, particularly in the sphere of socioeconomic planning, see Cyrus Schayegh, "1958 Reconsidered: State Formation and the Cold War in the Early Postcolonial Arab Middle East," *International Journal of Middle East Studies* 45 (2013): 421–43.

58. Traboulsi, *History of Modern Lebanon*, 136

59. Traboulsi, *History of Modern Lebanon*, 136.

60. Traboulsi, *History of Modern Lebanon*, 137.

61. Waddah Charara, interview by author, June 9, 2007, Beirut, Lebanon.

62. Waddah Charara, interview by author, June 9, 2007, Beirut, Lebanon.

63. The Syrian Social Nationalist Party, a radically secular organization advocating for a pan-Syrian union, aligned itself with President Chamoun and the Lebanese nationalists against the Arab nationalists Muslims during the 1958 civil clashes. Fawwaz Traboulsi, interview by author, August 2, 2008, Beirut, Lebanon.

64. Waddah Charara, interview by author, June 9, 2007, Beirut, Lebanon.

65. Husayn Muruwwa, *Wulidtu Shaykhan wa Amutu Tiflan: Sira Dhatiyya fi Hadithin Ajrahu maʿahu ʿAbbas Baydun* [I Was Born a Sheikh and I Will Die a Child: An Autobiography Undertaken as a Conversation with Abbas Beydoun] (Beirut: Dar al-Farabi, 1990), 9.

66. Muruwwa, *Wulidtu Shaykhan wa Amutu Tiflan*, 10.

67. Abbas Beydoun, interview by author, July 31, 2008, Beirut, Lebanon.

68. Abbas Beydoun, interview by author, July 31, 2008, Beirut, Lebanon. Mikhail Naimy (1889–1988), also a staple of the school curriculum, was an "influential Lebanese immigrant writer of the same period [as Khalil Gibran]. Born in Mount Lebanon in 1889, Naimy spent years studying in Palestine and then the Ukraine before moving to Washington State and eventually to New York. His publications, both in English and Arabic, also abound in the deification of the Lebanese terrain and reinforces themes that Gibran would make popular," in Elise Salem, *Constructing Lebanon: A Century of Literary Narratives* (Gainesville: University Press of Florida, 2003), 17. The stories of Maroun ʿAbbud (1886–1962) also deal with village life in Mount Lebanon: "The 'Lebanese' ʿAbbud writes about are Christian villagers who live deep within the rugged Maronite terrain. The inhabitants are very religious and have total faith in the powers of St. Maroun. The stories revolve around village characters and their beliefs, generational differences, shocking Western innovations, etc." Salem, *Constructing Lebanon*, 54.

69. Abbas Beydoun, *Blood Test*, trans. Max Weiss (Syracuse, NY: Syracuse University Press, 2008); Abbas Beydoun, interview by author, July 31, 2008, Beirut, Lebanon.

70. Abbas Beydoun, interview by author, July 31, 2008, Beirut, Lebanon.

71. Abbas Beydoun, interview by author, July 31, 2008, Beirut, Lebanon.

72. The comparison between the road to Najaf and the road to Damascus and Beirut—previously quoted—is extracted from the introduction to the book of biographical interviews that Abbas Beydoun conducted with Husayn Muruwwa entitled *Wulidtu Shaykhan Wa Amutu Tiflan* (1990). The title is based on a word pun. *Shaykhan* could either mean an old man or shaykh as in cleric, and the title plays on the double meaning, which could be rendered in English as "I was born an old man and I die a child" or "I was born a cleric and I die a child."

73. Abdel Latif Charara, however, unlike Husayn Muruwwa and his brother Muhammad, did not pursue a religious curriculum in Najaf, but graduated around the mid- to late 1930s from the "center for elementary school teachers" in Beirut, a Lebanese public institution for the preparation of primary school teachers.

74. Charara, *Transformations*, 3.

75. Charara, *Transformations*, 3.

76. This text, written in April 1967, three months before the June 1967 defeat, did not contain any index of the author's Marxist political militancy at the time. Socialist Lebanon was an underground organization.

77. Charara, *Transformations*, 94.

78. Waddah Charara, "al-Nisba al-Mutala'thima: Fusul min Sira (ma Qabl) Lubnaniyya" [The Faltering Belonging: Segments from a (Pre-) Lebanese Autobiography], *Abwab*, no. 2 (1994): 202–13. Hereafter cited in its English translation.

79. Charara, "Faltering Belonging," 203.

80. Charara, "Faltering Belonging," 207–8.

81. From the Arabic *Ahl*, which denotes those who are related either by blood ties, by inhabiting the same place, or by belonging to the same clan or tribe. It could also denote those united by a common occupation, such as the practice of a craft. Charara uses Ahli to denote mostly the communal—sectarian, regional, and kin—infranational solidarities at work in Lebanese society.

82. Charara, "Faltering Belonging," 213.

83. Frantz Fanon died in 1961.

84. Waddah Charara, interview by author, June 9, 2007, Beirut, Lebanon.

85. Waddah Charara, interview by author, June 9, 2007, Beirut, Lebanon.

86. Merleau-Ponty's exact sentence is "Nous n'avons pas le choix entre la pureté et la violence, mais entre différentes sortes de violence" [We don't have the choice between purity and violence, but between different kinds of violence], *Humanisme et terreur* (Paris: Gallimard, 1947), 118.

NOTES TO CHAPTER 2

1. Susan Buck-Morss, *Thinking Past Terror: Islamism and Critical Theory on the Left* (London: Verso, [2003] 2006), vii. Hereafter, this work is cited parenthetically as *TPT*.

2. Susan Buck-Morss, "The Second Time as Farce . . . Historical Pragmatics and the Untimely Present," in *The Idea of Communism*, ed. Costas Douzinas and Slavoj Žižek (London: Verso, 2010), 78. Hereafter, this work is cited parenthetically as STF.

3. Traboulsi, *History of Modern Lebanon*, 138–39.

4. Picard, *Lebanon, a Shattered Country*, 90.

5. "State Administration doubled in size through the employment of 10,000 new functionaries. . . . Under Sham'un, the Maronites constituted 29 per cent of the population but held at least half of the administrative posts; by the end of Shihab's mandate they held no more than a third." Traboulsi, *History of Modern Lebanon*, 140.

6. Picard, *Lebanon, a Shattered Country*, 90.

7. Traboulsi, *History of Modern Lebanon*, 139.

8. Picard, *Lebanon, a Shattered Country*, 90.

9. Waddah Charara, interview by author, June 9, 2007, Beirut, Lebanon.

10. In Lyon, he also met Hassan Hamdan (1936–87), six years his senior, who was studying philosophy. Hamdan later became the main theorist of the Lebanese Communist Party, known under his pseudonym, Mahdi 'Amil, and Charara's colleague at the Lebanese University.

11. The ANM's slogan at the time was "Unity, Liberation, Vengeance," while the Ba'thists' slogan was "Unity, Freedom, Socialism." It is, as would be expected, the term "Vengeance" that provoked accusations of fascism toward the ANM. It would later drop it, for "regaining Palestine." See Walid Kazziha, *Revolutionary Transformation in the Arab World: Habash and His Comrades from Nationalism to Communism* (New York: St. Martin's, 1975).

12. Kazziha, *Revolutionary Transformation*, 61.

13. Traboulsi, *Portrait of the Young Man in Red*, 36–37.

14. "The tableau of Ba'th was something different from the one you know now. It was a broad alliance that had everything in it, the Arab Spirit [Michel] Aflaq folks, the Algerian model people, and those supporters of armed struggle, as well as a large leftist bloc." Fawwaz Traboulsi, interview by author, August 2, 2008, Beirut, Lebanon.

15. Traboulsi, *Portrait of the Young Man in Red*, 40.

16. Traboulsi, *Portrait of the Young Man in Red*, 41.

17. Traboulsi, *Portrait of the Young Man in Red*, 41.

18. Traboulsi, *Portrait of the Young Man in Red*, 45. In the late 1950s, Yemen was in the last years of the Zaidi imams' rule. The 1962 revolution would give rise to the Yemen Arab Republic. The port of Aden, which fell under British rule in 1839, remained under British control until the establishment of the People's Democratic Republic of Yemen in 1967. See Messick, *Calligraphic State*, 8–12, for a synopsis of Yemeni history.

19. Tareq Y. Ismael, *The Arab Left* (Syracuse, NY: Syracuse University Press, 1976), 25.

20. Ismael, *Arab Left*, 26.

21. Among those Lebanese cadres who split was Waddah Charara's older cousin, Talal Charara, who was instrumental in Charara's Ba'thist experience and who will later play a role in introducing him to Fawwaz Traboulsi.

22. Mahmoud Soueid, interview by author, July 7, 2008, Beirut, Lebanon.

23. Ismael, *Arab Left*, 45.

24. Ismael, *Arab Left*, 45.

25. Traboulsi, *Portrait of the Young Man in Red*, 46.

26. Traboulsi, *Portrait of the Young Man in Red*, 47. After the coup, the new rulers engaged in "a policy of recrimination and physical liquidation against the Iraqi Communists, Qasimites [proponents of the deposed and executed president 'Abd al-Karim Qasim], and opponents to their rule." Ismael, *Arab Left*, 27.

27. Roneos, another name used for mimeographs, the predecessors of photocopiers, are duplicating machines that produce copies from a stencil. Roneos could not be bought without registering the machines; however, the group succeeded in obtaining a machine through a Jewish comrade who managed to buy it from a store that sold stationery, one of the last remaining Jewish stores in Beirut in the mid-1960s.

28. Fawwaz Traboulsi, interview by author, August 2, 2008, Beirut, Lebanon. The first issue was dated September 1966 and the last one in my possession (issue 17) was published in March 1970. Ahmed Beydoun granted me access to his personal archive from that period. Beydoun, who later became a distinguished historiographer, kept an extensive archive of their militant activity. I suspect, through the conversations I had with members of the group, that overall Socialist Lebanon may have published around twenty or twenty-one issues, that is, about three more issues after the one dated March 1970.

29. According to Fawwaz Traboulsi's present estimate, not records. Personal communication with Traboulsi, July 12, 2010.

30. Fawwaz Traboulsi, interview by author, August 2, 2008, Beirut, Lebanon. Hassan Qobeissi (1941–2006) studied philosophy at the Lebanese University, and later at the University Saint Joseph. He taught philosophy in Lebanese public high schools, and later at the Lebanese University, and assumed editorial functions. Qobeissi was also a prolific translator of philosophy and anthropology. He translated Jean-Paul Sartre, Claude Lévi-Strauss, E. E. Evans-Pritchard, and John Locke among other authors.

31. Fawwaz Traboulsi, interview by author, August 2, 2008, Beirut, Lebanon.

32. Union National des Etudiants de France, France's major university students' syndicate, which was active in support of Algerian independence in the 1950s.

33. Ahmad Beydoun, interview by author, July 11, 2007, Beirut, Lebanon.

34. Ahmad Beydoun, interview by author, July 28, 2008, Beirut, Lebanon. Pierre Bourdieu and Jean-Claude Passeron, *Les Héritiers: Les Etudiants et la Culture* (Paris: Les Editions de Minuit, 1964).

35. Lubnan Ishtiraki [Socialist Lebanon], "Ma'rakat al-Tullab al-Thanawiyyin al-Muqbila" [The Coming Battle of Secondary School Students], Issue 5, April 1967. Charara mentioned writing a text in support of the secondary students' struggles using Bourdieu at the time. And since "The Coming Battle" is clearly written under the sign of Bourdieu, but not signed, I am inferring that it is the same article he recalled writing—forty years later—in 2007.

36. See Dominic C. Boyer, "Foucault in the Bush: The Social Life of Post-Structuralist Theory in East Berlin's Prenzalauer Berg," *Ethnos* 66, no. 2 (2001): 207–36.

37. Waddah Charara, interview by author, June 30, 2009, Beirut, Lebanon.

38. The Dziga Vertov Group, a cinematographic collective that included Jean-Luc Godard, Jean-Henri Roger, and Jean-Pierre Gorin, for instance, was founded around the

time of student demonstrations and workers' strikes of May and June 1968 in France, around four years after the establishment of Socialist Lebanon. See Irmgard Emmelhainz, "From Third-Worldism to Empire: Jean-Luc Godard and the Palestine Question," *Third Text* 3, no. 5 (2009): 649–56.

39. Kristin Ross, *May '68 and Its Afterlives* (Chicago: University of Chicago Press, 2002), 81. Hereafter cited in the text as *May '68*.

40. When François Maspero stepped down, he handed the direction of the house to François Gèze on the condition that the name be changed. It became Éditions la Découverte.

41. *Le Monde Diplomatique*, still published on a monthly basis, was founded in 1954 by Hubert Beuve Marie, as Ignacio Ramonet, the monthly editor in chief from 1990 to 2000, noted, in order to give foreign affairs their due place. Until 1973, still according to Ramonet, the monthly followed *Le Monde*'s editorial line on international politics, itself a reflection of Beuve Marie's politics, which were characterized by "a late realization of the necessity of negotiation with the colonies independence movements, a cult of La Francophonie set up as a 'neutral' space facing the American and Soviet blocs as well as constant anti-communism balanced by a severe anti-Atlantism." Ignacio Ramonet, "Cinquante Ans" [Fifty Years], *Le Monde Diplomatique* 74 (April–May 2004). http://www.monde-diplomatique.fr/mav/74/RAMONET/10882.

42. Ahmad Beydoun, interview by author, July 28, 2008, Beirut, Lebanon.

43. Azza Charara Beydoun, who joined Socialist Lebanon in the late 1960s and married Ahmad Beydoun in 1969, was the first math teacher in the English language in the Lebanese public school system in the mid-1960s, revealing the dominance of French until that time in Lebanese public high schools.

44. Anouar Abdel Malek, *Egypte, Société Militaire* [Egypt, Military Society: The Army Regime, the Left and Social Change under Nasser] (Paris: Le Seuil, 1962); Hassan Riad, *L'Egypte Nassérienne* [Nasserite Egypt] (Paris: Les Editions de Minuit, 1964); Mahmoud Hussein, *La Lutte des Classes en Egypte de 1946 à 1968* [Class Conflict in Egypt from 1945 to 1970] (Paris: Maspero, 1969). Adel Rif'at, born Eddy Lévy, grew up in a Jewish Egyptian family. Rif'at, who worked at UNESCO, is a well-known essayist who has been collaborating with Bahgat al-Nadi for the past fifty years, both writing under the nom de plume Mahmoud Hussein. Rif'at is the older brother of Benny Lévy (1945–2003), known also under his pseudonym Pierre Victor, a student of Louis Althusser at the École Normale Supérieure and one of the main leaders and theoreticians of the Gauche Prolétarienne (Proletarian Left), the Maoist party. Charara was in touch with Rif'at and al-Nadi during his stay in Paris in the early 1970s and circulated in militant circles, which included members of the Gauche Prolétarienne. Benny Lévy was also the last personal secretary of the aging Jean-Paul Sartre from 1974 until Sartre's death in 1980. He later steered away from radical politics and began to study Judaism in the late 1970s. He relocated to Israel in 1995 and established the Institute for Levinassian Studies in Jerusalem, alongside two of the most media-present French "Nouveaux Philosophes," Bernard-Henri Lévy and Alain Finkielkraut. See Douglas Johnson, "Benny Lévy," *Guardian*, October 21, 2003, https://www.theguardian.com/news/2003/oct/21/guardianobituaries.booksobituaries.

45. Lubnan Ishtiraki, "Madkal li–qira'at al-Bayan al-Shuyu'i" [An Introduction to Reading the Communist Manifesto], *Dirasat 'Arabiyya* [Arab Studies], 5, no. 7 (1969): 38–80. Hereafter, this work will be referred to as the "Introduction," and cited parenthetically as IRCM.

46. Faleh A. Jabar, "The Arab Communist Parties in Search of an Identity," in *Post-Marxism and the Middle East*, ed. Faleh A. Jabar (London: Saqi Books, 1997), 93.

47. Jabar, "Arab Communist Parties in Search of an Identity," 93.

48. Jabar, "Arab Communist Parties in Search of an Identity," 94.

49. Dipesh Chakrabarty, *Provincializing Europe: Postcolonial Thought and Historical Difference* (Princeton, NJ: Princeton University Press, 2000), 8.

50. "When the army mobilized itself on July 23rd, it was expressing the people's hopes that for a long time the people had struggled for; its hopes for opening up new horizons over which the banners of 'Sufficiency and Justice' would flap . . . and today brothers, now that this road has been paved for us, and we have declared political democracy for the entire people, not for the people's enemies, and that we have declared social democracy and established socialism in our midst, and that we've declared that we will build a society on the basis of justice and sufficiency." These are excerpts from a speech delivered by President Nasser on December 19, 1961. *Khitab al-Ra'is Jamal 'Abd al-Nasir fi 'Id al-'Alam* [Speech of President Gamal Abdel Nasser on Flag Day], December 19, 1961. http://nasser .bibalex.org/Speeches/browser.aspx?SID=1006&lang=ar.

51. They translated writings by authors from the revolutionary tradition such as Karl Marx, Isaac Deutscher, V. I. Lenin, Leon Trotsky, Antonio Gramsci, John Berger, Mao Tse-Tung, and Cornelius Castoriadis.

52. Abd al-Ilah Bilqaziz, *al-Islam wa-l-Hadatha wa-l-Ijtima' al-Siyasi* [Islam, Modernity, and Political Sociality] (Beirut: Dar al-Wihda al-'Arabiyya, 2004), 78–79.

53. Abbas Beydoun, interview by author, July 31, 2008, Beirut, Lebanon.

54. See Benjamin, "Left-Wing Melancholy," 28–32, and Brown, "Resisting Left Melancholy," 19–27.

NOTES TO CHAPTER 3

1. United Nations Development Programme, *Arab Human Development Report 2003: Building a Knowledge Society* (New York: Regional Bureau for Arab States, cosponsored with the Arab Fund for Economic and Social Development, 2003), 125. Critics situate the trajectory of the Lebanese Rahbani Brothers, Lebanon's most famous postindependence composers and pioneers of musical theater, into two epochs, the pre-1967 one and the post-1967. See Muhammad Abi-Samra, "Zahirat al-Akhawayn Rahbani wa Fairuz" [The Rahbani Brothers and Fairuz Phenomenon] (master's thesis, Lebanese University, 1985).

2. Jastinder Khera, "Mashrou' Leila: The Band Out to Occupy Arabic Pop," *BBC News*, October 16, 2013. http://www.bbc.com/news/world-middle-east-24469243.

3. Cited in Ghassan Salamé, *Le théâtre politique au Liban (1968–1973): Approche idéologique et esthétique* [Political Theater in Lebanon (1968–1973): An Ideological and Aesthetic Approach] (Beirut: Dar al-Mashriq, 1974), 102.

4. "In so far as it manifests a rupture with external demands and a desire to exclude artists suspected of obeying them," Bourdieu writes, "the affirmation of the primacy of form over function, of mode of representation over the object of representation, is the most specific expression of the claim to the autonomy of the field and of its pretension to produce and to impose the principles of a specific legitimacy as much in the order of production as in the order of reception of the work of art.... The artist challenges any external constraint or demand and affirms his or her mastery over what defines him or her and what belongs to him or her by right, that is, the manner, form, style—*art* in short, thus established as the exclusive purpose of art." Pierre Bourdieu, *The Rules of Art: Genesis and Structure of the Literary Field*, trans. Susan Emanuel (Cambridge: Polity Press, 1996), 299–300. See Fadi A. Bardawil, "Art, War and Inheritance: The Aesthetics and Politics of Ziad Rahbani" (master's thesis, American University of Beirut, 2002) and Jessica Winegar, *Creative Reckonings: The Politics of Art and Culture in Contemporary Egypt* (Stanford: Stanford University Press, 2006).

5. Ibrahim Abu Rabi', *Contemporary Arab Thought: Studies in Post-1967 Arab Intellectual History* (London: Pluto Press, 2004), and Kassab, *Contemporary Arab Thought: Cultural Critique in Comparative Perspective* (New York: Columbia University Press, 2010).

6. Hereafter, I will refer to Abu Rabi''s book in the text.

7. Kassab, *Contemporary Arab Thought*, 2.

8. For a recent revisionist history of the 1967 defeat from the standpoint of the Arab New Left, see Sune Haugbolle, "The New Arab Left and 1967," *British Journal of Middle Eastern Studies* 44, no. 4 (2017): 920–34.

9. See Suzanne Kassab, "Summoning the Spirit of Enlightenment: On the Nahda Revival in Qadaya wa-Shahadat," in *Arabic Thought against the Authoritarian Age: Towards an Intellectual History of the Present*, edited by Max Weiss and Jens Hanssen (Cambridge: Cambridge University Press, 2018), 311–35.

10. See Sadik Jalal al-Azm, *Self-Criticism after the Defeat,* trans. George Stergios (London: Saqi Books, [1968] 2011) and Adonis, "*Bayan 5 Huzayran 1967*" [The June 5th, 1967 Manifesto], *Al-Adab*, Issues 7 and 8, July–August 1967.

11. For an early and prescient, pre-Arab revolutions (2011-) critique, of the crowning of the 1967 defeat as the cardinal event of contemporary Arab thought, see Yassin al-Haj Saleh, "Hazimat Huzayran: min Hadath Tarikhi ila Shart Thaqafi" [The June Defeat: From a Historical Event to a Cultural Condition], *al-Hiwar al-Mutamaddin*, Issue 1936, June 4, 2007. http://www.ahewar.org/debat/show.art.asp?aid=98676&nm=1. For an illuminating discussion of nationalist influences on the historiographies of nationalism in the Middle East, see Rashid Khalidi, "Arab Nationalism: Historical Problems in the Literature," *American Historical Review* 96, no. 5 (1991): 1363–73.

12. Ahmad Beydoun, interview by author, July 11, 2007, Beirut, Lebanon.

13. Muhsin Ibrahim, interview by author, August 4, 2008, Beirut, Lebanon.

14. Lubnan Ishtiraki "Mulahazat Hawl al-Ittifaq al-Akhir Bayn al-Thawra al-Kurdiyya wa-l-Hukuma al-'Iraqiyya" [Notes on the Last Agreement between the Kurdish Revolution and the Iraqi Government], Issue 1 (mid-September 1966), 14–23. Hereafter, Lubnan Ishtiraki will be cited in notes in its English translation, Socialist Lebanon. On their first mention, articles will be transliterated, from the second onwards I will use their English translation.

15. Socialist Lebanon, "Notes on the Last Agreement," 15–16.

16. "Nasser Accuses Arab Reds Again: Says They Plotted to Split U.A.R., Seize Iraq and Form 'Fertile Crescent,'" Reuters, April 16, 1959, http://www.nytimes.com/1959/04/17/archives/nasser-accuses-arab-reds-again-says-they-plotted-to-split-u-a-r.html?_r=0.

17. Socialist Lebanon, "Musahama fi Niqash Ittijahat al-'Amal al-Fida'i al-Filastini (al-Qism al-Awwal)" [A Contribution to the Discussion of the Directions of Palestinian Fida'yi Action (Part One)], Issue 14, December 1968, 35.

18. Socialist Lebanon, "Muhawala li-Fahm al-Ahdath al-Akhira Fi Suria" [An Attempt to Understand the Recent Events in Syria], Issue 3, mid-December 1966, 10.

19. Socialist Lebanon, "An Attempt to Understand," 12. Socialist Lebanon held similar views on the Egyptian regime, whose nationalizations "transformed the ones in power into a core of a state bourgeoisie that controls, through ruling, the surplus production and consumes that surplus to the detriment of development issues and the building of the economic base." Socialist Lebanon, "Mawdu'at Awwaliyya fi Itar al-Ma'raka" [Primary Topics in the Context of the Battle], Issue 8, November 1967, 7. Instrumental to their critiques were the conceptual works of an older generation of Egyptian Marxist thinkers, written and published in France, that were critical of the Nasser regime; see chapter 2.

20. Socialist Lebanon, "al-Yasar al-Lubnani wa A'ba' al-Ma'raka" [The Lebanese Left and the Battle's Burdens], Issue 16, September 1969, 11.

21. Socialist Lebanon, "Lebanese Left and the Battle's Burdens," 11.

22. Socialist Lebanon, "Lebanese Left and the Battle's Burdens," 12.

23. Socialist Lebanon, "Lebanese Left and the Battle's Burdens," 11.

24. Socialist Lebanon, "Lebanese Left and the Battle's Burdens," 12.

25. Socialist Lebanon, "A Contribution to the Discussion," 23.

26. Lisa Wedeen, "Ideology and Humor in Dark Times: Notes from Syria," *Critical Inquiry* 39, no. 4 (2013): 843.

27. Said, *Out of Place*, 293.

28. Said, *Out of Place*, 279.

29. Edward Said, "My Guru," *London Review of Books* 23, no. 24 (December 13, 2001), http://www.lrb.co.uk/v23/n24/edward-said/my-guru.

30. Said, "My Guru." The American sociologist Janet Abu-Lughod (1928–2013), née Lippman, was married to Ibrahim Abu-Lughod from 1951 to 1991.

31. Timothy Mitchell, "The Middle East in the Past and Future of Social Science," in *The Politics of Knowledge: Area Studies and the Disciplines*, ed. David L. Szanton, University of California International and Area Studies vol. 3, article 3 (2003), 12.

32. Mitchell, "Middle East in the Past and Future of Social Science," 12.

33. Mitchell, "Middle East in the Past and Future of Social Science," 12.

34. Mitchell, "Middle East in the Past and Future of Social Science," 12.

35. al-Azm met Edward Said during the 1970 Association of Arab-American University Graduates conference, which provided an institutional space of encounter between intellectuals at home and those in the diaspora who were supportive of the Palestinian struggle. They became good friends, until the publication of al-Azm's critical review of

Orientalism in 1981—that I look into in chapter 6—after which Said severed his relation with al-Azm, refusing to resume contact despite a number of attempts by common friends to reunite them. Sadik Jalal al-Azm, interview by author, August 4, 2008, Beirut, Lebanon.

36. Ghada Talhami, "An Interview with Sadik al-Azm," *Arab Studies Quarterly* 19, no. 3 (1997): 117.

37. Talhami, "Interview with Sadik al-Azm," 114.

38. The first went through "ten printings between 1968 and 1973 (despite being forbidden and confiscated in many countries) excluding the independent printings that took place in the Occupied Palestinian Territories." Sadik Jalal al-Azm, "Taqdim ba'd Tul Inqita'" [A Preface after a Long Absence], in *Al-Naqd al-Dhathi ba'd al-Hazima* [Self-Criticism after the Defeat] (Damascus: Dar Mamduh 'Idwan li-l Tiba'a wa-l-Nashr, 2007). Both books were published by Dar al-Tali'a in Beirut. The publishing house, owned by the Beiruti "Liberal" Ba'thist Bashir al-Da'uq, also issued the vibrant journal *Dirasat 'Arabiyya*, to which al-Azm and the members of Socialist Lebanon contributed collectively, or individually, with pseudonyms.

39. The philosophy department chair who opposed Sadik al-Azm was Charles Malik (1906–87)—see chapter 1 for a brief synopsis of Malik's political career. On a different register, Malik was married to the first cousin of Edward Said's mother and played an important role in his intellectual and political growth before their subsequent political divergences: "From Uncle Charles, as we called him, I learned the attractions of dogma, of the search for the unquestioning truth, of irrefutable authority. From him I also learned about the clash of civilizations, the war between East and West, communism and freedom. In addition to telling us about this in Dhour, he played a central role in formulating all this for the world stage. Along with Eleanor Roosevelt, he worked on the Universal Declaration of Human Rights; names like [Andrei] Gromyko, [John Foster] Dulles, Trygve Lie, [Nelson] Rockefeller, and [Dwight] Eisenhower were the common currency of his conversation, but so too were [Immanuel] Kant, [Johann Gottlieb] Fichte, [Bertrand] Russell, Plotinus and Jesus Christ." Said, *Out of Place*, 265–66.

40. Talal Asad, "Review of *Orientalism* by Edward Said," *English Historical Review* 95, no. 376 (July 1980): 648.

41. See chapter 2 for the different answers provided by Socialist Lebanon and the Arab Nationalist Movement in Lebanon.

42. "To say, therefore, that the Arab is a victim of imperialism is to understand the statement as not only to the past, but also to the present, not only in war and diplomacy but also Western consciousness. There are signs, however, that with much of the Third World, the Arab has now fully recognized this as his predicament: he is demanding the West, and of Israel, the right to reoccupy his place in history and in actuality." Edward Said, "The Arab Portrayed," in *The Arab-Israeli Confrontation of June 1967: An Arab Perspective*, ed. Ibrahim Abu-Lughod (Evanston, IL: Northwestern University Press, 1970), 9.

43. Sadik Jalal al-Azm, *Al-Naqd al-Dhathi ba'd al-Hazima* [Self-Criticism after the Defeat] (Beirut: Dar al-Tali'a, 1968), 69. Hereafter the book is cited in its English translation.

44. al-Azm, "Self-Criticism after the Defeat," 78.

45. al-Azm, "Self-Criticism after the Defeat," 78.

46. al-Azm, "Self-Criticism after the Defeat," 140.

47. Tareq Y. Ismael and Jacqueline S. Ismael, *The Communist Movement in Syria and Lebanon* (Gainesville: University Press of Florida, 1998), 54.

48. The Lebanese Communist Party was established in 1924 during mandate Lebanon. It spread its activities toward Syria in the following year, founding the Communist Party of Syria and Lebanon in 1925. In the next four decades the party would split and reunite a number of times. In January 1944, a month after Lebanese independence from France, a decision was taken to split the two parties, keeping a common central committee though. In 1950, Khalid Bikdash, the secretary general of the Syrian party, who held control over both parties with an iron fist since he gained the secretariat in the 1930s, feeling his power under threat, decided to reunite the two parties. In 1958, in the wake of the union, Bikdash split the party again and fled to Eastern Europe.

49. Tareq Y. Ismael, *The Communist Movement in the Arab World* (London: Routledge Curzon, 2005), 22.

50. Ismael, *Communist Movement in the Arab World*, 36.

51. Ismael and Ismael, *Communist Movement in Syria and Lebanon*, 59.

52. Ismael and Ismael, *Communist Movement in Syria and Lebanon*, 78. The relationships with Arab nationalists was not always confrontational. In 1954, Khalid Bikdash won a parliamentary seat in Damascus as part of a progressive front that included the Ba'th, which had won sixteen seats. This rapprochement with the national forces was in alignment with the post-Stalinist doctrine of the Communist Party of the Soviet Union. By 1955, the Soviet Union began establishing close links with Nasser, its inaugural iconic moment being the approval of Czech-Egyptian arms deal (1955). In the aftermath of the twentieth Communist Party of the Soviet Union Congress (1956), during which the collaboration with progressive factions in the Third World was confirmed, dropping the Stalinist requirement of the dictatorship of the proletariat, "the USSR often paid little attention to the needs and conditions of Arab Communists." Arab communist parties were stuck between the hammer of the national regimes' repression and the anvil of allegiance to the Soviet Union, which was allied to their oppressors. See Ismael, *Communist Movement in the Arab World*, 22–23.

53. Waddah Charara did not mention this episode in any of our numerous meetings.

54. Traboulsi, *Portrait of the Young Man in Red*, 53.

55. The argument for joining the opposition wing of the Lebanese Communist Party, according to Traboulsi, revolved around the idea that Socialist Lebanon was a small group, so why not join the Lebanese Communist Party and try working from the inside to influence it. Fawwaz Traboulsi, interview by author, August 2, 2008, Beirut, Lebanon.

56. Socialist Lebanon, "al-'Amal al-Yasari al-Lubnani 'ala Bisat al-Bahth min Jadid" [Lebanese Socialist Action under Consideration Once More], Issue 9, February 1968, 6.

57. Socialist Lebanon, "'Lubnan al-'Ishtiraki' wa-l–Yasar" ["Socialist Lebanon" and the Left], Issue 3, December 1966, 2.

58. The early precursor to the Lebanese National Movement of the 1970s was mainly composed of Jumblatt's Progressive Socialist Party, the Lebanese Communist Party, and the Arab Nationalist Movement.

59. Socialist Lebanon, "al-'Amal al-Yasari al-Lubnani 'ala Bisat al-Bahth min Jadid" [Lebanese Leftist Practice under Discussion Once More], Issue 9, February 1968, 2.

60. Socialist Lebanon, "Nusus Mukhtara min 'Ma al-'Amal?' Linin, 1902" [Selected Texts from "What Is to Be Done?" Lenin, 1902], Issue 4, February 1967, 11.

61. In *The Organization of Lebanese Socialists, What For? (The Arab Nationalist Movement from Fascism to Nasserism): An Analysis and a Critique* (1970), Muhsin Ibrahim in a gesture of auto-critique of the ANM's Nasserite past, writes, "The movement had practiced a pro-unity policy that was romantic and foggy. [This policy] was characterized by severe verbal persistence [in advocating] unity. Such an attitude manifested itself in slogans like 'Unity regardless of the Price,' or 'Unity comes first and last' and/or 'Unity is the path to Liberation and the Key to all Problems Confronting the Arab Society.' This made the movement unable to see the Unity slogan in its proper historical context. It stripped the slogan of all progressive class contents. . . . Again when the movement declared its full support of the establishment of the United Arab Republic, it failed to see its petty-bourgeois contents." Cited in Ismael, *Arab Left*, 70–71.

62. There were 2 *fida'yi* operations launched from southern Lebanon in 1967, 29 in 1968, and 150 in 1969. See Kassir, *La Guerre du Liban*, 63.

63. The guerrillas made their entry into the village of Khiam, the first to welcome them in 1968, accompanied by the inhabitants of the village who occupied the head-quarters of the army intelligence in the village, expelling its occupants. Kassir, *La Guerre du Liban*, 64.

64. Kassir, *La Guerre du Liban*, 64.

65. Kassir, *La Guerre du Liban*, 64. Between 1968 and 1974, Israel violated Lebanese territory three thousand times, and eight hundred Palestinian and Lebanese victims fell as a result of Israeli aggression.

66. Wade R. Goria, *Sovereignty and Leadership in Lebanon 1943–1976* (London: Ithaca Press, 1985), 95. Israeli air raids, "which were to become Israel's privileged tool in the coming years, intervening regularly in Southern Lebanon against Palestinian camps and Lebanese villages," were used for the first time on July 30, 1969. Kassir, *La Guerre du Liban*, 65.

67. Kassir, *La Guerre du Liban*, 71.

68. Fawwaz Traboulsi, *A History of Modern Lebanon* (London: Pluto Press), 153–54.

69. Traboulsi, *History of Modern Lebanon*, 154.

70. The accords recognized the Palestine guerrillas' right to "be present on and move around Lebanese territory, especially to and from the 'Arqub region, and provided a form of extra-territoriality for the Palestinian camps, long under the heavy hand of the Lebanese security services, and recognized a Higher Palestinian Commission, headed by a Palestinian veteran Shafiq al-Hut, as a *de facto* Palestine embassy in Lebanon." Traboulsi, *History of Modern Lebanon*, 154.

71. A few months after the promulgation of the agreement, "Phalangist militants attacked a Palestinian convoy in Kahalé (March 25th, 1970), which was followed by clashes in the suburbs of Beirut." Kassir, *La Guerre du Liban*, 73.

72. Waddah Charara, interview by author, July 4, 2008, Beirut, Lebanon.

73. Socialist Lebanon, "Al-Muqawamatan: Al-Lubnaniyya w-al-Filastiniyya" [The Two Resistances: The Palestinian and the Lebanese], Issue 16, September 1969, 1. Hereafter cited in the text.

74. Underlined in the original. "The entity," as in the Lebanese entity, is a designation used pejoratively by political commentators and actors wishing not to bestow legitimacy and recognition. Israel, for example, is sometimes referred to as the Zionist entity, while fervent Syrian nationalists refer to Lebanon as the Lebanese entity.

75. Karl Marx and Friedrich Engels, *The Communist Manifesto*, trans. Samuel Moore (Moscow: Progress Publishers, 1969), https://www.marxists.org/archive/marx/works /download/pdf/Manifesto.pdf.

76. Underlining in the original. Socialist Lebanon, "The Lebanese Left and the Battle's Burdens", 16. Hereafter cited in the text.

77. Underlining in the original.

78. There were around 1,000–1,500 Organization of Lebanese Socialists members as opposed to less than 100 for Socialist Lebanon. Estimates of previous adherents note that Socialist Lebanon (1964–70) did not move beyond thirty to forty members in the first few years of work, inflated to less than a hundred members by the time of fusion with the Organization of Lebanese Socialists in 1970.

79. Abbas Beydoun, interview by author, July 31, 2008, Beirut, Lebanon. *Al-Hurriyya*, a weekly magazine, was the mouthpiece of the Arab Nationalist Movement, founded in 1960 and edited by Muhsin Ibrahim in the 1960s. After the radicalization of the move-ment and its splintering post-1967, it was shared by its Lebanese faction, the Organ-ization of Lebanese Socialists (OLS), and the Democratic Front for the Liberation of Palestine (DFLP). After the union of SL and OLS in 1970, it would become the common platform of the Organization of Communist Action in Lebanon and the DFLP until 1977, when it became associated only with the latter.

80. Abbas Beydoun, interview by author, July 31, 2008, Beirut, Lebanon.

81. Abbas Beydoun, interview by author, July 31, 2008, Beirut, Lebanon.

82. Muhsin Ibrahim, "George Hawi Ibn al-Nahda al-Yasariyya al-Lubnaniyya wa Ahad Abraz Sunna'iha al-Kibar" [George Hawi: The Son of the Lebanese Leftist Renaissance and One of Its Great Producers], *Bayrut al-Masa'*, Issue 572, August 13, 2005. The two points are also cited in Talal Salman, "Muhsin Ibrahim wa Naqd al-Tajruba . . . hayth la Yajru' al-Akharun!" [Muhsin Ibrahim and the Critique of the Experience . . . Where Others Do Not Dare!], *Al-Safir*, August 8, 2005, http://elaph.com/Web/NewsPapers /2005/8/81930.htm?sectionarchive=NewsPapers.

83. Anouar Abdel Malak, "Introduction," *Contemporary Arab Political Thought*, ed. Anouar Abdel Malak (London: Zed Books, 1984), 19–20. I would like to thank Samer Frangie for prompting me to revisit this volume.

84. "A date [1982] that certain authors are not hesitant to propose as the endpoint of the adventure of the Nahda, understood in its wider historical sense. It is true, that until then, the spirit of the Renaissance remained constantly present in the Arab world." Samir Kassir, *Considérations sur le Malheur Arabe* [Being Arab] (Paris: Actes Sud), 67.

85. See Farouk Mardam-Bey and Elias Sanbar, *Etre Arabe: Entretiens avec Christophe Kantcheff* [Being Arab: Interviews with Christophe Kantcheff] (Paris: Actes Sud, 2005),

for 1967 as a second Nakba; and for 1967 as the defeat of the second Nahda, see Elias Khoury, "For a Third Nahda," in *Arabic Thought against the Authoritarian Age: Towards an Intellectual History of the Present*, ed. Max Weiss and Jens Hanssen (Cambridge: Cambridge University Press, 2017), 357–69.

86. Darraj cited in Barbara Harlow, "Introduction to Kanafani's 'Thoughts on Change and the 'Blind Language,'" *Alif: Journal of Comparative Poetics*, no. 10 (1990): 132.

87. Darraj cited in Harlow, "Introduction to Kanafani's," 132.

88. Josette Zouëïn and Thierry De Rochegonde, "Rencontre avec un traducteur en Arabe, Georges Tarabishi" [A Meeting with a Translator from Arabic, Georges Tarabishi], *Che vuoi?*, no. 21 (2004): 96.

89. Faysal Darraj, "Rahin al-Hazima/Rahiniyyat al-Kitab al-Naqdi" [The Actuality of Defeat/The Endurance of the Critical Book], in *Al-Naqd al-Dhathi ba'd al-Hazima* (Damascus: Dar Mamduh 'Adwan, 2007), 21.

90. Darraj, "Rahin al-Hazima," 20.

91. Darraj, "Rahin al-Hazima," 21.

92. Stephen Sheehi, *Foundations of Modern Arab Identity* (Gainesville: University Press of Florida, 2004), 2–3.

NOTES TO CHAPTER 4

1. See Dipesh Chakrabarty, "The Legacies of Bandung: Decolonization and the Politics of Culture," in *Making a World after Empire: The Bandung Moment and Its Political Afterlives*, ed. Christopher Lee (Athens: Ohio University Press, 2010), 46.

2. The merger between the two organizations took place in 1970, and the common body was referred to as the "unified organization." A year later, and in the aftermath of the nascent organization's first conference, the Organization of Communist Action in Lebanon was officially declared.

3. Abbas Beydoun, interview by author, August 31, 2008, Beirut, Lebanon.

4. Traboulsi, *Portrait of the Young Man in Red*, 122.

5. Traboulsi, *Portrait of the Young Man in Red*, 129.

6. Traboulsi, *Portrait of the Young Man in Red*, 115.

7. Among the SL cadres that left were Hassan Qobeissi, Jinan Sha'ban, Rashid Hassan, and Roger Nab'a. Abbas Beydoun, interview by author, July 31, 2008, Beirut, Lebanon.

8. Waddah Charara, interview by author, July 4, 2008, Beirut, Lebanon.

9. Abbas Beydoun offers a retrospective interpretation of the split and Charara's departure, noting: "No one was aware of this, but he was very disturbed [by the split]. He may have woken up to the fact that what happened was directed against him essentially. The split was against him. If you want to interpret it now away from class analysis and political yammering, it was a battle against him . . . and I think between him and those who were there, there were enmities that are still present." Abbas Beydoun, interview by author, July 31, 2008, Beirut, Lebanon.

10. Abbas Beydoun, interview by author, July 31, 2008, Beirut, Lebanon. Gauche Prolétarienne, a French Maoist group, was established in the wake of May 1968. It

rejected the Leninist organizational model, and advocated following the masses, namely through the principle of établissement: "the implanting of its (mainly intellectual) members in factories.... Its slogans in the workplace were direct and simple: slowdowns, sabotage, and direct action against bosses and supervisors in the form of sequestrations; they even went so far as to call for the lynching of Deputies. They hated the existing unions (particularly the Communist-led CGT) and, as one of their internal bulletins said: 'Demands, unions and lists of demands smell of the reformist litany.'" Mitchell Abidor, *La Gauche Prolétarienne*, http://www.marxists.org/history/france/post-1968 /gauche-proletarienne/introduction.htm. Gauche Prolétarienne (Proletarian Left), a hub of militant intellectuals, combined its call to follow the masses with high visibility in Parisian intellectual circles, establishing relations with Sartre, Foucault, de Beauvoir, and Althusser. Benny Lévy, who was briefly mentioned in chapter 2, known as Pierre Victor at the time, was one of its main leaders.

11. *Al-Hurriyya*, Issue 628, July 16, 1973.

12. "Fusion with the Palestinian struggle in this conjuncture is a decisive element between defeat and preparation for future battles. Since the [observation of] forces being prepared by imperialism make every position that does not prepare, starting today, for a certain confrontation, an ostrich's position and one of national abandonment." *al-Majmuʿa al-Mustaqilla ʿan Munazzamat al-ʿAmal al-Shuyuʿi Tudih Wijhatu Nazariha* [The Group Independent from the "Organization of Communist of Action" Clarifies Its Point of View], 94. It was widely known among the comrades as al-Kirras al-Azraq [The Blue Pamphlet]. The text is divided into three major sections of approximately thirty pages each that follow a preface written by Ahmad Beydoun and an introduction. The tripartite structure begins with a history and narrative—an auto-critique—that seeks to answer the question "Where has the OCAL gotten to?" The second section moves out from the internal issues of the OCAL toward providing a theoretical and political examination of the major battles of the "movement of the masses." The third section, building on the auto-critique and the analysis of the second section, draws the appropriate political conclusions, calling for "a national mass line."

13. Ahmad Beydoun, interview by author, July 11, 2007, Beirut, Lebanon.

14. Traboulsi, *Portrait of the Young Man in Red*, 127–28. In addition to these two major splits, in the summer of 1972 the organization also witnessed the exit of one of its student groups, which joined the Maoist tendency within Fatah. It also witnessed the split of Muhammad Kishli, one of the OLS's cadres, at the head of a small group, who joined the DFLP.

15. Traboulsi, *Portrait of the Young Man in Red*, 128.

16. Traboulsi, *Portrait of the Young Man in Red*, 129.

17. See Traboulsi, *History of Modern Lebanon*, 164–70, for a breakdown of the major protest activities according to the three sectors. Hereafter cited in the text.

18. Organization for Communist Action in Lebanon, Traboulsi is using the short-hand OCA instead of OCAL. Recent accounts cast doubt on the accepted narrative of al-Khawaja's membership in the LCP: see the film *Shuʿur Akbar min al-Hubb* [A Feeling Greater Than Love], directed by Mary Jirmanus Saba, 2017.

19. "A private franchise-holding company since 1935, whose franchise was extended until 1973, the *Régie* also held the exclusive right to export Lebanese-produced tobacco, import cigarettes and produce local cigarettes." Traboulsi, *History of Modern Lebanon*, 165.

20. Waddah Charara, interview by author, July 3, 2007, Beirut, Lebanon.

21. *The Blue Pamphlet*, 38. Hereafter referred to as TBP and cited in the text.

22. "And it should be clear that this critique is an auto-critique at the same time. For we have participated fully in the revisionisms we are now criticizing, and some of us bear the greatest part of responsibility in them, which in our view consolidates our critique and gives it a practical basis" (TBP, 7).

23. Socialist Lebanon, "Madha Ya'ni Rafi' Shi'ar "al-Kifah al-Musallah" fi al-Marhala al-Rahina" [What Does Branding the Slogan of "Armed Struggle" Entail in the Current Juncture?], Issue 8, November 1967, 15. Underlining in the original.

24. Although the text does not name specific individuals one can infer from the descriptions that one of the main targets of *The Blue Pamphlet* in the leadership is Muhsin Ibrahim, the leader of the Organization of Lebanese Socialists, who later on during the Lebanese war became the secretary general of the OCAL. Initially, the OCAL had a central committee and a politburo but no secretary general.

25. The precursor to the Lebanese National Movement, which included Kamal Jumblatt's Progressive Socialist Party and the LCP. The rally was launched officially in June 1973 in opposition to a draft law on political parties, under Prime Minister Salam, which "greatly curtailed freedom of thought and association." See Traboulsi, *History of Modern Lebanon*, 174.

26. Waddah Charara, interview by author, July 4, 2008, Beirut, Lebanon.

27. Charara does not mention Trotsky's book *Our Political Tasks* (1904), in which he criticizes substitutionism. That said, Charara's critique bears a close resemblance to Trotsky's. The latter writes, "In the internal politics of the Party these methods lead, as we shall see below, to the Party organisation 'substituting' itself for the Party, the Central Committee substituting itself for the Party organisation, and finally the dictator substituting himself for the Central Committee." https://www.marxists.org/archive/trotsky/1904/tasks/.

28. Waddah Charara, interview by author, June 21, 2007, Beirut, Lebanon.

29. Traboulsi, *Portrait of the Young Man in Red*, 134. Hereafter referred to as *PYMR* and cited in the text.

30. Muhsin Ibrahim, interview by author, August 4, 2008, Beirut, Lebanon.

31. "In all the practical work of our Party, all correct leadership is necessarily 'from the masses, to the masses.' This means: take the ideas of the masses (scattered and unsystematic ideas) and concentrate them (through study turn them into concentrated and systematic ideas), then go to the masses and propagate and explain these ideas until the masses embrace them as their own, hold fast to them and translate them into action, and test the correctness of these ideas in such action. Then once again concentrate ideas from the masses and once again go to the masses so that the ideas are persevered in and carried through. And so on, over and over again in an endless spiral, with the ideas becoming

more correct, more vital and richer each time." Mao Tse-Tung, cited in Donald Reid, "Etablissement: Working in the Factory to Make Revolution in France," *Radical History Review* 88 (2004): 89.

32. Jean-Luc Godard during his Maoist phase described himself as a receiver-transmitter. See Julien Bourg, "Principally Contradiction: The Flourishing of French Maoism," in *Mao's Little Red Book: A Global History*, ed. Alexander C. Cook (Cambridge: Cambridge University Press, 2014), 231.

33. See Ross, *May '68*.

34. Jacques Rancière, *Althusser's Lesson*, trans. Emiliano Batista (London: Continuum Lesson, [1974] 2011), xiv. See Stuart Hall, *Familiar Stranger: A Life between Two Islands*, ed. Bill Schwarz (Durham, NC: Duke University Press, 2017).

35. Mao Tse-Tung, "Report on an Investigation of the Peasant Movement in Hunan," in *Selected Works of Mao Tse-Tung*, vol. 1 (Peking: Foreign Languages Press, 1965), https://www.marxists.org/reference/archive/mao/selected-works/volume-1/mswv1_2.htm.

36. Charara translated his dissertation, "Le Discours Arabe sur l'Histoire," into Arabic and published it as *al-Mas'ala al-Tarikhiyya fi al-Fikr al-'Arabi al-Hadith* [The Question of History in Modern Arab Thought] (Beirut: Ma'had al-Inma' al-'Arabi, 1977).

37. Socialist Lebanon, "Al-Muqawamatan: Al-Lubnaniyya w-al-Filastiniyya—al-Qism al-Thani" [The Two Resistances: The Palestinian and the Lebanese—Part II], Issue 17, March 1970, 4.

38. Michele Salkind and Fawwaz Trab[o]ulsi, "Organization for Communist Action: An Interview with Fawwaz Trab[o]ulsi," *Middle East Research and Information Project Reports (MERIP)*, no. 61 (1977): 6.

39. Reid, "Etablissement," 86.

40. Ross, *May '68*, 95.

41. "With the opening up of the Arab domain, the Lebanese bourgeoisie appears it is really is, i.e. as the result of exploiting the whole Arab area. This is what stops it [the bourgeoisie] from restricting its battle with the masses to the isolating Lebanese, sectarian, frame. In this case, its defense of its interests and privileges appears clearly as a political, interest-based defense that cannot veil itself with sectarianism. This transforms a sectarian war into a civil war." Socialist Lebanon, "The Two Resistances: The Palestinian and the Lebanese", 7.

42. See "People's War" in *Quotations from Chairman Mao Tse-Tung* (Peking: Foreign Languages Press, 1966), 88–99.

43. Waddah Charara, *Fi Usul Lubnan al-Ta'ifi: Khatt al-Yamin al-Jamahiri* [Origins of Sectarian Lebanon: The Right-Wing's Mass Line] (Beirut: Dar al-Tali'a, 1975). Hereafter cited in the text.

44. For a much later critique that shares points of contact with Charara's, see Dipesh Chakrabarty, "Labor History and the Politics of Theory: An Indian Angle on the Middle East," in *Workers and Working Classes in the Middle East: Struggles, Histories, Historiographies*, ed. Zachary Lockman (Albany: State University of New York Press, 1993), 321–33.

45. Ussama Makdisi, *The Culture of Sectarianism: Community, History, and Violence in Nineteenth-Century Ottoman Lebanon* (Berkeley: University of California Press, 2000).

1. Traverso, *Left-Wing Melancholia*, 52.

2. Michaelle Browers, "The Civil Society Debate and New Trends on the Arab Left," *Theory and Event* 7, no. 2 (2004).

3. See Salim Tamari, "Left in Limbo: Leninist Heritage and Islamist Challenge," *Middle East Report* 179 (1992): 16–21.

4. Traboulsi, *History of Modern Lebanon*, 183.

5. Charara's flatmate at the time, who was also a leftist, was influenced by the Iranian Revolution in 1979. He exited from Marxism and became a Shiʿi cleric. The circle is closed. While in the 1940s southern Shiʿi clerics were dropping their religious garb and joining pro-Soviet communist parties, their non-Soviet-aligned New Left children under the influence of the Iranian Revolution dropped their "guerrilla" fatigues back for the robes. While the first story can be mapped as a "tradition" to "modernity" story during the high tides of anticolonialism; the second story is more symptomatic of the postcolonial moment of revival of religious traditions, which in the case of the Iranian Revolution was coupled with militant anti-imperialist politics and discourses articulated in an Islamic idiom.

6. Waddah Charara, interview by author, July 3, 2007, Beirut, Lebanon.

7. Traboulsi, *History of Modern Lebanon*, 192. Old Lebanese identification cards had the citizen's religious affiliation inscribed, facilitating the sectarian sorting out of Christians from Muslims at checkpoints.

8. Waddah Charara, *Hurub al-Istitbaʿ aw Lubnan al-Harb al-Ahliyya al-Daʾima* [Wars of Subjugation: Lebanon the Permanent Civil War] (Beirut: Dar al-Taliʿa, 1979), 225–26. Hereafter I will refer to the book's title in translation, *Wars of Subjugation*, and cited in the text. The book is a collection of essays published between the autumn of 1974 and the winter of 1976. All citations are from the book, but I will refer in the body of the text to the initial dates of publication of the articles since it is crucial for detecting Charara's shifting theoretical and political positions, from his prewar years to the beginning of the war.

9. "Isolationist" was the term by which the LNM referred to the Christian Phalange Party. In his memoir, *A Portrait of the Young Man in Red* (158), Traboulsi engages in a retrospective auto-critique of the LNM's policy advocating the isolation of the Phalanges, that is, the isolationists: "The biggest mistake committed by the LNM that the communists were drawn to and theorized was the slogan of isolating the Phalange: the call to refuse the participation of representatives of that party in the ministers' cabinet, and to isolate it as a punishment for its role in the massacre of ʿAyn al-Rummana [The Bus Incident], and finally the call for an Arab boycott of the party. We spent a lifetime calling for the isolation of the Phalange. And in reality it was not the Phalange who were isolated in the Arab world, but us. Regardless, instead of convincing the 'isolationist' Phalange to break their isolation and open up to the rest of the Lebanese, and to accept a dialogue with them, and this is the important thing, we called for . . . their isolation." And in *A History of Modern Lebanon* (188), Traboulsi the historian notes, "That slogan [isolation of the Phalange] only led to increasing the influence of the Phalange among the Christian public."

10. Salkind and Trab[o]ulsi, "Organization for Communist Action," 5.

11. Salkind and Trab[o]ulsi, "Organization for Communist Action," 5. The program was mainly formulated by Muhsin Ibrahim, who had become the main leader of the OCAL by the beginning of the war; George Hawi, the assistant to the secretary general of the LCP at the time; and Kamal Jumblatt, the LNM's leader. The veteran Palestinian historian Walid Khalidi in 1979 described the Lebanese Nationalist Movement thus: "All were at least left of Center. Most were undeflectedly confrontational. Their overriding target was a revolution in the status quo. Their battering ram: deconfessionalism. Their enemy: both the Maronite and the Muslim establishments. Their strategic ally: the Palestinian commandos. Their patron saint and mentor: Kamal Jumblatt." Walid Khalidi, *Conflict and Violence in Lebanon: Confrontation in the Middle East* (Cambridge, MA: Center for International Affairs, Harvard University, 1979), 75–76.

12. Fawwaz Traboulsi, *Portrait of the Young Man in Red*, 153. The program called for "the abolition of the system of political and administrative sectarian quotas; a voluntary civil code for personal status; a new electoral law based on proportional representation in which Lebanon would become a single electoral district; extensive administrative decentralisation and the convocation of a constituent assembly on a non-sectarian basis." Traboulsi, *A History of Modern Lebanon*, 189.

13. Bold in the original text.

14. Charara and al-Azmeh cotranslated Gramsci's *The Modern Prince* in 1970, publishing it under their pseudonyms: Zahi Cherfan (Waddah Charara) and Qays al-Shami (Aziz al-Azmeh), Antuniu Ghramshi, "al-Amir al-Hadith: Qadaya fi 'Ilm al-Marksiyya" [The Modern Prince: Issues in Marxist Science], tarjama [translation] Zahi Shirfan wa Qays al-Shami (Beirut: Dar al-Tali'a, 1970).

15. Aziz al-Azmeh, "The Progressive Forces," in *Essays on the Crisis in Lebanon*, ed. Roger Owen (London: Ithaca Press, 1976), 65. Hereafter cited in the text.

16. Rosenthal, the translator of Ibn Khaldun's *Muqaddimah*, renders *iltiham* as close contact and *istitba'* as subservience; see Ibn Khaldun, *The Muqaddimah: An Introduction to History*, trans. Franz Rosenthal (Princeton, NJ: Princeton University Press, [1967]1989). I am translating *iltiham* as fusion and *istitba'* as subjugation.

17. Antonio Gramsci, *The Antonio Gramsci Reader*, ed. David Forgacs (New York: New York University Press, 2000).

18. This is what Dipesh Chakrabarty's work does very well. Take for instance Chakrabarty's critical engagement with the elementary categories of political economy: price, labor efficiency, and land. Chakrabarty mentions the contested genealogy of the category of land, particularly in settler colonial societies, such as Australia, where "it is both a tool of disinterested analysis and at the same time a tool of ideological and material domination if not also of epistemic violence." Dipesh Chakrabarty, "Can Political Economy Be Postcolonial? A Note," in *Postcolonial Economies*, ed. Jane Pollard, Cheryl McEwan, and Alex Hughes (London: Zed Books, 2011), 31. See also Dipesh Chakrabarty, *Rethinking Working Class History, Bengal, 1890–1940* (Princeton, NJ: Princeton University Press, 1989); and Chakrabarty, *Provincializing Europe*.

19. In this sentence, Charara inserted a footnote referring to his usage of "bourgeoisie." He wrote, "I am using this designation from the angle of a function limited by the

confines of a specific role" (ws, 240). It's a convoluted formulation reminding the reader of the "technical" usage of the "bourgeoisie" in this context, one that the author sought to distance from the ideological normative charge this concept carries in Marxist political literature.

20. Charara attached a footnote to the above-cited sentence in parenthesis, noting in a gesture of auto-critique: ". . . in which [i.e., the illusions of the Left] the author of this effort has enthusiastically participated" (ws, 246). The three dots (". . .") at the beginning of the footnote are inserted to connote the author's detachment from, and regret about, his past political enthusiasms—an "auto-critique" in a footnote. The author, no longer a militant leader who ought to justify how his past analysis led to a political deadlock that the present political line would deliver him and his comrades from, and no longer writing from within and accountable to a political collectivity, recovered his past after the closure of political activity as a personal enterprise, to which a mention in a footnote sufficed.

21. This is probably why *Wars of Subjugation* neither refers to *Origins'* argument nor cites the book.

22. Ahmad Beydoun, "Waddah Sharara: 'Dimuqratiyyat' al-Dawla aw "Umq' al-Hurriyya" ["Waddah Charara: 'The Democracy' of the State or 'The Depth' of Freedom?"], in *Madakhil wa Makharij: Musharakat Naqdiyya* [Entry Points and Ways Out: Critical Interventions] (Beirut: al-Mu'assasa al-Jami'iyya li-l-Dirasat wa-l-Nashr wa-l-Tawzi', 1985), 136–67. The review was written in August 1979 and first published in the November 1979 issue of *Dirasat 'Arabiyya*.

23. Ahmad Beydoun, *Identité confessionnelle et temps social chez les historiens Libanais contemporains* [Confessional Identity and Social Time among Contemporary Lebanese Historians] (Beirut: Publications de L'Université Libanaise, 1984), 463.

24. "Al-Haraka al-Tullabiyya fi Zawahiruha al-Jadida, min al-Haraka al-Qita'iyya 'ila al-Haraka al-Siyasiyya" [The Student Movement in Its Recent Manifestations: From a Sectorial Movement to a Political One], in ws.

25. Beydoun, "Waddah Charara," 150.

26. Beydoun, "Waddah Charara," 151.

27. Beydoun, "Waddah Charara," 152.

28. Waddah Charara, interview by author, June 30, 2009, Beirut, Lebanon.

29. "Man 'Allamani . . . Madha? (Sira Ta'limiyya Jiz'iyya)" [Who Taught Me . . . What? (A Teacher's Partial Autobiography)], in ws, 163–224.

30. See Charara's second autobiographical essay regarding his days of militancy, "al-Rifaq" [The Comrades], originally published in *Dirasat 'Arabiyya* in July 1980 and reprinted in *Isti'naf al-Badi': Muhawalat fi al-'Ilaqa ma bayn al-Tarikh wa-l-falsafa* [The Resumption of Beginnings: Essays in the Relationship between History and Philosophy] (Beirut: Dar al-Hadatha, 1981), 11–55.

31. I borrow the notion of distilling political experiences into texts from Russell Jacoby, who wrote that Georg Lukács's *History and Class Consciousness* and Karl Korsh's *Marxism and Philosophy*, which were both published in 1923, "distilled past political experiences." Russell Jacoby, *Dialectic of Defeat: Contours of Western Marxism* (Cambridge: Cambridge University Press, 1981), 83.

32. Stefan Collini, "Marxism and Form," *Nation*, December 12, 2005, http://www
.thenation.com/archive/marxism-and-form. Perry Anderson, *Spectrum: From Right to
Left in the World of Ideas* (London: Verso, 2005).

33. Collini, "Marxism and Form."

34. Collini, "Marxism and Form."

35. Collini, "Marxism and Form."

36. Collini, "Marxism and Form."

37. Ahmad Beydoun, interview by author, July 28, 2008, Beirut, Lebanon.

38. See Enzo Traverso, *Left-Wing Melancholia: Marxism, History, and Memory* (New
York: Columbia University Press, 2017).

39. Ahmad Beydoun, interview by author, July 28, 2008, Beirut, Lebanon.

40. Ahmad Beydoun, "Waddah Charara," 136–37.

41. Ahmad Beydoun, "Waddah Charara," 138.

42. Ahmad Beydoun, *Identité confessionnelle et temps social*, 308–9.

43. See Waddah Charara, *Al-Mas'ala al-Tarikhiyya fi al-Fikr al-'Arabi al-Hadith* [The
Question of History in Modern Arab Thought] (Beirut: Ma'had al-Inma'al-'Arabi, 1977).

44. Waddah Charara, *Dawlat Hizb Allah: Lubnan Mujtama'an Islamiyyan* [Hizbul-
lah's State: Lebanon, an Islamist Society] (Beirut: Dar al-Nahar li-l-Nashr, 1996).

45. Waddah Charara, interview by author, July 3, 2007, Beirut, Lebanon.

46. Sudipta Kaviraj, "Marxism in Translation: Critical Reflections on Indian Radical
Thought," in *Political Judgement: Essays for John Dunn*, ed. Richard Bourke and Raymond
Guess (Cambridge: Cambridge University Press, 2009), 178.

47. Kaviraj, "Marxism in Translation," 178.

48. Traboulsi, *Portrait of the Young Man in Red*, 125.

49. Charara is referring to the massacre of as many as five hundred unarmed men,
women, and children committed by US army troops in South Vietnam in March 1968.

50. The *New York Times*'s review of Solzhenitsyn's novel described it as "a non-fictional
account from and about the other great holocaust of our century—the imprisonment,
brutalization and very often murder of tens of millions of innocent Soviet citizens by
their own government, mostly during Stalin's rule from 1929 to 1953." The novel relies
on the author's own experiences between 1945 and 1953 in Soviet camps as well as the
testimonies of 227 survivors, "supplemented by information from official, samizdat, and
even several Western publications. They are assembled in a powerful narrative which
combines the prose styles of epic novelist, partisan historian and outraged moralist,
interspersed with Russian proverbs, black humor, prison camp language and parodies of
Soviet bureaucratese." Solzhenitsyn's argument in the novel rejects the view of the camps
as a Stalinist "aberration," relating them instead to "the original nature of the Bolshevik
revolution and Soviet political system—that there was a 'straight line' between the Lenin
and Stalin eras—and specifically from the Marxist-Leninist ideology." Stephen F. Cohen,
"The Gulag Archipelago," *New York Times*, June 16, 1974, http://www.nytimes.com
/books/98/03/01/home/solz-gulag.html?_r=1.

51. Gregory Elliot, "Parisian Impostures," review of *French Intellectuals against the Left:
The Anti-Totalitarian Moment of the 1970s*, by Michael Scott Christofferson, *New Left
Review* 41 (2006): 140.

52. Michael Scott Christofferson, *French Intellectual against the Left: The Anti-Totalitarian Moment of the 1970s* (New York: Berghahn Books, 2004), 103. Christofferson notes that both Lefort and Glucksmann wrote theses under Raymond Aron in the 1960s and were both involved in revolutionary politics and both reacted against communism.

53. André Glucksmann, *La cuisinière et le mangeur d'hommes: Essai sur l'etat, le Marxisme, les camps de concentration* [The Cook and the Man Eater: An Essay on the Relations between the State, Marxism and Concentration Camps] (Paris: Seuil, 1975); and Claude Lefort, *Un homme en trop: Réflexions sur l'Archipel du Goulag* [One Man Too Many: Reflections on *The Gulag Archipelago*] (Paris: Seuil, 1976). Michael Scott Christofferson, *French Intellectuals against the Left*, 100.

54. "The grounds for Clastres's exaggerated, and monomaniacal, hatred of the state are partly biographical. Many ex-communists have felt it. But Clastres took the fanatical suspicion of the state, familiar among some ex-communists, to an altogether new level of theoretical sophistication. And there is the circumstance of the 1970s in which he wrote, the years of Alexander Solzhenitsyn's *Gulag Archipelago*, and the widespread conviction in France that the rejection of totalitarianism counted as the beginning of political wisdom." Samuel Moyn, "Of Savagery and Civil Society: Pierre Clastres and the Transformation of Political Thought," *Modern Intellectual History* 1, no. 1 (2004): 72. Furet argued that the French Revolution "planted the seeds of twentieth-century totalitarianism. "'Today the Gulag forces us to rethink the Terror,'" he wrote, 'precisely because the two undertakings are seen as identical,'" quoted in Andrew Jainchill and Samuel Moyn, "French Democracy between Totalitarianism and Solidarity: Pierre Rosanvallon and Revisionist Historiography," *Journal of Modern History* 76, no. 1 (March 2004): 109.

55. Michael Scott Christofferson, "Quand Foucault appuyait les 'nouveaux philosophes'" [When Foucault Backed the 'Nouveaux Philosophes'], *Le Monde Diplomatique*, October 2009, http://www.monde-diplomatique.fr/2009/10/CHRISTOFFERSON/18219. Foucault erased the term "archipel carcéral" [carceral archipelago] from the later editions of the book, which according to Christofferson was probably related to his fear of it being used to confound all persecutions (i.e., between those taking place in the socialist East and the capitalist West) and to relieve the stress on the French Communist Party (and its relation to Moscow) by comparing institutions in the West to Soviet repression.

56. Peter Dews, "The Nouvelle Philosophie and Foucault," *Economy and Society* 8, no. 2 (1979): 128.

57. Benedict Anderson, *Imagined Communities: Reflections on the Origins and Spread of Nationalism* (London: Verso, 1983), 1.

58. Ernesto Laclau and Chantal Mouffe, *Hegemony and Socialist Strategy: Towards a Radical Democratic Politics* (London: Verso, [1985] 2001).

59. Laclau and Mouffe, *Hegemony and Socialist Strategy*, xii.

60. "Cold civil-communal peace" is borrowed from the title of Charara's magnum opus, *Al-Silm al-Ahli al-Barid: Lubnan al-Mujtama' wa-l-Dawla 1964–1967* [The Cold Civil/Communal Peace: Lebanon, the Society and the State 1964–1967] (Beirut: Ma'had

al-Inma'al-'Arabi, 1980). Charara resumes in this book the tradition of paradoxical titles he inaugurated in *Origins of Sectarianism: The Right-Wing's Mass Line.*

NOTES TO CHAPTER 6

1. See Dipesh Chakrabarty, "Foreword: The Names and Repetitions of Postcolonial History," in *The Ambiguous Allure of the West: Traces of the Postcolonial in Thailand*, ed. Rachel V. Harrison and Peter A. Jackson (Hong Kong: Hong Kong University Press, 2010): vii-xvii.

2. For a similar observation regarding the poverty of Western social and political theory and a conceptualization of the modalities of political practice in India, see Chatterjee, *Lineages of Political Society.*

3. See Ranajit Guha, *Dominance without Hegemony: History and Power in Colonial India* (Cambridge, MA: Harvard University Press, 1997); Guha's wonderful collection of essays, *The Small Voice of History*, ed. Partha Chatterjee (Delhi: Permanent Black, 2013); and Dipesh Chakrabarty, "A Small History of *Subaltern Studies*," in *Habitations of Modernity: Essays in the Wake of Subaltern Studies* (Chicago: University of Chicago Press, 2002): 3-19.

4. Peters, "Aspects of Rank and Status amongst Muslims in a Lebanese Village," and Peters, "Shifts in Power in a Lebanese Village."

5. It also constituted a personal watershed moment for thinkers such as Talal Asad, contributing to steering his critical excavations toward questions of colonialism and power. See Talal Asad, "Introduction," in *Anthropology and the Colonial Encounter*, ed. Talal Asad (Amherst, NY: Humanity Books, [1973] 1998), 9–19.

6. Sadik Jalal al-Azm, *Dirasat Naqdiyya li-Fikr al-Muqawama al-Filastiniyya* [A Critical Study of the Thought of the Palestinian Resistance] (Beirut: Dar al-'Awda, 1972).

7. Sadik Jalal al-Azm, interview by author, August 4, 2008, Beirut, Lebanon. See also Husayn Bin Hamza, "Sadiq Jalal al-'Azm: al-Mufakkir alladhi Dafa'a 'an (Hurriyyat) Salman Rushdi" [Sadik Jalal al-Azm: The Thinker Who Defended (the Freedom) of Salman Rushdie], *Al-Akhbar*, January 5, 2009. Fatah also withdrew a large number of copies of the book from the market and prevented the publisher from putting out a second edition.

8. Georges Tarabishi, *Sartr wa-l-Marksiyya* [Sartre and Marxism] (Beirut: Dar al-Tali'a, 1963).

9. Josette Zoueïn and Thierry De Rochegonde, "Rencontre avec un traducteur Arabe, Georges Tarabishi," *Che Vuoi?*, no. 21 (2004): 94.

10. Zoueïn and De Rochegonde, "Rencontre avec un traducteur Arabe, Georges Tarabishi," 97.

11. Zoueïn and De Rochegonde, "Rencontre avec un traducteur Arabe, Georges Tarabishi," 96.

12. Hassan Salman, "al-Mufakkir al-Suri Sadiq Jalal al-'Azm: al-'Almaniyya hiya al-Badil 'an al-Harb al-Ahliyya fi al-'Alam al-'Arabi" [The Syrian Thinker Sadik Jalal al-Azm: Secularism Is the Alternative to Civil War in the Arab World], *Asharq Al-Awsat*, August 15, 2007.

13. Salman, "al-Mufakkir al-Suri."

14. Salman, "al-Mufakkir al-Suri."

15. Kassir, *Considérations sur le malheur Arabe*, 39–40. My translation.

16. Al-Afif al-Akhdar, *Madha Qalat li al-Sawarikh al-Mutasaqita 'ala 'Asimat al-Rashid?* [What Did the Falling Missiles on Baghdad Tell Me?], posted on the Saudi website Elaph, March 23, 2003. Accessed through the website Ahewar.org. http://www.ahewar.org/debat/print.art.asp?aid=6276&ac=1.

17. Abu Jihad (Khalil al-Wazir, 1935–88), one the founders of the Palestinian national liberation organization Fatah and a key political and military figure of the Palestinian resistance, was assassinated by Israeli forces at his home in Tunis in April 1988. In 1962, in the wake of Algeria's independence Abu Jihad opened a bureau for Fatah in Algiers. Al-Afif al-Akhdar, who had close relations with the leaders of the Algerian Left, worked from 1962 to 1965 as a translator in Abu Jihad's Bureau. See Shakir al-Nabulsi, *Muhami al-Shaytan: Dirasa fi Fikr al-Afif al-Akhdar* [The Devil's Advocate: A Study of the Thought of al-Afif al-Akhdar] (Beirut: al-Mu'assasa al-'Arabiyya li-l-Tiba'a wa-l-Nashr, 2005), for a synopsis of al-Akhdar's intellectual and political trajectory.

18. Edward Said, *Covering Islam: How the Media and the Experts Determine How We See the Rest of the World* (New York: Vintage Books, [1981] 1997). Hereafter cited in the text.

19. Talal Asad, "The Idea of an Anthropology of Islam," Occasional Papers Series (Washington, DC: Center for Contemporary Arab Studies, Georgetown University, 1986), 1.

20. Ruhollah al-Musawi Khomeini, *A Call to Divine Unity* (Tehran: Institute for Compilation and Publication of Imam Khomeini's Works, 1989).

21. See Talal Asad, "Multiculturalism and British Identity in the Wake of the Rushdie Affair" and "Ethnography, Literature, and Politics: Some Readings and Uses of Salman Rushdie's Satanic Verses," in *The Genealogies of Religion: Disciplines and Reasons of Power in Christianity and Islam* (Baltimore: Johns Hopkins University Press, 1993), 239–306.

22. See Sadik Jalal al-Azm, *Dhihniyyat al-Tahrim: Salman Rushdi wa Haqiqat al-Adab* [The Tabooing Mentality: Salman Rushdie and Literature's Truth] (Damascus: Dar al-Mada, 1997), 45.

23. Nicolas Dot-Pouillard, "De Pékin à Téhéran en regardant vers Jérusalem: La singulière conversion à L'Islamisme des 'Maos du Fatah'" [From Peking to Teheran while Looking toward Jerusalem: The Singular Conversion to Islamism of "Fatah's Maoists"], *Cahiers de l'Institut Religioscope*, no. 2 (December 2008), 6.

24. Dot-Pouillard, "De Pékin à Téhéran," 10.

25. Dot-Pouillard, "De Pékin à Téhéran," 19.

26. Souheil al-Kache, "Convaincre discours de répression" [To Convince: A Discourse of Repression] (PhD diss., Université de Paris VIII Vincennes, 1979). The dissertation is not numbered. al-Kache defended his dissertation on November 29, 1979, under the supervision of François Chatelet and with a committee that included Jean-François Lyotard, the former member of Socialisme ou Barbarie.

27. al-Kache, "Convaincre discours de répression."

28. al-Kache, "Convaincre discours de répression."

29. Dot-Pouillard, "De Pékin à Téhéran," 10.

30. Sadik Jalal al-Azm, "Orientalism and Orientalism in Reverse," in *Orientalism: A Reader*, ed. A. L. Macfie (New York: New York University Press, 2000), 234.

31. Said, *Orientalism*, 328–29.

32. Said, *Orientalism*, 154.

33. See Aijaz Ahmad, "Orientalism and After: Ambivalence and Cosmopolitan Location in the work of Edward Said," originally published in 1992, and reprinted in *In Theory: Classes, Nations, Literatures* (London: Verso, 1994), 159–220.

34. For a discussion of these themes, see Edward Said's brilliant critical intervention, *The Text, The World, and the Critic* (Cambridge, MA: Harvard University Press, 1983).

35. Mahdi 'Amil, *Hal al-Qalb li-l-Sharq wa-l-'Aql l-il-Gharb? Marks fi Istishraq Idward Sa'id* [Does the Heart Belong to the Orient and the Mind to the West? Marx in Edward Said's *Orientalism*] (Beirut: Dar al-Farabi, [1985] 2006).

36. Samer Frangie, "Theorizing from the Periphery: The Intellectual Project of Mahdi 'Amil," *International Journal of Middle Eastern Studies* 44, no. 3 (2012): 465.

37. Mahdi 'Amil, *Muqaddimat Nazariyya* [Theoretical Prolegomena] (Beirut: Dar al-Farabi, 1980), 8.

38. 'Amil, *Hal al-Qalb li-l-Sharq*, 6.

39. 'Amil, *Hal al-Qalb li-l-Sharq*, 51. Emphasis in original.

40. *Orientalism*'s critique, which is predicated on the coupling of the West's knowledges and its will to dominate, when transposed to the theoretical and political stakes of al-Azm's Levantine problem-space, would lose the power part of the power/knowledge couple.

41. al-Azm, "Orientalism and Orientalism in Reverse," 231. Hereafter cited in the text.

42. Said, *Orientalism*, 107.

43. Gramsci, after all, was central to both Edward Said's and Waddah Charara's theories. The first put Gramsci to use, in showing how Orientalism is a hegemonic Western structure that keeps on reproducing itself, while the second concluded around the same time that the multiplicity of modalities of power at work in Lebanese society weakens the establishment of hegemony. Power in this case operates as a formal dominance that does not rework the internal relations of communities and fashions subjectivities, while Said underscored the power of Orientalism in fashioning the "Orient" and the "Oriental."

44. Said, *Orientalism*, 25.

45. Edward Said, *Culture and Imperialism* (New York: Vintage Books, 1993).

46. Ahmad Beydoun, "Idward Sa'id wa-l-Bahth fi al-Imbiriyaliyya" [Edward Said and the Examination of Imperialism], in *Kalamun: Min Mufradat al-Lugha ila Murakkabat-il-Thaqafa* [Kalamun: From Language's Words to Culture's Constructions] (Beirut: Dar al-Jadid, 1997), 339.

47. Beydoun, "Idward Sa'id wa-l-Bahth fi al-Imbiryaliyya," 339.

1. Bruno Latour, "Why Has Critique Run Out of Steam? From Matters of Fact to Matters of Concern," *Critical Inquiry* 30 (2004): 227.

2. Latour, "Why Has Critique Run Out of Steam?," 230. For an analysis of how Christian born-again language appropriates feminist language and left-liberal moves, see Susan Harding, *The Book of Jerry Falwell: Fundamentalist Politics and Language* (Princeton, NJ: Princeton University Press, 2000); for state discourse's appropriation of claims to the situatedness of scientific claims, which were marshaled by critics to call into question the imperialism of universal norms, see Timothy K. Choy, "Articulated Knowledges: Environmental Forms after Universality's Demise," *American Anthropologist* 107, no. 1 (2005): 5–18; for the media's insistence on granting equal time to climate change deniers, see Kim Fortun, "Ethnography in Late Industrialism," *Cultural Anthropology* 27, no. 3 (2012): 446–64.

3. John G. Gunnell, *History, Discourses and Disciplines*, ed. Christopher C. Robinson (New York: Routledge, 2017), 165. These debates, which Gunnell observes, are precipitated by works of the likes of "Thomas Kuhn and Rorty, who disclaims the ability of philosophy to supply the transcendental ground of scientific truth," are a "displacement of the theory/practice problem that haunts all meta-theoretical problems" (165–66). I am thankful to Lisa Wedeen and Linda Zerilli, who introduced me to the work of John Gunnell, which I read with great profit.

4. Gunnell, *History, Discourses, and Disciplines*, 166. In a similar vein, Didier Fassin calls into question his inflated account of the powers of critical theory on political developments in the world. "Is it not too hastily putting the guilt on and simultaneously giving credit to social scientists for the treacherous influence of their knowledge?," Fassin asks, before adding, "is it not complacently granting them too much indignity as well as too much honour?" Didier Fassin, "The Endurance of Critique," *Anthropological Theory* 17, no. 1 (2017): 4.

5. See Linda M. G. Zerilli, "This Universalism Which Is Not One," *Diacritics* 28, no. 2 (1998): 2–20. This scholastic perspective on the world, which fails to dialectically relate the multiple processes and contradictions at the heart of these societies to global capitalist expansion and projects of geopolitical hegemony, misses the simple fact that "universalism," as Ann Tsing pithily put it, "is implicated in both imperial schemes to control the world and liberatory mobilizations for justice and empowerment." Anna Lowenhaupt Tsing, *Friction: An Ethnography of Global Connection* (Princeton, NJ: Princeton University Press, 2005), 9.

6. "One sign of this," Talal Asad had noted a bit less than three decades ago, "is the fact that anthropological textbooks on the Middle East—such as Gulick's or Eickelman's—devote their chapter on 'Religion' entirely to Islam. Although Christianity and Judaism are also indigenous to the region, it is only Muslim belief and practice that Western anthropologists appear to be interested in. In effect, for most Western anthropologists, Sephardic Judaism and Eastern Christianity are conceptually marginalized and represented as minor branches in the Middle East of a history that develops elsewhere—in Europe, and at the roots of Western civilization." Asad, "Idea of an Anthropology of Islam," 3.

7. For example, see Hussein Ali Agrama, *Questioning Secularism: Islam Sovereignty and the Rule of Law in Egypt* (Chicago: University of Chicago Press, 2012); Lara Deeb, *An Enchanted Modern: Gender and Public Piety in Shi'i Lebanon* (Princeton, NJ: Princeton University Press, 2006); Charles Hirschkind, *The Ethical Soundscape: Cassette Sermons and Islamic Counterpublics* (New York: Columbia University Press, 2006); Saba Mahmood, *Politics of Piety: The Islamic Revival and the Feminist Subject* (Princeton, NJ: Princeton University Press, 2004).

8. Lara Deeb gives an illustrative thumbnail sketch of the historical and social-scientific scholarship on sectarianism in Lebanon. She writes: "Max Weiss shows how a Shi'i sectarian political identity and set of institutional practices were forged during the mandate period, via both top-down and ground-up processes. Scholars, including Joseph, Melani Cammett, Bassel Salloukh et al., Paul Kingston, Joanne Nucho, and Maya Mikdashi, among others, have also shown how sectarianism in contemporary Lebanon is maintained, reinforced, and reproduced at the levels of the state, municipality, civil society, elite networks, citizenship, and personal status law." Lara Deeb, "Til Sect Do You Part? On Sectarianism and Intermarriage in Lebanon," *Jadaliyya*, September 14, 2017, http://www.jadaliyya.com/pages/index/27137/-%E2%80%9Ctil-sect-do-you-part%E2%80%9D-on-sectarianism-and-interm.

9. Leila Ahmed poignantly highlights this dimension of colonial power in her encounter with US non-Muslim feminists who claim that they are able to articulate feminist positions from within their religious traditions, while Muslims have to give up their tradition to truly become feminists. Leila Ahmed, *A Border Passage: From Cairo to America—A Woman's Journey* (New York: Penguin Books, 2000), 292.

10. Talal Asad, "Conscripts of Western Civilization?," in *Dialectical Anthropology: Essays in Honor of Stanley Diamond*, vol. 1, ed. C. Gailey (Gainesville: University Press of Florida, 1992), 333–51.

11. Deeb, "Til Sect Do You Part?"

12. For an illuminating analysis of psychic disavowal in a colonial context, see Ranjana Khanna, *Dark Continents: Colonialism and Psychoanalysis* (Durham, NC: Duke University Press, 2003).

13. Lara Deeb, "On Representational Paralysis, or, Why I Don't Want to Write about Temporary Marriage," *Jadaliyya*, December 1, 2010, http://www.jadaliyya.com/pages/index/364/on-representational-paralysis-or-why-i-dont-want-t.

14. For a recent critique of metropolitan oppositional scholarship's focus on the critique of imperialism in the discussion of violence against women in the Muslim world as well as its denouncing of Muslim feminists as westernized, see Rachel Terman, "Islamophobia, Feminism and the Politics of Critique," *Theory, Culture and Society* 33, no. 2 (2016): 77–102.

15. Audra Simpson, writing on the contemporary ethnographies of Native North America, noted the disjunction between what was written about her own people and what mattered to them. In doing so, Simpson underlined the poverty of anthropological and postcolonial literatures that could not account for the multiple articulations of consciousness. "There was not a doubleness to their consciousness," Simpson writes, "a still-colonial but striving to be 'post-colonial consciousness' that denied the modern

self that Fanon, Bhabha and Giddens speak of and from." "There seemed rather to be a tripleness, a quadrupleness, to consciousness and an endless play," she adds, "and it went something like this: 'I am me, I am what you think I am and I am who this person to the right of me thinks I am and you are all full of shit and then maybe I will tell you to your face.'" Audra Simpson, "On Ethnographic Refusal: Indigeneity, 'Voice' and Colonial Citizenship," *Junctures* 9 (2007): 74.

16. For a discussion of the idealist and materialist predication of the subject, see Gayatri Chakravorty Spivak, "Practical Politics of the Open End," in *The Post-Colonial Critic: Interview, Strategies, Dialogues*, ed. Sarah Harasym (New York: Routledge, 1990).

17. Elyachar, *Markets of Dispossession*, 9.

18. The modern project of fashioning peasants into citizens, whether you call it a social reform or a disciplinary project, is also suffering from an additional set of complications. International organizations, since the Bretton Woods Agreement, have the authority "to oversee not only relations between states but the conditions of life of their citizens as well." This aspect of these organizations' work was reinforced when, in addition to their humanitarian effort to alleviate poverty, a concern for human rights was added to their mandate. "With this switch," Elyachar writes, "the person being counted became no longer a citizen of a nation-state but an individual in a universal humanity." Elyachar, *Markets of Dispossession*, 76.

19. Brown, "Resisting Left Melancholy," and Wendy Brown, *Undoing the Demos: Neoliberalism's Stealth Revolution* (New York: Zone Books, 2015).

20. See Wendy Brown, *Politics Out of History* (Princeton, NJ: Princeton University Press, 2001), cited in Saba Mahmood, *Politics of Piety: The Islamic Revival and the Feminist Subject* (Princeton, NJ: Princeton University Press, 2004), and David Scott, "Appendix: The Trouble of Thinking: An Interview with Talal Asad," in *Powers of the Secular Modern: Talal Asad and His Interlocutors*, ed. David Scott and Charles Hirschkind (Stanford: Stanford University Press, 2006), 243–304.

21. Pierre Bourdieu, *Pascalian Meditations*, trans. Richard Nice (Stanford: Stanford University Press, [1997] 2000).

22. This of course is not exclusive to the Arab world. "South Africans," James Ferguson writes, "responded to the 1990s academic critiques of modernism and enlightenment with the dismayed objection: 'You all are ready to abandon it before we've even gotten to try it!'" James Ferguson, "Theory from the Comaroffs, or How to Know the World Up, Down, Backwards and Forwards," "Theorizing the Contemporary," *Cultural Anthropology* website, February 25, 2012, https://culanth.org/fieldsights/271-theory-from-the -comaroffs-or-how-to-know-the-world-up-down-backwards-and-forwards.

Bibliography

ARCHIVE

Socialist Lebanon papers. Ahmad Beydoun Private Collection. Beirut, Lebanon.

INTERVIEWS

al-Azm, Sadik Jalal. Interview by Author. August 4, 2008. Beirut, Lebanon.
Beydoun, Abbas. Interview by Author. July 31, 2008. Beirut, Lebanon.
Beydoun, Ahmad. Interview by Author. July 11, 2007. Beirut, Lebanon.
Beydoun, Ahmad. Interview by Author. July 28, 2008. Beirut, Lebanon.
Beydoun, Azza Charara. Interview by Author. July 23, 2007. Beirut, Lebanon.
Charara, Waddah. Interview by Author. June, 9, 2007. Beirut, Lebanon.
Charara, Waddah. Interview by Author. June 21, 2007. Beirut, Lebanon.
Charara, Waddah. Interview by Author. July 3, 2007. Beirut, Lebanon.
Charara, Waddah. Interview by Author. July 4, 2008. Beirut, Lebanon.
Charara, Waddah. Interview by Author. June 30, 2009. Beirut, Lebanon.
Ibrahim, Muhsin. Interview by Author. August 4, 2008. Beirut, Lebanon.
Kawtharani, Wajih. Interview by Author. July 15, 2008. Beirut, Lebanon.
Soueid, Mahmoud. Interview by Author. July 7, 2008. Beirut, Lebanon.
Traboulsi, Fawwaz. Interview by Author. August 2, 2008. Beirut, Lebanon.

FILM

Shu'ur Akbar min al-Hub [A Feeling Greater Than Love] DVD. Directed by Mary Jirmanus
    Saba. Lebanon, 2017.

PUBLICATIONS

Abdel Malek, Anouar. *Egypte, société militaire* [Egypt, Military Society: The Army Re-
    gime, the Left and Social Change under Nasser]. Paris: Le Seuil, 1962.
Abdel Malak, Anouar. "Introduction." In *Contemporary Arab Political Thought*, edited by
    Anouar Abdel Malak, 1–26. London: Zed Books, 1984.
Abdel Nasser, Gamal. "Khitab al-Ra'is Jamal 'Abd al-Nasir fi 'Id al-Thawra al-Rabi' min
    al-Iskandariyya, 'Khitab Ta'mim Qanat al-Suways'" [Speech of President Gamal Abdel
    Nasser on the Fourth Anniversary of the Revolution in Alexandria, "The National-

ization of the Suez Canal Speech"], July 26, 1956. http://nasser.bibalex.org/Speeches
/browser.aspx?SID=495&lang=en.

Abdel Nasser, Gamal. Khitab al-Ra'is Jamal 'Abd al-Nasir fi 'Id al-'Alam [Speech of President Gamal Abdel Nasser on Flag Day], December 19, 1961. http://nasser.bibalex.org
/Speeches/browser.aspx?SID=1006&lang=ar.

Abidor, Mitchell. La Gauche Prolétarienne. Accessed September 1, 2017. http://www
.marxists.org/history/france/post-1968/gauche-proletarienne/introduction.htm/.

Abi-Samra, Muhammad. "Zahirat al-Akhawayn Rahbani wa Fairuz" [The Rahbani
Brothers and Fairuz Phenomenon]. Master's thesis, Lebanese University, 1985.

Abu-Lughod, Lila. "Zones of Theory in the Anthropology of the Arab World." Annual
Review of Anthropology 18 (1989): 267–306.

Abu Rabi', Ibrahim. Contemporary Arab Thought: Studies in Post-1967 Arab Intellectual
History. London: Pluto, 2004.

Adonis. "Bayan 5 Huzayran 1967" [The June 5th, 1967 Manifesto]. al-Adab, Issues 7 and
8, July–August 1967.

Agrama, Hussein Ali. Questioning Secularism: Islam Sovereignty and the Rule of Law in
Egypt. Chicago: University of Chicago Press, 2012.

Ahmad, Aijaz. "Orientalism and After: Ambivalence and Cosmopolitan Location in the
Work of Edward Said." In In Theory: Classes, Nations, Literatures, 159–220. London:
Verso, 1994.

Ahmed, Leila. A Border Passage: From Cairo to America—A Woman's Journey. New York:
Penguin Books, 2000.

Ahmed, Leila. Women and Gender in Islam: Historical Roots of a Modern Debate. New
Haven, CT: Yale University Press, 1992.

al-Akhdar, al-Afif. Madha Qalat li al-Sawarikh al-Mutasaqita 'ala 'Asimat al-Rashid?
[What Did the Falling Missiles on Baghdad Tell Me?]. Elaph, March 23, 2003. http://
www.ahewar.org/debat/print.art.asp?aid=6276&ac=1.

Allen, Lori. The Rise and Fall of Human Rights: Cynicism and Politics in Occupied Palestine. Stanford: Stanford University Press, 2013.

al-Nabulsi, Shakir. Muhami al-Shaytan: Dirasa fi Fikr al-Afif al-Akhdar [The Devil's Advocate: A Study of the Thought of al-Afif al-Akhdar]. Beirut: al-Mu'assasa al-'Arabiyya
li-l-Tiba'a wa-l Nashr, 2005.

'Amil, Mahdi. Hal al-Qalb li-l-Sharq wa-l-'Aql li-l-Gharb? Marks fi Istishraq Idward Sa'id
[Does the Heart Belong to the Orient and the Mind to the West? Marx in Edward
Said's Orientalism]. Beirut: Dar al-Farabi, [1985] 2006.

'Amil, Mahdi. Muqaddimat Nazariyya [Theoretical Prolegomena]. Beirut: Dar al-Farabi,
1980.

Anderson, Benedict. Imagined Communities: Reflections on the Origins and Spread of
Nationalism. London: Verso, 1983.

Anderson, Perry. Spectrum: From Right to Left in the World of Ideas. London: Verso, 2005.

Asad, Talal. "Anthropological Texts and Ideological Problems: An Analysis of Cohen on
Arab Villages in Israel." Economy and Society 4, no. 3 (1975): 251–82.

Asad, Talal. "Anthropology and the Analysis of Ideology." Man 14, no. 4 (1979):
607–27.

Asad, Talal. "A Comment on Translation, Critique, and Subversion." In *Between Languages and Cultures: Translation and Cross-cultural Texts*, edited by Anuradha Dingwaney and Carol Maier, 325–32. Pittsburgh: University of Pittsburgh Press, 1995.

Asad, Talal. "Conscripts of Western Civilization?" In *Dialectical Anthropology: Essays in Honor of Stanley Diamond*, vol. 1, edited by C. Gailey, 333–51. Gainesville: University Press of Florida, 1992.

Asad, Talal. "Ethnographic Representation, Statistics and Modern Power." *Social Research* 61, no. 1 (1994): 55–88.

Asad, Talal. *Formations of the Secular: Christianity, Islam, Modernity*. Stanford: Stanford University Press, 2003.

Asad, Talal. *The Genealogies of Religion: Disciplines and Reasons of Power in Christianity and Islam*. Baltimore: Johns Hopkins University Press, 1993.

Asad, Talal. "The Idea of an Anthropology of Islam." Occasional Papers Series. Washington, DC: Center for Contemporary Arab Studies, Georgetown University, 1986.

Asad, Talal. "Introduction." In *Anthropology and the Colonial Encounter*, edited by Talal Asad, 9–19. Amherst, NY: Humanity Books, [1973] 1998.

Asad, Talal. Review of *Orientalism* by Edward Said. *English Historical Review* 95, no. 376 (July 1980): 648–49.

al-Azm, Sadik Jalal. *Dhihniyyat al-Tahrim: Salman Rushdi wa Haqiqat al-Adab* [The Tabooing Mentality: Salman Rushdie and Literature's Truth]. Damascus: Dar al-Mada, 1997.

al-Azm, Sadik Jalal. *Dirasat Naqdiyya li-Fikr al-Muqawama al-Filastiniyya* [A Critical Study of the Thought of the Palestinian Resistance]. Beirut: Dar al-'Awda, 1972.

al-Azm, Sadik Jalal. *Al-Naqd al-Dhathi ba'd al-Hazima* [Self-Criticism after the Defeat]. Beirut: Dar al-Tali'a, 1968.

al-Azm, Sadik Jalal. "Orientalism and Orientalism in Reverse." In *Orientalism: A Reader*, edited by A. L. Macfie, 217–38. New York: New York University Press, 2000.

al-Azm, Sadik Jalal. *Self-Criticism after the Defeat*. Translated by George Stergios. London: Saqi Books, [1968] 2011.

al-Azm, Sadik Jalal. "Taqdim ba'd Tul Inqita'" [A Preface after a Long Absence]. In *Al-Naqd al-Dhathi ba'd al-Hazima*, 9–15. Damascus: Dar Mamduh 'Idwan li-l–Tiba'a wa-l-Nashr, 2007.

al-Azmeh, Aziz. "The Progressive Forces." In *Essays on the Crisis in Lebanon*, edited by Roger Owen, 59–72. London: Ithaca Press, 1976.

Bardawil, Fadi A. "Art, War and Inheritance: The Aesthetics and Politics of Ziad Rahbani." Master's thesis, American University of Beirut, 2002.

Bardawil, Fadi A. "Forsaking the Syrian Revolution: An Anti-Imperialist Handbook." *al-Jumhuriya*, December 22, 2016. https://www.aljumhuriya.net/en/content/forsaking-syrian-revolution-anti-imperialist-handbook.

Benjamin, Walter. "Left-Wing Melancholy (on Erich Kästner's New Book of Poems)." *Screen* 15, no. 2 (1974): 28–32.

Beydoun, Abbas. *Blood Test*. Translated by Max Weiss. Syracuse, NY: Syracuse University Press, 2008.

Beydoun, Ahmad. *Identité confessionnelle et temps social chez les historiens Libanais contemporains* [Confessional Identity and Social Time among Contemporary Lebanese Historians]. Beirut: Publications de L'Université Libanaise, 1984.

Beydoun, Ahmad. "Idward Saʿid wa-l-Bahth fi al-Imbiryaliyya" [Edward Said and the Examination of Imperialism]. In *Kalamun: Min Mufradat al-Lugha ila Murakkabat al-Thaqafa* [Kalamon: From Language's Words to Culture's Constructions], 333–40. Beirut: Dar al-Jadid, 1997.

Beydoun, Ahmad. "Waddah Charara: 'Dimukratiyyat' al-Dawla aw "Umq' al-Hurriyya ["Waddah Charara: 'The Democracy' of the State or 'The Depth' of Freedom?"]. In *Madakhil wa Makharij: Musharakat Naqdiyya* [Entry Points and Ways Out: Critical Interventions], 136–67. Beirut: al-Muʾassasa al-Jamiʿiyya li-l-Dirasat wa-l-Nashr wa-l-Tawziʿ, 1985.

Bhabha, Homi. *The Location of Culture.* New York: Routledge, 1994.

Biehl, João, and Peter Locke. "Deleuze and the Anthropology of Becoming." *Current Anthropology* 51, no. 3 (2010): 317–51.

Bilqaziz, ʿAbd al-Ilah. *al-Islam wa-l-Hadatha wa-l-Ijtimaʿ al-Siyasi* [Islam, Modernity, and Political Sociality]. Beirut: Dar al-Wihda al-ʿArabiyya, 2004.

Bin Hamza, Husayn. "Sadik Jalal al-Azm: al-Mufakkir alladhi Dafaʿa ʿan (Hurriyyat) Salman Rushdi" [Sadik Jalal al-Azm: The Thinker Who Defended (the Freedom) of Salman Rushdie]. *Al-Akhbar,* January 5, 2009.

Bishara, Amahl. *Back Stories: US News Production and Palestinian Politics.* Stanford: Stanford University Press, 2012.

Bourdieu, Pierre. *Distinction: A Social Critique of the Judgment of Taste.* Translated by Richard Nice. Cambridge, MA: Harvard University Press, [1979] 1984.

Bourdieu, Pierre. *Pascalian Meditations.* Translated by Richard Nice. Stanford: Stanford University Press, [1997] 2000.

Bourdieu, Pierre. *The Rules of Art: Genesis and Structure of the Literary Field.* Translated by Susan Emanuel. Cambridge: Polity Press, 1996.

Bourdieu, Pierre, and Jean-Claude Passeron. *Les héritiers: Les etudiants et la culture* [The Inheritors: French Students and Their Relations to Culture]. Paris: Les Editions de Minuit, 1964.

Boyer, Dominic C. "Foucault in the Bush. The Social Life of Post-Structuralist Theory in East Berlin's Prenzalauer Berg." *Ethnos* 66, no. 2 (2001): 207–36.

Browers, Michaelle. "The Civil Society Debate and New Trends on the Arab Left." *Theory and Event* 7, no. 2 (2004). https://muse.jhu.edu/article/52894.

Brown, Wendy. *Politics Out of History.* Princeton, NJ: Princeton University Press, 2001.

Brown, Wendy. "Resisting Left Melancholy." *boundary 2* 26, no. 3 (1999): 19–27.

Buci-Glucksmann, Christine. "A voix nue par Sandrine Treiner." *France Culture,* February 13, 2012. https://www.franceculture.fr/emissions/voix-nue/christine-buci -glucksmann-15.

Buck-Morss, Susan. "The Second Time as Farce . . . Historical Pragmatics and the Untimely Present." In *The Idea of Communism,* edited by Costas Douzinas and Slavoj Žižek, 67–80. London: Verso, 2010.

Buck-Morss, Susan. *Thinking Past Terror: Islamism and Critical Theory on the Left.* London: Verso, [2003] 2006.

Butler, Judith, Ernesto Laclau, and Slavoj Žižek. *Contingency, Universality, Hegemony: Contemporary Dialogues on the Left.* London: Verso, 2000.

Carré, Oliver. *Le nationalisme Arabe*. Paris: Payot, [1993] 1996.

Chakrabarty, Dipesh. "Can Political Economy Be Postcolonial? A Note." In *Postcolonial Economies*, edited by Jane Pollard, Cheryl McEwan, and Alex Hughes, 23–35. London: Zed Books, 2011.

Chakrabarty, Dipesh. "Foreword: The Names and Repetitions of Postcolonial History." In *The Ambiguous Allure of the West: Traces of the Postcolonial in Thailand*, edited by Rachel V. Harrison and Peter A. Jackson, vii–xvii. Hong Kong: Hong Kong University Press, 2010.

Chakrabarty, Dipesh. "Labor History and the Politics of Theory: An Indian Angle on the Middle East." In *Workers and Working Classes in the Middle East: Struggles, Histories, Historiographies*, edited by Zachary Lockman, 321–33. Albany: State University of New York Press, 1993.

Chakrabarty, Dipesh. "The Legacies of Bandung: Decolonization and the Politics of Culture." In *Making a World after Empire: The Bandung Moment and Its Political Afterlives*, edited by Christopher Lee, 45–68. Athens: Ohio University Press, 2010.

Chakrabarty, Dipesh. *Provincializing Europe: Postcolonial Thought and Historical Difference*. Princeton, NJ: Princeton University Press, 2000.

Chakrabarty, Dipesh. *Rethinking Working Class History: Bengal, 1890–1940*. Princeton, NJ: Princeton University Press, 1989.

Chakrabarty, Dipesh. "A Small History of *Subaltern Studies*." In *Habitations of Modernity: Essays in the Wake of Subaltern Studies*, 3–19. Chicago: University of Chicago Press, 2002.

Charara, Waddah. *Dawlat Hizb Allah: Lubnan Mujtama'an Islamiyyan* [Hizbullah's State: Lebanon, an Islamist Society]. Beirut: Dar al-Nahar li-l-Nashr, 1996.

Charara, Waddah. *Fi Usul Lubnan al-Ta'ifi: Khat al-Yamin al-Jamahiri* [Origins of Sectarian Lebanon: The Right-wing's Mass Line]. Beirut: Dar al-Tali'a, 1975.

Charara, Waddah. *Hurub al-Istitba' aw Lubnan al-Harb al-Ahliyya al-Da'ima* [Wars of Subjugation: Lebanon, the Permanent Civil War]. Beirut: Dar al-Tali'a, 1979.

Charara, Waddah. *Isti'naf al-Badi': Muhawalat fi al-'Ilaqa ma bayn al-Tarikh wa-l-falsafa* [The Resumption of Beginnings: Attempts at an Encounter between History and Philosophy]. Beirut: Dar al-Hadatha, 1981.

Charara, Waddah. *al-Mas'ala al-Tarikhiyya fi al-Fikr al-'Arabi al-Hadith* [The Question of History in Modern Arab Thought]. Beirut: Ma'had al-Inma'al-'Arabi, 1977.

Charara, Waddah. "al-Nisba al-Mutala'thima: Fusul min Sira (ma Qabl) Lubnaniyya" [The Faltering Belonging: Segments from a (Pre-) Lebanese Autobiography]. *Abwab*, no. 2 (1994): 202–13.

Charara, Waddah. *al-Silm al-Ahli al-Barid: Lubnan al-Mujtama' wa-l-Dawla 1964–1967* [The Cold Civil/Communal Peace: Lebanon, the Society and the State 1964–1967]. Beirut: Ma'had al-Inma'al-'Arabi, 1980.

Charara, Waddah. *Transformations d'une manifestation religieuse dans un village du Liban-Sud (Ashura)* [Transformations of a Religious Manifestation in a Village of Southern Lebanon (Ashura)]. Beirut: Publications du Centre de Recherches de L'Institut des Sciences Sociales, 1968.

Chatterjee, Partha. "Anderson's Utopia." *Diacritics* 29, no. 4 (Winter 1999): 128–34.

Chatterjee, Partha. *Lineages of Political Society: Studies in Postcolonial Democracy*. New York: Columbia University Press, 2011.

Chaudhary, Zahid R. "Subjects in Difference: Walter Benjamin, Frantz Fanon, and Postcolonial Theory." *Differences* 23, no. 1 (2012): 151–83.

Chen, Kuan-Hsing. *Asia as Method: Toward Deimperialization*. Durham, NC: Duke University Press, 2010.

Chow, Rey. *The Age of the World Target: Self-Referentiality in War, Theory, and Comparative Work*. Durham, NC: Duke University Press, 2006.

Choy, Timothy K. "Articulated Knowledges: Environmental Forms after Universality's Demise." *American Anthropologist* 107, no. 1 (2005): 5–18.

Christofferson, Michael Scott. *French Intellectuals against the Left: The Anti-Totalitarian Moment of the 1970s*. New York: Berghahn Books, 2004.

Christofferson, Michael Scott. "Quand Foucault appuyait les «nouveaux philosophes»" [When Foucault Backed the "New Philosophers"]. *Le Monde Diplomatique,* October 2009. http://www.monde-diplomatique.fr/2009/10/CHRISTOFFERSON/18219.

Clifford, James. *The Predicament of Culture*. Cambridge, MA: Harvard University Press, 1988.

Clifford, James, and George Marcus, eds. *Writing Culture: The Poetics and Politics of Ethnography*. Berkeley: University of California Press, 1986.

Cohen, Stephen F. "The Gulag Archipelago." *New York Times*, June 16, 1974. http://www.nytimes.com/books/98/03/01/home/solz-gulag.html?_r=1.

Collini, Stefan. "Marxism and Form." *Nation*, December 12, 2005. http://www.thenation.com/archive/marxism-and-form.

Comaroff, Jean, and John L. Comaroff. "Theory from the South: A Rejoinder." "Theorizing the Contemporary," *Cultural Anthropology* website, February 25, 2012. https://culanth.org/fieldsights/273-theory-from-the-south-a-rejoinder.

Comaroff, Jean, and John L. Comaroff. *Theory from the South: Or How Euro-America Is Evolving towards Africa*. New York: Routledge, 2016.

Crapanzano, Vincent. *Tuhami: Portrait of a Moroccan*. Chicago: University of Chicago Press, 1980.

Da Col, Giovanni, and David Graeber. "Foreword: The Return of Ethnographic Theory." *HAU: Journal of Ethnographic Theory* 1, no. 1 (2011): vi–xxxv.

Dakhli, Leyla. "The Autumn of the Nahda in Light of the Arab Spring: Some Figures in the Carpet." In *Arabic Thought beyond the Liberal Age: Towards an Intellectual History of the Nahda*, edited by Jens Hanssen and Max Weiss, 351–72. Cambridge: Cambridge University Press, 2016.

Darraj, Faysal. "Rahin al-Hazima/Rahiniyyat al-Kitab al-Naqdi" [The Actuality of Defeat/The Endurance of the Critical Book]. In *Al-Naqd al-Dhathi ba'd al-Hazima*, 17–25. Damascus: Dar Mamduh 'Adwan, 2007.

Deeb, Lara. *An Enchanted Modern: Gender and Public Piety in Shi'i Lebanon*. Princeton, NJ: Princeton University Press, 2006.

Deeb, Lara. "On Representational Paralysis, or, Why I Don't Want to Write about Temporary Marriage." *Jadaliyya*, December 1, 2010. http://www.jadaliyya.com/pages/index/364/on-representational-paralysis-or-why-i-dont-want-t.

Deeb, Lara. "Til Sect Do You Part? On Sectarianism and Intermarriage in Lebanon." *Jadaliyya*, September 14, 2017. http://www.jadaliyya.com/pages/index/27137/ -%E2%80%9Ctil-sect-do-you-part%E2%80%9D-on-sectarianism-and-interm.

Deeb, Lara, and Jessica Winegar. "Anthropologies of Arab-Majority Societies." *Annual Review of Anthropology* 41 (2012): 537–58.

Deeb, Lara, and Jessica Winegar. *Anthropology's Politics: Disciplining the Middle East* Stanford: Stanford University Press, 2016.

Dews, Peter. "The Nouvelle Philosophie and Foucault." *Economy and Society* 8, no. 2 (1979): 127–71.

Di-Capua, Yoav. *No Exit: Arab Existentialism, Jean-Paul Sartre, and Decolonization.* Chicago: University of Chicago Press, 2018.

Dot-Pouillard, Nicolas. "Boire à Hamra: Une jeunesse nostalgique à Beyrouth?" [Drinking in Hamra: A Nostalgic Youth in Beirut?]. In *Jeunesses Arabe—Du Maroc au Yémen: loisirs, cultures et politiques* [Arab Youth—From Morocco to Yemen: Entertainments, cultures and politics], edited by Laurent Bonnefoy and Miriam Catusse, 125–33. Paris: La Découverte, 2013.

Dot-Pouillard, Nicolas. "De Pékin à Téhéran en regardant vers Jérusalem: La singulière conversion à l'Islamisme des 'Maos du Fatah'"[From Peking to Teheran While Looking towards Jerusalem: The Singular Conversion to Islamism of "Fatah's Maoists"]. *Cahiers de l'Institut Religioscope*, no. 2 (December 2008).

Durkheim, Emile. *The Elementary Forms of Religious Life.* New York: Free Press, [1912] 1995.

Elliot, Gregory. "Parisian Impostures," Review of *French Intellectuals against the Left: The Anti-Totalitarian Moment of the 1970s*, by Michael Scott Christofferson. *New Left Review* 41 (2006): 139–45.

El Shakry, Omnia. *The Arabic Freud: Psychoanalysis and Islam in Modern Egypt.* Princeton, NJ: Princeton University Press, 2017.

El Shakry, Omnia. "'History without Documents': The Vexed Archives of Decolonization in the Middle East." *American Historical Review* 120, no. 3 (2015): 920–34.

Elyachar, Julia. *Markets of Dispossession: NGOs, Economic Development, and the State.* Durham, NC: Duke University Press, 2005.

Emmelhainz, Irmgard. "From Third-Worldism to Empire: Jean-Luc Godard and the Palestine Question." *Third Text* 3, no. 5 (2009): 649–56.

Fassin, Didier. "The Endurance of Critique." *Anthropological Theory* 17, no. 1 (2017): 4–29.

Fassin, Didier. "La politique des anthropologues: Une histoire Française" [The Politics of Anthropologists: A French History]. *L'Homme* 185–86, no. 6 (2008): 165–86.

Ferguson, James. "Theory from the Comaroffs, or How to Know the World Up, Down, Backwards and Forwards," Theorizing the Contemporary, *Cultural Anthropology* website, February 25, 2012. https://culanth.org/fieldsights/271-theory-from-the-comaroffs -or-how-to-know-the-world-up-down-backwards-and-forwards.

Fernea, Robert A., and James M. Malakey. "Anthropology of the Middle East: A Critical Assessment." *Annual Review of Anthropology* 4 (1975): 183–206.

Fortun, Kim. "Ethnography in Late Industrialism." *Cultural Anthropology* 27, no. 3 (2012): 446–64.

Foucault, Michel. *Les mots et les choses: Une archéologie des sciences humaines* [The Order of Things: An Archeology of the Human Sciences]. Paris: Gallimard, 1966.

Frangie, Samer. "Theorizing from the Periphery: The Intellectual Project of Mahdi 'Amil." *International Journal of Middle East Studies* 44, no. 3 (2012): 465–82.

Gaonkar, Dilip Parameshwar, and Elizabeth A. Povinelli, "Technologies of Public Forms: Circulation, Transfiguration, Recognition." *Public Culture* 15, no. 3 (2003): 385–97.

Geertz, Clifford. *The Interpretation of Cultures*. New York: Basic Books, 1973.

Glucksmann, André. *La Cuisinière et le mangeur d'hommes: Essai sur l'etat, le Marxisme, les camps de concentration* [The Cook and the Man Eater: An Essay on the Relations between the State, Marxism and Concentration Camps]. Paris: Seuil, 1975.

Goria, Wade R. *Sovereignty and Leadership in Lebanon 1943–1976*. London: Ithaca Press, 1985.

Gourgouris, Stathis. "Antisecularist Failures: A Counterresponse to Saba Mahmood." *Public Culture* 20, no. 3 (2008): 453–59.

Gourgouris, Stathis. "Detranscendentalizing the Secular." *Public Culture* 20, no. 3 (2008): 437–45.

Gramsci, Antonio [Antuniu Ghramshi]. "al-Amir al-Hadith: Qadaya Fi 'Ilm al-Marksiyya" [The Modern Prince: Issues in Marxist Science]. Translated by Zahi Cherfan and Qays al-Shami. Beirut: Dar al-Tali'a, 1970.

Gramsci, Antonio. *The Antonio Gramsci Reader*. Edited by David Forgacs. New York: New York University Press, 2000.

Guha, Ranajit. *Dominance without Hegemony: History and Power in Colonial India*. Cambridge, MA: Harvard University Press, 1997.

Guha, Ranajit. *The Small Voice of History*. Edited by Partha Chatterjee. Delhi: Permanent Black, 2013.

Gunnell, John G. *History, Discourses and Disciplines*. Edited by Christopher C. Robinson. New York: Routledge, 2017.

Hage, Ghassan. *Alter-Politics: Critical Anthropology and the Radical Imagination*. Melbourne: Melbourne University Press, 2015.

al-Haj Saleh, Yassin. "Hazimat Huzayran: min Hadath Tarikhi ila Shart Thaqafi" [The June Defeat: From a Historical Event to a Cultural Condition], *al-Hiwar al-Mutamaddin* Issue 1936, June 4, 2007. http://www.ahewar.org/debat/show.art.asp?aid=98676&nm=1.

Halabi, Zeina G. *The Unmaking of the Arab Intellectual: Prophecy, Exile and the Nation*. Edinburgh: Edinburgh University Press, 2017.

Hall, Stuart. *Familiar Stranger: A Life between Two Islands*. Edited by Bill Schwarz. Durham, NC: Duke University Press, 2017.

Harding, Susan. *The Book of Jerry Falwell: Fundamentalist Politics and Language*. Princeton, NJ: Princeton University Press, 2000.

Harik, Iliya. *Politics and Change in a Traditional Society: Lebanon, 1711–1845*. Princeton, NJ: Princeton University Press, 1968.

Harlow, Barbara. "Introduction to Kanafani's "Thoughts on Change and the 'Blind Language.'" *Alif: Journal of Comparative Poetics*, no. 10 (1990): 132–36.

Haugbolle, Sune. "The New Arab Left and 1967." *British Journal of Middle Eastern Studies* 44, no. 4 (2017): 497–512.

Hirschkind, Charles. *The Ethical Soundscape: Cassette Sermons and Islamic Counterpublics.* New York: Columbia University Press, 2006.

Hirschkind, Charles, and Saba Mahmood. "Feminism, the Taliban, and the Politics of Counter-Insurgency." *Anthropological Quarterly* 75, no. 2 (2002): 107–22.

Hourani, Albert. "Albert Hourani." In *Approaches to the History of the Middle East: Interviews with Leading Middle East Historians,* edited by Nancy Gallagher, 19–45. Reading, UK: Ithaca Press, 1994.

Hourani, Albert. *Arabic Thought in the Liberal Age, 1798–1939.* Cambridge: Cambridge University Press, [1962] 1983.

Hussein, Mahmoud. *La lutte des classes en Egypte de 1946 à 1968* [Class Conflict in Egypt from 1945 to 1970]. Paris: Maspero, 1969.

Ibn Khaldun. *The Muqaddimah: An Introduction to History.* Translated by Franz Rosenthal. Princeton, NJ: Princeton University Press, [1967] 1989.

Ibrahim, Muhsin. *George Hawi Ibn al-Nahda al-Yasariyya al-Lubnaniyya wa Ahad Abraz Sunna'iha al-Kibar* [George Hawi: The Son of the Lebanese Leftist Renaissance and One of Its Great Producers]. *Beirut al-Masa',* no. 572 (August 13, 2005).

Ismael, Tareq Y. *The Arab Left.* Syracuse, NY: Syracuse University Press, 1976.

Ismael, Tareq Y. *The Communist Movement in the Arab World.* London: Routledge Curzon, 2005.

Ismael, Tareq Y., and Jacqueline S. Ismael. *The Communist Movement in Syria and Lebanon.* Gainesville: University Press of Florida, 1998.

Jabar, Faleh A. "The Arab Communist Parties in Search of an Identity." In *Post-Marxism and the Middle East,* edited by Faleh A. Jabar, 91–110. London: Saqi Books, 1997.

Jackson, Michael. "Ajàlá's Heads: Reflections on Anthropology and Philosophy in a West African Setting." In *The Ground Between: Anthropologists Engage Philosophy,* edited by Veena Das, Michael Jackson, Arthur Kleinman, and Bhrigupati Singh, 27–49. Durham, NC: Duke University Press, 2014.

Jacoby, Russell. *Dialectic of Defeat: Contours of Western Marxism.* Cambridge: Cambridge University Press, 1981.

Jainchill, Andrew, and Samuel Moyn. "French Democracy between Totalitarianism and Solidarity: Pierre Rosanvallon and Revisionist Historiography." *Journal of Modern History* 76, no. 1 (2004): 107–54.

James, Laura M. "Whose Voice? Nasser, the Arabs, and 'Sawt al-Arab' Radio." *Transnational Broadcasting Studies,* no. 16 (June–December 2006). http://archived.tbsjournal.arabmediasociety.com/James.html.

Jayusi, Salma Khadra. *Modern Arabic Poetry: An Anthology.* New York: Columbia University Press, 1987.

Johnson, Douglas. "Benny Lévy." *Guardian,* October 21, 2003. https://www.theguardian.com/news/2003/oct/21/guardianobituaries.booksobituaries.

al-Kache, Souheil. "Convaincre: discours de répression" [To Convince: A Discourse of Repression]. PhD diss., Université de Paris VIII Vincennes, 1979.

al-Khomeini, Ruhullah al-Musawi. *A Call to Divine Unity*. Tehran: Institute for Compilation and Publication of Imam Khomeini's Works, 1989.

Kassab, Elizabeth Suzanne. *Contemporary Arab Thought: Cultural Critique in Comparative Perspective*. New York: Columbia University Press, 2009.

Kassab, Elizabeth Suzanne. "Summoning the Spirit of Enlightenment: On the Nahda Revival in Qadaya wa-shahadat." In *Arabic Thought against the Authoritarian Age: Towards an Intellectual History of the Present*, edited by Max Weiss and Jens Hanssen, 311–35. Cambridge: Cambridge University Press, 2018.

Kassir, Samir. *Considérations sur le malheur Arabe* [Being Arab]. Paris: Actes Sud, 2004.

Kassir, Samir. *La Guerre du Liban: De la dissension nationale au conflit régional 1975–82* [The Lebanon War: From National Strife to a Regional Conflict 1975–82]. Paris: Karthala, 1994.

Kaviraj, Sudipta. "Marxism in Translation: Critical Reflections on Indian Radical Thought." In *Political Judgement: Essays for John Dunn*, edited by Richard Bourke and Raymond Guess, 172–200. Cambridge: Cambridge University Press, 2009.

Kazziha, Walid. *Revolutionary Transformation in the Arab World: Habash and His Comrades from Nationalism to Communism*. New York: St. Martin's, 1975.

Khalidi, Rashid. "Arab Nationalism: Historical Problems in the Literature." *American Historical Review* 96, no. 5 (1991): 1363–73.

Khalidi, Rashid. "The Legacies of *Arabic Thought in the Liberal Age*." In *Arabic Thought beyond the Liberal Age: Towards an Intellectual History of the Nahda*, edited by Jens Hanssen and Max Weiss, 375–86. Cambridge: Cambridge University Press, 2016.

Khalidi, Walid. *Conflict and Violence in Lebanon: Confrontation in the Middle East*. Cambridge, MA: Center for International Affairs, Harvard University, 1979.

Khanna, Ranjana. *Dark Continents: Colonialism and Psychoanalysis*. Durham, NC: Duke University Press, 2003.

Khera, Jastinder. "Mashrou' Leila: The Band Out to Occupy Arabic Pop." BBC News, October 16, 2013. http://www.bbc.com/news/world-middle-east-24469243.

Khoury, Elias. "For a Third Nahda." In *Arabic Thought against the Authoritarian Age: Towards an Intellectual History of the Present*, edited by Max Weiss and Jens Hanssen, 357–69. Cambridge: Cambridge University Press, 2018.

Khuri-Makdisi, Ilham. *The Eastern Mediterranean and the Making of Global Radicalism, 1860–1914*. Berkeley: University of California Press, 2013.

Koselleck, Reinhart. *Futures Past*. Translated by Keith Tribe. New York: Columbia University Press, [1979] 2004.

Laclau, Ernesto, and Chantal Mouffe. *Hegemony and Socialist Strategy: Towards a Radical Democratic Politics*. London: Verso, [1985] 2001.

Latour, Bruno. "The Recall of Modernity: Anthropological Approaches." Translated by Stephen Muecke. *Cultural Studies Review* 13, no. 1 (March 2007): 11–30.

Latour, Bruno. "Why Has Critique Run Out of Steam? From Matters of Fact to Matters of Concern." *Critical Inquiry* 30 (2004): 225–48.

Lefort, Claude. *Un homme en trop: Réflexions sur l'Archipel du Goulag* [One Man Too Many: Reflections on *The Gulag Archipelago*]. Paris: Seuil, 1976.

Limadha Munazzamat al-Ishtirakiyyin al-Lubnaniyyin (Harakat al-Qawmiyyin al-'Arab min al-Fashiyya 'ila al-Nassiriyya): Tahlil wa Naqd [The Organization of Lebanese

Socialists, What For? (The Arab Nationalist Movement from Fascism to Nasserism): An Analysis and a Critique]. Beirut: Dar al-Tali'a, 1970.

Lyotard, Jean-François. *The Postmodern Condition: A Report on Knowledge*. Minneapolis: University of Minnesota Press, [1979] 1984.

Mahmood, Saba. "Is Critique Secular? A Symposium at UC Berkeley." *Public Culture* 20, no. 3 (2008): 447–52.

Mahmood, Saba. *Politics of Piety: The Islamic Revival and the Feminist Subject*. Princeton, NJ: Princeton University Press, 2004.

Mahmood, Saba. "Secular Imperatives?" *Public Culture* 20, no. 3 (2008): 461–65.

Mahmood, Saba. "Secularism, Hermeneutics, and Empire: The Politics of Islamic Reformation." *Public Culture* 18, no. 2 (2006): 323–47.

Makdisi, Ussama. *The Culture of Sectarianism: Community, History, and Violence in Nineteenth-Century Ottoman Lebanon*. Berkeley: University of California Press, 2000.

Malley, Robert. *The Call from Algeria: Third Worldism, Revolution, and the Turn to Islam*. Los Angeles: University of California Press, 1996.

Mao Tse-Tung. "People's War." In *Quotations from Chairman Mao Tse-Tung*, 88–99. Peking: Foreign Languages Press, 1966.

Mao Tse-Tung. "Report on an Investigation of the Peasant Movement in Hunan." In *Selected Works of Mao Tse-Tung*, vol. 1. Peking: Foreign Languages Press, 1965. https://www.marxists.org/reference/archive/mao/selected-works/volume-1/mswv12.htm.

Mardam-Bey, Farouk, and Elias Sanbar. *Etre Arabe: Entretiens avec Christophe Kantcheff* [Being Arab: Interviews with Christophe Kantcheff]. Paris: Actes Sud, 2005.

Marx, Karl, and Friedrich Engels. *The Communist Manifesto*. Translated by Samuel Moore. Moscow: Progress Publishers, 1969. https://www.marxists.org/archive/marx/works/download/pdf/Manifesto.pdf.

Massad, Joseph A. *Desiring Arabs*. Chicago: University of Chicago Press, 2007.

Mbembe, Achille. *Critique of Black Reason*. Translated by Laurent Dubois. Durham, NC: Duke University Press, 2017.

Merleau-Ponty, Maurice. *Humanisme et terreur* [Humanism and Terror]. Paris: Gallimard, 1947.

Messick, Brinkley. *The Calligraphic State: Textual Domination and History in a Muslim Society*. Berkeley: University of California Press, 1993.

Mitchell, Timothy. "The Middle East in the Past and Future of Social Science." In *The Politics of Knowledge: Area Studies and the Disciplines*, edited by David L. Szanton. University of California International and Area Studies, vol. 3, article 3 (2003).

Morris, Rosalind. "Introduction." In *Can the Subaltern Speak? Reflections on the History of an Idea*, edited by Rosalind Morris, 1–20. New York: Columbia University Press, 2010.

Moyn, Samuel. "Of Savagery and Civil Society: Pierre Clastres and the Transformation of Political Thought." *Modern Intellectual History* 1, no. 1 (2004): 55–80.

Murthy, Viren. "Looking for Resistance in All the Wrong Places? Chibber, Chakrabarty, and a Tale of Two Histories." *Critical Historical Studies* 2, no. 1 (2015): 113–53.

Muruwwa, Husayn. *Wulidtu Shaykhan Wa Amutu Tiflan: Sira Dhatiyya fi Hadithin Ajrahu Ma'ahu 'Abbas Baydun* [I Was Born a Sheikh and I Will Die a Child: An Autobiography Undertaken as a Conversation with Abbas Beydoun]. Beirut: Dar al-Farabi, 1990.

"Nasser Accuses Arab Reds Again; Says They Plotted to Split U. A. R., Seize Iraq and Form 'Fertile Crescent.'" *New York Times*, April 17, 1959.

Perreau, Bruno. *Queer Theory: The French Response.* Stanford: Stanford University Press, 2016.

Peters, Emrys L. "Aspects of Rank and Status amongst Muslims in a Lebanese Village." In *Mediterranean Countrymen*, edited by Julian Pitt-Rivers, 159–200. The Hague: Mouton, 1963.

Peters, Emrys L. "Shifts in Power in a Lebanese Village." In *Rural Politics and Social Change in the Middle East*, edited by Richard Antoun and Iliya Harik, 165–97. Bloomington: Indiana University Press, 1972.

Picard, Elizabeth. *Lebanon, a Shattered Country: Myths and Realities of the Wars in Lebanon.* Translated by Franklin Philip. New York: Holmes and Meier, 1996.

Piot, Charles. *Nostalgia for the Future: West Africa after the Cold War.* Chicago: University of Chicago Press, 2010.

Ramonet, Ignacio. "Cinquante Ans"[Fifty Years]. *Le Monde Diplomatique* 74, April–May (2004). http://www.monde-diplomatique.fr/mav/74/RAMONET/10882.

Rancière, Jacques. *Althusser's Lesson.* Translated by Emiliano Batista. London: Continuum Lesson, [1974] 2011.

Rancière, Jacques. *The Philosopher and His Poor.* Translated by John Drury, Corinne Oster, and Andrew Parker. Durham, NC: Duke University Press, [1983] 2004.

Reid, Donald. "Etablissement: Working in the Factory to Make Revolution in France." *Radical History Review* 88 (2004): 83–111.

Riad, Hassan. *L'Egypte Nassérienne* [Nasserite Egypt]. Paris: Les Editions de Minuit, 1964.

Ross, Kristin. *May '68 and Its Afterlives.* Chicago: University of Chicago Press, 2002.

Said, Edward. "The Arab Portrayed." In *The Arab-Israeli Confrontation of June 1967: An Arab Perspective*, edited by Ibrahim Abu-Lughod, 1–9. Evanston, IL: Northwestern University Press, 1970.

Said, Edward. *Covering Islam: How the Media and the Experts Determine How We See the Rest of the World.* New York: Vintage Books, [1981] 1997.

Said, Edward. *Culture and Imperialism.* New York: Vintage, 1993.

Said, Edward. "My Guru." *London Review of Books* 23, no. 24 (December 13, 2001). http://www.lrb.co.uk/v23/n24/edward-said/my-guru.

Said, Edward. *Orientalism.* New York: Vintage Books, [1978] 1994.

Said, Edward. *Out of Place: A Memoir.* New York: Knopf, 1999.

Said, Edward. *The Text, the World, and the Critic.* Cambridge, MA: Harvard University Press, 1983.

Salamé, Ghassan. *Le théâtre politique au Liban (1968–1973): Approche idéologique et esthétique* [Political Theater in Lebanon (1968–1973): An Ideological and Aesthetic Approach]. Beirut: Dar al-Mashriq, 1974.

Salem, Elise. *Constructing Lebanon: A Century of Literary Narratives.* Gainesville: University Press of Florida, 2003.

Salibi, Kamal. *A House of Many Mansions: The History of Lebanon Reconsidered.* Berkeley: University of California Press, 1990.

Salkind, Michele, and Fawwaz Trabulsi. "Organization for Communist Action: An Interview with Fawwaz Trabulsi." *Middle East Research and Information Project Reports (MERIP)*, no. 61 (1977): 5–8, 21.

Salman, Hassan. "al-Mufakkir al-Suri Sadiq Jalal al-Azm: al-'Almaniyya Hiya al-Badil 'an al-Harb al-Ahliyya fi al-'Alam al-'Arabi" [The Syrian Thinker Sadik Jalal al-Azm: Secularism Is the Alternative to Civil War in the Arab World]. *Asharq al-Awsat*, August 15, 2007.

Salman, Talal. "Muhsin Ibrahim wa Naqd al-Tajruba ... Hayth la Yajru' al-Akharun!" [Muhsin Ibrahim and the Critique of the Experience ... Where Others Do Not Dare!]. *al-Safir*, August 8, 2005. http://elaph.com/Web/NewsPapers/2005/8/81930.htm?sectionarchive=NewsPapers.

Schayegh, Cyrus. "1958 Reconsidered: State Formation and the Cold War in the Early Postcolonial Arab Middle East." *International Journal of Middle East Studies* 45 (2013): 421–43.

Schofield, Hugh. "Algerian Novelist Kamel Daoud Sparks Islamophobia Row." BBC News, March 7, 2016.

Scott, David. "Appendix: The Trouble of Thinking: An Interview with Talal Asad." In *Powers of the Secular Modern: Talal Asad and His Interlocutors*, edited by David Scott and Charles Hirschkind, 243–304. Stanford: Stanford University Press, 2006.

Scott, David. *Conscripts of Modernity: The Tragedy of Colonial Enlightenment.* Durham, NC: Duke University Press, 2004.

Scott, David. "Criticism and Culture: Theory and Post-Colonial Claims on Anthropological Disciplinarity." *Critique of Anthropology* 12, no. 4 (1992): 371–94.

Scott, David. "David Scott by Stuart Hall." *Bomb* 90 (Winter 2005). https://bombmagazine.org/articles/david-scott/.

Scott, David. *Refashioning Futures: Criticism after Postcoloniality.* Princeton, NJ: Princeton University Press, 1999.

Scott, David. *Stuart Hall's Voice: Intimations of an Ethics of Receptive Generosity.* Durham, NC: Duke University Press, 2017.

Shaery-Eisenlohr, Roschanak. *Shi'ite Lebanon: Transnational Religion and the Making of National Identities.* New York: Columbia University Press, 2008.

Sheehi, Stephen. *Foundations of Modern Arab Identity.* Gainesville: University Press of Florida, 2004.

Simpson, Audra. "On Ethnographic Refusal: Indigeneity, 'Voice' and Colonial Citizenship." *Junctures* 9 (2007): 67–80.

Skinner, Quentin. "An Interview with Quentin Skinner." *Cogito* 11, no. 2 (1997): 69–76.

Spivak, Gayatri Chakravorty. "Can the Subaltern Speak?" In *The Post-Colonial Studies Reader*, edited by Bill Ashcroft, Gareth Griffiths, and Helen Tiffin, 28–37. New York: Routledge, 1995.

Spivak, Gayatri Chakravorty. "Practical Politics of the Open End." In *The Post-Colonial Critic: Interview, Strategies, Dialogues*, edited by Sarah Harasym, 95–112. New York: Routledge, 1990.

Talhami, Ghada. "An Interview with Sadik al-Azm." *Arab Studies Quarterly* 19, no. 3 (1997): 113–26.

Tamari, Salim. "Left in Limbo: Leninist Heritage and Islamist Challenge." *Middle East Report* 179 (1992): 16–21.

Tarabishi, Georges. *Sartr wa-l-Marksiyya* [Sartre and Marxism]. Beirut: Dar al-Tali'a, 1963.

Terman, Rachel. "Islamophobia, Feminism and the Politics of Critique." *Theory, Culture and Society* 33, no. 2 (2016): 77–102.

Traboulsi, Fawwaz. *A History of Modern Lebanon*. London: Pluto, 2007.

Traboulsi, Fawwaz. *Surat al-Fata bi-l-Ahmar: Ayyam fi al-Silm wa-l-Harb* [A Portrait of the Young Man in Red: Days of Peace and War]. Beirut: Riad el-Rayyes Books, 1997.

Traverso, Enzo. *Left-Wing Melancholy: Marxism, Memory, Culture*. New York: Columbia University Press, 2016.

Trotsky, Leon. "Our Political Tasks [1904]." https://www.marxists.org/archive/trotsky/1904/tasks/.

Tsing, Anna Lowenhaupt. *Friction: An Ethnography of Global Connection*. Princeton, NJ: Princeton University Press, 2005.

Tsing, Anna Lowenhaupt. "Is There a Progressive Politics after Progress?" *Cultural Anthropology* website. Accessed June 26, 2018. https://culanth.org/fieldsights/1133-is-there-a-progressive-politics-after-progress.

Tully, James. *Meaning and Context: Quentin Skinner and His Critics*. Princeton, NJ: Princeton University Press, 1989.

United Nations Development Programme. *Arab Human Development Report 2003: Building a Knowledge Society*. New York: Regional Bureau for Arab States, cosponsored with the Arab Fund for Economic and Social Development, 2003.

Walker, Gavin. *The Sublime Perversion of Capital: Marxist Theory and the Politics of History in Modern Japan*. Durham, NC: Duke University Press, 2016.

Wedeen, Lisa. "Ideology and Humor in Dark Times: Notes from Syria." *Critical Inquiry* 39, no. 4 (2013): 841–73.

Weiss, Max, and Jens Hanssen. "Introduction: Arabic Intellectual History between the Postwar and the Postcolonial." In *Arabic Thought against the Authoritarian Age: Towards an Intellectual History of the Present*, edited by Jens Hanssen and Max Weiss, 1–35. Cambridge: Cambridge University Press, 2018.

Wilder, Gary. *Freedom Time: Decolonization and the Future of the World*. Durham, NC: Duke University Press, 2015.

Winegar, Jessica. *Creative Reckonings: The Politics of Art and Culture in Contemporary Egypt*. Stanford: Stanford University Press, 2006.

Zerilli, Linda M. G. "Feminism, Critique, and the Realistic Spirit." *Philosophy & Rhetoric* 50, no. 4 (2017): 589–611.

Zerilli, Linda M. G. "This Universalism Which Is Not One." *Diacritics* 28, no. 2 (1998): 2–20.

Zoueïn, Josette, and Thierry De Rochegonde. "Rencontre avec un traducteur en Arabe, Georges Tarabishi" [A Meeting with a Translator from Arabic, Georges Tarabishi]. *Che vuoi?*, no. 21 (2004): 93–99.

Index

Page numbers in italics refer to figures.

Front of National and Progressive Political Parties, 98
Furet, François, 161, 233n58

Geertz, Clifford, 8, 203n19
geopolitics, 18, 169, 173, 191, 237n5
Ghandour strike, 117–18, 120, 123
Ghazi, Christian, 97
Gibran, Khalil, 47–48, 213n68
global interconnectedness, 13–15
global Left, 53, 54–55
Global South, 5, 6, 77; North/South binary, 13–15, 67–68, 78
Glucksmann, André, 161, 233n56
Godard, Jean-Luc, 78, 162, 216n38, 228n34
Gramsci, Antonio, 145–46, 163, 167, 180, 236n43
Guevara, Che, 5, 63, 67, 173
Guha, Ranajit, 167
Gulag Archipelago (Solzhenitsyn), 160–61, 232n54, 233n58
Gunnell, John, 188, 237n3

al-Hafiz, Yasin, 60, 82, 92, 107
Hamdan, Hassan (Mahdi 'Amil), 108, 177, 179–81, 184, 215n10
Harootunian, Harry, xvii
Hawi, George, 106, 124, 144, 230n11
hegemony, 10, 166, 237n5; Charara on, 157–58, 162, 185, 236n42; power and dominance, 145–46, 167; Said and, 177, 184, 236n42; universality and, 163; Western or European, 12, 20, 189, 205n35, 236n43
Helou, Charles, 56, 99
al-Helou, Farajalla, 96
historical dis(continuity), 27–28, 135, 176
historical reconstruction, 22, 80, 208n73
historicism, 20, 21, 165, 172; Marxist, 3, 70, 133, 178, 179, 183
Hizbullah, 4, 157–58, 163, 209n11. *See also* Shi'i community
holistic doctrines and critique, 84, 106, 109
Hourani, Albert, 20, 27–29
human rights, 20, 160, 170, 188, 212n55, 239n18
Hussein, Mahmoud. *See* al-Nadi, Bahgat; Rif'at, Adel

Ibn Khaldun, 145–46, 148, 166, 175–76, 185
Ibrahim, Hassan, 57
Ibrahim, Muhsin, 223n61, 230n11; and ANM, 42–43, 46, 224n80; and LNM, 123–24, 143; and Nasser, 43; on the New Left, 87, 106; and OCAL, 42, 121, 123, 227n24
ideas: history of, 27
identity: Arab, 210n24; Lebanese, 99; Muslim, 176; religious, 33; sectarian, 130, 136, 238n8
ideological distinctions, 12, 16–17, 181
imaginary: cultural and literary, 39, 47–48; Socialist Lebanon's, 68, 80, 129; of workers, 127–28, 165

imperialism, 23, 55, 86, 160; American, 20, 78, 93, 98; cultural, 93, 221n42; French, 103, 129; Kurds and, 87–88; Marxist critiques of, 4, 85; power and, 18, 185–86, 189–90; Western, 167–68, 184. *See also* anti-imperialism
individual-historian, 156–57
intellectual labor, 151, 154, 171
intellectuals: 'Amili, 47–49; diasporic, 16, 85, 91–94, 166–70, 179; French or Parisian, 67, 160–61, 226n10, 233n56; and the masses, 125, 127–28, 131; organic, 156, 171; public, 12–13, 91, 107, 158, 180, 183; role of, 155. *See also* Arab thought/thinkers; New Left militant intellectuals
internationalist solidarity, 4, 8, 14, 15, 161, 162
intervention: reconstructing the character of, 21–22, 208n73; Western/non-Western, xv–xviii, 18, 94
Iranian Revolution (1979), 17, 49, 161, 170–71, 229n5; and Marxists/Maoists, 175–76, 181, 184; and militant Islam, 4, 166, 169, 176–77, 209n11
Iraq, 57, 169; Ba'th power, 60, 188, 216n26; Communist Party, 49, 216n26; Kurdish self-rule, 87; US invasion, xiii, 173, 211n26
Islam: term usage, 182
Islamic revival. *See* Islamist militancy
Islamism: Buck-Morss on, 53–54; discourses of difference, 189; Marxist/Maoist conversion to, 175–76, 184; nationalism and, 107; representations of, 174–75
Islamist militancy, 110, 166, 173, 209n11; anti-imperialism, 4, 94, 169, 184; Shi'i, 157–58, 163, 180
isolation, 142, 229n9
Israel, xvi, 34, 85, 170; air raids, 100, 223n66; formation of state (1948), 6, 107; invasion of Lebanon, 4, 100, 105, 107, 140, 171, 179, 223nn65–66; Nasser and, 212n47. *See also* June 1967 defeat

Jabar, Faleh A., 69–70
al-Jabarti, Abd al-Rahman, 126, 157
Jackson, Michael, 9
Jacoby, Russell, 1, 232n34
Jahel, Nazir, 175–76
al-Jamal, Khalil, 99
Jambet, Christian, 53
Japan, xvii
Jihad, Abu, 173, 235n17
Jordan, 94, 101, 170
Judaism, 189, 217n44, 238n6
Jumblatt, Kamal, 70, 98, 121, 123, 124, 222n58; assassination, 139–40; duality, 160; LNM leadership, 142, 230n11; and political change, 143, 230n12
June 1967 defeat, 1, 37, 99, 170, 173; al-Azm on, 92–93, 94–95; contemporary Arab thought and, 83–85, 109; historiography of, 107–9; importance of, 82; Said on, 90–91; Sartre on, 171–72; Socialist Lebanon and, 90, 95. *See also* Israel

pragmatics, 55, 77
problem-spaces, 27, 32, 99, 139, 167, 180; of beginnings, xii; of French political anthropology, 208n75; ideological and political, 93; Scott's concept, 21–22
production: relations of, 66, 70, 125, 148–50, 163
progressive regimes, 86–87, 94, 109, 113, 143, 169–70
Progressive Socialist Party, 98, 222n58, 227n25
proletariat, 78, 139, 163, 222n52; Gauche Prolétarienne, 116, 161, 225n10. *See also* working class
pro-Western Lebanese nationalism, 34, 51, 99, 163
pseudonyms, 68, 152–53, 170, 179, 217n44
publishing houses, 13, 67–69, 161, 221n38, 234n7

Qobeissi, Hassan, 61, 68, 216n30, 225n7
queer theory, 204n32
Qutb, Sayyid, 53, 54–55, 74, 75, 77

racism, 18, 92, 93, 184, 185–86
radio, 46, 211n36; Sawt al-'Arab, 39, 40
Rahbani Brothers, 218n1
Rally of National Parties and Forces, 121, 123, 227n25
Rancière, Jacques, 80, 187
reflexive critical practice, 158–59, 179
refugees, 6, 35–36, 210n23
religion: ahistorical notion of, 31; anthropological studies and, 189, 238n6; culture and, 93, 173, 185; in Lebanon, 32–34, 210nn22–23; political ideologies and, 31–32, 49–50, 51, 107; tradition, 55, 94–95, 229n5, 238n9. *See also* sectarianism; *specific religious communities*
representation: of the Arab world, 93, 182–83; epistemic, 124, 125, 184; of Islam, 169, 174–75; meanings of, 19, 219n4; object of, 19; political, 34, 133, 143, 184; provisional confessional, 33
representational paralysis, 191
Resnais, Alain, 78
revolutionary theory and practice, xii, xvi, 4, 16, 71, 86, 110, 129; Charara and, 140, 167; fragmentation, 171–72; gap between, 94; Lenin on, 73, 125; and linguistic translations, 13–14, 74–75; Maronite movement and, 134, 136–37; masses and, 115, 132, 165; power and, 179; sectarianism and, 135; traveling, 161. *See also* critical theory; political practices; theory and practice
Riad, Hassan (Samir Amin), 68
Rif'at, Adel (Eddy Lévy), 68, 217n44
right-wing ideology, 16, 134, 137. *See also* Phalanges
Roneos, 61, 216n27
Ross, Kristin, 66–67, 78, 128
Rushdie, Salman, 174

Sa'd, Ma'ruf, 46
al-Sadat, Anwar, 41, 44, 90, 120, 174
Saghieh, Hazem, 175
al-Sa'id, Ahmed, 40

Said, Edward, xvi, 12, 18, 23, 169, 184, 221n39; "The Arab Portrayed," 91, 174, 221n42; and al-Azm, 220n35; and Charara, 168, 185; contemporary Arab thinkers and, 6–7, 202n11; *Covering Islam*, 174–75; critical public interventions, 92, 93, 180; *Culture and Imperialism*, 185–86; reaction to 1967 defeat, 37, 85, 90–91, 170. *See also Orientalism* (Said)
Sartre, Jean-Paul, 57, 67, 171–72, 216n30, 217n44
Sawt al-'Arab, 39, 40
schools, 64, 153; Arab nationalism and, 43–44; languages of instruction, 47, 68, 205n38, 217n43; public and private, 12, 205n38; strikes, 118. *See also* student protests
Scott, David, 21–22, 208n73
sectarianism: bourgeoisie and, 105, 149; Charara and, 133–36, 147, 151; class struggle and, 131; critical scholarship on, 190–91; and Lebanese political structure, 33, 103–5, 129–31, 139, 151, 228n44, 238n8; solidarity, 144. *See also* religion; *specific religious communities*
secular nationalism, 83–84, 177. *See also* anticolonial nationalism; Arab nationalism; pro-Western Lebanese nationalism
Self-Criticism after the Defeat (al-Azm), 92, 94–95, 108
self-Orientalization, 5, 15, 20, 183, 185
self-referentiality, xvii
September 11, 2001, attacks, xii, 53, 175
Shari'ati, Ali, 54–55, 74, 75, 77
Shi'i community, 31, 51, 168, 209n11, 212n45; administrative positions, 210n22; clerics, 229n5; sectarian organizations, 144, 238n8; types, 50; writers and intellectuals, 47–48, 156. *See also* Hizbullah
Simpson, Audra, 239n15
Skinner, Quentin, 21–22, 208n65, 208n73
social fabric: and the political, 2, 145, 151–52, 163, 166, 168
socialism: Abdel Nasser and, 71; achieving, 171; Arab, 41, 57–58, 60, 94, 99, 138, 215n11; political stages of, 69–70
Socialist Lebanon (Lubnan Ishtiraki), xi, 12–13, 23, 55, 96, 105, 120; diagnosis of regimes, 84–85, 87–90, 95, 109, 220n19; engagement with Marxism, 62, 69–70, 72–73, 109; ethos, 80–81; focus on the political present, 70–71, 79; founding and theoretical practice, 2, 36, 46, 56, 61–64, 113, 126–27; leftists and, 97–99; membership, 224n79; and OLS, 46, 113, 115–16, 224n80, 225n2; political practice, 122, 128–29; readings and translation practices, 67–68, 72–74, 79, 168. *See also* Organization of Communist Action in Lebanon (OCAL)
Socialist Lebanon (bulletin): articles, 64, 65, 75, 76, 87, 216n35; production and distribution, 61, 66, 216n28; "The Theoretical Education Corner," 64, 98–99; "The Two Resistances," 101, 102, 103–5

social mediation, 159–60
social movements, 117–18, 162
social sciences, 10, 17, 188
social structure, 50, 108
social theory, 147, 167, 185
Solzhenitsyn, Alexander, 160–61, 232n54, 233n58
Soueid, Mahmoud, 35–36, 42, 46, 58, 60, 211n32
sovereignty: Arab national, xiii, xv, 29, 30, 85; Lebanese, 99, 163, 187, 211n26; state, xii, 150
Soviet Union, 96, 138, 158, 160, 222n52, 232n54
Spengler, Oswald, 168
Stalin, Josef, 63, 69, 161, 222n52, 233n54
studding (tarsi'), 52
student protests, 45, 64, 66, 74, 80, 152. See also schools
subjugation: logics of, 3, 151–52, 156–59, 166, 167, 185
substitutionism, 121, 227n27
al-Sulh, Riad, 33
su'luk, 156–57
Sunni community, 32–33, 45, 103, 144, 210nn22–23
Syria: Ba'th rule, 4, 60, 87, 89, 187, 211n26; Egyptian union (1958), 40–42, 59–60, 86, 96; French Mandate rule, 32–33, 205nn35–36; Lebanese relations, 100, 211n26; Marxist thinkers, 60, 92; refugees, 210n23; revolution (2011), 88, 169, 184, 196, 210n23
Syrian-Lebanese Communist Party, 1, 96, 222n48
Syrian Nationalists, 42, 46, 87, 213n63

takhwin, 87–88
Tarabishi, Georges, 107–8, 171–72
Les Temps Modernes, 13, 67–68
theory and practice, 66, 136, 161; anthropologist's, 8–11; gap between, 94, 126, 133; leftist militant, 125–27; Maoist, 114–15; Marxist tradition of, xi, xii, 86, 113, 206n47; politics of, 16, 73, 181; questions about, xi–xii. See also critical theory; political practices; revolutionary theory and practice
Thinking Past Terror (Buck-Morss), 53–55, 75
Third Worldist militants, 4, 5, 160, 176; writings and publishing houses, 62, 68, 78
tobacco production, 118, 226n119
top-down politics, 123, 133, 143, 151, 152, 166, 238n8
Traboulsi, Fawwaz: and Algeria, 37, 58; Ba'th membership, 57–58, 60; at Brummana high school, 46; on Chamoun, 43; on Chehab, 56; education and travel, 12, 57–58; family hotel, 37; History of Modern Lebanon, 117–18; and LCP, 97, 222n55; and LNM, 142–43, 229n9; on OCAL, 117, 123, 127; and Socialist Lebanon, 2, 61–62, 63
translation, acts of, 205n39, 206n41; Bourdieu and, 64, 66; Buck-Morss and, 75; Marxist texts and, 13–14, 73–74; Socialist Lebanon and, 68–69, 73, 218n51
traveling theories, 77, 159, 179, 181

Traverso, Enzo, 138–39
Trotsky, Leon, 5, 63–64, 227n27
Tsing, Anna, 237n5
turath (traditions), 1, 172, 175

Union National des Etudiants de France, 63, 216n32
unions, 117–18
United Arab Republic, 56, 57, 58, 59, 96, 113, 223n61
United States: foreign policy, 45, 163; interventions, xv–xvii, 18; invasion of Iraq, xiii, 173, 211n26; Islam and, 174, 175; Middle East scholarship and, 91, 190; military, 44–45
unity: Arab, 42, 57, 58, 86, 171, 212n47
Universal Declaration of Human Rights, 212n55, 221n39
universals/universality, xiii–xiv, 14–15, 17, 20–21, 29, 176; categories, 147, 167–68; celebration of, 188; hegemonic, 158, 163; of Marxism, xii, 73; Olympian, 154, 157, 159; particularity and, 130; Tsing on, 237n5
universities, public and private, 12, 205nn37–38. See also American University of Beirut (AUB); Lebanese University; schools

Victor, Pierre (Benny Lévy), 217n44
Vietnam, 77–79, 160, 232n53
violence, 52, 118, 132, 152, 174, 214n86; Charara on, 141–42, 147, 150–51, 160, 166; colonial, 10; communal, 169; epistemological and ontological, 10, 20, 125, 167–68, 187, 188, 231n21; against women, 238n14

Wars of Subjugation (Charara), 152, 229n8; "Archipelagos" in, 160; first-person plural in, 154; importance of, 159; Lebanese capitalism in, 148–50; logic of the state in, 150–51, 152; minoritarian critique, 143, 155; schematics, 151; social and political entanglements in, 144–47, 167; violence in, 141–42
Weiss, Max, 238n8
Western consciousness, 93, 221n42
Western knowledges, 16, 18–19, 21, 85, 92, 166; in Orientalism, 179–83, 236n40
Western philosophical tradition, 53–54
Wittgenstein, Ludwig, 21
women, xiii, 37, 117, 206n42, 238n14. See also feminists
workers' sector, 115–18, 149
working class, 75, 117, 124, 140, 154; and "burning stages," 69–70, 80; estrangement of intellectuals and, 127–28; French figure of, 66; solidarity, 133; struggles, 121, 131–32. See also proletariat

Yemen, 58–59, 215n18